RAILWAYS
OF THE WORLD

RAILWAYS OF THE WORLD

BRIAN HOLLINGSWORTH

MAGNA BOOKS

Published by Magna Books
Magna Road
Wigston
Leicester, LE8 2ZH

Produced by Bison Books Ltd
Kimbolton House
117A Fulham Road
London SW3 6RL
England

ISBN 1 85422 037 3

Printed in Hong Kong

Reprinted 1989

CONTENTS

Below: Operating relic: Serra do Mar inclines in Brazil. A steam brake van in action.

PREFACE

It is the intention of this book to present to the reader, country by country, an account of the world's railways. In addition to covering historical and technical aspects, an attempt has been made to bring serious instruction into relief by considering aesthetic, pleasurable and even idiosyncratic attributes – almost raising railways to an art form, without forgetting their folklore.

Except when they are the principal line of one particular country or are of exceptional international interest, railways of less than 100 miles or with less than 25 locomotives have had to be omitted. 'Exceptional interest' in this context means those which have earned the title 'first' or 'only' in some particular way. 'Public' or 'Common Carrier' railways receive a more generous interpretation of this rule than do private or industrial ones.

The geographical sections are preceded by a general description of the development and historical effect of railways in the world. In the same way the account of each country's railways begins with a short history. There follows an account of what the system is like today, emphasizing differences from the rest of the world rather than stating similarities. Special mention is made of features which were developed in a particular country which have become standard practice worldwide. Where a country contains a number of railway systems, the account begins with a general description of its railways and their effect on its history.

Two points remain: first, traditional Imperial weights and measures are used; second, where a railway system spans two countries or continents, its entry is placed according to the location of its headquarters.

One characteristic common to railways the world over is a love of statistics, both meaningful and meaningless. Railway reference books and annual reports are full of them. Great care is needed in interpretation – there is, for example, a noticeable correlation between the decrease of steam traction on British Railways and the decline in its profitability – but, alas for steam lovers, it does not mean that modernization was a great mistake. The few statistics which appear in this book are given more with the idea of showing the kind of railway being described rather than making a contribution to the store of absolute truth.

For example, a railway will, with utter confidence, declare on an Atlas of World Railways' questionaire, that it has, say, 138,624 wagons; but on Judgement Day it would have to admit it does not really know exactly how many. Some are being built, others are being scrapped, some have been reported scrapped but are still around, others have been scrapped or destroyed but not reported. There is usually an interesting group which has one number on one side and another number on the other side, even on the best regulated lines! It might in fact be more sensible to give the figure as 139,000 – meaning, between 138,500 and 139,499 – and this is what has been done in this book. The same applies to other statistics; even the length of route or track is uncertain. Does a railway line cease to be included in statistics when it goes out of use or when – possibly years later – the rails are pulled up?

Anyone wishing to play around with figures and obtain a mass of fascinating information regarding railways, is referred to two excellent annually published works of reference:

The Railway Directory and Year Book, published by IPC Transport Press, Dorset House, Stamford St, London SE1 9LU.

Jane's World Railways and Rapid Transit Systems, published by Jane's Yearbooks, Paulton House, 8 Shepherdess Walk, London N1 7LW.

Above: Early railroading in America: The Santa Fe express halts at Virginia City in 1885, headed by Virginia & Truckee 4-4-0 No 11 Rene.

Editor's Note

The maps were supplied by George Philip Printers Limited from their *Modern School Atlas*. The railways drawn on them are as up to date as possible but in the areas which are covered densely with railways, the main lines only are shown.

INTRODUCTION

There is a plaque on the wall of the original railway station at Stockton, County Durham, England, which reads modestly as follows: 'Here in 1825 the Stockton and Darlington Railway Company booked the first passenger thus marking an epoch in the history of mankind.' While the claim as stated is not pedantically correct – regular steam passenger trains did not come for another five years – the truth remains that the coming of steam railways did have an immense effect on the way people lived.

This is not surprising when one considers that both the cost and the speed of transport were improved at one stroke by a factor of at least four. On the credit side, no longer would most inland people stay all their lives in the place where they were born; no longer need they live within horse-and-cart range of the land on which their food was grown. On the

debit side, governments found a fatal ability to move armies from place to place in days rather than weeks, detraining the troops reasonably fresh and ready for battle, rather than footsore and weary from continuous forced marches. But would William of Normandy have got ashore at Hastings in 1066 if King Harold's army had moved by train from his victory over the Scandanavians in Yorkshire a few days earlier?

The political and economic power generated by the new railways meant that they were used for the unification and development of nations. In this way the world found itself the richer, but many green and pleasant lands were spoiled by dark satanic mills in the process.

Above: The first public railway to use regular steam traction was the line from Stockton to Darlington.

The Origins and Development of Railways

Sometime in the dawn of civilization some unsung hero must have, for the first time, laid strips of wood – still called rails when used in fences – on the ground to allow his horse to pull a heavier load. And if the wheels of his cart were fixed outside the shafts, whose spacing was in turn determined by the width of the animal's buttocks, then the distance between these wooden strips would approximate to the width between the rails of most of the world's railways today.

After a diversion into 'plateways' using cast-iron flanged plates, there came wrought-iron rails and finally steel rails. At the same time the living horse had to give way to the iron one.

By the early 1800s railways and plateways were quite common in mining areas, while steam power was also commonly in use for driving pumping machinery. The marriage of the two and hence the first steam locomotive is attributed to Richard Trevithick, a mine captain from Cornwall, England. Trevithick's locomotive, built in 1804 at Pen-y-darran in South Wales as a wager, was tried out on a local mine tramway. While it seems to have worked quite well, the cast-iron plates which formed the track were not strong enough.

William Hedley's *Puffing Billy* of 1813 which ran on a tramway at Wylam near Newcastle-on-Tyne was one of the earliest successful uses of steam traction. *Puffing Billy* was good enough to continue in use until 1859, well into the photographic age.

The first use of steam on a public railway was George Stephenson's *Locomotion* on the Stockton and Darlington in 1825, but the term 'public' then had a literal meaning; it meant that anyone could run his train on the railway by paying the appropriate toll. A high proportion of S&D traffic, including all regular passenger workings, was hauled by horses supplied and operated by independent contractors, just as if the railway was a canal. So we come to the first public railway – in the modern and more restricted sense – the Liverpool and Manchester of 1829.

The Liverpool and Manchester Railway had every element of a modern railway. Its trains were propelled by mechanical means and ran on metal wheels guided by flanges running inside pairs of rails set 4ft 8½in apart. All trains ran to a timetable, were operated by the company, stopping only at its own stations, manned by its own staff. Perhaps the most significant way in which this railway fell short of a modern one was its speed. The 38 miles between the two cities were booked to be covered in two hours and six minutes, an average of eighteen mph.

Only fourteen years later, however, we find Daniel Gooch, locomotive superintendent of the Great Western Railway, personally driving Queen Victoria's husband, Prince Albert, home from Bristol to London after launching Brunel's new steamship, the *Great Britain*. The 118 miles were covered in two hours and four minutes, an average speed which would still be out of reach on many railways even today.

By 1850 many hundreds of miles of railway had been opened in most of the countries of the civilized world and, indeed, the speed of extension during the next thirty years took the form of railway mania. In 1869 the continent of America had been spanned, in 1902 – with the opening of the Trans-Siberian railway – came Asia's turn. Australia had to wait until 1917, while Cecil Rhodes' dream of an African Cape-to-Cairo line has yet to be fulfilled. By World War I in most parts of the world the network was complete.

We may note, however, that a young man, Henry Ford, in the early 1900s had the idea of making motorcars not as playthings for the wealthy, but as cheap transport for such as you and I. By the time Ford Model 'T' production ended in 1927, after fifteen million vehicles had been made (plus untold numbers of other

makes), railways were finding their customers coming to them by choice rather than necessity. The same applied to traders and shippers as well as those without cars; they had the alternative of trucks and motor buses.

The effect on the main lines was very marked, but that on branch and local railways was catastrophic. A few small countries abandoned railways completely, while in others, great reductions in mileage were made. In France, for example, 15,000 miles of local interest railways were abandoned and in the USA the slaughter of inter-urban local lines amounted to a similar figure over this period.

The shortage of oil during World War II signalled a reprieve; the development of aircraft during that conflict led (by the 1960s) to the jet airliner. The speed of the big jets more than compensated for the superior comfort and roominess of long-distance trains.

Thus, between road and air competition the railways suffered greatly; indeed, after just over a century of existence their very survival as providers of general transportation was in doubt. The situation was compounded in many countries by continuing and inflexible systems of regulation dating from monopoly days.

However, today it has become clear that, for a whole series of reasons, the world is entering a new railway age. Ten years ago, this would have been speculation, but it is now firmly rooted in certainty.

Firstly, the exhaustion of the world's oil supplies is an event which is likely to be of concern to people living now; therefore any means of transport which does not depend on oil – or uses less oil than others – is one which should be fostered.

Secondly, it is recognized that the economics of hauling things in long trains, which flanged steel wheels guided by steel rails permit, make a railway by far the cheapest form of land transport, provided that the trains are long enough and/or frequent enough to pay for the fixed costs of what is, after all, a very specialized form of highway.

Thirdly, technology is once again on the side of the railway, with such notions as crewless freight trains or aircraft-speed passenger trains becoming practical possibilities.

Fourthly, growing concern for the environment is encouraging for railways, bearing in mind that one extra freight train on the railway means fifty juggernaut trucks off the roads.

Thus, 150 years after the first inter-city line, the future of railways can be viewed with considerable optimism. Only a tiny fraction of the world's countries are without railways; and several of these have indicated their intention of becoming members of the railway club.

The Development of Motive Power and Rolling Stock

Steam

Steam power dominated traction on the world's railways for the first 120 years of their existence, that is until the 1950s. In some places of course, it still does. Indeed serious new construction continued at least until 1978, when this was written. The final product, the *March Forward*

or 'QJ' class 2-10-2, built by and for the Chinese National Railways, was typical of the tradition of steam construction in the world. Accordingly, it is illuminating to compare the *March Forward* with the *Rocket* of the Liverpool and Manchester Railway, which took to the road 147 years earlier. It is no surprise that what impresses one is the similarities not the differences, at any rate in fundamentals. The path of evolution from *Rocket* to *March Forward* is remarkable as much for the small number of forward steps as for the large number taken sideways or on branch lines.

Rocket already had a fire-tube boiler with multiple tubes, water space round a firebox and a fire which was drawn up by exhaust steam blasted up the chimney. The more steam was used, the more the fire was drawn. There were two cylinders linked to driving wheels by connecting rods, all outside the frames in full view.

Major progress came straight away with some of *Rocket*'s immediate successors of 1830. *Phoenix* had a smokebox and with *Northumbrian* the previously separate water space round the firebox was integrated with that of the rest of the boiler, exactly as in *March Forward*.

The *Invicta*, built the same year for the Canterbury and Whitstable Railway in England, had the cylinders which, although still inclined, were placed at the front end and, in addition, her four wheels were coupled.

With the *Planet*, built later in 1830 for the L&M, Stephenson (and most British locomotives) left the main line of evolution for a branch. The cylinders were placed inaccessibly under the smokebox, the drive being provided by an expensive double crank in the driving axle. This branch line was a long one, locomotives of this layout being supplied – some by Robert Stephenson and Company – 120 years later to an order placed by the Western Region of British Railways. It will be appreciated that not only had the cranks and connecting rods to be accommodated between the frames but also two sets of gear to actuate the valves.

The cylinders temporarily reached their final horizontal outside forward position with the 2-2-0 locomotive *Vauxhall* built for the Irish Dublin & Kingstown Railway in 1834 by a Liverpool engineer called Forrester. They remained in Ireland permanently and were adopted in the USA from 1835 on. Bogies first appeared under William Hedley's *Puffing Billy* of 1813; during the time (1815–1831) it was altered from a four-wheeler to an eight-wheeler. This double-power-bogie arrangement is today – with diesel or electric drive – by far the commonest in the world.

The idea of pivoted wheels for guidance originated in the USA. The great Mathias Baldwin of Philadelphia produced a bogie 4-2-0 design as early as 1834, but bogies and pony trucks with side movement did not develop until the 1860s. On the other hand the bogie tender of our Chinese 2-10-2 is an arrangement which appeared in the USA early in the 1830s, as being suitable for America's lightly laid tracks.

Eugène Walschearts of Belgium in 1854 devised the valve gear that bears his name, but it saw little use for many years. Early in this century, however, it came suddenly into fashion and in the end became virtually universal for the last forty years of steam construction. The gear that bears Stephenson's honoured name can be arranged to give excellent steam distribution, but it is awkward to place it in an accessible position outside the wheels, whereas Walschearts' fits in very conveniently and remains in full view.

Brilliant engineers unfortunately can conceive complicated designs but a Frenchman called Henri Giffard in 1851 produced his injector – a simple and static arrangement of cones – whereby steam is used to squirt water directly into the boiler. In this way the expense of troublesome feed pumps became a thing of the past. Actually in making his invention, Giffard had steam aircraft in mind but this early spin-off from the space age has been of great benefit to the cause of steam.

Flat or 'slide' valves were normal in the 1800s, but around the turn of the century they began to give way to the less friction-bound piston type.

Complexity and the steam locomotive never agreed. For example, the compound principle was tried over a period – short in Britain, long

Top: This contemporary print shows the opening of another very early railway, the Canterbury and Whitstable, 3 May 1830. The locomotive Invicta *has been preserved.*

Above: The causeway connecting the line from Hamburg, Germany to the island of Sylt crosses the open sea. This composite picture (in the form of a popular postcard) is rather more dramatic than the actual case.

An American train runs alongside the Mississippi River in Minnesota.

in France – whereby a second set of cylinders was provided which would take in the steam exhausted from the first ones and extract additional work from it. The process had achieved big savings when applied to steam engines in factories and ships. But, for two reasons, compounding never (not even in France) became universal practice: firstly, the gain in efficiency was reduced when, as in a railroad, the demand for power constantly varied; secondly, the extra machinery needed extra maintenance and the savings were not enough to justify this. Similar remarks applied to other multiple-cylindered locomotives which did not use the compound principle.

Wilhelm Schmidt of Germany in 1891 fitted a locomotive with what was called a super-heater. By the laws of physics water boils at a temperature precisely dependent on the pressure; hence, since efficiency is improved by working at a higher temperature and increasing the pressure leads to problems in making the boiler strong enough, Schmidt thought that further heating the steam after it had left the boiler might do the trick. His simple arrangement of tubular elements inside enlarged fire-tubes worked well and superheating became a universal feature from the early years of the century onwards.

Early in the new century, therefore, the

made in the cost of running the conventional Stephenson steam locomotive. In stark contrast was the failure, in spite of many attempts by the most skilful designers and engineers, to improve the basic Stephensonian principles.

One thing does remain to be said about steam and that is to refer to the passionate and almost unbelievable love that it evokes in men beyond any bounds of logic or reason. In all the countries which have dispensed with steam, iron horses have been preserved for pleasure purposes, to the tune of several thousand in total, many of them in working order. The effort put into this is some measure of the strength of feeling for one of mankind's most beneficial and attractive creations.

Diesel

As a competitor of steam, the diesel engine was a late-comer; the principle dates back to a type of heat engine devised by a certain *Herr Doktor* Diesel of Berlin, Germany in 1893. Like other internal combustion engines, it is capped by a fundamental weakness and it is this: unless the engine is turning, no force is produced. In traction of course, a big force is needed when stationary; this basic unsuitability has not, however, prevented diesel-driven locomotives from dominating the railway scene today.

Four solutions of gradually increasing complexity have been considered and experimented with; it is strange that while in steam-locomotive engineering the simplest of alternative solutions has usually prevailed, with diesel the most complex has been the winner. The first answer to this problem of coupling a spinning shaft to a stationary wheel is the familiar motor-car clutch and gearbox – a mechanical solution in fact. This works very well for low powers, up to say 200 horsepower, but in spite of some brave attempts, no higher.

One idea which seemed promising was to use a diesel engine to compress air. The compressed air in its turn could be used to drive the locomotive – in one 1932 German experiment an actual steam locomotive was used. However, the excess heat produced in the process proved in the end to be both troublesome and wasteful.

The coupling of the engine to the wheels hydraulically has had modest success and many diesel-hydraulic locomotives run on the world's railways. Most originate either directly or indirectly from Germany.

Nevertheless, today the standard locomotive of the world is the diesel-electric which is, in fact, an electric locomotive which carries its own power station. We note an early successful application of the principle to some low-power Swedish railcars in 1913 and experiments, some of which became successes, in many countries during the 1920s, but most of the credit of turning a dubious and complex box of tricks into a world-beater must go to General Motors of the United States of America during the 1930s. The complication of the solution may be gauged from the fact that diesels cost three times as much and some had (as a measure of their complexities) sixteen times as many cylinders as steam locomotives of equivalent performance, but the advantages prevailed.

The advantages of diesel locomotives over steam sprung much less from direct savings – when modern diesels were compared with modern steam power, these were often negligible – than from indirect ones. Diesels are push-button power – no lighting up, hours before they are needed. They are also building-block power, capable of being made up to any power required by adding units, without needing extra crews. The servicing time is also much less and there is a small bonus in smoke abatement. All these things added up to a good case and furthermore, even railway magnates are vulnerable to the 'keeping-up-with-the-Jones' syndrome.

Electric

For most railway traffic, however, dieselization is not a long-term solution. Electrification, which goes back further in time, is likely to be applied to all railways in the future where the density of movement is sufficient to justify the high fixed costs. Put another way, when there are enough trains, it is better to take power stations off the locomotives and build instead bigger and fewer ones on the ground. The inventor of electric traction was a Scotsman called Davidson from Edinburgh, who demonstrated an electrically propelled vehicle as early as 1834. On the other hand the first practical electric railway was one demonstrated at the Berlin exhibition of 1879 by the firm of Siemens and Halske. This led in 1881 to a line 1.5 miles long near Berlin and very quickly thereafter to a proliferation of electric inter-urban and local railways. The only survivor from these days is Volk's Electric Railway at Brighton, England. The gestation period for practical electric traction was therefore much longer than for steam or diesel, but its childhood much shorter.

The first major main-line, big-time, electric railway was the Swiss Bernese Alps line (now called the Bern–Lötschberg–Simplon), which opened in 1913. After the 1914 war, railways in numerous countries electrified quite long sections of main line. By 1930 it was, for example, possible to travel the 500 miles from Geneva, Switzerland to Salzburg, Austria by electric train.

Where is the longest such journey now? It goes from near the Finnish-Russian frontier at Vyborg via Leningrad, and the Trans-Siberian Railway as far as Karymskay 1993 miles from Vladivostok on the Pacific Ocean. The overall distance is just short of 4500 miles. Alas, while Czarist *laissez-faire* provided one uniform track gauge throughout this journey, Communist planning has led to two incompatible electrification systems, direct current and alternating current, over different parts of the route.

This highlights a conflict between high-voltage alternating current systems (cheap fixed equipment, costly locomotives) and medium voltage direct current (more costly fixed equipment, cheaper locomotives) which has gone on since electrification began. If compatibility with older systems is no problem, the solution of using newly developed solid-state conversion equipment on DC locomotives,

steam locomotive reached its final form. It remained to improve the materials and the details. As an example of what could be done, one could cite an improved axlebox bearing introduced in the 1930s on a British Railway – the London, Midland & Scottish – by a locomotive engineer from rival Great Western. Failures due to overheated axleboxes on the seventy principal 'Royal Scot' express locomotives fell from eighty per year to seven in consequence. Such an instance illustrates the kind of improvements in repair and maintenance costs that could be and were achieved by careful study of every detail. In this way enormous reductions were constantly being enabling them to use AC transmission, has recently resolved the matter. It has also become very much easier to build multi-current locomotives, capable of running under both DC and AC systems.

Passenger Carriages
The Liverpool and Manchester Railway commenced operations with what were effectively stage-coach 'inside' bodies in threes on four-wheeled rail chassis. This compartmented layout (with eight or more 'bodies' forming each coach, and in due time modernized with a side corridor), remained the norm in Britain until the 1960s. Early American railroads favoured the open coach – which most of the world's railways have now adopted – in which the passengers sit either side of a central aisle, entering and exiting by doors at the ends. Rougher tracks across the Atlantic led to the mounting of carriage bodies on the now-familiar four-wheel trucks or bogies as early as 1840. The present-day layout of railway carriages, therefore, evolved very early and development has taken the form of improvements and refinements rather than change. Stronger construction and automatic brakes have improved safety; air-conditioning, heating and better bogies have improved comfort out of all recognition. One major improvement involved communication between adjacent

vehicles. Access to and between open carriages was originally via open and draughty platforms at each end. By the early 1900s these were beginning to be made into closed vestibules and the vehicles joined to one another by flexible corridor connections. This feature is now virtually universal.

In the first years of railways, passengers generally either brought their own food or snatched what they could in dining rooms during stops. Similarly, they slept as best they could in carriage seats when overnight journeys were involved. In due time, dining, buffet and sleeping cars evolved to meet these needs.

The extra comforts of sleeping berths as well as meals on the move, were (and to some extent are still) catered for by two famous companies, both household words in their own sphere of influence. They were Pullman, mainly in the USA, and Wagons-Lits, mainly in Europe. Other lines, particularly those under British influence, used their own cars.

The first recorded regular provision of sleeping accommodation in a train was well ahead of its general provision. There was a 'bed carriage' on the London and Birmingham Railway in 1838, while the first regular public dining car operated by the Great Western Railway of Canada (now part of Canadian National) in 1867. Such facilities (as appropriate) are now normal on most overnight

and long-distance trains the world over. There were facilities on the Liverpool and Manchester Railway to bring one's own road carriage with one on the train; it is a pleasure to record that in recent years (after a long absence) these have now returned, on a small scale in the USA under the name Autotrain, but quite extensively – as Motorail – in Europe.

Many special types of passenger carriage have existed, such as dance cars, observation cars, gymnasiums, fresh and salt-water bath cars, and so on, but they give pleasure to the student of curiosities rather than play a serious role in the evolution of modern passenger transport. An exception is the class of vehicles built for the heads of state and other VIPs; in some countries and in the early years what was right for Kings and Queens in one decade became available for their subjects in the next. Sometimes it worked the other way; before her recent Jubilee Queen Elizabeth II of Britain used a train which included vehicles dating back to her grandfather's time and, in consequence, she could sometimes be seen travelling on the 'slow' lines at their maximum speed of 70 mph while her subjects roared by on the fast ones at 100 mph.

Left: A five-unit diesel crosses the Olifants River Bridge with an iron-ore train on the new Sishen-Saldanha line in South Africa.

Left: A steam-hauled goods train crosses the arches of a masonry viaduct.

Extreme left: A narrow-gauge 4-8-4 climbs the Raurimu spiral in New Zealand.

The Development of Operations and Services

With this development of passenger accommodation came improvements in two main areas. First, overall speeds steadily increased. In steam days, 70 mph average speeds and 100 mph maximum speeds were reached, but with diesel and electric power a thirty percent improvement on that has so far been the best that can be achieved. There seems reason to suppose that, above 150 mph, the flanged steel wheel on a steel rail begins to run into difficulties. The idea of tilting the carriages to maintain a comfortable ride at high speeds round sharp curves is being developed in several countries.

The second main area of improvement has been the development of passenger trains which run without change, over the metals of several administrations. That a traveller should be able to remain in his seat or berth while moving from one country's or one company's line to another, instead of facing all the tedium and hazards of changing trains, is one of the greatest possible benefits. Awkward problems have had to be solved, compatibility of equipment being the least of them.

Having said all this, it must be added that, regarding railroads in general, passenger services take very much second place to freight movement. Most types of goods wagon or

freight car now in use have been around since the early days of railways, (including containers and 'piggy-back') but the size and load carried has steadily increased. A typical rail freight vehicle, which might a century ago have carried ten tons, now might carry fifty. This is not an unmixed blessing – what do you do if you have only ten tons to send?

Not only do individual vehicles have this much higher capacity, but trains also can be made up to much higher loads, carrying, perhaps, 10,000 tons instead of 200. This time the railway companies have the problem and what do they do? Wait until they have accumulated 10,000 tons for one destination and delay the traffic, or send what they have at the time and increase the cost?

Safety has been a foremost concern of railways ever since an English Member of Parliament was killed on the opening day of the Liverpool and Manchester Railway in 1830. Soon enough it was realized that something better than just the train driver's eyes was needed for these fire-chariots, when running at their mind-boggling speeds of 30 mph.

At first, policemen were appointed to signal to drivers that a preceding train had passed less than or more than so many minutes ago – time-interval working, it was called. After the invention and installation of the electric telegraph, it was possible to signal back from the

station ahead that a particular train had passed, thereby confirming the line was clear. This was called the Block System; it was installed in special places very early on and became general in the late 1800s. Also, in due time, fixed mechanical signals of various types (disc, ball, semaphore) replaced hand signals. Further development of mechanical signalling gave interlocking with points and switches, so that a signal could not show clear unless the route had been set correctly.

A device called the track circuit, which detects the presence of a train on a line electrically, led the way, first to preventing signals being put to all-clear when there was a train on the line ahead, second to putting them automatically to danger as a train went past. This has led to a large degree of automation in the signalling of trains; almost all rail routes of any importance are now controlled in this way, with human intervention at junctions, usually from remote-control locations.

A quite different philosophy of train safety still exists in many different parts of the world, notably the US although it is on the wane. It applies particularly to single lines. The basis of this system is that trains should run according to the timetable and, that the timetable should be worked out so they shall not collide with one another.

Common to all systems is the requirement

for trains to be able to stop when they need to. For this reason automatic brakes, applicable to all vehicles on a train and self-applying in the case of malfunction, are compulsory in practically all countries. A much less universal but growing contribution to safety is an automatic connection between the signals and the brakes on a train to which they apply. If a train passes a signal at 'caution', brakes are automatically applied and the driver, of course, warned.

In general, safety considerations have had precedence over financial ones, but the latter govern the continued existence of most railways. Recognizing this, people are curious to know the score and one is often asked about a particular railway, 'does it pay?' Accordingly, official figures have, wherever possible been given, expressed usually in the form of expenses as a percentage of receipts.

A warning was given earlier that official statistics of quite solid things like mileage of route and number of wagons are a trifle suspect, but when it comes to so sensitive a matter as a railway's finances, we really enter the realms of fiction. Oddly enough, capitalist-owned railways seem to give more plausible figures than ones owned by governments, which have the power to play all sorts of tricks. Subsidies for certain traffic, money lent free of interest, over-generous payments for social services may improve results; free carriage for, say, military traffic, continuance of uneconomic services for political ends, and the like may make them worse. Even so, a very good percentage figure gives some indication of a well-run railway and a very bad one an indication that the railway is one with problems.

The permanent way at the approaches to a great terminus.

Europe	Great Britain	Netherlands
General Information	British Railways	Netherlands Railways
Compagnie Internationale des Wagons-Lits	The Pullman Car Company	
International Sleeping Car Company	*Bradshaw's Railway Guide*	Norway
	Bluebell Railway	Norwegian State Railways
Albania	Festiniog Railway	Spitzbergen
Albanian State Railways	Isle of Man Railways	
	London Transport	Poland
Austria	Middleton Railway	Polish State Railways
Austrian Federal Railways	Northern Ireland Railways	
Styrian Provincial Railways (and other lines)	Post Office Railway	Portugal
	Romney Hythe & Dymchurch Light Railway	Portuguese Railway Company
Belgium	Tallyllyn Railway Company	
Belgian National Railways	Volk's Electric Railway	Rumania
		Rumanian State Railways
Bulgaria	Greece	
Bulgarian State Railways	Hellenic Railways	Spain
		Spanish National Railways
Cyprus	Hungary	
	Hungarian State Railways	Sweden
Czechoslovakia		Swedish State Railways
Czechoslovak State Railways	Ireland, Republic of	
	Irish Transport Company	Switzerland
Denmark	Irish Peat Board	Swiss Federal Railways
Danish State Railways		Berne – Lötschberg – Simplon Railway
	Italy	Independent Swiss Railways
Finland	Italian State Railways	Wengernalp Railway
Finnish State Railways		Rhaetian Railway
	Liechtenstein	
France		USSR
French National Railways	Luxembourg	USSR Railways
Paris Transport Authority	Luxembourg National Railways	Moscow Metro
Other French Railways		
	Malta	Yugoslavia
Germany		Yugoslav Railways
German Federal Railway (West Germany)	Monaco	
German State Railway (East Germany)		Vatican City
Wuppertal Suspension Railway		

In no sense, other than a wishful one, can the railways of Europe be regarded as an entity; they are divided into many compartments, not so much by national barriers as by technical, political and geographical ones. For example, Britain is cleanly separated from the rest of Europe by a thirty-mile stretch of water, a fact that Britons have been thankful for on many occasions in the past. In the railway sense the island is also separated, because, while the distance between the rails is the same, the size of the space available through tunnels and under bridges – what a railwayman would call the 'structure gauge' – is much smaller. Hence most European rolling stock, which in general conforms in size to what is called the 'Bern Gauge', cannot run in Britain. Specially built smaller vehicles do, of course, run from Europe into Britain over two train-ferry links, from Zeebrugge in Belgium to Harwich and from Dunkirk in France to Dover.

A tunnel under the English Channel has been projected since Napoleonic times – the Duke of Wellington personally opposed one of the early proposals – and numerous subsequent schemes have also foundered. The strata of chalk through which the tunnel is to be bored is ideal for tunnelling; easy to cut, yet solid enough to stand up on its own. The condition of the bores made in connection with various false starts made in the past bears this out.

The last attempt came to grief (in 1974) because of over-idealistic planning. This led the project designers to escalate the cost by including in it a new high-speed 'Bern Gauge' railway from the Channel coast to London; a high proportion of this new line was, for environmental reasons, also to be in the tunnel. The Channel Tunnel itself was to be large enough to carry full-size road trucks on railway wagons.

It is pleasant to record that, at the time of writing, a simpler and more sensible Channel Tunnel scheme is currently being launched, with minimum facilities and, to begin with, only a single line of normal rail size. This is feasible because it so happens that the peak periods of travel in each direction do not coincide.

Political barriers are more difficult to cross. Outstanding is the notorious Iron Curtain which splits the railway map of Germany and cuts the majority of the many tracks which crossed its line. The few trains which do run on the routes which remain are subject to lengthy frontier formalities, especially in the westward direction; each eastern government takes special precautions against anyone trying to leave its socialist paradise.

A little way beyond and behind the Iron Curtain comes a technical barrier in the form of a change of track gauge, from the Stephenson standard of 4ft 8½in between the rails, to the Soviet standard of 5ft 0¼in. A similar barrier cuts off the Iberian Peninsula because the Spanish gauge is 5ft 6in. Limited movement of trains across both these rail frontiers is made possible by wheel- and bogie-changing arrangements. In the case of passenger workings, the cars, complete with occupants, are lifted on board.

Nevertheless, the railways of continental Western Europe are making serious attempts to act as one entity. Of course, those in Eastern Europe act in uniform subservience to 'dad' in Moscow, but west European railways' voluntary co-operation is all the more creditable. The principal instrument of co-operation is the *Union International des Chemins de Fer*. In theory, any railway can belong, but in practice only European systems do so and, of them, those outside continental central Western Europe regard many UIC deliberations with a certain detachment. Nevertheless, one particular matter which is gaining ground at the moment is the production of rolling stock to a common specification under the title Co-rail.

In spite of all the barriers, a remarkable series of through trains and carriages connects the major centres of Europe. Up market, and in Western Europe only, are the Trans-Europe Expresses, which provide fast luxury day services, first-class only with supplement; excellent catering is a feature. Both self-propelled and locomotive-hauled trains are included; most are equipped to run on more than one electrical system. One, the 'Catalan Talgo', even has its wheel-sets changed enroute, to run from Geneva in Switzerland to Barcelona in Spain.

The other express trains of Europe are also very remarkable, particularly regarding the complexity of their composition. This was a tradition handed down from the old Wagons-Lits Company, but the new trains have another dimension in that, since they are no longer *trains de luxe*, they carry ordinary and couchette coaches in addition to sleeping cars. As an illustration of this one could cite the 'Italia Express' which runs basically from Hamburg to Rome, but carries cars to and from numerous

places over various stretches of its journey *viz*

Amsterdam–Rome
Hamburg–Ventimiglia (for the Riviera)
Calais–Rome
Brussels–Rome
Oberhausen–Rome
Frankfurt–Rimini

There is a dining car from Hamburg to Frankfurt and a buffet car from the Swiss border to Rome.

Soviet sleeping cars from Moscow penetrate to most continental Western European capitals, usually two or three times a week. They seem to be characterized by exceptional drabness (even by normal European standards) and, although quite comfortable inside, appear to be very little patronized. Since they clearly have little commercial or 'show the flag' use, one cannot but speculate on their true purpose.

However, freight is much more important than passengers. For many years wheel standards, air brakes, buffers and screw-couplings have been standardized so that standard wagons can circulate freely between all the countries of Europe, except Britain, the USSR, Spain and Portugal, without any physical difficulty. It is

artificial hindrances at frontiers that are the trouble. Even here people have found the way round – Anthony Fokker relates in his biography *Flying Dutchman* how he smuggled the contents of his aircraft factories by the trainload from Germany into his native Holland, during 1919. Officials were persuaded to look the other way as train after train rumbled through their stations, by gifts of sewing machines, which he had been producing as a substitute for war-planes. One should perhaps add that such occurrences are not at all typical of the way in which freight is nowadays passed from one European country to another – nevertheless, the paperwork, sorting and shunting that goes on at the frontiers causes delays that are a sizeable fraction of overall transit times.

Page 18-19: A train steams across a bridge on the Gotthard line in the Swiss Alps.

INTERNATIONAL SLEEPING CAR COMPANY – CIWLT

Compagnie Internationale des Wagons-Lits et du Tourisme,
53 Boulevard Clovis,
Brussels.

Once upon a time, everywhere in Continental Europe and in many places in Africa and Asia too, could be seen (for our comfort and pleasure) a fleet of magnificent saloon, dining and sleeping cars, bearing the sonorous original full name of their owners, the *Compagnie Internationale des Wagons-Lits et des Grands Express Européens* – written here in French, but also appearing in fourteen other languages according to the working of the particular car in question. Half close your eyes as you look into the corridor and you get a glimpse of Marlene Dietrich disappearing with the secret plans.

The Wagons-Lits Company was founded in 1876, taking over 53 sleeping cars from a previous enterprise, Mann's Railway Sleeping Carriage Company. Wagons-Lits was already accepted by the major French and German railways and in the 1880s expanded into Italy, Spain and Portugal. The founder, Georges Nagelmackers, already envisaged bogie-changing to give through running on to the wider 5ft 6in gauge of the Iberian peninsula, but it was over eighty years before this was accomplished.

The 'Orient Express' began running in 1883 between Paris and Bucharest, Rumania. Istanbul (then Constantinople) was reached in 1889.

In 1885 the Prussian State Railways (in true 'scrap of paper' tradition) broke the contracts, causing serious problems with attempts to link up with Russia. Eleven years later the Prussians relented, in time for an uninterrupted connection with the 'Trans-Siberian Express' which was inaugurated in 1898.

From 1889 onwards, Wagons-Lits began operations in Africa. There were sleeping and dining cars in Algeria, Egypt, Morocco, Senegal and Tunis. There were also services in northern China on the Russian-owned Chinese Eastern Railway. The Chinese services, which had carried on somehow in the face of wars, invasions and revolutions, ended abruptly in 1948 – the company's image was not perhaps entirely compatible with the Thoughts of Chairman Mao.

World War I played havoc with Wagons-Lits operations. All its assets in Germany were confiscated and used to form a rival organization, Mitropa, which lasted until 1945. Those in the USSR were just confiscated.

In 1922 the famous blue steel cars appeared on the 'Calais-Mediterranée Express'. One was even specially adapted for the use of HRH the Prince of Wales. The public (but not the company) immediately christened it the 'Blue Train'. Before this, all cars had been built and finished in varnished teak, including, of course, the famous dining car in which the Armistices of 1918 and 1940 were signed.

Between the wars the Company expanded into Turkey. Baghdad was reached in 1940 on completion of the standard gauge railway. Sleeping-car service also expanded into Britain

in 1938, when the London-Paris and London-Brussels Night Ferry service was inaugurated. A service between Peking and Shanghai was operated for a short time in the 1930s.

By the end of the 1930s the Company owned 2260 cars: 710 dining, 1180 sleeping, 200 saloons or Pullmans and 170 baggage vans. In addition to countries mentioned already, services were operated in Denmark, Finland, Estonia, Latvia, Lithuania, Poland, Czechoslovakia, Austria, Hungary, Bulgaria, Greece, Yugoslavia, Switzerland, Palestine, Syria, French Equatorial Africa, Angola and the Belgian Congo. By 1939 two Pullman cars had actually arrived in Hong Kong for a service to Canton, but it never started.

At their peak in 1930, the following *trains de luxe*, that is, those with sleeping, dining or saloon accommodation only, were operated:–

Pullman Trains

'Golden Arrow'	Calais-Paris
(Pullman train)	Calais-Brussels
'Etoile du Nord'	Paris-Brussels
'Oiseau Bleu'	Paris-Brussels-Antwerp
'Edelweiss'	Amsterdam-Zurich-Lucerne
'Andalucia Express'	Seville-Granada and Malaga
'Côte d'Azur'	Paris-Menton
'King Carol 1'	Bucharest-Constanza
'Dunarea'	Bucharest-Galatz
'Sunshine'	Cairo-Luxor
'Golden Mountain Express'	Montreux-Gstaad-Zweisimmen (narrow-gauge)

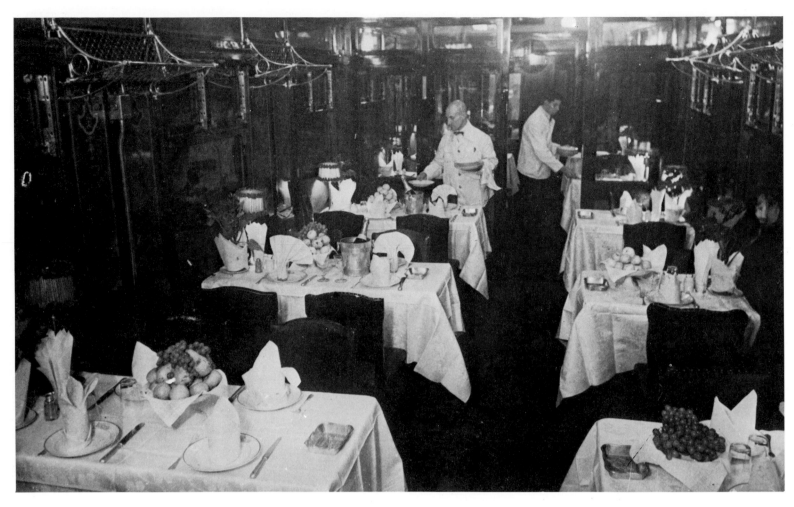

(Pullman train)	Ostend–Cologne
(Pullman train)	Milan–San Remo–Nice–Cannes

Trains of Sleeping Cars

'Barcelona Express'	Paris–Port Bou
'P&O Bombay Express'	Boulogne–Marseille
'Engadine Express'	Boulogne and Paris–Chur (for St Moritz)
'Oberland Express'	Boulogne and Paris–Interlaken
'Nord Express'	Ostend, Calais and Paris–Riga & Warsaw
'Orient Express'	Calais and Paris–Bucharest
'Ostend–Vienna–Orient Express'	Ostend & Amsterdam–Bucharest & Istanbul
'Côte d'Argent'	Paris–Iran
'Rome Express'	Paris–Rome
'Simplon–Orient Express'	Calais–Paris–Istanbul, Bucharest & Athens
'Riviera Express'	Berlin–Cannes
'Anatolian Express'	Haydarpasa–Ankara
'Taurus Express'	Haydarpasa–Rayak (for Cairo) and Nusaybin (for Baghdad)
(Sleeping Car Train)	Paris and Boulogne–Prague and Karlovy Vary
(Sleeping Car Train)	Ostend–Karlovy Vary
(Sleeping Car Train)	Rome–Milan
(Sleeping Car Train)	Rome–Genoa–Turin
(Sleeping Car Train)	Vienna–San Remo–Nice–Cannes–Rome–Palermo and Syracuse

Note:
Some of these trains were combined with other *trains de luxe* (but rarely with plebeian trains) over certain sections of their routes.

After 1945, Communist governments in eastern Europe took over internal services, although through ones were allowed to continue. Expansion brought Wagons-Lits into Sweden and into the Lebanon. The provision of sleeping cars on Europe's Motorail services was another new area of activity.

Over the last few years, many other railway administrations have taken over the Company's cars, of which there were over 700 in 1974, but it is already expanding again into such enterprises as hotels, motels and airline catering. Even in the last-named business, Wagons-Lits has over fifty years of experience, having provided the first lunch ever served on a public Paris–London flight.

The memories of the superb travel offered by 'Madame la Compagnie' are enshrined in the consciousness of an older generation and brought to the notice of the younger by such films as *From Russia with Love* and *Murder on the Orient Express*. Two organizations have acquired some of the traditional blue cars and Pullmans and offer nostalgic excursions back into the past. Intraflug AG of Tugernstrasse 12a, 8127 Forch, Zurich, Switzerland, runs very de luxe trips to Athens, Istanbul (once they went on to Baghdad), Bordeaux (for the vintage) and elsewhere. The other is expecting to offer a regular *trains de luxe* service to and from Paris and London, starting in 1979.

Top left: Sleeping cars of the Compagnie Internationale des Wagons-Lits on the 'Blue Train' at Beaulieu-sur-Mer.

Above: The interior of a dining car of the International Sleeping Car Company in 1923.

ALBANIA

See map on pages 86-87.

ALBANIAN STATE RAILWAYS
Drejtoria e Hekurudhave,
Tirana.

The railway age came late to Albania; not until 1947 was the first line from the port of Durres to Pegin opened. In 1949 the capital, Tirana, became rail connected and by 1977 there were 135 miles of routes radiating from Durres to five different termini. Extensions are in progress and a connection between the northernmost of these and the Yugoslavian Belgrade-Bar line is contemplated. Very few foreigners have travelled in the system's trains of four-wheel, and now sometimes bogie, carriages, hauled by Czech-built diesels. Recent visitors have not reported any sign of the original steam-powered Polish-built 2-8-2Ts of the standard Tkt2 design of the Polish State Railways.

AUSTRIA

See map on pages 26-27.

The railway map of Austria bears sad witness to the fact that the country was, only sixty years ago, the central province of a great unified empire in which the Imperial and Royal State Railways (*Kaiserlich und Koeniglich Staats Bahnen* or KK St B) conducted its operations with a royal and imperial air. Defeat in World War I led to the loss of lines in what are now Hungary, Rumania, Poland, Czechoslovakia, Yugoslavia and Italy. Hitler's *Anschluss* in 1936 meant the further degrading of the republican railways to a mere division of the German Reichsbahn. But since the regaining of independence in 1945, an almost totally wrecked system has been built up into the excellent system in existence today.

Excellent, of course, is a broad term; in this case the lightening of the heart that accompanies a crossing of any of the nineteen rail routes that lead into Austria is due more to the welcoming by the people (nowhere better reflected than in their railways) than any significant increase in mere efficiency or comfort.

The 4000 miles of railway in Austria are administered by ten organizations but the Austrian Federal Railways system dominates nine miles out of every ten.

Austria had its own school of locomotive design with many excellent features, but it had little direct influence outside the country. However, in one field, that of on-track mechanical permanent way-maintenance equipment, Austria has considerable world influence. The lifting, tamping and lining machines exported by the firm of Plasser and Theurer can be found in most parts of the world.

AUSTRIAN FEDERAL RAILWAYS – OeBB
Oesterreichische Bundesbahnen,
Elisabethstrasse 9,
A1010 Vienna.

Dominating – literally so – the operations of the Federal Railways are the mountains of which the greater part of present-day Austria consists. A further major factor lies in the fact that the capital and most industries are concentrated near the eastern frontier of a country that measures 400 miles from east to west and averages a mere seventy miles from north to south. All the main lines, 1620 miles in all, amounting to 48 percent of the network, are electrified on the standard Central Europe system of 15,000v AC, $16\frac{2}{3}$ cycles, and the state-owned branch lines include not only 280 miles of narrow (2ft 6in) gauge but also two tourist-carrying mountain rack-and-pinion lines. Other lines are worked by diesel power and to a minor extent by steam.

History and Development
The first steam railway in Austria was the Kaiser Ferdinand Nordbahn, opened in 1837, which ran northward from Vienna into what is now Czechoslovakia. The state took a hand in the next decade or so and various railways, including the famous Semmering main line (1851) over the mountains, linking Vienna to Trieste and Italy, were constructed under its auspices. Later the pendulum swung back and private enterprise built (and took over) some important lines, including the Kaiserin Elizabeth Railways from Vienna to Salzburg (1852) and the Franz Josef line linking the capital to Belgrade (1860). Finally, in 1880 the KK St B state system was formed; this organization gradually took over the private lines, including the Semmering, one of the earliest state lines but which later strayed from the fold being the last (under the name Sudbahn) to return in

1924. By this time the KK St B had become the Austrian State Railways, its size having shrunk from 9500 miles in 1914 to around 3000 after the peace treaties.

In 1889 the opening of the 6.3-mile Arlberg tunnel completed rail communication from the Swiss Frontier at Buchs right across the country. The Tauern route, involving the 5.4-mile Tauern tunnel and other major works, opened north-south communication in 1910.

Electrification began in earnest after World War I with the conversion of the trunk routes in the mountains west of Salzburg; the main line to Vienna had to wait until after World War II, when the system took its present title after liberation from the Germans.

Civil Engineering
In any mountainous country where the civil engineer has had to force a passage for the iron road, considerable civil engineering works will be found; Austria is no exception. The two major tunnels have been mentioned, but the mile-long Semmering tunnel of 1851 was at least as great a feat when one considers the primitive explosives and other equipment available at the time.

Railway destruction in Austria in 1945 was very comprehensive. The scale of reconstruction can be judged by the fact that from 1945 to 1949, 367 bridges of a length aggregating 8.5 miles were rebuilt. The Semmering tunnel itself had been damaged to a point where a new bore had to be pierced. Tracks and buildings also suffered damage on a similar vast scale.

Locomotive Landmarks
In 1837 Robert Stephenson and Company of England supplied the first locomotives to Austria, two 2-2-0s for the Kaiser Ferdinand Nordbahn. A certain John Haswell who accompanied them rose to be the head of the Vienna locomotive works and responsible for much early development in Austria. His 0-8-0

Below: Steam over the Semmering route. This
important route from Vienna to the south was
electrified by 1959. In steam days trains were assisted
over the steep inclines by pilot locomotives; large
tank locomotives were kept specially for this purpose
at Glognitz at the foot of this incline.

need for steam. There was no costly panic-stricken rush to the new forms of motive power and, indeed when it happens the process of steam elimination will have taken nearly sixty years to complete. Even in 1978 over 100 steam locomotives were in daily use in Austria.

Electric traction in Austria followed very closely both the practices and the development stages of her neighbours, Germany and Switzerland. The same high-voltage low-frequency alternating current system was used and, while freight locomotives akin to the famous Swiss 'crocodiles' were built, passenger ones were more in the German style. Even the dun-coloured livery was the same. Recent construction has followed world fashion for bogie locomotives, again of quite conventional construction and appearance. As in the case of steam, the majority of Austrian electric and diesel locomotives are home-built, many under licence from firms in larger countries. The non-electrified routes of the OeBB are the secondary ones and, correspondingly, diesel traction has only a secondary role to play in Austria.

Train Services

The Austrian timetables are dominated by the tremendous main line from the Swiss frontier to Vienna. The great 'Arlberg Express' from Vienna to Paris takes 10.5 hours for the 470 miles with 26 stops, which, when one considers the amount of mountainous terrain and single line west of Salzburg, is quite remarkable. The light, high-speed Vienna–Basel 'Transalpin' does even better with a truly superb 8.25-hour trip. The problem of keeping these and many other fast express trains to time over hundreds of miles of single-line track in the mountains occasionally gets the better of the controllers, but waiting is always made pleasant by the world-famous Austrian *gemutlichkeit*, often at its best in crowded station bars.

The writer, having once – with some diffi-culty in atrocious winter weather – reached

for the locomotive trials, held to decide on a suitable type for working heavy trains over the Semmering line, was only a partial success, but its derivatives became the basis of what was effectively a European standard type.

The first European 0-10-0s of 1900 were the work of Karl Golsdorf, who became locomotive chief in 1893. Most of Golsdorf's locomotives were either two- or four-cylinder compounds, with his simple automatic system of direct admission of steam to the compound cylinders for starting. Some 2-6-4 high-power locomotives with big fireboxes, necessitating a four-wheel trailing truck and of very distinctive lineaments, appeared in 1908. Reflecting the

nature of the country, the first 2-12-0 appeared in 1910.

Golsdorf's death in harness in 1916 was followed by the construction of a big batch of simpler non-compound 2-8-0s. Some 2-10-0s, 4-8-0s and some high-speed 2-8-4s built in the 1920s completed, in the face of a major electrification programme, Austrian steam construction. All these late-comers were also simples. At the time of the *Anschluss* the steam locomotive stock stood at 2610.

German standard types – particularly 2-10-0s – came in during the Hitler period. After World War II, further electrification and, later, dieselization steadily reduced the

-CENTRAL EUROPE-

NORTH SEA

BALTIC

NETHERLANDS

GERMANY

BELGIUM

LUX.

CZECHOSL

FRANCE

SWITZERLAND

AUSTRIA

ITALY

ADRIATIC SEA

Projection : Conical with two standard parallels

East from Greenwich

Langen station (at the mouth of the Arlberg Tunnel) in good time on his way home, was surprised and delighted to find the train already in. It turned out to be the previous day's, running 23.5 hours late.

A high proportion of Austrian express trains are international, including the famous and original 'Orient Express' (reports of whose recent demise were, like Mark Twain's, greatly exaggerated) and, because the present frontier lines were drawn after the railways were built, numbers of local trains are also international. They meander in and out of neighbouring countries, even Communist Hungary, taking Austrians home to their villages.

STYRIAN PROVINCIAL RAILWAYS – StmLB (and other lines)

Steiermärkische Landesbahnen
Radetzystrasse 31,
Postfach 553,
A8011, Graz.

Nowhere in the world is the charm of the narrow-gauge local railway more compelling than in Austria, where many such lines still meander through beautiful valleys. Almost 300 miles (eleven separate lines) have been sucked into the maw of the Federal Railways, but many others remain independent, although very similar in character and appearance. The 2ft 6in gauge is almost universal.

The Styrian Provincial Railways operate a group of seven separate lines (mostly in narrow gauge in the south of the country) which justify

Top: A stone arch and steel bridge on the Austrian State Railways route over the Brenner Pass.

Above: The Ybbstalbahn. Now dieselized, this Austrian narrow-gauge line used this standard Krauss 0-6-2T for its motive power. Similar steam locomotives still work trains over slim-gauge tracks in Austria today.

inclusion here on the grounds of having 34 locomotives (sixteen diesel, twelve steam and five electric) and a total mileage of 120. About 500,000 tons of goods and 900,000 passengers are carried annually but, alas, not profitably, for expenses are 2.5 times the receipts.

Over half the system was opened in 1892-93; the last section – from Birkfeld to Ratten – was complete in 1930. The longest line is the fifty-mile Murtalbahn from Unzmarkt to Mauterndorf.

As on all sections of the Austrian narrow gauge, 0-6-2Ts by Krauss of effectively a standard design were the commonest, but much variety from 0-6-0 tender tank locomotives to 0-10-0Ts with flexible wheel-base was used also. Steam is now virtually relegated to tourist or pleasure use, the Murtalbahn going so far as to offer 'self-drive-hire' with a small 0-4-0T! The independent Zillertalbahn near Innsbruck also offers this exceedingly rare service.

Neat diesel locomotives now handle most StmLB trains, except on two sections which have ancient electrifications.

BELGIUM

See map on page 94.

Belgium is a densely populated and heavily industrialized country with a railway system to match. Virtually the whole network belongs to the 2500-mile state main-line system, the only significant exception being a 140-mile remnant of the state local (*vicinaux*) transport administration which, before it took to the road, administered over 3000 miles of railway. The density (at 2.9 miles per 100 square miles of territory) of railways in Belgium is the highest in the world.

The boundaries of Belgium have remained virtually constant since the first steam railway in continental Europe was opened from Brussels to Malines in 1835. However, the country and its railways suffered exceptional devastation in both world wars. After World War II, the destruction was so complete that rapid modernization was facilitated.

BELGIAN NATIONAL RAILWAYS – SNCB
Société Nationale des Chemins de Fer Belgiques
85 Rue de France,
1070 Brussels.

Origins and Development
The coming of the railway age coincided with the formation of the Belgian state in 1830. Accordingly, to foster unity, the government made itself responsible for constructing the majority of the main lines in Belgium, thereby pioneering state ownership of railways in the world. Even so, some lines, for example Liège-Namur, were built by foreign interests. Indeed, until World War II, this line was operated by the French Nord Company. The state system expanded rapidly and by 1843, Brussels was connected to Antwerp, to Ostend via Ghent, to Namur, to France via Mons and to Germany via Liège.

The state railways were reorganized as the Belgian Railway Company in 1926. Electrification began on a small scale in 1935 with conversion of the Brussels-Antwerp main line and after the war was extended rapidly to include all the principal main lines; 800 miles, one-third of the total, are now completed, including, of course, all the lines with the heaviest traffic. The system chosen, 3000v DC, is alas, incompatible with those of all Belgium's neighbours.

Civil Engineering
Belgium is by no means flat but it could not be described as mountainous either. Accordingly, no exceptional feats of civil engineering were involved in building the railways. One major achievement is the Brussels Junction line, connecting the Nord and Midi stations – previously termini – with a six-track railway right

The 'Arlberg Express' between Zell-am-See and Salzburg.

through the centre of the city, partly elevated and partly underground. Construction began in 1911, but economic circumstances and two wars delayed completion until 1958.

Locomotive Landmarks

The original stud for the Brussels–Malines line consisted of three locomotives supplied by Tayleur and Company of England: 2-4-0 *L'Eléphant*, 2-2-2s *Stephenson* and *La Flèche*. Later, locomotive builders in Belgium emerged – in the 1900s there were as many as eleven, a large number for so small a country – and they supplied most of the country's needs, but relatively little abroad.

Fairly conventional engineering was often combined with very unusual appearance: for example there were some 2-4-2s produced in the late 1900s with square chimneys, which seemed like a bad dream to locomotive men from any other country. In the early 1900s

following the gold medal win by a Caledonian Railway 4-4-0 at the Brussels Exhibition of 1897, over 700 4-4-0s and 0-6-0s of Scottish design but mostly of Belgian construction – far more than ever existed in their native land – were put into service.

Simultaneously some French inspired de Glehn compound 4-4-2s and 4-6-0s were built, but by 1910 the Belgian Jean Flamme had put into service some 4-6-2s, which again looked like nothing on earth, for the smokebox was located behind the four cylinders and bogie. This apparently was not enough to emphasize Belgium's individuality for, in addition, the chimney sported a startling and immense capuchon. In fact, of course, no nation that included the honoured names of Walschearts and Belpaire (inventors, respectively, of the valve gear and firebox that bear their names) among its locomotive engineers needed to do anything further to assert its personality. At

Above: A modern diesel unit at the head of a passenger train at Brussels' Midi station.

Left: A British-style 4-4-2T pulls a local train to Luttre out of Manage in 1963. Note the extra coal carried on the cab roof. Many early Belgian steam locomotives were of basic British design.

the same time 100 2-10-0s to Flamme's design were built – this at a time when, in Britain, for example, 0-6-0s were the norm for new construction in the field of heavy freight haulage.

World War I was followed by an influx of standard German designs under reparations and, later, a relatively small amount of new construction of relatively straightforward conception.

Electrification and dieselization in Belgium followed very conventional – and incidentally very successful – lines with the usual bogie locomotives supplied by Belgian constructors. The majority of the diesels had highly developed power plants from General Motors of the USA, mostly built under licence. Steam was phased out in 1960, apart from a few post-World War II American-built 2-8-0s kept as a strategic reserve, but occasionally run on pleasure trips.

Train Services

The range of international destinations served by through trains from Brussels includes Moscow, Copenhagen, Vienna, Zurich, Berne, Rome, London (via ferry), Berlin and Warsaw, an indication of Belgium's importance in the European network. As appropriate to a small densely populated country, internal services consist mainly of fast electric multiple-unit trains, running in many cases to regular-interval timings.

All sleeping, dining and on-train refreshment services are operated by the Wagons-Lits organization, which is of Belgian origin.

BULGARIA

See map on pages 86-87.

Independence from a long period of Turkish domination came in 1878, as did, more or less, the first railway. The railways even had royal patronage. Before World War II, a period when most European railways suffered some degree of neglect, Bulgaria's were protected by the fact that King Boris was a great railway enthusiast, holding, (it is said) his own engine-driver's ticket. On one occasion at least when he was a passenger and the engine-driver was taken ill, the King immediately took over the throttle.

Bulgaria is not a poor country; this is reflected in a modernized and efficient railway system and a prosperous and enjoyment-loving populace. The cyrillic script in use is confusing to western visitors at first but once this is mastered, unintelligible notices often dissolve into recognizable and useful words – for example, *pectopaht* becomes *restaurant*. (The thing which takes longer to get used to is the fact that a Bulgarian nod means 'no' and a shake of the head 'yes'.)

As befits a Marxist government, all Bulgarian railways are operated by the state.

Below: The façade of the Bulgarian Railways station at Ruse on the Bulgarian border with Rumania.

BULGARIAN STATE RAILWAYS – BDZ
Iwan Wazov Strasse 3, Sofia.

As elsewhere, the first railway in Bulgaria owes its existence to the geographical fact that some of the world's most navigable rivers (and the Danube rates high in this regard) are much less navigable near their mouths or deltas, so a by-pass railway from Ruschuk (now Ruse) 139 miles to Varna was opened in 1866. The original station at Ruse is now the National Railway Museum. The main line across the country from Dragoman via Sofia and Plovdiv to Silvengrad (leading directly to Istanbul) opened in 1888. This was the famous 'Orient Express' route.

Since World War II, approximately half the 2500-mile system has been electrified.

Civil Engineering

Much of Bulgaria is mountainous and one notes six spiral tunnels, four on the Septembri narrow-gauge line in the south, and two others on the main north-south link in the centre of the country. The great bridge over the Danube at Ruse, leading into Rumania, was completed in 1954. It is 150 miles nearer the river's mouth than the next bridge over the Danube.

Locomotive Landmarks

The first locomotives to run in Bulgaria were 0-6-2Ts by Couillet of France but locomotives of standard German designs and manufacture predominated in the days of steam. Actually,

Bulgaria went beyond anything normally built for the Fatherland with 4-10-0 tender and 2-12-4 tank designs. Passenger power took the form of 4-8-2s but the ubiquitous standard German 2-10-0s predominated in the later years of steam, still not quite over in 1978. Even on the 2ft 6in gauge the standard locomotives were Germanic 2-10-2Ts of Polish build. The handsome lines of all these locomotives are enhanced by a bright green livery complete with golden wings on the smokebox.

Electrification did not begin until well after World War II and accordingly, Bulgaria began by using the high voltage standard frequency AC system. Skoda of Czechoslovakia supplied the first bogie 25,000v 50-cycle locomotives. Lines with lesser traffic are being dieselized.

Train Services

One hundred million passengers are carried on BDZ annually plus 79 million tons of freight, hauled an average distance of 120 miles. The successors and the derivatives of the famous 'Simplon Orient Express' finally dwindled away in 1976 when the three-times-a-week Paris-Istanbul sleeper was withdrawn. Instead, solid trains of Soviet sleeping cars run daily from Moscow to Sofia and to the Black Sea resorts in season.

CYPRUS

See map on pages 250-251.

In the early 1900s the then-British island of Cyprus had a 67-mile 2ft 6in gauge railway which ran from Famagusta on the east coast, passed a mile or so away from Nicosia, the capital, and reached Morphou on the north coast. It was opened on 21 October 1905 and closed on 31 December 1951. Among the twelve-strong locomotive fleet were four noble 4-8-4Ts from Kitsons of Leeds. There were (possibly are) also two short private mineral lines.

Above: The main line of the Cyprus Government Railway ran from the port of Famagusta to the capital, Nicosia. This 2ft 6in gauge line tottered on into the 1950s but by then its ageing Nasmyth Wilson 4-4-0s and even its rattling railcars were anachronisms. This picture of the midday train from Nicosia was taken in April 1946.

Below: A Bulgarian 2-12-4T steam locomotive hauls an empty mineral train back to the mines.

Left: The 76cm narrow-gauge Bulgarian line to Septembri now uses smart red diesels in place of the huge green 2-10-2 tanks which sometimes ran in pairs in earlier years.

CZECHOSLOVAKIA

See map on pages 26–27.

CZECHOSLOVAK STATE RAILWAYS – CSD

Ceskoslovenské Státní Dráhy
Příkopy 33,
Prague 1.

Until 1918 Czechoslovakia was part of the Austro-Hungarian empire. From a railway historian's point of view, Austria and Hungary were separate entities and, accordingly, the provinces of Bohemia and Morovia should be regarded as originally part of Austria; Slovenia as part of Hungary. Since Vienna and Budapest were the respective focal points of these railways, the new republic had to alter the railway maps to suit a new country whose capital was Prague. Some 100 miles of new line were built and some 125 miles more upgraded from single-line branches to double-track main lines; in this way east-west communication was improved, in line with the new direction of political control.

All significant public railways were taken over by the new state and this involved several major privately owned concerns as well as part of the Austrian and Hungarian state railways. In gratitude to the man who helped create the nation, the centre of the new system in Prague was called the Wilson Station; under Communist rule even the most benevolent of American presidents are anathema – the central station is now called Hlavni.

One small but significant step for the new nation was to make some order out of a motive power fleet that consisted of 184 locomotive classes. Each class was allocated a number which – unlike those allocated to modern aircraft and computers – contained a code which still tells anyone with a certain mathematical ability something useful concerning the locomotive.

For a locomotive foreman with a strange engine on his hands it is important to know the maximum load on any axle, which governs the lines on which the locomotive can work: too heavy an axle-load and damage could be done to the track. If you added ten to the righthand or 'units' digit, this gave the axle-load in tons.

The centre digit gave a clue to the locomotive's maximum speed – add three and multiply by ten and there it was in kilometres per hour. The hundreds digit simply told the number of coupled axles. Hence a class 498 'Albatross'

Left: The 2ft 6in gauge 2-10-2 and narrow-gauge train on the banks of the Danube near Oryakhovo.

Above: The 498 class 4-8-2s were Czechoslovakia's pride and joy – and with good cause as they were magnificent modern machines, lasting in regular service into the mid-1970s. Here is one with the 'Saxonia Express' in July 1965.

locomotive had four coupled axles – in fact they were 4-8-2s, among the best and most modern in the world – was allowed to run at 75mph and had an axle-loading capacity of eighteen tons.

This excellent and quite unique classification system was a mere reflection of the superb quality of Czech locomotive building, which has continued (mainly through the well-known firm of Skoda) into the diesel and electric era. Steam is currently (1978) still in use but on a small and rapidly decreasing scale.

World War II came and went with much destruction, but with the Czech borders and railway system more or less as they were before the notorious Munich Pact (Hitler said 'I have no more territorial claims to make in Europe' but the German tradition of ignoring scraps of paper proved too much for him) of 1938. The system now comprises 8150 miles of standard-gauge route, 62 miles of broad (Soviet) gauge and 110 miles of narrow-gauge line. Fifteen hundred miles are electrified, most at 3000v DC, but more recently at 25,000v AC.

Incidentally, the first ever recorded railway (horse-drawn with wooden rails) occurred in what was then Hungary but is now southern Czechoslovakia. It appears as embroidery on a sacred altar cloth dating from around 1500. (Where, however, does one end in moving away from what we now know as a railway; do

the grooves for chariot wheels in the stone-paved streets of Roman cities count?)

Freight traffic in Czechoslovakia now exceeds 320 million tons annually, needing a fleet of around 150,000 wagons. Passenger traffic, using a fleet of over 10,000 carriages, is three times what it was before World War II.

DENMARK

See map on pages 38–39.

DANISH STATE RAILWAYS – DSB
Danske Statsbaner
40 Solvgade,
1349 Copenhagen K.

Denmark's railway *system* began on 27 June 1847, when the locomotive *Odin* (a 2-2-2 from Sharp-Stewart of Manchester) hauled a train on the Zeeland Railway Company's line from Copenhagen to Roskilde. This was not the first railway in Denmark as then constituted, for a line was opened the previous year from Altona to Kiel in the province of Schleswig-Holstein, which in 1864 was grabbed by Prussia to form part of a greater Germany.

The original lines were privately owned, but

in the later years of the century the trunk routes were taken over by the state. In 1885 the present Danish State Railways was formed; local railways remained (and to some extent still remain) unnationalized. This 'non-doctrinaire' approach, typical of the Danish way of doing things, pervades the story of Danish railways.

Denmark presented few problems to railway builders regarding hills and valleys. Her difficulty lay in the fact that the places to be linked by rail lay on several separate islands. For many years the most important routes were interrupted by train ferries: for example between Copenhagen (on Zeeland) and Esjberg (on Jutland) there were two ferry rides and, hence, a journey time of seven hours for the 194 miles. Between the wars efforts were made to fill in some of the gaps. First, in 1935, was the 0.75-mile bridge across the Little Belt, which enabled DSB to introduce diesel-electric 'lightning trains' (*Lyntog* in Danish) which reduced that seven-hour timing to four. In 1938 came the two-mile Storstrom bridge connecting Zeeland with Lolland, an island which is a stepping-stone on the route south from Copenhagen into Germany. Both these bridges are in the world class with main spans of 450ft and 722ft respectively. At the same time, the DSB still finds employment for modern ferries taking trains across the sixteen mile Great Belt and across the Baltic and the Skaggerak to Germany and Sweden.

Danish steam was distinctive, handsome and not allowed to pass away in unwanted disrepute. Indeed, one of the last steam trains to run in Denmark was the recent funeral train of King Frederick; he was a life-long railway enthusiast and had actually specified this form of transport for his last journey. Distinction lay deeper than the band of national colours which Danish steam locomotives carried round their chimneys; older locomotives frequently had the rare Allan straight-link valve gear in full view outside the frames and later ones (such as the elegant compound 4-4-2s) had big wind-cutter wedge-fronted cabs.

Some of the 4-4-2s were rebuilt as 4-6-2s, but the most powerful Danish express locomotives, also compound 4-6-2s, actually came from Sweden, which was disposing of them because of electrification. The economics of compounding made sense in a country which had to import its coal.

There was no Gadarene rush into dieselization, which cost so many unthinking railways so much. In fact, the Danes spent over forty years on the job. Hence no scrapping of brand-new steam locomotives or, for that matter newish but unwisely ordered diesels, which characterized the process in Great Britain and other countries. Of the Western European systems, the DSB was the first to begin dieselization, in 1927 – and one of the last to complete, in 1970. In Denmark the word 'complete' is correct, as main-line electrification has not yet begun there, understandable in a country which has neither coal, water-power, nor mountain grades. There is a 1500v DC suburban electrification around Copenhagen, using 283 electric motor coaches, but elsewhere a fleet of 298 diesel locomotives and 105 railcars reign supreme.

The early amalgamation of third-class and second-class accommodation into a 'general' passenger class, anticipated similar moves in the rest of Europe by many years.

Top: The striking and unusual lines of a Danish 4-4-2 steam locomotive.

Centre and left: Over forty years ago Danish Railways were putting diesel-electric power into service. The locomotive (above left) was built in 1937 and the one on the left is a modern diesel locomotive at Jutland station.

Extreme left: The five hundredth engine, No T679, emerges from the Nové Zámky (Czechoslovakia) locomotive works on 9 July 1973.

Scandinavia

ICELAND
on the same scale
as general map

1:5 000 000

Projection: Conical with two standard parallels

Right: A Lyntog train leaves the Great Belt train ferry at Nyborg across the channel from Korsör.

Below: The circulating area of the great hall of Copenhagen's Central Station is typical of the general Germanic design found from the Baltic to the Black Sea.

FINLAND

See maps on pages 38–39 and 118–119.

FINNISH STATE RAILWAYS – VR
Valtionrautatiet,
Vilhonkatu 13,
00100 Helsinki 10.

Finland is a land without mountains – except for some high hills in the extreme north called mountains by courtesy. However, little of it is flat; the typical landscape is of many low hills of granite, ground down by ice-age glaciers, covered by forest and many lakes, some forming large navigable systems. The south is relatively mild and fertile, but conditions get harder further north. Although the railway system does not penetrate as far as the Arctic coast, two lines go well beyond the Arctic circle.

History
Although there is a large Swedish-speaking minority, Finland was a part of Imperial Russia until it seized its independence in 1918. A large part of the east of the country was regained by the USSR through conquest in 1945, but Finland retains a genuine independence and is, in fact, the only Western democracy to have any border with Russia itself (apart from a short Norwegian frontier length in the Arctic). A legacy of Soviet dominion is witnessed by the fact that the Finnish railway system is built to the Soviet gauge of 5ft.

The first railway in Finland, from Helsinki to Hameenlinna, was opened in 1862. Connection was made to St Petersburg (Leningrad) by 1870, and construction, almost all undertaken directly by the state, continued steadily up to 1918 and thereafter. Indeed, two important new lines, improving and shortening major routes, have been opened during the 1970s, chief of which is the 75-mile Tampere-Seinajoki link. The present route mileage is 3750.

Locomotive Development
Even more than in the USSR proper, early Finnish locomotive design was much influenced by American practice. Later on, German influence predominated. Right up till the end of steam traction, woodburners outnumbered coalburners, since wood is the only home-produced fuel, and it was only after the 1920s that coalburners came to work most of the heavier duties. Designs tended to be hampered by axle-load restrictions, and conditions did not require any remarkable machines to be developed; the steam fleet consisted mainly of handsome but fairly conventional 2-6-0s, 4-6-0s and 2-8-0s, with 2-8-2s, 4-6-2s and a few US-built 2-10-0s coming in from the late 1930s onwards. Dieselization had begun by the early 1950s, but was not rushed and not completed for twenty years by which time electrification was well in hand on the busiest lines in the south. However the Finns remain nervous about the strategic 'wisdom' of dependence on imported oil or easily bombed hydro-electric complexes (with good reason in their short national history) and still maintain a large number of woodburning locomotives in reserve.

Train Services and Rolling Stock
Considering the relatively sparse population, passenger train services in Finland are very good, quite fast and frequent. To some extent this occurs because of reliance on diesel railcars, but even during the steam age the picture was much better than might have been expected. One reason might be the fact that roads are not as good as they can be in kinder climates; frost in the sandy soil tends to destroy most road surfaces unless they are very strong and expensive. Until the last decade most passenger coaches were wooden-bodied, and shared with Soviet railways a very large loading gauge giving plenty of space inside. However, heating has been by steam for many years, and the Soviet practice of having a separate coal stove in each coach is not followed. Recent coaches, railcars, and multiple units (both diesel and electric) have been in line with current European practice. The only international passenger service is from Helsinki to Leningrad, where no gauge problem arises; there is some limited use of axle-changing to accommodate standard-gauge freight vehicles at the connection with the Swedish railways at Tornio at the head of the Gulf of Bothnia, and at the ice-free port of Hangö whence a train ferry operates to the East German port of Travemünde.

Operations and Signalling
Traditional Finnish signalling is German in equipment, and somewhat American in method. Racquet-shaped upper-quadrant semaphores, with numbers of arms coding divergent routes, plus wire-worked frames and points are Germanic, and single-line working by train

order and telephone are American. More modern installations, on both single and double line, tend more to the international norm of CTC, and automatic block. One feature which remains doggedly in stations and yards is an absence of remote control of points, due to the impossiblity of keeping wires and rods clear and working during icebound weather; most points therefore had to be hand-worked and locally indicated. A few modern power-worked, propane-heated points do exist.

Administration and Finance

The Finnish State Railways is now under the control of the Ministry of Communications. Some minor railways, including several of 75cm and 60cm gauge, were privately owned, but no independent undertaking now survives. There is an annual deficit of some thirty percent.

Top: Diesel shunter and electric commuter trains at Helsinki. Today Finland's trains are diesel hauled and steam no longer appears on its 5ft gauge tracks.

Centre right: Further north in Finland, where the traffic is comparatively sparse, passengers are catered for in blue and cream railcars which run between wooden clapboard stations. Here is a car waiting to depart from Oulu to Kemi.

Right: More modern than their spark arresting stacks make them appear, Finland's 2-8-0 1100 class woodburners are mainly confined to shunting duties further north, where copious supplies of fuel are available for little cost. Here at Rouveniemi, No 1150 sets the coaches for the overnight train to Helsinki.

Above: A steam-hauled freight train at Esjberg in Denmark.

Above: Gare de Lyon, Paris, France.

Right: French signals glow in the night.

FRANCE

See map on pages 46-47.

Except for the industrialized belt running along the Belgian and Luxembourg frontiers from Lille towards Strasbourg, France, with a total population of 53 million, is the least densely populated country of Western Europe, excluding the Scandinavian and Iberian peninsulas. There are of course great cities, especially Paris, and industrial and mining areas, but most of the nation is farmland, forest, or mountain, so that it is not too difficult to escape from urban pressures. The largest area of flat plain lies in a great 180° arc south of Paris, to a radius of perhaps 100 miles; to the north the landscape varies from gently rolling to hilly, but with little that could be called mountainous. The southern centre comprises the Massif Central, high hills often wild and broken, showing here and there signs of volcanic origin; and along the southern and southeastern borders, facing Spain, Italy and Switzerland, are (generally) very rugged alpine areas, including the Pyrenees and the Savoy Alps themselves. In these regions the great river valleys mark the lines of communication, indeed of most development of any kind.

FRENCH NATIONAL RAILWAYS – SNCF

Société Nationale des Chemins de Fer Français,
88 Rue St.-Lazare,
75436 Paris.

Greater distances and smaller population meant that the French railway network was slower to become established than the British. Gallic logic ensured that once it was commenced, it was designed and carried out in a much more comprehensive and cohesive form; and Gallic tradition insisted that its whole philosophy and policy in every department had to spring from different roots and develop uniquely French objects and attributes. Since the seventeenth century, the French state had concerned itself with constructing the best system of roads, and later canals, in Europe; once the British had demonstrated the feasibility of a national railway system, several years were needed to work out how one could be established in accordance with French legal and political principles, although a few lines were commenced earlier by impatient small companies. The Railway Law of 11 June 1842 is probably the grandest and most ambitious programme of organization and construction ever launched anywhere, with the possible exception of the recent American Interstate Highway system.

Firstly, the 1842 Law established the basic principle that the state was to own all public railways without exception, just as it owned the roads. This fixed its right to determine what lines were built as well as to supervise their operation. However, private enterprise would be invited to work the railways under lease;

Top left: On 28 March 1955 the French Railways (SNCF) broke the World Rail Speed Record at 205 mph using electric locomotive CC.7107 – seen here during the run passing the level crossing at Labouheyre.

Left: Two of France's top expresses, 'L'Aquitaine' and 'Le Capitôle' (together with relief trains) await departure from Paris Austerlitz station on a peak traffic day.

Top: SNCF electric locomotive BB9004, joint holder with CC7107 of the World Rail Speed Record of 205 mph hauls a fast train between Paris and Savoy.

Above: A Clermont-Ferrand to Paris Express accelerates after leaving Vichy in April 1967. These superb 241P class 4-8-2s were based on a PLM design and though not so efficient as the Chapelon 240P locomotive, gave a very good account of themselves.

45

FRANCE

each line, once built by the state, would be put up to tender and the company offering the largest rent and the shortest lease (within a maximum of 99 years) would be given the concession.

Secondly, the 1842 scheme ordained a network of seven main lines radiating from Paris, plus two transverse routes; these still form the foundation of the system. These lines ran from Paris to Belgium via Amiens and Lille; to Marseille via Lyon; to Bordeaux and Spain via Orleans; to the Massif Central, also via Orleans; to Brittany via Chartres and Rennes; and to Normandy via Rouen. The transverse lines were to run from Bordeaux to Marseille via Toulouse and Narbonne; and from Dijon, between Paris and Lyon, to Mulhouse, Basel and Strasbourg.

As the network developed, the 1842 Plan was modified by schemes of (principally) 1859, 1865 and 1879. Ultimately the intention developed, and was almost achieved, that there should be a standard-gauge railway to every Sous-Préfecture, or roughly every town of over 1500 inhabitants, with feeders of standard or narrow gauge generously filling in the gaps (about a third of the 1914 route-mileage in France was metre-gauge). Working these rail-

FRANCE
DEPARTMENTS
1:8 000 000

1. VAL d'OISE
2. YVELINES
3. ESSONNE
4. HAUTS-DE-SEINE
5. SEINE-ST. DENIS
6. VAL-DE-MARNE
7. VILLE DE PARIS

1 : 4 000 000

CORSICA
on same scale

COPYRIGHT. GEORGE PHILIP & SON. LTD.

East from Greenwich

Below: The Mont-Doré portion of the Clermont-Ferrand to Paris Express tackles the long climb (eighteen miles at 1 in 40) to Vauriat Summit in March 1949. The engine is one of a batch built by the North British Locomotive Company in 1916/17 as class 141TA. The design was based on a very successful class built by SLM Winterthur for the Thunersee Railway in Switzerland.

Below: The Lyon–Nantes 'Corail' train on the Montciand viaduct near Arfeuilles in October 1976. This is one of the fastest cross-country services in France.

ways were private companies whose dividends were, in general, guaranteed by the state, which took in exchange for the guarantee, two-thirds of any greater profits. Some lines were, however, worked by the state itself, usually because of the failure of the original leaseholding company. After 1930 this dense railway network needed pruning as road transport developed. Almost all the narrow gauge has now gone, mainly through closure; the national route mileage has declined by about forty percent to its present figure of around 25,000 miles. Similarly, the financial difficulties which had begun to face the old companies, most of which had worked happily and uneventfully for eighty years, led to their nationalization in 1938 and formation of the present Société Nationale des Chemins de Fer Français, an act carried out by a socialist government but with a minimum of the bitter quarrelling, obstruction and disappointment which marked the nationalization of the British network ten years later.

However, since the old companies have left their mark both physically and in folklore forty years later, short accounts of the main ones are

in order. There were six of them, following an initial period of regrouping, which had settled by 1857, and they still in large part are mirrored by the six regions of the modern SNCF.

Chemin de Fer de l'Est

This company was incorporated in 1845 as the Chemin de fer de Strasbourg, when it received the concession for the Paris-Strasbourg trunk line. It changed its name in 1854 on obtaining the concession for the parallel route from Paris to Basel via Chaumont. It covered, exclusively, the eastern quadrant of the nation centring on these lines, without sending any branches out of the area, and it remained reasonably affluent throughout. The main event in its corporate history was the purchase – forced, but for real money – by the victorious Prussians after 1870, of its lines in the seized provinces of Alsace and Lorraine; on the return of these territories to France in 1919, the railways (somewhat Prussianized meanwhile and converted to right-hand running) were administered until 1938 by a separate state organization as the Réseau de l'Alsace et de Lorraine.

Chemin de Fer du Nord

This company received the concession for the line to Belgium in 1842, and prospered happily thereafter, coming to monopolize the area between the territory of the Est and the Channel coast (including but not going far beyond the Paris-Calais line). It did send one tentacle westwards for the important freight route from Amiens to Rouen. Its prosperity was originally such that not only did the company repay the whole cost of building its main lines to the government but until war came in 1914 it never had to ask the government to make up its dividend to the level of the guarantee and so never had to surrender any of its profits. Being so rich, it always had the reputation of being the best-run line with the best equipment, not unjustly.

Chemin de Fer Paris-Lyon-Méditerranée

The PLM was nearly as continuously well-off as the Nord, and arguably as well run. It was formed in 1857 as the result of a series of amalgamations of smaller companies which had not only come to own the whole of the trunk line from Paris via Dijon and Lyon to Marseille – the *Ligne Imperiale* – but also included the then-unfinished parallel line via Vierzon and Clermont Ferrand to Nimes which the 1842 Plan had intended should go to an ill-fated rival concern, the Grand Central. Following further growth and take-overs, the PLM came to monopolize the whole of its area as well, eastwards to the Swiss and Italian borders and westward to a less distinct line running northwards from the unimportant town of Sète on the Mediterranean coast, between Toulouse and Marseille. By far the biggest and most conspicuous railway company, the PLM came to typify French railway practice; where the other companies did things differently, as they quite often did (even in things like signalling), these variations were regarded as departures from a PLM norm.

Chemin de Fer Paris–Orléans

This company had been set up in 1838 to build the short line indicated by its title, but in 1842 it obtained the concession for the Paris–Bordeaux route and began to grow. Its two

principal main lines were from Paris to Bordeaux and to Toulouse (via Limoges), and it monopolized the area west of the PLM country as far as the Bordeaux main line. However, westwards of that things got a little complicated, (discussed below). Until 1934 the Orléans company also had the important line from Tours to Nantes and Quimper, and so held half the Breton peninsula, but as part of that year's rearrangements lost it.

Chemin de Fer du Midi

The only one of the major companies not to serve Paris, the Midi was established in 1852 to work the transversal line from Bordeaux to Toulouse and the Mediterranean (meeting the PLM end-on at Sète). It came to own all the other railways south of this line, but its only important venture to the north of it was the long and mountainous branch from Béziers to Neussargues, right on the PLM/Orléans borders. Always closely associated with the Orléans company, from 1934 the two railways were worked as one and the companies thus amalgamated in everything but legal form. However,

the Midi is historically important for two matters. One is that, dissatisfied with its unreal eastern terminal at Sète, it fought hard with the government for the right to build a line of its own to Marseilles, ultimately losing, and so confirming the principle of the 1842 legislation that directly parallel and competing railways would not be allowed. The other is that the Midi was the first French railway to go all-out for electrification; even by the 1920s its policy was to electrify everything, and this was largely achieved by 1934 (with the major exception of the easy Bordeaux–Toulouse main line, on which the company's steam locomotives were to serve out their time). Following 1934 the policy was taken up by the combined undertakings; although checked by the war, by 1948 a map of French main-line electrification still closely resembled a map of the PO-Midi.

And in the West

This brief account so far omits any mention of the corporate history of the railways of the western part of the country, between the Nord and the Orléans. This is because it was complicated. In the beginning were the Normandy and Brittany companies, holding the concessions under the 1842 Plan. They did not prosper and amalgamated in 1855 to form the Chemin de fer de l'Ouest which, surprisingly enough, did not prosper either. However, it struggled along from bankruptcy to reorganization and back until 1909, and contrived to operate (after some fashion) the main lines from Paris to Brest, le Havre and Cherbourg, and in the area surrounding. Much less respectable were the various small companies which maintained, in a kind of state of statutory brigandage, the majority of the lines in the area west of the Bordeaux main line and south of Nantes; ultimately during the 1870s things reached such a pass that the government cancelled their concessions and ran their lines itself.

Having just smacked down the Midi for wanting a rival line to Marseilles, the government then changed the rules in its own favour. In 1883 in an endeavour to make these lines in the Vendée pay, the government linked certain lines together with others obtained in exchange from the Orléans company, and demanded from the Ouest running powers from Chartres into Paris. It then established itself as the

operator of a rival and competing main line from Paris to Bordeaux, the only example of direct mainline competition in French railway history. This continued until after 1938. The state system having thus been linked with the Compagnie de l'Ouest, when that sank into bankruptcy again in 1909 it was nationalized and the two concerns then operated as the Réseau de l'Etat. It remained something of a byword for most kinds of malpractice until finally taken in hand in the 1930s; the Paris–le Mans electrification of 1937, with its associated line and junction improvements for high speed running, set new standards worldwide.

With the 1938 unification under the SNCF, most of the old and unique legal foundation for the French railway network became of academic interest, but not all. It still colours the French official and public attitude, and in many ways they speak of 'our' railways much more meaningfully than elsewhere in Western Europe. After all, the main lines never were privately owned, and commercial motives have never been allowed to outweigh social and political ones; but yet the operator has always stood aside from politics and been firmly independent. Few other countries have managed

Bottom right: A modern stainless-steel train on the Paris Métro.

Below: French speed is electric.

this balance so well, and its roots in France lie still in the 1842 system.

Civil Engineering

Since the state undertook the original construction of the main-line networks, there is a certain consistency of style about them, particularly in the older buildings. But, although they were later relaxed when the time came to build branch lines and routes over which heavy traffic was never likely to pass, the fundamental specifications of all lines – maximum grade, sharpest curve – was decided *ab initio* and centrally, quite independently of the financial state of the company which ultimately worked the line. Nothing was therefore ever skimped, and large and expensive works were undertaken without trepidations. In the 1840s the civil engineering of French railways was much influenced by the ideas of Joseph Locke, who built several early lines including that from Paris to le Havre. Locke was much more willing to accept steep gradients (by which he meant something around 1 in 125) than his mentor George Stephenson (who liked to avoid anything steeper than about 1 in 250, or else concentrate it dramatically into a short pitch

designed for cable working). On the other hand, Locke shunned tunnels; but both engineers undertook very large viaducts and earthworks, and liked to avoid sharp curves. Locke's lines therefore tended to be rather cheaper to construct at the price of involving gradients which in steam days proved demanding against fast and heavy traffic, but yet were solid and well adapted to speeds of up to 60 or 75 mph even through fairly difficult country; and this, in effect, well describes the character of French main lines built up to about 1870. Later, more faith was put in tractive effort, and main lines built in the 1880s and 1890s, such as the direct route from Limoges to Toulouse, are quite difficult.

But state financing had its most dramatic effect on some of the spectacular engineering undertaken in hilly areas, even on lines of no great importance at all. It having been decided, for instance, that railway policy required the construction of a line from Volvic to Lapeyrouse, west of Clermont-Ferrand, it followed that the then-highest viaduct in the world was unavoidably necessary; no commercial concern would ever have built the Fades viaduct, carrying the tracks 430ft above the bottom of a

limestone gorge, but the line was felt to be needed even though little traffic would use it. Some of the other high viaducts in the Massif Central are equally impressive, both as engineering works of art and as, in some sense, sledgehammers to crack nuts. Perhaps the most remarkable example of mountain railway building never in fact got finished; construction of the line from le Puy to Lalevade d'Ardeche was suspended in 1914, never to be resumed, with the long summit tunnel at St Cirgues (two miles) finished and much else, but not the southern descent of the mountains which would have included some extraordinary gyrations inside the vast crater of a primeval volcano, involving two distinct spirals within a third; quite a unique feature.

Locomotive Landmarks

Just as the legal and political foundations of French railways were unique, so was their locomotive practice, particularly in steam days. Fundamental to their approach was the idea that a locomotive driver had to be quick, sure, and dependable, master of a complex machine, and that it was therefore a job for a young man. None of the gradual promotion through the grades of cleaner, fireman, and passed-fireman universal elsewhere – a driver was trained directly for his job, including classes in scientific theory, and workshop practice. After twenty years on the footplate he retired on a good pension, and it was nothing to see an engine crew with the fireman twenty or thirty years older than the driver. On the other hand, discipline was strict, and no excuses acceptable; for example, if a driver passed a danger signal by mistake, he never drove again.

With men of this calibre to operate them, French steam locomotives therefore tended to be more complex and sophisticated. Elsewhere the sheer difficulty of getting crews to understand its finer points, quite as much as any question of maintenance costs, made the steam locomotive into a rather crude and simple tool. The French team made it possible to turn it into an exact instrument for extracting the last ounce of power from every ton of coal burned, and a complex system of bonuses motivated the crew to make the effort. There was, for example, a worthwhile bonus for saving fuel, but a very much larger one for making up time (within speed limits) lost for other reasons. This system reached its zenith with the big mainline locomotives of the 1920-1950 period, almost all four-cylinder compounds. On nationalization in 1938 the great André Chapelon was placed in charge of steam locomotive research and development. Unfortunately the war and postwar changes prevented him, very narrowly, from actually achieving any new construction of engines designed to take full

advantage of his ideas, but his utter transformations of older machines by rebuilding them made a series of dramatic impressions. Not least the last. In 1947 the die had already been cast in favour of widespread electrification and cessation of steam construction, and plans were almost ready to build the first series of powerful express passenger electric locomotives. Then Chapelon wheeled out his experimental 4-8-4, a rebuild of a twenty-year-old 4-8-2, which put up a dazzling performance and clearly outclassed anything that the new electric would be capable of. The modernists scurried, panic-stricken, back to their drawing boards, and the 5000hp 2D2 9100 series of electrics which ultimately emerged in 1950 had been very much beefed up as a result of this rude experience.

Steam has now gone, of course, but something of its panache remains all the same. The designers of the latest 8000hp (continuous rating) electrics, and some of the more powerful main-line diesels, have achieved the nearly impossible by producing machines which combine – almost uniquely – high performance with a distinctive and acceptable exterior styling. For all of us but the specialists, a diesel is a diesel is a diesel – unless perhaps it's French.

New Construction and Electrification
As we have seen, the Midi and the Paris-Orléans led the way in electrification before 1938, establishing the 1500v DC overhead system firmly in the south-west. The first great

postwar conversion, the Paris-Lyon-Marseille trunk route, was also carried out on this system. However, before it was completed a cheaper method had been developed by SNCF engineers, using 25,000v 50 cycles AC. This has, since 1950, covered most of the north and east of the country, with some lines also in the west and south. No DC lines have been converted to AC, as in Britain, because it was felt that this would be wasted effort; indeed DC lines are still being extended here and there in a small way. Problems at change-of-voltage points have been avoided instead by the development of adequate numbers of locomotives able to run on both systems although the majority of machines are confined to one or the other.

Electrification, coupled with more advanced signalling systems, brought about large increases in line capacity as well as average speeds. However, it has been felt that further improvements are called for, particularly on the most important main line between Paris and Lyon, where the original route of the 1840s is beset with curves through the hills of Burgundy and unsuitable for speeds over 100 mph as well as being congested with traffic. A completely new railway suitable for 170 mph is now being built between the outskirts of Paris and Lyon, cutting the 320 miles via Dijon down to about 260 miles. This is going to be a real space-age railway, the first of its kind in Europe; it is interesting to note that since modern power-to-weight ratios enable gradients of up to one in thirty or so to be used freely, vertical curvature has become as much of a consideration as

Left: The once-huge network of the metre-gauge Côtes du Nord system in Brittany had been reduced to a single branch by 1956 – that from St Brienc to Paimpol. Trains were mostly autorails (railcars) with trailer cars but on high days and holidays the maroon 0-6-0 tanks came out again. Here is one such day – an enthusiasts' excursion from England.

Right: Although it was the Réseau Breton which had pride of place with 0-6-6-0 Mallet tanks, the SNCF's now-dieselized lines out of Tulle used 0-4-4-0s until the mid 1960s. Here is an Argentat freight climbing towards the county terminus in June 1963.

ordinary horizontal curvature and much trouble has therefore had to be taken to ensure that there are no sudden changes of inclination. But unlike the Japanese Shinkansen lines, the nearest comparison, this new railway will form part of the national network, used by through trains to other destinations.

Train Services and Rolling Stock

For most of the steam age, distances between Paris and most provincial cities were such that there were only two times each day during which trains linking them could run; either they left quite early in the morning and travelled all day, or in the evening and travelled all night. Traditionally, therefore, the time-table shaped itself round an infrequent service of long-distance trains radiating from Paris, meeting connections at all junctions which was, of course, easier when so few main-line trains were involved. As traffic grew, to avoid disturbing this complex pattern of connections, main-line trains became extremely heavy and tended to run in 'flights', a series only a few minutes apart with long gaps between. In the last few decades of steam, faster running first made possible a midday flight of trains which could still reach their destinations before midnight, and ultimately a few extra-fast evening flyers, generally charging extra fares, were also put on (a process taken much further after electrification). The French tradition was therefore one of heavy, fast, but infrequent long-distance services, which still remains the norm to a large extent, although the need to compete with the car and the aircraft are bringing about a shift to the more usual European pattern of more frequent regular-interval services on the most important lines.

French railways were in the 1920s and 1930s among the first in Europe to standardize all-steel construction for main-line passenger stock, and the typically rather spartan but immensely strong and heavy vehicles of that era are only now being replaced by new stock, somewhat more comfortable. However, the vehicles used on the relatively few prestige trains have always been up-to-date and luxurious.

Freight services have always been efficient and relatively intensive, with modern ideas being adopted without delay. On the other hand, traditional wagonload and sundries traffics, although less profitable, have been promoted and improved just as keenly, and a real effort made to maintain freight services on a wide scale even where passenger trains have been replaced by buses.

Operations and Signalling

Traditional French signalling was radically different in conception to British, not least in making a distinction unknown to British practice, between a 'stop' signal given for the reason that there was some positive blockage or conflicting train ahead, and one given just for the reason that there was another train ahead proceeding in the same direction. In the latter case, 'stop and proceed' was the normal rule, although the distinction was made manifest by the use of a different type of signal. Modern practice has developed from this base, and has tended therefore to be fundamentally rather cheaper and simpler than the mammoth and expensive complexities of current large installations in Britain or Germany, for example. Safety, however, is maintained at a very high level by the system of monitoring and recording drivers' actions, standard for many years. For example the system makes a chart automatically of each run noting not only that the driver has obeyed all speed restrictions and signal indications, but that he has signalled in good time to the apparatus his intention to do so. Any rule-breaking or even bad habits can thus be detected and put right long before an accident results. This system is in use on all SNCF trains, on branches as well as main lines.

Administration and Finance

Looked at simply in the light of the total sum declared to be paid over each year by the French state to the SNCF, the French railways have proportionately quite a large deficit by European standards. However, leaving aside the question of whether the declared sum in France and every other country is the amount including past capital write-offs (perhaps the biggest single factor making simple comparisons of this kind wildly misleading), or indeed whether any useful point can be made by crudely comparing totally non-comparable figures just because they are called the same thing, it can be noticed that in France this total sum includes compensation to the SNCF for

many items, including subsidized charges for many disadvantaged groups, accepted as a state concern for many years. In addition, the 1842 legislation allowed for the fact that certain lines could never be commercially viable or worth building, and found an ingenious method of having them operated by successful commercial enterprises all the same, by accepting a large share of state responsibility from the outset. One can only, nowadays, judge by results; and during the last decade, passenger traffic (both long-distance and suburban) and freight traffic on the SNCF have both shown a rising tendency. There is no sign that the deficit is out of control, and indeed the state has shown its continued faith in the vitality of the railway system by funding the construction of the new Paris–Lyon high-speed line, as well as other improvements.

PARIS TRANSPORT AUTHORITY – RATP
Regie Autonome des Transports Parisiens,
53 Quai de Grands Augustins,
75271 Paris.

The most important non-SNCF railway undertaking in France is the CF Métropolitain de Paris. The original conception of the Paris Métro was much that of an underground tramway, with many routes, frequent stations, shallow tunnels or sometimes low viaducts, sharp curves, and therefore slow running. All this of course survives with great character and charm, particularly on those lines still worked by fifty-year-old trains rather than their sometimes rubber-wheeled replacements. However, the city has grown beyond its old Métro, and in the last few years a new and much grander, longer-distance system has begun to be superimposed on it, the Réseau Express Régional. The RER trains are high-speed, compatible with those on SNCF lines, and run right across the urban map. They tend to use ex-SNCF lines in the suburbs, but in the centre they run in new deep-level tunnels, laid out for fast running, and with widely spaced stations connecting with the older system. The older Métro lines are not quite the most antiquated of their kind in the world (Madrid, Buenos Aires, New York are in the running for this), but the RER is certainly the most modern.

Other French Railways

The narrow gauge is now all but extinct in France, though the SNCF still runs two electric metre-gauge lines of great scenic attraction, one in the Alps and one in the Pyrenees. A few other minor outposts survive, including much of the Corsican system. The most important of them is the last section of the old Chemins de Fer de Provence, 95 miles from Nice to Digne. Serving a spectacular part of the Savoy Alps, it still runs an efficient all-diesel passenger and freight service, under the pre-1938 rules, at the prime financial responsibility of the local authorities in fact, though in form centrally subsidized. Like the other lines mentioned, it still offers a year-round transport service so

perhaps it is remarkable not that so much has gone but that so many narrow-gauge lines still manage to perform this function.

Perhaps this is the reason why there are only relatively few narrow- (or even standard-) gauge 'entertainment' railways in France, running strictly for tourists and generally with steam traction. However, they do include perhaps the most successful operation of its kind in Continental Europe, the twenty-mile line from Tournon in the Rhône Valley to Lamastre. This is a surviving fragment of the old metre-gauge Réseau du Vivarais, which at its peak had over 120 miles of track winding and climbing over the high and broken rocky country along the watershed of the Atlantic and the Mediterranean. Resurrected in 1971, there is something very French about this railway now, for every Sunday morning a stately procession of trains, some hauled by restored ex-Vivarais 0-6-6-0T Mallets, climbs to Lamastre, a small town with more notable restaurants per cobbled street than any other in Europe.

Among the select list of railways opened in the world during 1978 was one which, although just another 'daisy-picking' line, is notable for having bumped the English Romney, Hythe & Dymchurch Railway from its position as the 'smallest (ie, having the least distance between the rails) statutory public railway in the world'. This is the 12in gauge four-mile steam-operated Réseau Guerledan at Mur-de-Bretagne near Pontivy in Brittany. Because lengths of rail had survived at level crossings, statutory powers were inherited from the old metre-gauge Réseau Breton, on whose road-bed the new line was laid.

GERMANY

See map on pages 26–27.

GERMAN FEDERAL RAILWAY – DB
Deutsche Bundesbahn,
Friedrich-Ebert-Anlage 43–45,
Frankfurt (Main).

GERMAN STATE RAILWAY – DR
Deutsche Reichsbahn
Voss Strasse 33,
108 Berlin.

Railways in Germany are said to have begun on 14 February 1834 when King Ludwig I of Bavaria gave his assent to the construction of a four-mile line between Nuremburg and Furth. Fredrich List, the 'Father of German railways', had been involved in railway development in the USA and built there a 21-mile coal-hauling line (Tamaqua to Port Clinton, Pennsylvania). He then had the idea of building railways in Germany. He opened the Nuremburg-Furth line on 7 December 1835 and, four years later, the first long-distance line in Germany, running 75 miles from Leipzig to Dresden.

The total length of railway in operation then

A West German Co-Co electric locomotive hauls a freight along the banks of the Rhine.

was a mere 92 miles, but subsequent development was rapid. By 1850 the figure was almost 4000, by 1870 over 12,000 and by the turn of the century approached 40,000 miles. The main lines were administered by five states, (Prussia, Bavaria, Saxony, Mecklenburg and Hesse), which had taken over from private companies in the 1875–1900 period, and three (Wurtemburg, Oldenburg and Baden) which had owned their railways from their inception.

After World War I, the lines (then 34,000 miles in extent) were formally unified and became the Deutsche Reichsbahn. The loss of Alsace-Lorraine in 1919 was counterbalanced by the gain of Austria in 1936. In fact, authoritarian Germany had for many years before 1920 used the railways as a single instrument to secure overriding power for the central government and, above all, to wage war.

For the Germans the availability of rail transport coincided in a remarkable way with the beginning of the series of wars of aggression which marked German history from 1860 to 1945. An attack by Prussia on Denmark in 1863, on Austria in 1866 (the Seven Weeks War) and on France in 1870 led to the King of Prussia being proclaimed Emperor of the then-enlarged German Confederation in 1871. Railways played an increasingly important part as this aggrandisement took place.

World War II found the German railways in excellent shape, well prepared for the struggle which was to put virtually the whole European railway system under German control. The use of it to transport six million non-Aryans from their homes to far-away extermination camps was a new (on this scale) use for railways. And in addition, the normal but immense military needs were satisfactorily catered for. Had the armies penetrated deeper into the USSR, supply lines would have become even longer. Plans had been drawn up for a 9ft 10in (3-metre) gauge trunk line to reduce the effort needed for mass transportation over the great distance involved.

Defeat in 1945, involving railway destruction on a vast scale, led to partition as well as loss of territory to Poland. The lines in the West became the Bundesbahnen or Federal Railways, while the railways in the Soviet Zone, now East Germany, kept the Reichsbahn title.

The first German locomotive *Der Adler* (the Eagle) was a standard Robert Stephenson 2-2-2 from England which arrived complete with driver. In his role as the nineteenth-century equivalent of a Concorde pilot his salary was twice the general manager's.

German locomotive practice is best known for the excellent standard range of simple locomotives – most of them of the 'world standard form', that is, two outside cylinders and Walschearts valve gear – which were produced in large numbers and in different shapes and sizes to cover all the duties on the railway. Outstanding were the *Kriegslok* (War Loco) 2-10-0s; 11,879 were produced in two and a half years, beginning in September 1942, by an industry already fully committed to war production, an achievement on a scale unequalled elsewhere. The same standards of

Above: Trans-Europ Express (TEE) No 10 'Rembrandt' (Munich–Amsterdam).

Left: A modern Bundesbahn electric train races along the Rhine.

Right: The new control tower outside the huge arched roof of the Frankfurt (Main) Hauptbahnhof.

Below: Eating the Mitropa way.

Right: The dining and sleeping cars on West German Railways are owned and run by the German Sleeping Car Company, DSG.

design were applied to locomotives exported to many countries, particularly those in eastern Europe. Turkey was a case in point, even after it had ceased to lie in the path of the German drive to the east.

German thoroughness ensured that the possibilities of constructing steam locomotives more thermally efficient than conventional ones, were thoroughly explored. As has been found elsewhere with less thorough investigations, the conclusion was drawn that the savings did not justify the extra cost of maintainance of such things as condensers, super-pressure boilers and compound cylinders.

Postwar practice produced few significant new developments – in fact locomotive building capacity was removed wholesale from East Germany to the USSR. In so far as there was new construction, the two administrations were careful to dovetail their numbering systems. Some steam still operates in the East. In the West it came to an end in 1977.

Electrification began early with a demonstration of the first-ever electric railway in public service at the Berlin exhibition of 1879. The inventor, Werner von Siemens, gave his name to a firm which is still a famous name in the electrical world. Some remarkable electric traction trials were carried out on an experimental line from Zossen to Marienfelde in 1901–03, when electric cars reached speeds of up to 135 mph, eclipsing steam in this regard forever. The first main-line electrification proper was completed in 1922, when 15,000v $16\frac{2}{3}$ cycles AC locomotives went into public service between Breslau and Görlitz. By 1932, 1200 miles were in operation.

The prewar total has since been well surpassed, all principal main lines (6200 miles) in West Germany now being turned over to this form of traction. In the East relatively little electrification or re-electrification has been done, in all, only one tenth of that in the West.

In talking of Germany and diesel traction it almost suffices to say that Dr Rudolf Diesel, the inventor in 1897 of the original engine of ⟋ the kind that now bears his name, was a German born in Paris. Numerous experiments were necessary before his invention became adapted as a practical instrument of rail traction, but perhaps a landmark was 15 May 1933 when the diesel-electric 'Flying Hamburger' went into service between Berlin and Hamburg, scheduled to run the 178 miles in 138 minutes, an average speed of 77.4 mph. This was, at the time, the fastest scheduled run in the world and the attention it drew from the public led to a widespread consideration of the possibilities of diesel-electric traction.

Since the war, Germany has specialized in diesel locomotives with hydraulic transmission. On the face of it, it would seem that such a system – a kind of grown-up 'fluid flywheel' – would be simpler, cheaper and less prone to failure than an electric transmission system. In fact, this has not proved to be the case but, in West Germany anyway, the manufacturers have not yet given up their speciality. In the East there has been a tendency to rely on Soviet-built diesel-electrics.

Train Services and Operations

The main problem faced by the West German system is the re-orientation of traffic flows. North–south lines that were once mere cross-country routes have now become main arteries (one could add also that grass grows undisturbed on many west–east lines leading into East Germany that were once main arteries). Proposals for high-speed lines to by-pass the worst sections together with upgrading elsewhere are in hand and this should lead to very-much-reduced journey times and more frequent express services.

A feature of both DB and DR is that branch-line and local passenger services are maintained at present (though there are signs of change) to a much greater degree than, for example, in Britain or France. But, on DB certainly, the concentration of effort and investment is directed at the long-distance traveller, making what is already an excellent service (with, incidentally, particularly good restaurant car meals, very reasonably priced) even better. DB carries 632 million passengers a year, using a fleet of 17,700 carriages and 1000 railcars of various kinds. In West Germany 2600 electric and 3100 diesel locomotives provide the haulage (East Germany provides no information), covering of course, both passenger and freight traffic. As might be expected in one of the world's greatest industrial countries, freight traffic in Germany is on a vast scale; it is relatively denser in the East, no doubt because of the lesser use made of road transport in the Soviet-dominated area. The figures for 1976 illustrate the position (see page 60).

Above: A modern diesel express under the great arched roof of Leipzig station, East Germany.

Top: Hamburg station in June 1966 with an East German 01 class Pacific heading a train for Berlin. These engines were still at work in 1978.

Extreme left: Diesel express at Saalfeld in East Germany.

Left: Diesel maintenance in East Germany.

Below: A traditional steam train hauled by a class 38 4-6-0 crosses the Hohenzollern Bridge at Cologne.

Figures for 1976	DB West Germany	DR East Germany
Length of route, miles	17,980	8910
Length electrified, miles	6260	880
Tons hauled annually, millions	326	286
Average distance hauled, miles	122	108

Below: A train at Altermarkt station on the Wuppertal Suspension Railway.

A recent development on DB is the fitting of a type of automatic coupler to certain wagons in circuit service. This is the coupler which, having been chosen as the European standard, is intended to become universal in Europe in due course, replacing the primaeval and familiar side buffers and screw-couplings.

WUPPERTAL SUSPENSION RAILWAY
Bromberger Strasse 39,
56 Wuppertal 2.

In the 1960s, there was a transient fashion for promoting monorails. Conventional railways were unfashionable and schemes for promoting them had to be packaged under such names as 'duo-rail'. But very few monorails indeed have achieved any extended existence. In fact, the only significant one is an eight-mile line, suspended above the Wupper River, which has carried the citizens of Barmen and Elberfield about their business ever since 1900, except for a three-year hiatus at the end of World War II. Forty-four electric cars carry 28 million passengers annually.

GREAT BRITAIN

See maps on pages 64 and 69.

Ninety-five out of every hundred miles of railway line in Britain belong to the state railway system and of the remainder the three largest systems (Northern Ireland Railway, London Transport and the National Coal Board) are also publicly owned. Much British early railway history is also World Railway history and hence has already been mentioned in the introduction. Maybe it is a result of being citizens of a country that was the birthplace of railways that the British have such an extravagant passion for them. This is reflected in various ways. For example, the British public demands, expects and is willing to maintain a well-equipped national rail system, much larger than purely plain economic considerations should allow. The other way in which this extraordinary love shows itself is in the growth of railways built or preserved for pleasure. This has been a feature of the last twenty years and in it Great Britain has played the leading role. None of the 143 pleasure lines currently operating in the United Kingdom qualifies for inclusion here on the grounds of length – in fact a mileage even in double figures is rare – but several (Bluebell, Festiniog, Isle of Man, Middleton, Romney Hythe & Dymchurch, Talyllyn, and Volks) do so on the grounds of world 'firsts' or 'onlys' of one kind or another.

The past influence of Great Britain in the world of railways is reflected in the amount of railway material manufactured there for use in other countries. Even more important was the export of ideas; the influence of past British railway engineers and managers can be seen on many systems which have long since ceased to depend on any British-made material.

The political stability of the mainland has meant a climate in which steady development could occur, but the enforced neglect and over-use of the railways in two world wars have been setbacks, the effect of which can still be felt. As regards the Republic of Eire (Southern Ireland), which ceased to be part of the United Kingdom in 1921, the railways there had always been independent of those in England, Scotland and Wales. Accordingly this event had little effect on the railway map.

BRITISH RAILWAYS – BR
222, Marylebone Road,
London NW1.

The 11,000-mile network of British Rail routes interconnect the larger towns and serve the basic industrial customers. During the last twenty years, BR has, on the whole, withdrawn from serving smaller towns and villages as well as the less concentrated industries. At the same time every aspect of railway operation has been transformed; the complete elimination of steam (except for one tiny line), multi-aspect colour-light signalling on most main routes, continuous welded rails, new and faster diesel and electric trains, computer control of freight

Formation of the Principal pre-1923 Railway Companies

Company name	Date of formation	Constituents on formation	Opening date of first section
Great Western	1835		1838
London & South Western	1839	London & Southampton	1838
Midland	1844	Birmingham & Derby Junction	1839
		North Midland	1840
		Midland Counties	1840
North British	1844		1846
Caledonian	1845		1848
London & North Western	1846	Liverpool & Manchester	1830
		Grand Junction	1837
		London & Birmingham	1838
Great North of Scotland	1846		1854
London, Brighton & South Coast	1846	London & Brighton	1841
Great Northern	1845		1850
Furness	1846		1846
North Staffordshire	1846		1846
Lancashire & Yorkshire	1847	Manchester & Leeds	1841
Glasgow & South Western	1850	Glasgow, Kilmarnock & Ayr	1840
		Glasgow, Dumfries & Carlisle	1843
North Eastern	1854	York, Newcastle & Berwick	1839
		York & North Midland	1841
		Leeds Northern	1849
Great Eastern	1862	Eastern Counties	1839
		Northern & Eastern	1842
		Eastern Union	1846
		Norfolk Railway	1846
Cambrian	1864	Llanidloes & Newton	1859
		Oswestry, Ellesmere & Whitchurch	1863
		Newton & Machynlleth	1863
		Oswestry & Newton	1864
		Aberystwyth & Welsh Coast	1864
Highland	1865	Inverness & Aberdeen Junction	1858
		Inverness & Perth Junction	1863
Great Central	1897	Manchester, Sheffield & Lincolnshire	1841
South Eastern & Chatham	1899	South-Eastern	1842
		London, Chatham & Dover	1859

operations and many new or refurbished stations, have combined to give BR a completely new ambience and image. Regretably, this modernization has been accompanied by a fairly steady deterioration in railway finances, but it would appear that the British people, on the whole, are prepared to underwrite their affection for railways by putting their hands fairly deeply into both their fare-paying and their tax-paying pockets. The result, even if expensive, is good. While a few countries have trains as fast and as comfortable, very few indeed have them as frequent.

History and Development
Early British railway promotors, far from being encouraged by the government and establishment, had to fight every sort of opposition, reasonable and unreasonable, legal and illegal, in order to obtain the right to build their lines. The outcome was a fairly haphazard kind of development, but by 1850, as shown on the map on page 64, virtually all the principal cities were linked to the capital by rail. By 1860 the majority of the great railway companies (until the government-dictated 'grouping' of 1923) had already emerged by name.

The Great Western company was the first

(and, as we shall see, the last), having been incorporated as early as 1835, but its 118-mile 7ft $\frac{1}{4}$in gauge main line from London to Bristol was not completed until 1841. By this time the original 1830 inter-city route between Liverpool and Manchester had, in 1836, been joined to Birmingham, by the first main line, known as the Grand Junction Railway and in the following year, the first 100-mile plus line in Britain, the London and Birmingham, opened to traffic. The table above shows how the old companies emerged.

Big profits made by the early companies led in the 1840s to an excessive amount of railway promotion – a period known as the 'Railway Mania' – but the subsequent 'crash' did not slow things up for long. As the century progressed the network was completed not only by the construction of lines competing for traffic between most important places but also by the building of comprehensive networks of country branches. With the completion of a competitive main line known as the Great Central from Nottingham to Marylebone station, London in 1899, new main-line railway construction in Britain came to an end. The Great Western Railway (then known as the 'Great Way Round') still had a few corners to cut off, and

A British Railways' country station on the Dolgellan–Llangollen line which is now closed. Note level crossing gates shut across the line.

Inset, bottom right : A British Railways express on the London–Edinburgh route, hauled by a 'Deltic' diesel-electric locomotive.

BEWARE OF TRAINS

DRWS·Y·NANT

Way out

there was some suburban and rapid transit work to do, but otherwise, the show was at an end. In seventy years 20,000 miles of railway had been laid and few places, however small, failed to have a railway station.

Rural railways in Britain (with a few honourable exceptions) were operated by the big companies. Often, a branch line would be sponsored and financed locally but, once built, a wise management would make arrangements for the main-line company to work it for, say, a percentage of the receipts. In due time the shares of the little company would be exchanged for shares in big brother and what had then become a mere paper existence would finally be extinguished. A few bold spirits decided to go it alone, but often their fate was that of the Culm Valley Railway in Devon. This line, after a few unhappy years on its own, was taken over by the Great Western for a price that was 'the best that could be expected between a seller that had to sell and a buyer who did not want to buy' as the GWR's official history put it. In other cases the big companies did it all. But however they came into being, the rural railways of Britain were, it must be said in salute to their memory, a particular delight, from the polished levers in the signal boxes to the roses in the flower-beds.

One of the reasons for this attractiveness was their solid main-line construction; they had to be built, manned and signalled to very expensive full main-line standards, when low speeds and infrequent trains would have made something simpler more appropriate. In 1898 the Light Railways Act was passed, which allowed local railways contemplated after the turn of the century to be promoted more easily – without a private Act of Parliament – as well as built to less exacting standards and thus much more cheaply. Fifty years before, this Act would have been of great use; fifty years later, as we shall see, it was.

Incidentally, one effect of this application of main-line standards to branch-line railways was that narrow-gauge lines were very rare in Great Britain except in one specific area, North Wales. Here, in fact, the worldwide use of narrow gauge for public railways was pioneered.

All the 'golden age' companies except one came to the end of the line in 1923, when by an Act of Parliament they were grouped into four big groups; the London Midland & Scottish, the London & North Eastern, the Southern and the Great Western but only the latter kept its name and entity.

The purpose of the 'grouping' was to strengthen the weaker companies, which had

been badly affected by over-use and enforced neglect during the 1914-18 war, by amalgamating them with the stronger ones. The main constituents of each group appear below.

All these pre-'grouping' railways had their own ways of doing things and their own designs for everything from uniform buttons to steam locomotives. Replacement by new and (in some cases) rather brash styles was a sad blow to those who took pleasure in such matters,

although much pre-'grouping' railway material is still in use over fifty years after the event and even more is now housed in sixteen railway museums, working and stationary (see table opposite).

The 'grouping' may have helped some weaker lines to survive, but the burdens came near bankrupting the stronger ones. Ordinary railway shares (previously the safest 'widow and orphan' investment) quickly fell into the wall-

British railways built up to 1841
British railways built up to 1850

The 'Grouping' of 1923

London, Midland & Scottish	London & North Eastern	Southern	Great Western
London & North Western	Great Northern	South Eastern & Chatham	Great Western
Midland	Great Eastern	London, Brighton & South	Cambrian
Lancashire & Yorkshire	Great Central	Coast	South Wales
Caledonian	North Eastern	London & South Western	'pit-to-port' lines
Glasgow & South Western	North British		
Highland	Great North of Scotland		
Furness			
North Stafford			

Principal Museums with Major Railway Exhibits

Name & Location of Museum	Speciality
National Railway Museum, York*†	
Steamtown, Camforth, Lancashire*†	International
Cranmore, Near Shepton Mallet, Somerset*†	—
Great Western Society, Didcot, Oxfordshire*†	Great Western
Birmingham Railway Museum, Tyseley, W Midlands*†	—
Dinting Railway Centre, Near Manchester*†	London, Midland & Scottish
Bulmer's Railway Centre, Hereford*†	Great Western
Scottish Railway Preservation Society, Falkirk*	Scottish Railways
Science Museum, London	Early locomotives
Great Western Museum, Swindon, Wiltshire	Great Western
Bressingham Hall, Diss, Norfolk†	—
North of England Open Air Museum, Beamish, County Durham†	North-Eastern
Darlington North Road Railway Museum, Co Durham	Stockton & Darlington
Quainton Railway Society, Near Aylesbury Buckinghamshire†	—
Birmingham Museum of Science & Industry	London, Midland & Scottish
Glasgow Museum of Transport	Scottish Railways

* operation facilities on BR   † facilities for steaming and demonstration

paper category – except inevitably those of the Great Western, in whose re-structuring there had been the smallest element of political meddling. The sixteen lean years until 1939 passed in absorbing the stresses of this enforced reorganization. Such modernization as was done had largely to be carried out with government assistance.

The 1939-45 war brought even severer strains on the railways of Britain and so, perhaps inevitably, it was followed in 1948 by nationalization, thereby bringing the United Kingdom into step with virtually all countries outside North America. With 650,000 staff and 6000 stations, 18,000 miles of route, 19,000 locomotives and over a million carriages and wagons, British Railway was a vast and even more indigestible meal for the administrators. After a long and costly process of trial and error on its part, today's smaller system (200,000 staff, 2000 stations, 11,000 miles of track, 4500 locomotives and 250,000 cars) meets the present-day demand for a lesser quantity but a higher quality of rail transport.

On the whole the stations and lines that

The main west-coast line from London to Scotland had two major obstacles to surmount – Shap Fell in Westmorland and Beattock, just over the border into *Scotland. Now that this line has been electrified they pose no problems to trains but in steam days, locomotives were hard pressed, often needing banking* *assistance, as is the case with this LMS 'Patriot' class 4-6-0 heading a fast freight.*

Above: A train leaves Porthmadog Harbour station hauled by Fairlie articulated locomotive along the narrow-gauge Festiniog Railway.

closed were rural, but some duplicate main stations and main lines went as well. Included was the last to be built, the Great Central line of 1899 from Nottingham to London.

Not all the 7000 miles of closed railway line were abandoned. Scattered about the country and aggregating almost 100 miles are a dozen or so sections of line which groups of enthusiasts, semi-professionals and businessmen have restored to run old-fashioned steam trains. They obtained powers to do so under the handy provisions of the previously little-used Light Railways Act of 1898. One can journey back into nostalgia, travelling not only in early BR and post-'grouping' style but also in that of the old pre-'grouping' companies, in trains which use their locomotives, their coaches, their tracks and their stations. In rural England, this is the new railway age. The pioneer was the Bluebell Railway, which is separately described; the complete list is as follows:

British Rail Lines Restored as Museum or Pleasure Lines

Re-opening date	Name and Location	Length (miles)	Old Company
1960	Bluebell; Sheffield Park, Sussex	4.5	London, Brighton & South Coast
1961	Welshpool Llanfair; Llanfair Caerenion, Powys	5.5	Great Western
1968	Keighley & Worth Valley: W Yorkshire	5	Midland
1969	Dart Valley; Buckfastleigh, Devon	7	Great Western
1970	Severn Valley; Bridgnorth, Shropshire	12.5	Great Western
1970	Lochty: near Ardeer, Fife, Scotland	1.5	North British
1971	Torbay & Kingswear; Paignton, Devon	6	Great Western
1973	Lakeside & Haverthwaite; Newby Bridge Lancashire	3.5	Furness
1973	North York Moors; Pickering, N Yorkshire	18	North Eastern
1974	Kent & East Sussex; Tenterden, Kent	4	Kent & E. Sussex
1975	Wight Locomotive Society; Haven St., Isle of Wight	2	Isle of Wight
1976	Great Central; Loughborough, Leicestershire	6	Great Central
1976	North Norfolk; Sheringham, Norfolk	4	Great Eastern
1977	Strathspey; Aviemore, Scotland	4	Highland
1977	West Somerset; Minehead, Devon	5	Great Western
1977	Mid-Hants; Alresford, Hampshire	3	London & S.W.
1977	Nene Valley; Peterborough, Cambridgeshire	3	London & N.W.
1978	Midland Railway; Butterley, Derbyshire	3	Midland

Civil Engineering

In Britain the task of constructing 20,000 miles of railway in a short seventy years was made easier because during the previous seventy years many miles of canal had been built, involving the solution of many similar problems. In fact the name 'navvy' given to the men – and later to the machines – who built the railways, derives from the term 'navigator' which was first applied to those who built the canals.

Bridges and viaducts made of stone or iron were entirely familiar to the engineers of the time and such problems as did arise occurred largely because of an increase in scale. Nothing like the bridge on the Irish Mail route across the Menai Straits with its two iron box-girder spans of 46oft each had been made before. (The Admiralty were unhappy about the obstruction which would have been caused by a bridge with many short spans, well within then current technology.) Robert Stephenson's ability as an engineer is well illustrated by the fact that the bridge lasted, carrying the much heavier trains of later years, until, in 1970, some small boys destroyed it by setting light to timbers

inside. Still existing today and younger by nine years is Brunel's Royal Albert Bridge of 1859 across the River Tamar at Saltash near Plymouth. This ingenious combination of the arch and suspension bridge principle crossed a similar water gap with two spans of almost identical length, but at a cost per track of thirty percent less.

Since 1859 there has been a requirement for only one large-span railway bridge on the scale of these two; this is the Forth Bridge between Edinburgh and Dundee with its two cantilever spans of 1710ft, which of course completely eclipses both Menai and Saltash.

Locomotive Landmarks
Steam

In a country where dozens of workshops have built hundreds of thousands of locomotives for hundreds of customers at home and abroad, it is impossible to single out individual landmarks of design. One can only look at families of design.

In the nineteenth century the typical British locomotive was a six-wheeler, either 2-4-0, 2-2-2, 0-6-0 or occasionally 0-4-2. It had two

Above: Built to the design of Robert Stephenson, the Britannia tubular bridge linked the island of Anglesey with the mainland of Wales. The weight of each of the four large tubes was 1800 tons and the smaller ones 1000 tons.

Top: The Forth Bridge on the railway connecting Edinburgh with Aberdeen.

inside cylinders and valve gear (Stephenson or Joy) out of the way between the frames. It was considered indecent to expose the works.

A landmark event occurred at the turn of the twentieth century when there came to one of the sleepiest and most conservative of companies a *volte-face* that fixed the layout of most British locomotives for their last fifty years of domestic steam construction. Locomotive superintendent Churchward of the Great Western Railway introduced 4-6-0, 2-8-0 and 2-6-2T types of advanced design, incorporating a combination of the best US and British practice.

They were respectively for express, freight and suburban trains; fifty years later locomotives of similar appearance and layout (but not quite so much brass and copper decor) were still handling most of Britain's rail traffic in these different fields.

Another great landmark was the introduction of the big (for Britain) engine with the wide firebox. Ivatt of the Great Northern produced his 4-4-2 'large Atlantic' in 1905. His successor Gresley in 1922 developed this idea with the first of the famous LNER family of 4-6-2s, a type that was also introduced by the LMS and SR companies, as well as British Railways to the tune of, in all, fifteen designs.

Apart from two experimental Gresley wide-firebox 2-8-2s built in 1925, the big freight engine had to wait until 1952, when the famous '9F' 2-10-0 was introduced. Steam construction on BR came to an end (saving a replica for the Liverpool & Manchester's 150th anniversary in 1980) in 1960 when *Evening Star* of this design was put into service.

Of main-line locomotive types, the one which was both the most numerous and the last steam survivor was the LMS company's legendary 'Black Five' 4-6-0. The 842 examples of the class were equally satisfactory on passenger trains at 80+mph as on slow and heavy freights.

No one could describe steam designers as unadventurous – twentieth-century British locomotive history was remarkable for many brave but unavailing attempts to improve the poor thermal efficiency of the Stephenson type steam engine, by using the greater range of temperatures and pressures typical of those found in steam plant in ships and power stations. Compounding was tried by many and even adopted by a few of the companies in the 1880–1914 period, but only the Midland (and its successor the LMS) persevered for more than a decade or so. Perhaps the LNER *Hush-Hush* compound 4-6-4 No 10,000, completed in 1929 with a Yarrow water-tube boiler pressed to 500lb/sq in, was the bravest among some twenty major attempts by private firms and by the main-line railways. But none, in any sort of overall sense, approached the economy of the simple Stephenson type.

Diesel

Diesel traction on British Railways and its predecessors began in the 1930s on a very small scale by first developing a low-power diesel shunting locomotive and then proceeding to

greater things. The first serious order for more than one or two main-line prototypes was placed with British manufacturers in 1957 but, before a reasonable time for evaluation had passed, the then-BR management unwisely decided to ignore their engineers' advice and proceed with large production orders. During the painful and expensive process of turning the resulting fleet into one on which the operators could rely, the reputation of the railways fell to a low ebb, which recent developments, such as the 125-mph high-speed train (HST), are at last beginning to retrieve. Currently there are 3500 diesel locomotives (including the single-unit Deltic diesels with individual horsepowers as high as 3300) and a large fleet of self-propelled diesel trains.

Electric

Electric locomotives were a rarity on the constituents of British Rail; in fact, at nationalization in 1948 only six were active. On the other hand, electric motor coaches from multiple unit sets numbered almost 5000 including such rare designs as the powered Pullman parlour cars of the 'Brighton Belle'. All the grouped railways except the Great Western had electric trains of their own design.

There was also great experience with electric traction in the export field and when the time came to go ahead with long-distance electrifica-

Top: Another form of large-span bridge – this time a combination of the arch and suspension principles – the Royal Albert Bridge links Devon with Cornwall over the River Tamar at Saltash. Designed by Isambard Kingdom Brunel and completed in 1859, it is still extant in its original form.

Centre: One of the larger signal boxes of semaphore days is Preston No 1 of the London Midland and Scottish Railway.

Above: The modern train control power box at New Street Station, Birmingham.

Right: A map of the British Railways system at its greatest extent in the 1950s.

An electrically hauled freight threads the English countryside.

Left: An electric express on the London–Glasgow route.

Right: A diesel-electric High Speed Train at 120 mph on the London–Bristol route.

tion schemes, few difficulties were experienced in putting into service an electric locomotive fleet now numbering 350, most of which operate at 25,000v AC on the London to Glasgow main line which also serves Birmingham, Liverpool and Manchester.

In the south, British Rail inherited a third-rail 750v DC electrification from the old Southern Railway (the largest suburban electric system in the world) and this has been extended. It now connects London with Bournemouth, Portsmouth, Brighton, Dover and Margate and serves a maze of lines in between. Two interesting features are rare enough to mention. First, the locomotives are fitted with auxiliary diesel generators which permit slow movement in unelectrified sidings, as well as enabling a locomotive which has come to rest on one of the inevitable gaps in the third rail, to re-start. Second, the majority of powered units on the Southern region are arranged to run in multiple with each other; that is, a train formed of, say, a diesel locomotive, an electric train and a diesel train can be worked from any of the cabs of any of the units.

Operations and Services

Passenger services in Britain have for many years been remarkable for two things; first the frequency with which they operate, and second, that the lowest class of passenger has been admitted to virtually all the trains – including the fastest and best – that run. One compares, for example, fast hourly two-class service between London and Newcastle (268 miles) with, say, that between Paris and Lyons (320 miles) where intervals of as much as $2\frac{1}{2}$ hours exist between successive trains during the day and the best ones are first-class only. The new High Speed Train services, currently being introduced, follow these two excellent traditions and, what is new, provide standards of speed and comfort (but not of cuisine) that have few rivals worldwide. Some 715 million passengers are carried annually in 23,000 passenger carriages.

Freight operations on BR suffer fundamentally from the fact that (equally fundamentally) they are confined within a small island. Hence, the average length of haul (73 miles) is not sufficient for it to be worthwhile making up the long trains that take full advantage of the potentialities of rail. Nevertheless, 176 million tons of freight is transported, handicapped by the strange anachronism that many of the 220,000 wagons are not fitted with continuous brakes. On the other hand, the reliability and economy of BR's freight service is greatly enhanced by the use of a sophisticated freight-movement computer control system known as TOPS, based on that developed by the Southern Pacific railroad of America.

International Standard containers are moved in Britain by specially built unit trains of fixed formation known as freightliners. In this way the railway can effectively be brought to any small factory or farm.

Safety has always had a high priority (over convenience and economy) in Britain and the methods of train signalling evolved there are

Above: Preston, on the west-coast line from London to Scotland appears much the same in this 1965 photo as it was in the Edwardian era.

Top: Barmouth Bridge, the Cambrian Railway trestle and swing bridge, fords the Mawddach estuary. Originally constructed to safeguard river traffic, the swing section was little used as the railway down the side of the river effectively killed this mode of transport.

Centre, above right: New Street Station, Birmingham, after rebuilding in 1967 and electrification.

widely used in the world. Specially characteristic is the method of signalling trains on single lines by a physical token (staff, key or tablet) which must be in the driver's possession when he enters the single-line section. The system is arranged so that a second token is not available from the instruments at either end of the section until the first one has been put back, also at either end. An objection is that all crossing places on single lines need to have staff in attendance even when very few trains are run, but the safeguard of having to be in possession of a physical object before proceeding is a very sure one.

In addition to trains British Rail operate a large fleet of ships (most sea-going), ferries and hovercraft. They are large hotel owners and have a multitude of road vehicles.

The Pullman Car Company

Pullman of the USA operated in Britain as the Pullman Palace Car Company from 1874 until 1907, providing both the first dining-car service in Britain – *Prince of Wales* on the Great Northern in 1879 – and, in 1881, the first electrically lit carriage in the world. This was *Beatrice* running between London and Brighton. Sleeping cars were provided for a time on the Midland and East Coast routes to Scotland, as well as on the Highland Railway. When, in 1907, the HR followed the example of the others and replaced the cars with its own; the last Pullman *sleeper* service in Europe had ended, but *parlour* cars continued.

Also in that year, G M Pullman's executors sold out to an Englishman called Davidson Dalziel (pronounced 'DL'), who quickly put into service the first daily all-Pullman train, the famous 'Southern Belle' – later the 'Brighton Belle'. The first British-built Pullman cars were made for this train.

In general, the arrangements were that Pullman provided the cars, staffed them, maintained them above the underframes and collected the supplements as well as anything paid for meals. The railway companies hauled them, maintained the running gear and took the basic fares. The extra comfort and superb service made it worth people's while to pay the extra, except where the standard of ordinary service was particularly high.

After 1922, of the 'big four' companies, only

Left: This evocative photograph shows the famous (or infamous) 1-in-37.7 Lickey Incline on the old Midland Railway main line from Bristol and Gloucester to Birmingham and the North. In steam days, every train needed banking assistance using one, two or even three helper engines. This is an example of how an early saving on capital cost can result in years of heavy running expenditure.

Above: The reconstruction of New Street Station, Birmingham, 1965–67.

Top: Diesels at Bristol's Temple Meads station in March 1978. On the left is a west to north express and on the right the 125 mph High Speed Train is leaving for London (Paddington).

the LNER and the Southern were consistently happy to run Pullmans. It was possible to travel from Bournemouth to Glasgow by all-Pullman train – except for crossing London. (Pullmans did, in fact, run on the London Underground, but not to connect the 'Bournemouth Belle' with the 'Queen of Scots.') The electrified 'Brighton Belle' entered service in 1933; the naming of cars marked a change, in tune with the times, from high-born ladies like the *Duchess of Connaught*, *Lady Dalziel* and *Zenobia* to ordinary and probably nicer ones like *Audrey*, *Gwen*, and *Hazel*.

The Pullman Car Company was bought by British Railways in 1952 and a brief flare-up of expansion took Pullmans (of a kind) to Swansea, Birmingham, Liverpool and Man-

chester. Alas, the beautiful brown and cream lined-out livery, many of the trains and much of the standard of service, disappeared, like many other good things, after a few years of nationalization. In 1978 only the Manchester, Liverpool and Hull services still run, although some purveyors of nostalgia can offer vintage Pullman travel.

BRADSHAW'S RAILWAY GUIDE

From 1841 until 1961 there appeared a monthly publication whose fame was such that its name became part of the English vocabulary.

Bradshaw's Railway Guide gave the reader details of all the passenger trains on all the railways in the British Isles. From 1839 to 1841 it came out intermittently. However, glancing at the centenary issue for July 1939, one finds a small fat volume of 1300 pages with peculiarly Bradshavian numbering (for example, page 182 ran from 182a to 182f, while 296 to 315 was all one). Bradshaw, a Quaker, disapproved of pagan names for the months and all issues prior to 1939 referred to them by number, *viz*: 7th. Mo. (July). Every table is festooned with pointing hands and references to complex tables of notes, such as 'U-runs alternate Mondays and cattle sale days at Wadebridge only' or 'b-stops to take up for beyond Montrose or to set down passengers holding ordinary return', 'm-monthly return tickets for Edinburgh, Glasgow or beyond who may wish to break their journey' and so on. Nine thousand stations are included in the index and one can plan, say, twenty different journeys between the five stations at Oldham (Clegg St, Mumps, Glodwick Road, Werneth and Central) or, perhaps, one from French Drove and Gedney Hill to Fleur-de-lis Platform. Bradshaw puzzle enthusiasts suffered a great sense of loss when his guide ceased publication. Until 1939 there was also a *Bradshaw's Continental Guide*. Reprints of selected issues of the time-table are available.

BLUEBELL RAILWAY LIMITED
Sheffield Park Station,
Uckfield, Sussex.

In 1960 a group of amateurs made world history when they took over and began to run a length of full-size standard-gauge railway as a tourist attraction. Previously this had only been done with narrow-gauge lines. The line in question connected East Grinstead and Lewes in Sussex and has always been known as the Bluebell line. A 4.5-mile section between Horsted Keynes and Sheffield Park was chosen as the path for this live rural railway museum. Seventeen steam locomotives, mostly survivors from the Southern Railway and its constituents, have been acquired although only one at a time is normally needed for operation. Vintage carriages offer nostalgic vintage transport to passengers, who have kept coming in sufficient numbers for the line to survive, greatly to the surprise of sceptics and professionals, especially in the early days. With a minimum of paid staff, the Bluebell Railway is a complete pleasure railway; not only do its travellers travel for pleasure but most of its workers work for pleasure too. The style was set for many other full-size preserved railways in Britain and elsewhere in the world.

FESTINIOG RAILWAY COMPANY
Harbour Station,
Porthmadog, Gwynedd.

Although only thirteen miles long, the Festiniog Railway has its place in railway history

Above: British Railways' only steam-operated line is the 1ft 11½in gauge section from Aberystwyth to Devils Bridge in Wales. Three 2-6-2 tank locomotives are used to work this summer-only passenger service.

Top centre: This rather rare photograph shows an ex-Great Central Railway 'Director' class 4-4-0 Gerrard Powys Dewhurst *on the old Great Northern Railway line. The train is the Harrogate Pullman – note somersault signals.*

Left: One of the diminutive London Brighton & South Coast 'Terrier' 0-6-0T locomotives in use on the Bluebell Line.

as the pioneer of steam traction, passenger-carrying and common-carrier operation on a narrow gauge, in this case as little as 1ft 11½in. Opened in 1836 as a tramway for slate transport (gravity downhill, horse traction uphill) the historic metamorphosis into a full railway came in 1864.

After a period of disuse following World War II, it was restored (an operation in which volunteers played a significant part) progressively from 1955 to 1979 as a steam pleasure line. The route from Porthmadog to Blaenau Ffestiniog in North Wales is superbly scenic. On a 2.5-mile deviation opened in 1978 to avoid a new reservoir, there is not only a new 330-yd tunnel but also the only railway spiral in Britain.

The locomotive fleet in use includes one of the original 1865 locomotives – 0-4-0T *Prince* – and, uniquely in the world, two Fairlie articulated double engines. Both of the latter were built in the line's own Boston Lodge works and completed in 1879 and 1979 respectively. Currently in use are six steam and two diesel locomotives.

Passengers carried (most of whom travel in July and August) amount to some 400,000 annually and, in the peak period, trains are run at half-hour intervals. Buffet and observation cars are usually present.

Above: Double Fairlie locomotive Merddin Emrys *negotiates the new deviation line on the Festiniog Railway in June 1978. The old course of the line is now engulfed by the waters of the reservoir seen in this picture.*

Top right: Middleton Railway – locomotives at the depot in Leeds.

Below: One of London Transport Metropolitan Railway's dark red Bo-Bo electric locomotives on the Baker Street to Aylesbury line.

ISLE OF MAN RAILWAY

The Railway Station,
Douglas.

The Isle of Man Railways have few rivals in maintaining almost continuous passenger service with the same steam locomotives for more than one hundred years. The first route of this 3ft-gauge network was from Douglas to Peel, a distance of 11.5 miles, and was opened in 1873.

An inspection train prior to the opening was hauled by the Beyer Peacock 2-4-0 locomotive *Sutherland* which was derailed while running round the train at Peel. Despite this inauspicious beginning *Sutherland* is still hauling trains of tourists on the line to Port Erin. This 15.5 mile route was opened in 1874 and *Loch*, one of the locomotives delivered for that new service, is still in use.

In 1879 a separate company built a 16.5-mile railway from Ramsey to connect with the Douglas–Peel line at St Johns. Finally, the 2.5-mile branch from St Johns to Foxdale was opened in 1886. Although this was primarily for freight traffic from the lead and silver mines in the area, it also provided a regular passenger service until 1942. In 1961 the whole of the Foxdale branch was still in position although scarcely used and while the rest of the network was still in use it was with a much reduced level of service. This year also saw delivery of the last new rolling stock – two second-hand diesel railcars from County Donegal. By this time the major traffic was summer tourists and from the autumn of 1965 the railway closed for the winter. The railway did not re-open in 1966 but services were resumed during the summer of 1967. In 1969 the lines to Peel and Ramsey were finally closed.

Now only the Port Erin line remains with two of the centenarian locomotives, assisted by the Septuagenarian *Maitland* and the diesel railcars, gamely maintaining a service for the summer visitors – an eloquent demonstration of the lasting quality of Victorian engineering design and construction.

LONDON TRANSPORT

55 Broadway,
London SW1H 0BD.

The original section of the Metropolitan Railway (now part of the Metropolitan Line), the first underground city railway in the world, was opened in January 1863 in London from a junction with the Great Western Railway at Paddington to Farringdon (now Barbican) via Euston Square and King's Cross. It was steam operated, originally on the 7ft-0¼in gauge (apparent very clearly if one looks carefully at the tunnels on this section of line) and almost wholly in cut-and-cover tunnel, that is, just below street level. With surface extensions the 'Met' and its slightly younger companion the 'District' now cover 99 miles. Electrification began in 1890; the last steam-operated section from Rickmansworth to Amersham was electrified in 1960. Steam was used for works trains until 1970.

The deep level tubes began with the City

and South London Railway in 1890 and their extension is still in progress. The name 'tube' arose from the small-diameter circular tunnels, cut in the London clay, in which the trains ran. An extension of the C & SLR, called the Northern line, includes the longest railway tunnel in the world, seventeen miles from Archway to Morden. To permit running in the small tube tunnels, tube trains are only 9ft 6in in height, although standard gauge.

The system has been unified since the formation of the London Passenger Transport Board in 1933 and the total length of line now operated is 236 miles, making it the largest rapid transit system in the world. The great days of Pullman-car trains have now passed, and the 600 million passengers carried annually are now transported in elegant one-class aluminium-coloured electric multiple-unit trains.

In the sulphurous days of steam underground, the mainstays of the services were Beyer-Peacock condensing 4-4-0Ts. Handsome 4-4-4Ts handled trains on the fifty-mile open-air extension to Verney Junction via Aylesbury.

Trains for this outpost of empire left London behind handsome electric Bo-Bo's bearing names such as *Sherlock Holmes* whose lodgings at 221B Baker Street would (had they existed) have overlooked the Metropolitan's station and headquarters on the opposite side of the road. From 1920 to 1939 Pullman cars *Mayflower* and *Galatea* ran on these trains.

Steam locomotives were fortunately unknown in traffic in *deep level* tube lines such as the Central London Railway. Known in its early years as 'the tuppenny tube' – on account of a uniform fare – it had, to begin with, some noble electric locomotives. Their vibra-

tions were the cause of complaints and claims from property owners above and lighter self-propelled trains soon replaced them.

An American called Samuel Yerkes had a good deal to do with the London systems and his influence can still be felt in the use of such terms as 'westbound' and 'eastbound' instead of the more usual British 'up' and 'down', and also in the early adoption of open cars in place of compartment carriages on the District, Inner Circle, and the tube lines. Compartment stock remained on the Metropolitan line until 1960.

The last complete new tube, the Victoria line from Brixton to Walthamstow, opened in 1965. A new feature was the automatically controlled train; the train-man needs only to initiate the start. The most important recently opened station is Heathrow (London Airport), to which the Piccadilly line was extended in 1977. Just completed is the first stage of the Jubilee line from Baker Street to Charing Cross; this new tube is intended to relieve congestion.

MIDDLETON RAILWAY

Garnet Road,
Leeds LS11 5JY.

Although very short, this railway was old when the Stockton & Darlington was new; now in its 222nd year, it was running steam locomotives commercially when the battle of Waterloo was fought in 1815. A group of enthusiasts centred at Leeds University rescued the three-mile line from oblivion in 1958 and it is now run partly for freight and partly (at weekends) as a pleasure line. Of ten industrial steam locomotives and four diesels, all standard gauge, none actually is original MR, but all are representative of factory and works power.

Above: Steam in the Isle of Man. Now a
government-sponsored tourist line and using only a
truncated section of its original network (Douglas-
Port Erin) this 3ft 0in gauge railway has always been
unique. Its locomotives, all 2-4-0 tank engines (bar
one), were built by Beyer Peacock of Manchester and
a typical example of that firm's Victoriana; its
coaches were equally ancient. Today these museum
pieces travel the tracks during the summer as part of
the Island's holiday attractions. This photograph was
taken in 1956 and shows the terminal station at
Douglas when trains ran to Port Erin, Peel and by
the circuitous route to Ramsey.

Right: Of all Ireland's broad-gauge (5ft 3in)
railways the Great Northern was probably the finest.
Its main line ran from Belfast to Dublin and to
Londonderry, its express engines were painted in sky
blue and scarlet (and named) and its coaches were
finished in varnished teak. Here is a Belfast to
Londonderry express at Dungannon in the Six
Counties (Northern Ireland) in 1957.

NORTHERN IRELAND RAILWAYS COMPANY LIMITED – NIR
1 York Road,
Belfast, BT15 1NG.

The Northern Ireland Railway is a 225-mile remnant of three companies which thirty years ago operated 900 miles of broad (5ft 3in) and forty miles of narrow (3ft) gauge within the province. Apart from a few container trains, nowadays only passenger traffic is handled, the majority by means of a fleet of 132 diesel rail-cars and trailers. In very few countries has such wholesale slaughter of railway facilities taken place.

When Ireland was partitioned in 1921, the railways north of the new border were not affected regarding ownership. The major system wholly within the province was the 120-mile Northern Counties Committee (NCC) Railway owned by the Midland Railway of England, shortly to become the London Midland & Scottish. The efficient Great Northern Railway of Ireland had one half of its 617 miles of route north of the border and there was also a small system, local to the capital, called the Belfast & County Down (B&CDR).

On nationalization of the LMS in 1948, the NCC was incorporated, together with road transport interests, in the Ulster Transport Authority. When the Great Northern ran out of revenue in 1955, the portion north of the border came into the UTA as did the B&CDR in 1950. The present company was formed in 1967.

The NCC ran charming broad-gauge Irish versions of standard Midland and LMS trains; they just had less distance between their terminals, and more between the rails. On the narrow gauge, delightful two-cylinder compound 2-4-2 tanks handled the traffic, including corridor boat trains out of Larne.

The GN was another fine concern dating from 1862 – lovely sky-blue 4-4-0s were its pride and joy. Its trains had, even as late as the 1950s, a completely Edwardian aspect once one was away from the Belfast–Dublin main line; they had Edwardian virtues such as comfort and convenience also.

The Belfast and County Down was not an Edwardian but a Victorian survivor when most of the system was closed down in 1950, leaving one dieselized run out of Belfast to Bangor, County Down.

POST OFFICE RAILWAY
King Edward Building, Newgate Street,
London, E1.

Under the streets of London for a distance of 2.5 miles runs a railway with ten stations which is thought to be unique in that its trains are not only driverless but also crewless. Work began in 1913, but was suspended in World War I. During that war the tunnels were used for storing national treasures. The line opened in 1927 and currently the fleet of thirty 2ft-gauge electric units run 1.75 million miles each year carrying mail. The techniques used, with some updating, make a nationwide unmanned

freight transport system an economic and practical possibility. But alas, no politician is prepared to tell one of the most powerful trade unions in the country, that their members' services are no longer required and, accordingly, the proposals have foundered.

ROMNEY HYTHE & DYMCHURCH LIGHT RAILWAY COMPANY
New Romney Station,
New Romney, Kent.

The fifteen-mile 15in-gauge Romney, Hythe and Dymchurch Railway is, by a substantial margin, *the longest miniature railway in the world* and until 1978 was the only such railway with statutory or common-carrier status. The gauge is 1ft 3in and all nine steam locomotives built for the line since it opened in 1927 are still in use there (plus one other steamer).

Double track from Hythe to New Romney facilitates the operation of a half-hourly service. A buffet car is provided on some trains and, in all, some 300,000 passengers are carried each year; most take the journey for pleasure, but a school train service is also included.

TALYLLYN RAILWAY COMPANY
Wharf Station,
Tywyn, Gwynedd.

Although a mere eight miles long, this 2ft-3in-gauge railway made history in 1951 when, 86 years after it had opened, it was taken over by a group of volunteers called the Talyllyn Railway Preservation Society. They have run the

Above: Post Office Railway's engine and trucks in a tunnel at Western District Office, London. The Railway runs by remote control for over 6.5 miles across central London, seventy feet below ground, at a speed between stations of 35 mph. Over 40,000 bags of mail are carried each day.

Top: A Romney, Hythe & Dymchurch train enters Dymchurch station.

This photo of the Talyllyn Railway taken in 1951 during the first year of enthusiastic operation shows 0-4-0T Dolgoch *crossing the brick viaduct over the Dolgoch Gorge.*

line as a tourist attraction ever since and this was the first time that amateurs successfully managed to take over the running of a railway.

Both the original 1865-built steam locomotives are still in use, supplemented by four more acquired elsewhere. One hundred thousand passengers are now carried each year, involving (in the peak period) twelve trips each way daily.

The TRPS inspired many other amateur take-over operations all over the world, including standard-gauge lines, where the problems are considerably more daunting. (The premier British ones are referred to in the British Rail entry.)

VOLK'S ELECTRIC RAILWAY
Marlborough House,
Old Sterne, Brighton.

Least in length of the independently worked lines described in this book, but one of the greatest in its significance to world railway development is the 2.5-mile 2ft-8½in-gauge Volk's Electric Railway on the sea-front at Brighton. This is because it is the *oldest electric railway in the world* and was the first to achieve any sort of permanent existence. There are nine electric cars, run singly or in pairs, providing a frequent service in the summer season. The line is now owned and run by the Brighton Corporation.

GREECE

See map on pages 86–87.

HELLENIC RAILWAYS ORGANIZATION LIMITED

*1 Karolou Street,
Athens 107.*

Civilization in Greece stretches back 2500 years, yet main-line railways did not appear until the twentieth century. The first railway, between Athens and the port of Piraeus, was a local concern and opened in 1869. The six-mile line was electrified in 1904 and still remains outside the state system.

The first section of what was to become the Hellenic State Railways standard-gauge network, eventually to connect Athens with the rest of Europe, was French owned. It was not opened until 1904. The actual link at Salonika (now Thessaloniki) was made in 1916, at a time when through running involved trespassing on the battlefields of what is now northern Greece but which before the war was Turkish territory. The State Railways were formed in 1920, when three French companies were absorbed. A long line runs eastwards through Macedonia to a much-disputed point where Bulgaria, Turkey and Greece meet.

South of Athens a separate metre-gauge noose-like system serves Peloponnesus, home of an even more ancient civilization than that of Greece, and technically an island since 1892 when the four-mile wide Isthmus of Corinth was cut through by a canal. These lines were absorbed into the state system after World War II.

At present there are 1000 miles of standard-gauge and 600 miles of metre-gauge line, on which run 188 diesel locomotives, 480 passenger carriages (only six restaurant cars) and 11,000 freight wagons.

Not all the narrow gauge was in the south; there were both metre and 1ft 11½in gauge lines north of Athens. All three gauges met in the town of Volos, where there was an interesting (and possibly unique) stretch of triple mixed-gauge track.

Much heavy civil engineering characterizes the railways of Greece; there was also much destruction in World War II and the troubles which followed it. For some years after the war trains in the Peloponnesus pushed mine-exploding wagons in front of them and moved only in the daytime.

As the railway north from Athens came nearer to becoming a trunk route, the Greeks in 1914 did what they should have gone on doing and ordered some down-to-earth American 2-8-2s from the American Locomotive Company of Schenectady. Commonsense did not, however, prevail and over the years the system accumulated the products (in some cases, the discarded products) of Germany, Austria, Britain and Italy as well. Steam is now virtually at an end.

Athens is the starting point for several international trains. Destinations include West Germany and Turkey; through sleeping cars have ceased running to Paris but have begun running to Moscow by two routes. The annual carriage of passengers is twelve million, while four million tons of freight is hauled an average distance of 230 miles by Hellenic Railways trains.

Bottom: Bralos viaduct on the Athens to Salonika main line of the Greek State Railways.

Below: A Peloponnesian Railway train leaves Patras behind a 1952 postwar Italian-built 2-8-2 locomotive built by Breda, as one of a class of reparation engines.

Above: The Peloponnese Express at Corinth.

Top right: A diesel-electric locomotive backs down onto its train at Waterford, Ireland.

HOLLAND
See Netherlands

——HUNGARY——

See map on pages 26-27.

HUNGARIAN STATE RAILWAYS – MAV
Magyar Allamvasutak,
Népköztársaság Utja, 73-75,
1940 Budapest, VI.

At the time modern railway history opened, Hungary was a reluctant partner in the Hapsburg Austro-Hungarian Empire, although there are records (the earliest known) of railways with wooden rails in the gold and silver mines of Upper Hungary, now part of Czechoslovakia, as early as 1500, before the Turkish invasion of 1530 and well before the Hungarian throne fell to Austria.

Shortly after the first section of the Budapest-Vienna railway – the first steam railway in Hungary – was opened in 1846, the Hungarians rebelled once again against foreign domination. Although the Austrians (like the Russians 110 years later) put it down with ferocity, they took a more enlightened view in the long term and gave Hungary internal self-government in 1867; Emperor Franz Josef of

Austria was crowned King of Hungary. This was the signal for the state to begin constructing new lines and taking over old ones. The present MAV initials first appeared in 1869, though an additional adjective, *kiralyi* (royal) was included until 1914, in the full title. In that fateful year there were almost 14,000 miles of railway in Hungary, but the fully independent republic set up after the war contained under 6000 miles because so much territory was lost to newly independent Czechoslovakia and Yugoslavia, as well as to Rumania. A small amount of territory was temporarily regained between 1938 and 1942, but the present frontiers of the country remain virtually the same as imposed in 1919.

The Hungarian Railways, Ganz of Budapest and electrical engineer de Kando were jointly responsible in 1933 for the very first main-line high-voltage industrial-frequency alternating-current electrification – the present world standard. Convertors – rotary ones in those days – on the locomotives converted this type of current supply to more digestible form (initially this was three-phase AC) for the traction motors. The location was the 120-mile Budapest to Vienna main line, as far as the Austrian frontier station of Hegyeshalom. Since 1954, a further 700 miles of railway have been electrified on the same system, but using locomotives of more conventional type with static convertors to convert AC to DC.

Hungarian steam locomotives have always

Above: Eight of the ubiquitous class 424 4-8-0 locomotives await their turns of duty at Budapest in 1967.

locomotives. The famous 424 class 4-8-0s handle heavier assignments – some of these were built as late as 1959. They have been exported to Czechoslovakia, Yugoslavia, the USSR and either China or North Korea (there are conflicting reports).

Present-day Hungary is easy locomotive country, but mountain territory now ceded to others, bred, in 1914, a sixty-strong class of 2-6-6-0 Mallet articulated locomotives, the most powerful ever to run in Hungary.

On the diesel side may be noted locomotives of Soviet, American (via the Swedish firm NOHAB) and homemade origin. Electrification has so far not proceeded far enough to relegate diesel traction to a secondary role.

A feature of Hungarian passenger operations is the use of locomotives on long push-pull trains, controlled from a cab on the leading coach when the locomotive – which can be electric, diesel or steam – is pushing. Common elsewhere with electric traction, it is rare to find this arrangement with diesels and virtually unique today with steam.

Currently there are 4870 miles of railway in Hungary, including 175 miles of 2ft 6in gauge and 23 miles of Soviet broad gauge on a connecting line near the frontier. Almost 133 million tons of freight are carried an average distance of 110 miles per year as well as 320 million passengers.

been distinctive (at times hideously so). Today they are distinctive by merely remaining in well-cared-for existence, backing up electric and diesel operation in an economical way.

Very old but entirely serviceable 0-6-0s and 0-6-0Ts of early standard MAV design survive on station pilot duties. For secondary lines there are Edwardian 2-6-2s and on the branch lines 2-4-2s and two sizes of 2-6-2 tank

Above: Budapest West station in 1974 with one of the frequent suburban push and pull sets passing the signal box at the platform's end. At that time these services ran partly by steam (424 class) and partly by electric locomotives but the service is now all electric and the whole station (bar the façade to the street) is being rebuilt.

Right: A 424 class 4-8-0 locomotive with a fast train at Budapest East station in 1967.

IRELAND

IRISH TRANSPORT COMPANY – CIE
Coras Iompair Eireann,
Houston Station,
Dublin 8.

The first railway in Ireland ran from Dublin to Kingstown (now Dun Laoghaire) and was opened on 17 December 1834. Development proceeded piecemeal but once one route had been built there was no reason, in a sparsely populated land, to build a competitive one. Originally the separate lines were built to several separate gauges. A Royal Commission decided that the best way to settle the matter without fear or favour would be to take the average – hence the gauge of 5ft 3in. In the remoter districts, construction took place under government subsidy or profit guarantee. At the time of independence from Britain – in 1921 – four major companies existed. The Midland and Great Western radiated from Dublin to Sligo and Galway; the Dublin & South Eastern went to Rosslare, Waterford and Wexford; the Great Southern & Western served Cork and Killarney. One could travel across the new border by Great Northern to Londonderry and Belfast.

Once the Civil War of 1923–24 ('The Troubles') was over, the government rationalized the situation by grouping all the lines wholly inside the border into a new company, the 2200-mile Great Southern Railways. In addition to those already mentioned several small lines, including several of local interest built to 3ft gauge, were included in the new company.

Until 1950 the railways of Ireland presented an incredibly fascinating and varied spectacle, quite out of proportion to the small scale on which their operations were conducted. For example, there were 143 different types of locomotive among the 700-strong fleet. These varied from the superb 'Irish Queen' 4-6-0s *Maedb*, *Macha* and *Tailte*, as modern and up-to-date as any steam locomotives in Europe, down to surviving 2-2-2 single drivers on the Waterford and Tramore line. The Londonderry and Lough Swilly line had narrow-gauge tank locomotives which were the only 4-8-4s in the British Isles and faithful hay-burners still plodded their way along the GN's horse-operated Fintona branch until the 1950s. One might also cite such delights as Limerick Junction (nowhere near Limerick) where no train could leave without reversing or the Tralee & Dingle narrow gauge which only ran trains once a month in connection with the cattle fairs.

Full nationalization came in 1950 (the change of title from GSR to CIE came in 1944) and included integration with road and water transport. Other closures followed – nationalization meant a 35 percent reduction in mileage – including the eclipse of all the narrow gauge – and then came modernization involving the early replacement of steam (and horse) traction by diesel. The present system is as efficient as it can reasonably be, but it is not possible to run at a profit nor, alas, has it been possible to retain the particular charm of the old days.

County Donegal Railways' diesel railcar climbs through the Barnesmore Gap, Ireland in 1952.

Italy & the Balkans

1 : 5 000 000

50   0   50   100 miles

50   0   50   100   150 km

Initial dieselization came to Ireland in 1931 on the Donegal narrow-gauge lines. The reduction in expenses by some pioneer light-weight bus-type railcar units made this system into the only profitable line in the Republic – and it was half owned by the British government as successors to the London Midland & Scottish Railway. The LMS had been joint owners with the Great Northern of Ireland.

Currently the CIE owns 221 diesel locomotives and 39 railcars, 582 passenger and 8599 freight cars plus 3500 road vehicles. In 1974 it carried 190 million passengers and 5.4 million tons of goods. The expenses represented 125 percent of the receipts.

IRISH PEAT BOARD
Bord na Mona,
28 Upper Pembroke Street,
Dublin 2.

The peat bogs of Ireland have in recent years been developed as sources of mechanically dug fuel, mainly for electric power stations. Trucks are not too satisfactory when used on the bogs so 3ft gauge railways are used for transport. The fleet of 250 diesel locomotives exceeds in number those in the national railway system. The 600 miles of track that exists also exceeds the amount of public narrow gauge that ever existed in Ireland. Numerous experiments were made on burning peat in locomotives, both on the peat railways and on the main lines, but with no lasting success. During World War II, it had to be used, but steam production was very uncertain.

Top: The Valencia Harbour branch of the old Great Southern & Western Railway was Ireland's most westerly 5ft 3in gauge line. This photograph was taken around the turn of the century.

Right and above right: New coaches for a new image on Ireland's diesel-hauled express.

ITALY

See maps on pages 86–87.

ITALIAN STATE RAILWAYS – FS
Ferrovie dello Stato,
Piazza della Croce Rossa,
Rome.

When railways first became a practicable proposition, back in the 1830s, Italy was not a political entity but a collection of kingdoms, states and areas under foreign (Austrian) domination. The first one to have a railway was the Kingdom of Naples, in which a line, five miles long from Naples to Portici, was opened on 3 October 1839.

The first inter-city main line was completed in 1854. It ran from Turin to Genoa in Piedmont under the joint encouragement of King Victor Emmanuel and Prime Minister Cavour. Five years later these two were to embark on the hazardous venture of freeing the whole of Italy from foreign domination and unifying the country. By then Piedmont had over 600 miles of railway (nearly half the Italian total) and this enabled the Piedmontese army and its French allies to concentrate against the Austrians. The Austrian army lacked a well-developed railway system and could not be deployed in the same rapid manner. Accordingly, they suffered decisive defeats at Magenta and Solferino.

The price exacted by the French for their support was the transfer to France of the Piedmontese provinces of Nice and Savoy. One consequence was that the Mont Cenis tunnel project, under way since 1860, became a joint French and Italian one instead of being purely Italian.

Subsequently Parma, Modena and Tuscany all agreed to join a united kingdom of Italy, while Garibaldi sailed from Genoa with a thousand men to win over Sicily and Naples. He was so welcome in the south that he was actually able to enter Naples by train, well ahead of his army.

King Victor Emmanuel and his new Italian government encouraged railway construction, mainly by means of generous concessions to private companies. By 1866 it was possible to travel by train between every Italian city, except a few in the far south, to this day an impoverished area. By 1871 Rome had become the capital, the 8.5-mile Mont Cenis tunnel leading into France was open, the Austrians had been driven out of the northeastern province of Venetia, and the Pope's once-vast temporal domains had shrunk to that of the Vatican City in Rome.

In addition to the unification of the country, successive steps were taken towards the unification of the main-line railways, under laws promulgated in 1865, 1885 and 1905 respectively. The last of these provided for the formation of the present state railway system, the Ferrovie dello Stato or FS, which came into being on 1 July 1905, with almost 7000 miles of route. Numerous lines of local interest remain

outside the FS network, which currently extends to 10,000 miles.

Volta, of 'volt' fame, was an Italian and, if one notes the fact that the tricky arithmetic of justifying electrification was particularly favourable in coal-less Italy, it is not surprising that electric traction there went ahead very rapidly and very early.

Early electrification was three-phase AC, very simple electrically, but involving fixed running speeds and two contact wires. This was particularly complicated at junctions. The first line was converted from steam traction in 1900 and by 1928, when the more flexible 3000v DC system was adopted for new work, over 1600 miles had been converted. This was by far the largest and the longest lasting application of the three-phase system – it did not finally disappear until 1971. After 1928 DC electrification was pushed ahead very rapidly (remember this was the reign of Mussolini who

Above: The inaugural Italian Direct Current train arrives at Genoa. Locomotives were fitted with a special pantograph to collect current from what had once been three-phase double overhead equipment.

Top: The Franco-Crosti boiler gives some Italian steam locomotives an appearance that takes some getting used to

Above: The station concourse at Rome, Italy is spacious and always clean.

Right: An exterior view of the Rome Terminus. The building is not only a pleasure to look at but is functional as well.

'made the trains run to time'). By 1939 it was possible to travel 690 miles from Bologna all the way to Reggio di Calabria in the toe of Italy by electric train. Currently electric traction extends 5230 miles, all the original three-phase sections having been converted to DC. Nineteen hundred electric locomotives handle the bulk of Italy's rail traffic.

Italian steam locomotives, which still exist to the tune of 600 or so but perform only reserve duties, are very distinctive. There are some with the strange looking Franco-Crosti boiler and others with inside cylinders but outside valve chests and valve gear. Because of the electrification programme, virtually no steam locomotives were constructed after 1925.

Diesel traction also came early to coal-less Italy, in the form of railcars (there are currently 1500 in service) and this experience has led to complete self-sufficiency in diesel traction, although this form is, on the whole, confined to lines of secondary importance. There are almost 1000 diesel locomotives at present in service.

Italian trains are also very fast, frequent, cheap and comfortable – and well filled too, one might add, reflecting a level of fares that only bring in just over half the cost of running them. Their Achilles heel is punctuality. Before European railways began running almost identical carriages, the wise traveller on an international train would choose an Italian vehicle in preference – and not only for the charming stained-glass windows in the lavatories. Luxury electric trains such as the 'Settebello' with observation saloons front and rear, set new standards for other nations to follow.

FS is carrying annually, with its fleet of 16,000 passengers and 120,000 freight vehicles, almost 400 million passengers and sixty million tons of freight. The latter is hauled an average distance of 200 miles.

During the interwar period, huge efforts were made to complete one of the greatest-ever feats of railway engineering, the Bologna – Florence direttissima ('most direct') railway, which had been begun in 1908. The Great Apennine Tunnel – only one of the great artifacts on this line – opened in 1934, was then as now the second longest mountain railway tunnel in the world, and because of the nature of the ground encountered, one of the most difficult to bore. The distance between the two

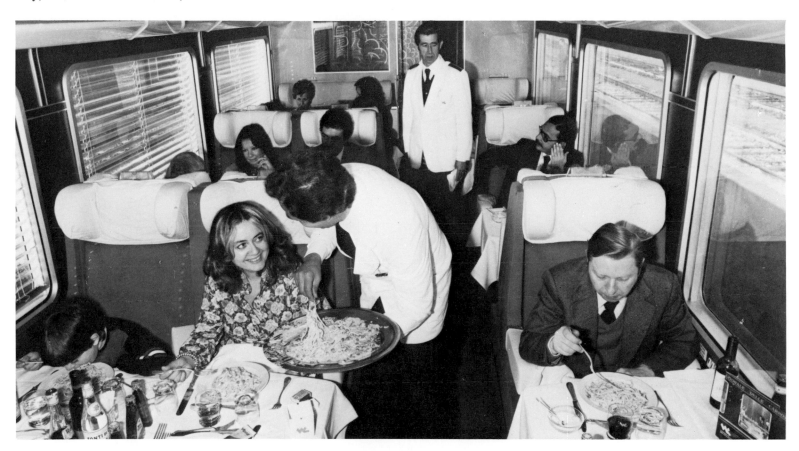

Above: Carrozza Ristorante – *eating the Italian way on an Italian TEE internal train.*

Left: View of the recently completed new Rome–Florence direttissima *railway.*

LIECHTENSTEIN

See map on pages 26–27.

LIECHTENSTEIN RAILWAY
The Chancellery,
Vaduz.

As the great 'Arlberg Express' gathers speed out of Switzerland into Austria immediately on leaving the frontier station of Buchs, it rapidly enters and leaves the sovereign principality of Liechtenstein on a line twelve miles long, which was completed in 1872. Alas, only local trains stop at stations like Schaan-Vaduz for the capital. Austria provides all railway services but there is a customs union with Switzerland.

LUXEMBOURG

Above: The 'Settebello Express' is the Rome to Florence electric express train. The driver's cab is raised above roof level with an observation lounge below.

Top: A typical Italian State express train on the viaduct at Lustra.

cities was reduced from 82 to sixty miles and the height to be climbed by almost 1000ft. The running time for passenger trains was reduced from $2\frac{1}{4}$ hours to 66 minutes.

Another *direttissima*, now under construction, is that between Rome and Florence, with a view to upgrading the whole Milan–Rome–Naples route (elsewhere local improvements in alignment will suffice) for 150 mph running.

See map on page 94.

LUXEMBOURG NATIONAL RAILWAYS – CFL
Société Nationale des Chemins de Fer Luxembourgeois,
9 Place de la Gare,
Luxembourg.

Right: One of the delights of Europe in the 1950s was the availability of so many narrow-gauge railway systems. Here is CFL 0-6-0 tank No 341 on the metre-gauge line from Luxembourg Central station to Remisch.

The Luxembourg Railways may be small in size (170 miles) but their traffic (thirteen million passengers and 23 million tons of freight) makes them proportionately among the busiest in the world. They were founded in 1946 from lines owned by the Guilliaume – Luxembourg Railway, which were operated by the French National Railways and a Belgian-owned company, the Prince Henri Railway and Mines Company. Also included were some state-owned narrow-gauge lines, now closed. As a result, the French and Belgian governments have each, to this day, a 24.5 percent share-holding in the system.

There are at present 56 diesel and nineteen electric locomotives (the Belgian 3000v DC and French 25,000v AC systems meet at Luxembourg station, with special switching arrangements), eighty carriages and 3500 freight cars. Expenses are currently 101 percent of receipts.

MALTA

See map on pages 86-87.

A short 7.5-mile metre-gauge railway was opened on the island of Malta in 1883. It ran from the capital, Valetta, to Citta Vechia in the centre of the island. The line was not a cheap one to build – for example the approach to the terminus at Valetta involved elaborate tunnelling. Bankruptcy came almost at once and the state took the line over in 1892. Barely viable in opposition to animal transport, the Malta Railway fell an early victim to the bus and private car, closing in 1931. There were three 0-6-0s and six 2-6-4 tank locomotives.

MONACO

See map on pages 46-47.

MONACO RAILWAY
Le Commissaire près la SNCF, Ministère d'Etat,
Monaco Ville, Monaco.

The Principality of Monaco is one-up on that of Liechtenstein, for at least the 'Blue Train' actually stops at the new Monte Carlo station in Monaco. In 1964 the main line was removed from the sea-front and put in a tunnel under the town; electrification followed in 1969. The rather choice old vintage station, which had echoed to the tread of so many famous (and infamous) feet, is now a memory. The one-mile length of railway in Monaco is, to all intents and purposes, part of the French National system and has been since 1868.

Above: An ex-British Austerity 2-10-0 with an extended chimney shares the work with native steam engines and a Swiss-built electric locomotive at Utrecht in January 1949.

NETHERLANDS

See map on page 94.

NETHERLANDS RAILWAYS – NS
Nederlandse Spoorwegen,
Moreelsepark, Utrecht.

The Dutch nation just made it into the exclusive railway class of the 1830s, for the first line in Holland opened on 24 September 1839, from Amsterdam to Haarlem. Development was privately financed and in the course of time the various companies gradually merged. In fact, by 1920 the state had become the largest shareholder in the two remaining companies, the Holland Railways Company and the Netherlands State Railway Company. These two pooled their operations in 1925, but this failed to avoid bankruptcy in 1937; accordingly the nationalized Netherlands Railways came into being on 1 January 1938.

There was electric working for local trains between the Hague and Rotterdam as early as 1908. Rotterdam and Amsterdam were connected by electric trains in 1927 and by 1939, 320 miles of the 1800-mile system were electrified. The war gave rise to wholesale damage. Dutch railwaymen went on strike at a critical point in the Allied advance into Germany; following the failure to secure the Rhine Bridge at Arnhem in October 1944, the Ger-

mans had the leisure to indulge in the systematic wrecking of the network. In consequence there was great hardship, but the totality of the destruction led very quickly to complete rebuilding. By the early 1950s the Netherlands had one of the world's finest railway systems, the envy of many countries whose lines had come through with less damage but in a state where patching-up was possible. Electrification at 1500v DC now covered all 870 miles of the principal main lines, using an unusual double-contact wire arrangement.

The contours of the Low Countries present few obstacles to railway building, but natural and manmade water gaps abound. The longest bridge is over the Hollandsch Diep at Moerdijk; this structure is 3510ft long. There is also a bridge over the Lek River near Culemboorg with a 502ft span. Many of the rivers are used as highways of commerce and in consequence opening bridges are very common; 81 swing, 23 lifting and twenty draw bridges are in use. Some very subtle arrangements are provided to ensure continuity of the 1500v contact wires over such bridges on electrified lines.

LOW COUNTRIES

Projection: Conical with two standard parallels

East from Greenwich

COPYRIGHT GEORGE PHILIP & SON, LTD.

The great destruction of World War II has been mentioned; during World War I Holland was neutral, but even so the conflict had its effect on NSB structures. Steel supplies were unavailable and the present NS headquarters at Utrecht, then under construction, had to be built of vaulted arches. The grim and medieval aspect of its corridors became entirely appropriate when, in World War II as Gestapo headquarters, even grimmer and more medieval things were done within its walls.

Dutch steam power was unique on the continent of Europe for being and staying entirely British in style, even to a mass of brass and copper adornments. High 4-6-0s, many actually from Beyer-Peacock of Manchester but others locally built, ran the passenger trains and there were 4-8-4Ts for freight. After the liberation the survivors were supplemented by British and USA War Department locomotives, but they were not granted the traditional staying power of stop-gaps.

The way in which a new motive power fleet was fitted to the system requirements after World War II is a classic. Instead of accepting the usual situation of warring departments, each intent on doing the best for itself, the Dutch did what other railways should have done and put one capable engineer in total charge. One example will suffice as an example of General Manager F Q den Hollander's thinking. In Holland most freight trains are run at night and for these general-purpose locomotives were needed. For passenger services (which in Holland run almost entirely during the day) self-propelled trains were to be used, except sufficient to occupy surplus locomotives from night-time freight trains. The consequence is a fleet of 470 self-propelled streamlined electric train sets and 112 main-line electric locomotives, and enough passenger cars for fifty or so trains. Many international expresses terminate in Holland and these, of course, are locomotive-hauled also. The trains have provided an interconnecting frequent regular-interval service for 8.5 million passengers annually covering all parts of Holland over the last 25 years; the only fault is, perhaps, that their styling has become a little dated. This is not concealed by garish and varied liveries – wide diagonal stripes of blue on bright yellow, for example – and their use as mobile advertisement hoardings. Startling decor on the front end is necessary as a warning to men on the line, of course. A Dutch electric train appeared on the world's television screens in 1976 when one was hijacked for several days complete with train load of passengers.

Freight operations in the Netherlands suffer competition not only from road transport, but also from the excellent canal and river system. An efficient and original computerized control system does its best and eighteen million tons of freight are moved each year, but the average distance is less than 100 miles.

Above: A Netherlands State Railways electric train.

Top: Netherlands State Railways electric power at Roosendaal. The train on the right of the picture is an express from Amsterdam to Paris.

NORWAY

See map on pages 38-39.

NORWEGIAN STATE RAILWAYS – NSB
Norges Statsbaner,
Storgt. 33,
Oslo 1.

Many railways were built with the sole purpose of unifying nations. Norway, however, is an exception. In the early days of railways, Norway was united with Sweden. Its trunk railways connected Christiania (now Oslo) and Trondheim to Stockholm rather than to each other, although there was in fact a dubious narrow-gauge link considered good enough for an outlying province between the two. Independence was achieved in 1905 without significant bloodshed or lasting rancour and so, rather late in the day, the stupendous task of linking the new capital with the principal provincial cities was put in hand. It was to take 57 years.

Bergen was reached in 1907 (the route was made snowproof in 1909), Trondheim in 1921, Kristiansand in 1938, Stavanger by 1944 and Bødø in the far north in 1962. Electrification, based on the ample supplies of water power available in Norway began in 1922 (between Oslo and Drammen) and was complete on all these lines except the last-named by 1970, including the connections to the Swedish border in the directions of Stockholm and Göteborg, a total of 1500 miles. The high voltage low frequency AC system is used, as in Sweden.

In a country which has a population of less than four million and which extends more than a thousand miles from north to south, no form of transport can be profitable. The railways are no exception, expenses running currently at over 130 percent of receipts, but their operations are regarded as a service whose value has no direct relation to profitability.

Dotted lines showing 'railways proposed or under construction' are a feature of many countries' railway maps. Typically, because of the ineptitude and inertia of governments, they often remain that way for decades. Not so in Norway; the dotted lines once on the map are now solid and have resulted in the formation of a first-rate system, powered mainly by a self-replacing source of energy.

Norway is a tough country in which to build railways. The average snow-line, summer and winter, is a mere 3000 feet and most of the land area is mountainous. The workforce boring the

Gravehalsen Tunnel (3.3 miles) on the Bergen–Oslo line was cut off from the outside world for ten weeks at a time during the 1902–03 winter. Outside the tunnel, in the upper reaches of the line whose summit is at 4207ft, work could only proceed for three months of the year. After completion, many miles of snow-sheds had to be constructed before trains could run reliably throughout the year.

Although such an altitude was not to be reached again, longer tunnels were needed on the Stavanger or Sørland (Southland) line. These were: Gylard – 3.6 miles, Haegebostad – 5.3 miles and Kvineshei – 5.6 miles. Since then an even longer tunnel has straightened this route on its oldest stretch between Oslo and Drammen, the 6.7-mile Lierasin Tunnel, opened in 1973. On the Bergen line, the circuitous stretch immediately outside the town has recently been re-aligned with another long (4.8 mile) tunnel. Even so, this short catalogue

Extreme left, top: The 'Norlandsban' freight train approaches the Arctic Circle.

Extreme left, below: The Bergen line electric express approaches Finse in conditions typical of all seasons except high summer.

Left: A Bergen to Oslo train at Voss in 1953, double-headed by two 4-8-0s.

Below: An iron-ore train en route to Narvik on the Ofoten Railway hauled by a Norwegian 1-D+D-1 locomotive.

mentions only six out of 773 Norwegian railway tunnels. An urban tunnel to connect the east and west stations in Oslo is now under construction.

The bridges are not quite so outstanding. However, mention must be made of a beautiful arches-on-an-arch 146ft bridge in stone, on the Andalsnes branch. The Rauma River runs 200 feet below and gives its name to the line. There is a 190ft span steel bridge at Gvarv in the Telemark district.

Bødø station, the end of the line, 1262 miles from Oslo and 750 miles from Trondheim, is not the furthest north on NSB. To go further north by rail, it is necessary first to go back 725 miles and change at Hell. The next stage is to proceed north via Sweden. The line back into Norway is a single line of rails which carries two-thirds of the total freight traffic on the Norwegian State Railways – twenty million tons. This is the Ofoten Railway, built between

1885 and 1902 to bring Swedish iron ore to the ice-free port of Narvik. It was the ancestor of many recently constructed mineral hauling roads and a rare case in Europe because 5000-ton North American-sized trains are run. The line was electrified between 1919 and 1923. Since then motive power has been pooled between the Norwegians and Swedish sections of the line.

Many Norwegian steam locomotives were notable, for so small a country, in being home-made by Thune's of Oslo. Small and large 4-8-0s of Swiss inspiration dominated the workings. Some were four-cylinder compounds using the Woolf system, whereby only two sets of valves and gear were required. Finally, a set of 2-8-4s were built – the 'Dovregrubben' – or 'Dovre Giants' – for express trains on the Dovreban from Oslo to Trondheim. Examples of Norwegian steam are preserved in the museum at Hamar.

The mechanical parts of many Norwegian electric locomotives were also built in the country, but electrical equipment was generally supplied by ASEA of Sweden. Some notable rod-drive 9500hp 1-D+D+D-1 locomotives deal with traffic on the iron-ore line in the north.

The four principal lines are either a full day's or a full night's travel and accordingly a day train (with dining car) and a night train (with sleeper and buffet) form the basic service, supplemented by faster limited service in, say, the afternoon. International services run to Stockholm and Copenhagen.

Currently 160 electric and 89 diesel locomotives, with 890 passenger and 8800 freight cars handle 33 million passengers and 31 million tons of freight, of which twenty million tons is iron ore into Narvik.

There are few independent railways in Norway; included are two small museum lines, remnants of once-lengthy 2ft 5½in and 3ft 6in narrow-gauge lines. They are, respectively, at Sorumsand east of Oslo and near Kristiansand in the south-west.

SPITZBERGEN

A 1.5-mile 2ft 11in (three Swedish feet) gauge industrial railway on a Norwegian island might be thought to be of small account. The significance of the coal railway at King's Bay in Spitzbergen lies in the fact it was substantially the most northerly in the world, lying precisely on the 79° parallel of latitude. The line opened in 1917 and was closed from 1929 to 1945. Final closure came in 1965 after a mine explosion. There were five steam 0-4-0T locomotives.

POLAND

See map on pages 26–27.

POLISH STATE RAILWAYS – PKP
Polskie Koleje Panstowe,
ul. Chalubinskiego 4,
00-928 Warsaw.

Railway development has always been subservient to the course of history. Centuries of foreign domination and partition have done

little to destroy the Poles' sense of identity.

The Poland of 1919 was formed from provinces which had been part of Russia, Germany and Austria for generations, since well before the coming of railways. The railways in each province were, of course, part of the railway systems of each of these 'occupying' nations. (The ex-Soviet lines were of a different gauge, 5ft 0in instead of 4ft 8½in.) There had been much fighting in Poland and, as a measure of the destruction caused, it is noted that eight out of ten bridges were destroyed.

There was much for the new administration to do to the 10,300-mile system they had inherited; war damage and neglect had to be made good, Soviet-gauge lines converted and so on. In the Soviet areas, too, railways were much more sparse on the ground; this had to be corrected. Flows of traffic had also changed; new lines had to be built and others upgraded and doubled. A particular project was a 350-mile line to connect the Silesian coal fields to the new Polish port of Gdynia; by exception (because of a financial crisis in Poland) this was let out to a private French company, which completed the line in 1933.

There were 11,200 miles of standard-gauge railway and 1500 miles of narrow serving Poland's 35 million population in 1939 when partition again took place. Six years and (on some lines) four gauge conversions later, a new Poland emerged. The second war eliminated

people more than things: ten million Poles were killed but under half the railway bridges were destroyed this time. The whole country had been moved 150-200 miles westwards, ceding 69,000 square miles of territory to the USSR but gaining 39,000 from Germany. In spite of this net loss of territory, there was a net gain of railway mileage since ex-German country tended to have denser railway networks than ex-Russian. The new system extended to 13,000 miles of standard and 2500 miles of narrow gauge.

Only twice in the last sixty years, have Polish Railways' locomotive engineers been left to their own devices. They found their country populated with all manner of locomotives. Each time they have made do for as short a time as possible, restocking quickly with a 'no-frills' locomotive fleet of excellent quality, built in the locomotive factories which exist in Poland. These were notable for having produced such machines as the 2-12-4Ts for Bulgaria and much else for export. Hence, there was less dissatisfaction with steam than elsewhere and Poland has the largest steam fleet remaining in Europe by a factor of at least two; but naturally Poland's richness in coal and poverty in oil are also factors. Over 4000 strong a few years ago, it is thought that between 1000 and 1500 steam locomotives are in regular use. Diesel and electric locomotives are now also being produced in Poland. About

1200 of each are believed to exist.

Electrification has also proceeded well; the current total is 3500 miles. Electric traction handles a high proportion of the 1120 million passengers and 464 million tons of freight carried annually an average distance of 280 miles. Remarkable amounts of traffic are handled by a fleet of approximately 8000 passenger and 190,000 freight cars.

Above: Krakow station in Poland.

Top left: A new Swedish-built electric locomotive in service in Norway.

Above: The new Dautzig terminus at Warsaw, Poland.

Top right: A narrow-gauge Mallet 0-4-4-0T leaves Porto Trinidade Station, Portugal.

Above: Narrow-gauge tracks wind their way out of Tua towards the Spanish border at Bragança. For many years this branch was the sole preserve of little 2-4-0 tanks, some with copper-capped chimneys like this one shown here at Mirandella in 1970.

Top: Portugal has a number of metre-gauge lines in service, most running north from the Douro Valley. Until recently the Corgo line out of Regua had the monopoly of the 2-4-6-0 Mallet tanks, built by Henschel. Both trains shown were so hauled in 1970.

PORTUGAL

See map on page 102.

PORTUGUESE RAILWAY COMPANY – CP

Companhia dos Caminhos de Ferro Portugueses, Calçado do Duque 20, Lisbon.

Throughout history the Portuguese have done everything possible to emphasize how different they are from their overbearing Spanish neighbours. However, in a brief account such as this, one can get further by pointing out the similarities. Northern Portugal has much in common with northern Spain: moderately mountainous, with deep river gorges, and some excellent agricultural country. Southern Portugal has more in common with southern Spain, though the climate is tempered by a higher rainfall and the plains and low hills are therefore, on the whole, more prosperous. Lacking any great mining or industrial bases, the Portuguese have become a richer people than the Spanish partly through their more fertile soil and partly through foreign trade.

The three most important main lines run from Lisbon, the capital. The first runs north to the second city Oporto (215 miles) and the Spanish frontier near Vigo. Branching from the Lisbon-Oporto line at Pampilhosa, is the second main line which runs to the Spanish frontier at Vilar Formoso and connects Portugal via Salamanca and Irun with France and the rest of Europe. The third line runs from Barreiro, opposite Lisbon on the south bank of the Tagus (unbridged here until recently), via Funcheira 215 miles to Villa Real de Santo Antonio. There is also a direct connection between Lisbon and Madrid, leaving the Oporto line at Entroncamento (which means 'junction') and reaching the Spanish border at Valencia de Alcantara (153 miles). The supporting network of branch lines is still largely intact, even including most of the six separate metre-gauge systems in the Oporto area, four of which are feeders to the line running east from Oporto up the Douro valley.

History

The Portuguese railways are still formally owned by a company; the Companhia dos Caminhos de Ferro Portugueses, which was originally founded in the 1850s with French capital to build the Lisbon-Oporto main line. In 1926 the CP reversed the usual process by taking over the state-owned railways, chiefly the Sul e Sueste system (most lines south of the Tagus) and the Minho e Douro (lines north and east of Oporto). In 1948 it absorbed most of the remaining undertakings, including the Beira Alta (Lisbon-Coimbra-Vilar Formoso) and its narrow-gauge connection, the Vale di Vouga. In 1976 it completed its collection of all Portuguese railways with the absorption of the Estoril Electric Railway. However, to claim that the CP is still a private-enterprise undertaking as distinct from a nationalized one is nowadays to make a very fine semantic distinction, and certainly the management and direction have been wholly Portuguese for many years.

One important point to make is that although most works of reference quote the gauge of both Spanish and Portuguese railways as 5ft 6in, it is not in fact the same. More accurately, the standard Spanish gauge is 1.674 metres and the standard Portuguese gauge is 1.665 metres. The difference is relatively small, yet it means that in general rolling stock cannot run through between the two systems. It is possible to devise a wheel profile which will run on both gauges acceptably, at additional maintenance cost; only a limited number of vehicles, chiefly passenger stock on international services, takes advantage of this and the interworking of freight equipment is very restricted.

Locomotives

Although a fair number of the locomotives in early days were British-built (and some near-centenarian 0-6-0s by Beyer Peacock survived until almost the end of broad-gauge steam operation in the mid-1970s), as might be expected, French design predominated in Portuguese practice, even though many engines actually came from German builders. There were considerable numbers of de Glehn compound 4-6-0s and 4-6-2s among a locomotive stock of considerable variety (and noticeably less superannuated than the Spanish fleet); other types included a variety of tank engines, including some modern 2-6-4Ts and 2-8-4Ts, and a few heavy 2-8-2s from Alco in 1944. Worth special mention were the three large 4-8-0 compounds built by Henschel in 1931 for the Beira Alta company. During the 1960s French expertise assisted the electrification at 25,000v AC of the Lisbon–Oporto main line and a number of other connecting lines, and dieselization of the remaining broad-gauge lines was completed in the 1970s using predominantly French types.

The metre-gauge lines, whose only steam locomotives were tank types, offered an equally varied scene. Apart from a profusion of non-standard 0-6-0Ts and 2-6-0Ts, there were some fine modern 2-8-2Ts and numerous Mallets, most of which had the rare wheel arrangement of 2-4-6-0T. Dieselization of these lines has not yet been quite completed.

Train Services and Rolling Stock

Since electrification some show has been made with improved and accelerated trains between Lisbon and Oporto, but traditionally Portuguese train services can be described best as less slow and less infrequent than traditional (but not modern) Spanish ones. Rolling stock also avoided the spectacularly antique while not offering any remarkable features.

On the other hand, it would be misleading to give the impression through this negative description that Portuguese railways lacked character. On the contrary, they had a very distinct flavour. Most lines, broad and narrow gauge, were very lightly built and since they tended to run through difficult country, speeds

were low. Large engineering works were not lacking, notably the viaduct over the Douro near Oporto, built by Gustave Eiffel. But the physical similarities with Spanish railways were out-balanced by the impression of greater vigour and efficiency, making the most of equally limited resources.

Administrative and Financial

Apart from the comments above on the unusual course of Portuguese railway history, it remains to add that the total of 1775 route-miles of the CP system is still not far below its historical peak, and still includes 465 miles of metre-gauge line. Operating expenses before the recent political changes ran at 15–20 percent above revenue, ensuring state direction of the railways in fact if not in form, but putting CP in the upper group of European railway systems when judged by the degree to which they approach economic balance; in a relatively poor country with short hauls this is a creditable achievement.

Most Rumanian steam locomotives were of Germanic design but the huge 2-8-4 (below) was an adaption of Austria's 214 class of the 1930s. For many years this class hauled the principal expresses over CFR routes; one is seen here at Apahida in 1965.

See map on pages 26–27.

RUMANIAN STATE RAILWAYS – CFR
Căile Ferate Romane,
Boulevard Dinicu Golescu 38,
Bucharest 7.

The first railway in what was then Rumania ran southwards from the capital, Bucharest, 43 miles to Giurgiu on the River Danube. It opened on 19 October 1869. An older line ran out of the Black Sea port of Constanta, in country that was at that time in Turkish hands. Various other privately financed lines followed and by 1888, when they were nationalized the total mileage was 1550. Further construction followed and the acquisition of territory, particularly Transylvania, which was ceded by Hungary in 1919, brought the amount of railway up to 6960 miles after World War I. Before the war there had been only one-third of that amount of line in the country. This mileage has been maintained by new construction, despite the loss of Bukovina and Bessarabia to Poland and the USSR.

There are 370 miles of narrow gauge, mostly 2ft 6in. More than 860 miles have been electrified since 1965. The Carpathian Mountains and the Transylvanian Alps provided Rumanian railway engineers with reasonable facilities for exercising their skills as surveyors and constructors. In the world class is the 9440ft-long bridge over the River Danube at Cernavoda, on the main line between Bucharest

Spain
& Portugal

1 : 5 000 000

50   0   50   100 miles
50   0   50   100   150 km

Projection Conical with two standard parallels

COPYRIGHT GEORGE PHILIP & SON LTD

m   3000   2000   1500   1000   400   200   0   ft
ft   9000   6000   4500   3000   1200   600   0   200   600   m

Below: A Rumanian diesel-hauled express near Carlinesti.

Bottom: A Fiat long-distance luxury diesel train in Spain.

and Constanta. Known as the Saligny Bridge, it was completed in 1895.

German practice was followed in steam days, large numbers of standard Prussian 4-6-0 and 0-10-0 types – many produced in Rumania – being lent distinction by brass bands decorating the chimney and an unparalleled collection of cast metal insignia on the cab sides. Rectangular plates were provided for running number, repair date, maximum speed, home shed and (rather unnecessarily) to declare the owner. For the principal expresses, a simple version of the famous Maffei 4-6-2 designs for Bavaria and – late in the 1930s – copies of the then-new Austrian 2-8-4s were provided. Rumanian locomotives burn coal but supplementary heat can be provided by the use of oil from reserve tanks in the tender.

A selection of Hungarian steam power was ceded to Rumania as a result of the 1919 territorial rearrangement. Notable was a class of 2-8-2 rack-and-adhesion tank locomotives, used on a line with one in twelve gradients which ran out of Subcetate, a junction approximately fifteen miles south of the town of Simeria in Transylvania. Their appearance – like some other steam locomotives of Hungarian origin – almost might have led one to believe that Count Dracula had a hand in the design. It is noted that equipment was provided on these machines to suck water from line-side supplies at rail level, rather than allowing to to fall from the more usual raised tank! Rumanian steam can still be found, mainly on station pilot and works train duties.

The existence of Rumanian oil wells encouraged the early development of diesel traction and today Rumania is among that handful of countries that produces and exports main-line diesel power. The box in which the machinery is concealed is distinctive but the numbers in existence remain a state secret. Currently the CFR is handling 370 million passengers and 228 million tons of freight annually an average of 160 miles.

SPAIN

See map on page 102.

Most of the Spanish land-mass is a high plateau, broken here and there with ranges of hills and mountains, and elsewhere by large rivers whose valleys are often very wide and flat. Unless they follow such rivers, railways penetrating the interior from the coast tend to get involved in some fairly spectacular hill-climbing. Madrid, the capital, stands some 2000ft above sea level and to the north, south, east, and west, the coast-line is at least 200 miles away; three quarters of the west coast is occupied by Portugal. Mountain barriers block most routes radiating from Madrid, nowhere more than the Pyrenees lying along the French border. Land along the coasts tends to be well-watered and fertile; inland and especially on the high Castilian plain north of Madrid, there is little rain and the soil is poor. Industry and coal

Above: An express railcar on the Vigo-Madrid train alongside Vigo Bay.

Right: Celebrations surround the centenary of Spanish Railways at Barcelona.

Top right: The Ponferrada-Villablino's metre-gauge line in Northern Spain is still one hundred percent steam, as befits a coal-hauling road. The only member of its class, 2-6-0 Esteban Tenadas, hauls a train of empties up the grade to the station at Cubillos, in the late afternoon of 25 March 1974.

Right centre: The Majorca Railway was one of the oldest Spanish systems, dating from 1875. It had a strong British connection, as witness the gauge of 3ft 0in. This picture shows a train on the harbour branch about to enter the tunnel under the cathedral at Palma. The locomotive is a 4-6-0T built by the British firm of Nasmyth Wilson.

mining lie mainly along the north coast, around Santander and Bilbao, with an important outcrop around the second city, Barcelona. Metal ores, chiefly iron and copper, are mined none too prosperously in the south-west, but with isolated workings elsewhere. The total population is around 34 million.

SPANISH NATIONAL RAILWAYS – RENFE
Red Nacional de los Ferrocarriles Españoles,
Plaza de los Sagrados Corozones 7,
Madrid 16.

NARROW GAUGE RAILWAYS – FEVE
Ferrocarriles de Via Estrecha,
6 General Rodrigo Street,
Parque de las Naciones, Madrid.

During the nineteenth century Spain was poor and politically unstable, therefore backward. The first railway, a short line from Barcelona, was not opened until 1848, and it was not until the government passed laws making railway investment attractive to foreign capital in 1855 that construction really got started. It then continued fairly energetically, except for periods of disturbance, until by 1870 most of the trunk lines were completed. However, one major misfortune was the decision at an early

stage to adopt a broad gauge of six Castilian feet (approximately 5ft 6in). Apart from impeding international traffic, this put up the cost of building railways and of working them when built, a disaster for so poor a country. By 1930 the total route mileage of broad-gauge lines in the entire country was still not 8000; they were spread very thinly. Worse, the lines were built very lightly; the average cost of construction per mile by 1923 in Spain was roughly three-quarters of the average amount spent in the rest of Continental Europe. Light axle-loadings, sharp curves, and steep grades thus threw away the potential benefits of the broad gauge which had been dearly bought. Not surprisingly, nearly 3000 miles of narrow-gauge railway (mainly metre gauge, but including most widths between 60cm and 4ft 8½in) had been built in an endeavour to provide more general coverage at reasonable cost, but this made the network more unwieldy than ever. Finally, the main-line network was indirect and evasive, its ownership divided between companies whose route structure was usually illogical with the possible exception of the largest company, the Madrid-Zaragoza-Alicante, which had come to own two of the three most important main lines, from Madrid to Barcelona and Seville. The third, running zig-zag fashion from Madrid to

Bilbao and Irun, belonged to the second company, the Norte.

Already rundown and inadequate, the Spanish railways were savaged during the Civil War (1936–39). Recovery afterwards was long delayed by other concerns and the international cold-shouldering of Spain for some years after 1945. Although all the broad-gauge lines had been nationalized in 1939 and taken over by the Red Nacional de los Ferrocarriles Españoles, as late as the 1950s there was still plenty of unspeakably bad main-line track and steam locomotives a hundred years old still at work alongside the impressive new RENFE 4-8-4s, 4-8-2s and 2-10-2s which were the first signs of recovery. However, since 1940 another thousand miles of broad-gauge railway have been opened, including new and much more direct, better-engineered routes from Madrid to Burgos and the north, La Coruna in the north-west, and Valencia on the Mediterranean coast. Closures have been minor; lines of that sort tended not to have been built in the first place.

The history of narrow-gauge lines has been somewhat similar, although these were not nationalized generally but left with their former owners. In recent years a different state organization (Ferrocarriles de Via Estrecha, FEVE) has been set up to operate most of them.

Only along the north coast do they form anything like a system on a large scale; elsewhere they were generally isolated, short or middle-length lines, although the electrified suburban network at Valencia and the partly-electrified (and partly-underground) Catalan Railways at Barcelona deserve special mention. Many narrow-gauge lines have been closed in recent years, but a substantial mileage remains, and indeed the metre-gauge main line along the north coast from Oviedo to El Ferrol was not completed until 1970.

Locomotive Landmarks

The most singular thing about Spanish locomotive history is the fact that many of their steam locomotives were so long-lived that their working lives spanned the whole period between the construction of the lines they ran on and their replacement by diesels or electrics up to a century later. Coming into action relatively late, and presenting so often such difficult operational problems, Spanish railways needed and got the most advanced steam locomotives European technology could produce, and benefited accordingly. Not everything survived so long; the less successful experiments, and the hardest-worked machines, disappeared much earlier. But apart from a number of smaller machines, RENFE, at the start of the 1960s, was still running several types of 0-6-0 and 0-8-0 which represented the very best products of the 1850s and 1860s. Newer machines were, of course, much more numerous, including varieties of simple and compound 4-6-0s from the turn of the century, 2-8-0s and 4-8-0s from soon after, and 4-8-2s from 1925 on, as well as the advanced postwar types already mentioned. The 4-4-0s and 4-6-2s, although they could be found, were never as popular in Spain as elsewhere; both types lacked adhesion for their weight, and their comfortable running at speed was not of much use. Brute tractive effort at low speed was *de rigueur*. This being so, surprisingly little use was made of articulated locomotives, except by one smallish company, the Central of Aragon (which ran from Zaragoza to Valencia). This had 2-6-6-0 and 0-6-6-0 Mallets (the former in 1906 the first European locomotives to weigh over 100 tons) and also 2-8-2+2-8-2 and 4-6-2+4-6-2 Garratts from 1931, the latter the only European Garratts intended for passenger work. More of the former were built by RENFE in 1961, the last steam locomotives built for main-line service in Western Europe.

Narrow-gauge locomotives tended to the small and picturesque, although articulated types and tender 4-8-0s were used by some lines whose traffic warranted them. One rare type, more used in Spain than elsewhere although it originated in Austria, is the Engerth, with tender semi-articulated so that some of its weight is available for adhesion. A few metre-gauge examples, either 2-6-0s or 2-6-4Ts depending on how one argues the matter, are still at work on the last commercial user of steam power in Spain, the Ponferrada-Villablino.

Electrification, originally at 1500 but now

all at 3000v DC, commenced on certain mountain sections from 1923 (neglecting a 1911 three-phase curiosity near Almeria now abandoned). Some 2200 miles, mostly of the more important or difficult lines, are now electrified.

Train Services and Rolling Stock

Following their long-delayed recovery from wartime destruction, train services in Spain are now approaching a reasonable European norm. Two special singularities exist. One of them is the fleet of convertible-gauge vehicles; not only are many four-wheeled freight cars capable of having their wheels and axles quickly changed at the French border, but also a quantity of otherwise standard passenger coaches, mainly sleeping cars can be changed, enabling good through services, for example, between Madrid and Paris. The other and much more unique feature is the Talgo train. These trains were originally introduced to enable high speeds to be reached on bad track in comfort; hauled by a more or less conventional diesel locomotive, the entire train is articulated in short segments, each supported by only two wheels of its own and at the other end by resting on the next segment. Early Talgos could not run at any speed in reverse, but later models are fully reversible and, in fact, a convertible-gauge specimen instituted a through service between Barcelona and Geneva. The passenger-carrying part of the train is much lower and narrower than conventional vehicles. Some Talgos still exist, although with track improvements their *raison d'être* has largely gone. The type had no success outside Spain; some American experiments were dismal failures in the early 1950s.

Administration and Finance

Some account of the historical difficulties faced by Spanish railways has been given above. The picture on the broad-gauge lines is now simple; RENFE is nominally an independent government-owned corporation, some 85 percent of whose direct costs are met by revenue. Most of the surviving narrow-gauge lines, totalling over 1000 route-miles and including almost all the northern network, are operated now by FEVE, whose economics are less favourable.

Top: An electrically hauled passenger train passes through typical Swedish countryside.

Right: An iron-ore train in Lappland – note the track inspection car in foreground.

SWEDEN

See map on pages 38-39.

SWEDISH STATE RAILWAYS – SJ
Statens Järnvogär,
Central Station, S-105 50,
Stockholm.

'Happy is the country that has no history' is a saying which seems to be appropriate when considering Sweden and her railways. Construction began under state auspices in 1850 when rail transport was already well-established and therefore had come to be regarded as a boon rather than a threat. The first complete state line opened between Stockholm and Göteborg. Stephenson's standard gauge was adopted and by 1930 there were 4250 miles of main-line railway. There was no doctrinaire adherence to state ownership and a further 5000 miles owned by 72 private companies had also been built in this period. Of these more than half were standard gauge, the remainder narrow. There were small amounts of respectable 3ft 6in and 1ft 11½in (600mm) but most were three Swedish feet, that is 2ft 11in or 891mm.

Since that time SJ has gradually taken over the more important private lines and many of the others have been allowed to die. Currently only three are left, although the memory of the remainder is kept green by four vestigial remnants operated as steam pleasure or museum lines. Accordingly, SJ's mileage since 1930 has increased to 7300, including just over 100 miles of 2ft 11in gauge.

Sweden's railways were fairly easy to build – the only problems were the many river crossings but these were not of excessive size. There is a 48-span 2815ft-long bridge across the Göta near Göteborg which is the longest in Sweden. The longest tunnel is the 'Gardatunneln' of 1.3 miles near Göteborg.

The modernization which has become so necessary in recent years on most of the world's railways as a desperate last-ditch defence

Right: A standardized electric I-C-I locomotive at Åre on the Storlien train in Sweden.

Below right: A modern Bo-Bo electric locomotive hauls a Swedish express passenger train.

Extreme right, top: A freight train approaches the corkscrew alignment at Giornico on the southern ascent of the Gotthard main line, Switzerland.

Below: Sweden had two gauges below standard, 3ft 6in (mostly in the south) and the odd gauge of 2ft 11in. At one place, Växjö (below), there was even a small section of four rail track!

against extinction, has in Sweden been a steady and continuous process. Electrification, based on water power, began with the Lapland Iron Ore line from Lulea to the Norwegian border; this occurred in 1915 when most industrial countries were otherwise engaged. This northern line was completed in 1922. When, twenty years later, the Göteborg–Stockholm trunk railway was electrified, one could, for the first time in history, make a journey of more than 1000 miles by electric train, from Malmö in the south to Riksgransen east of Narvik, in the north. Currently 5000 miles are electrified, handling 90 percent of all rail traffic and using the 15,000v low-frequency AC system. There are 757 electric locomotives plus 170 railcars and motor-coaches. The technology which has resulted from this extraordinary achievement on the part of such a small nation is now a

major export, and the performance of the superb railway system is one of the major factors which has given Sweden one of the highest standards of living in the world. Sixty-five million passengers are now carried annually and 54 million tons of freight are hauled an average distance of 175 miles.

Steam traction in Sweden was not specially remarkable, except that most of it was home-made. One recently absorbed constituent of SJ, the ore-hauling Grängesberg (near Lud-vika)–Oxelösund Railway made railway history by using a fleet of steam turbine locomotives in normal service; this was both the first and the only such use in the world. Steam power was held in reserve in Sweden until around 1970; up to that time it had only seen marginal use.

A more imitated innovation was the privately owned Mallesta & Södermanlands Railway's

introduction, in 1913, of the first diesel-electric vehicle to run in regular public service. Diesel traction has a secondary role to play in Sweden; there are 690 locomotives and 180 railcars in use.

Swedish railway carriages and trains are exceptionally comfortable; this is mainly due to the extraordinary width (11ft 2in), one foot wider than allowed in Europe generally. The high standard of cleanliness and small amenities such as drinking water and ladies' retiring rooms play their part. When Europe had three classes of travel, Sweden was for many years the only system to provide sleeping accommodation in third class as well as first and second. More modestly dimensioned vehicles, including USSR sleeping cars from Moscow, enter Sweden on board train ferries from East Germany or Denmark.

SWITZERLAND

See maps on pages 26–27 and 46–47.

The Swiss Railways system is notable not only for an efficient intercity service, but for a remarkably comprehensive inter-village one as well. No other country in the world even begins to offer its remote corners such a magnificent service of fast and frequent electric trains. In other aspects of service, Swiss trains also have few peers; their safety, comfort, convenience and cleanliness all rate among the world's best.

Two reasons for this fortunate state of affairs must be noted: stable government and long-standing neutrality in war. The Swiss Confederation dates from 1815, well before the coming of railways. Since that time political changes have been minimal, in spite of the four language groups – German, French, Italian, Romansh – into which the population is divided.

The way in which the railways have become organized has also played its part. The Federal railways, with centralized control, are confined to the main trunk routes, while most regional needs are met by independent and provincially minded local companies – often described as private but in most cases and in truth public. Only 2934 of the miles of railways in Switzerland belong to the Swiss Federal Railways, the remainder being divided among 127 other administrations. Many of the minor railways are narrow gauge.

Although this fragmentation allows for local control, it is not allowed to invonvenience the passenger or trader. One ticket will cover a journey over two or more railways, and baggage checked through can be relied on to arrive simultaneously with the traveller, even after several changes of train.

SWISS FEDERAL RAILWAYS – SBB/CFF/FFS

Schweizerische Bundesbahnen – Chemins de fer Fédéraux-Ferrovie Federali Svizzera, Hochschulstrasse 6, CH 3030, Bern.

Left: Swiss mountain engineering is well illustrated by the bridge over the Bietschtal gorge between Brig and Irandersted.

Above: A Swiss inter-city express features the latest type Bo-Bo electric locomotive.

Above: A typical wayside station in the Swiss Alps.

Centre top: A Furka-Oberalp Railway steam train runs through a snow cutting in Switzerland higher than its chimney.

Centre: One solution to the snow problem is the steam rotary plough used here on the Bern–Lötschberg–Simplon Railway.

Right: A 6240 HP Bo-Bo locomotive handles 600 tons on a 1 in 38 gradient on the Bern–Lötschberg–Simplon Railway.

Extreme right, top: This railway map of Switzerland was drawn in 1958 but the routes have remained almost unchanged.

History and Development

The first railway to open in Switzerland – apart from the tip of a French tentacle which reached Basel in 1846 – was a line from Baden to Zurich which opened in 1847. It got to be known as the 'Spanish Bun Railway', from one of its original staple traffics. As was common in Europe, subsequent development took the form of private concessions rather than free-for-all competition. In this way the trunk railway system was developed by a number of companies. Three of them, the Swiss North-Eastern, the Weiss Central and the Swiss United, were incorporated into the Swiss Federal Railways in the year 1901. The Jura-Simplon followed in 1906 and the Gotthard in 1909; the only trunk route to escape nationalization was the Bern-Lötschberg-Simplon railway, which was not opened until 1913.

Belonging to a country without indigenous fuel supplies, Switzerland's railways suffered serious problems during World War I and, accordingly, immediately the conflict was over, electrification was undertaken. By 1925 on the SBB, only secondary routes remained. The SBB became totally electrified in 1965 and in

fact today, only four short private lines remain in the hands of other forms of traction.

In recent years much effort has been put into re-aligning and doubling sections of trunk route that were originally single and so sharply curved as to preclude fast running. Having regard to the terrain, this has involved very heavy expenditure.

Civil Engineering

The task of laying out a main-line railway system in country that would daunt a mule-train, has given Switzerland some of the world's greatest railway engineering, including the longest mountain railway tunnel which joins Brig in Switzerland to Domodossola in Italy. Strictly speaking the Simplon is two tunnels, the first single line bore being completed in 1906 and the second in 1912. It is 12.25 miles long. The double track 9.3-mile Gotthard tunnel, the previous longest, was built between 1880-1889.

As remarkable as the long tunnels are the helicoidal ones used to overcome height differences while still keeping the gradient down to an acceptable figure. The four double-track

ones on the approaches to the Gotthard tunnel are specially notable – and quite bewildering to the traveller.

The bridges and viaducts in the Swiss Alps are, as might be expected, also remarkable; particularly elegant are the arched masonry structures typical of construction in the days before 1914. The Swiss were among the pioneers in the use of reinforced concrete and structures built in connection with doubling and re-alignments – no new main lines have been built since 1913 – and have made much use of this method of construction.

The extensive use of steel sleepers is an unusual feature (for Europe) of Swiss railway track, although practice regarding renewals is now more in line with the rest of Europe. In either case the Swiss love of order and tidiness is reflected in a permanent way that can only be described as manicured.

Locomotive Landmarks

The Swiss developed their own school of locomotive design, influenced at the start by that of their larger neighbours, France and Germany. Until 1875 most Swiss locomotives were built abroad, but in that year the Swiss Locomotive Works of Winterthur, directed by an Englishman called Charles Brown, supplied its first main-line engine. This was a 2-6-0T for the North Eastern Railway. It is interesting to note that, having Walschearts' valve gear and two outside cylinders, this machine had the exact mechanical layout of the steam locomotive in its final form of a century later – well in advance of world thinking at the time. Most subsequent Swiss locomotives were constructed by the firm. A short flirtation with the Mallet principle for sharply curved mountain lines left little mark – the conclusion reached was that the complications were not worthwhile.

French influence was felt with the introduction of four-cylinder compounds from 1901 onwards. A long series of such 4-6-0s were built for the youthful Swiss Federal Railways. The culmination of Swiss main-line steam were the 2-10-0s of 1913-17. A 2-10-0 and a 4-6-0 survive in working order and are occasionally run.

Since World War I construction has been virtually confined to electric locomotives with specialist firms like Brown-Boveri and Oerlikon supplying electrical equipment. Originally construction followed steam principles with the wheels driven via coupling rods; the famous 'crocodile' articulated 1-c-c-1s for the Gotthard line were specially notable.

Although a few rod-drive locomotives still survive, the fleet built for general main-line electrification during the 1920s had (mostly) individual motors for each driving axle. The 2-Do-1s and 2-Co-1s supplied then, still give good service although more conventional Bo-Bos and Co-Cos are now the front runners. Powers as high as 1000hp per axle were pioneered in Switzerland during the 1950s.

Incidentally, the Swiss call a 2-Do-1 an Ae4/7 and a 1-C-C-1 a Ce6/8. The first letter is an indication of the maximum permitted speed, A being fast, C being slow, etc; e means electric; 4/7 means four axles driven out of seven. Hence, the steam 4-6-0s were B3/5 and the high speed Bo-Bos are Re4/4, R being chosen because there is no letter before A in the alphabet. Switzerland is the only country in the world which opts out of internationally recognized classifications for motive power types.

One form of Swiss traction, unique to the world, was a wartime expedient whereby an 0-6-0T shunting locomotive was fitted with electric heating elements and a pantograph collector. With almost all the electricity used coming from water power (many of the generators are over fifty years old and still efficient) this was not so extravagant a proceeding as it might otherwise seem.

Operations and Services

The amazing frequency, comprehensiveness, comfort and cleanliness of Swiss passenger train services has been mentioned. In statistical terms 210 million passengers are carried annually in a fleet of 3600 carriages.

Freight operation is dominated by Switzer-

land's position as the 'Turntable of Europe' and the consequent great flows of traffic over major international arteries such as the Gotthard line. Although such 'bridge route' operations are intrinsically profitable, there is another side to the coin; international trade can fluctuate enormously and cause such *debacles* as a fall from 46 million tons of freight carried in 1974 to 35 million carried in 1975. How can Switzerland's 26,400-strong wagon fleet be utilized efficiently in the face of such variations as these?

Although the fascinating giant signalling bells of the SBB are now history, Swiss signalling is still distinctive. Notable are the square distant or warning signals which indicate messages not only by colour but by the pattern of the lights. One-man locomotive operation has been a feature for many years; the safety precautions include not only the usual 'dead man's handle' but also a vigilance button, which the driver has to press at prescribed intervals to indicate his continuing awareness.

BERN-LOTSCHBERG-SIMPLON RAILWAY – BLS
11 Rue de Genève,
Bern.

Although working in close association with the Federal Railways, the Bern-Lötschberg-Simplon Railway is notable because it is the only section of the European trunk network not to be owned by a national government.

Of the main-line railways of the world, the Lötschberg, when it opened in 1913, was the first to be built as an electric railway from end to end. It was also among the very earliest to be worked electrically. The conception of the line resulted from the fact that Bern, the capital of Switzerland, was a railway cul-de-sac, whereas Geneva, Lausanne, Lucerne, Zürich, Basel and other places all lay on the great through routes that got Swiss rails known as the 'turntable of Europe'.

Getting no satisfaction from central government the citizens of Bern set out on their own to drive a main-line railroad, 75 miles long, through the Bernese Alps to reach the Simplon main line at the north end of the great tunnel. They raised the money and work began in 1902. The main task was the 9.1-mile Lötschberg tunnel and here for once the mountain gods decided to show who was master. An unsuspected cleft in the terrain was pierced and 25 men working at the tunnel face perished in the deluge – a mile of completed tunnel had to be abandoned and three curves introduced to form a wide kink in the alignment to avoid the trouble area.

The BLS also financed a cut-off line, which includes the 4.5 mile Grenchenberg tunnel, to shorten communication between Bern and the North. This, however, is only used by Swiss Federal Railways trains.

High-voltage single-phase AC electrification had then barely emerged from the laboratory and when electric trains began to run there were major difficulties with unexpected surges of power. Lots of volts and amps would

then go the wrong way – with dire results. Experience was quickly gained and the little Lötschberg railway was the pathfinder for the great Federal Railway electrifications of the 1920s. Rod drive 1-E-1 (2-10-2) locomotives were supplied first, supplemented between the wars by great articulated 1-Co-Co-1 machines. In 1947 the BLS pioneered a plain double-bogie locomotive with 1000 horsepower per axle, an amazing figure for the time; in due course the rest of the world followed.

Forty-five electric locomotives, 130 passenger carriages and 310 wagons are the main items in the rolling stock fleet. The last figure bears no relationship to the role of the BLS as an international carrier of five million tons of traffic; eight million passengers are also conveyed, expenses being 89 percent of receipts.

Independent Swiss Railways

This railway feat-of-arms, unparalleled elsewhere in the world, putting almost every Swiss hamlet and mountain top on the railway map, deserves a closer look. In the lowlands the independent lines tend to be a hybrid between a street tramway and a country branch line and are electric. The first Swiss electric line was the two-mile line from Grütschalp to Mürren, opened in 1891 and the first electric local (as opposed to mountain) railway was the three-mile line from Orbe to Chavornay, opened in 1893. Typically, the trains start from a tram stop in the street outside the main station, but take to their own right-of-way outside towns. Again typically, they are of metre gauge but standard-gauge freight cars can be hauled on transporter wagons. This is a type of railway which has almost disappeared from the rest of the world.

But Switzerland's mountain railways are what the country is famous for. Now there are four ways of climbing a mountain by rail. The first way (for very steep inclines) is to haul one car at a time with a cable. Such funicular railways are outside the scope of this book. The second way is to use a rack-and-pinion arrangement, a cog railway as it is sometimes called. The third way is to avoid 'artificial' aids and make the climb more gradual by extending the distance, either by making U-turns on steep mountain sides, or by building spiral tunnels inside them. The second and third ways can be combined to produce a railway that works by the rack on very steep sections and by adhesion elsewhere. Descriptions of outstanding lines in all these categories follow. And because it is Switzerland under discussion, outstanding means outstanding in the world.

WENGERNALP RAILWAY – WAB
Wengernalpbahn,
Interlaken.

The largest purely rack railway in the world (by a substantial margin) is the twelve-mile 2ft 7½in gauge Wengernalp Railway in the Bernese Oberland. It runs in full view of some of the greatest *Viertausender* (13,100+ft) peaks in the Alps. The line was built for sightseers in 1893 – winter opening for skiers was an afterthought which did not occur until over ten years later and in due course brought English names like 'The Bumps', 'Mac's Leap' and 'Slip Cartilage Corner' to certain points in WAB terrain.

The WAB is quite a complex system with junctions and elaborate station layouts. The arrangements at points whereby, since the motive power has no adhesion drive, the rack is kept continuous are fascinating to see. Steam ruled on grades up to one in four from the opening in 1893 until 1908, when electrification at 1500v DC was carried out. Separate locomotives were universal until after World War

Top centre: A steam tourist train crosses the stone arches-on-an-arch bridge at Wiesen near Davos on the Rhaetian Railway.

II; since then the ubiquitous power car has taken over. Trains are limited to two bogie vehicles and one four-wheel ski-and-luggage truck. Currently there are 24 railcars, eight locomotives, forty trailers and fifty goods vehicles; 2.3 million passengers are carried annually. Connection is made at the WAB's lower termini and (oddly enough) also at its highest point with metre-gauge rack-and-adhesion lines. Thus Kleine Sheidegg, altitude 6260ft, is connected by an extraordinary line – the Jungfrau Railway – which runs mainly inside the Eiger mountain, to the highest point (11,800ft) reached by rail in Europe.

Above: Jungfraujoch station on the Jungfrau RW.

Top right: A train en route to Zermatt ascends a 1 in 8 rack section near Tasch, Switzerland.

RHAETIAN RAILWAY – RhB
Rhätische Bahn – Chemin de Fer Rhetique – Ferrovia Retica – Viater Rietica,
CH-7002, Chur, Graubunden.

In saying that the Rhaetian Railway system in southeast Switzerland is justifiably world-famous in many ways, one must add that it is no more so than the country in which it was built. The canton of Graubunden (the 'Gray Leagues') was once ruled by a Prince-Bishop at Chur, but is now the largest canton of the Swiss Confederation. In deference to the locally spoken ancient Romansch tongue, the Rhaetian

Railway spells its name in that tongue as well as in German, French, Italian and English.

The RhB began life in 1889 as the Landquart-Davos Railway, bringing passengers from the main line up the Pratigau Valley to Klosters and Davos. In those days most visitors were connected with the tuberculosis sanitaria at Davos, but among them must be included early skiers who found a way down from the mountains above Davos to Küblis and for whom the Parsenn funicular was later built. Even now, Davos' winter holiday season is busier than its summer one – the RhB peak month is February.

The problems of climbing up to Davos (5280ft) were overcome (and rack sections avoided) by steepening the gradient to 1 in 22.5 (45 per thousand) but when the time came a few years later to connect world-famous St Moritz (altitude 6180ft) to the outer world by train, the traffic anticipated suggested the easier figure of 1 in 29 (35 per thousand). The penalty was civil engineering on an altogether different scale with breathtaking bridges and viaducts, four spiral tunnels (two placed one directly above the other) and finally the 3.7-mile Albula tunnel under the pass into the Engadine, the high valley in which St Moritz lies.

Extensions followed; the one in the so-called Lower Engadine, leading to Schuls-Tarasp on the Austrian border, was interesting in that it was completed in 1913 as an electric railway. It became a prototype for electrification of the whole Rhaetian system, which was completed in 1923. The low frequency AC system was used, with 11,000v (nominally) at the contact wire. Trains could descend the long inclines using their motors as dynamos to give braking and return power to the system; provision had to be made for disposing of surplus power (the hydro-electric power supply system was originally self-contained) when all trains on the railway were running downhill!

After an early affair with articulated Mallet locomotives, the RhB settled in steam days for a fleet of 29 noble 2-8-0s, two of which survive for the pleasure of rail fans. Their replacement in the 1920s with only fifteen equally noble C-C 'crocodile' electrics tells its own tale. More conventional bogie locomotives now haul the dining car expresses and most other trains.

Signalling on the RhB is particularly delightful; the passage of trains is marked by sonorous notes struck on giant block bells standing like enormous toadstools on station platforms. The original revolving disc signals have now nearly all been replaced by coloured lights.

Currently there are sixty electric locomotives, forty electric railcars, 300 passenger cars and 1100 freight cars. These carry 7.5 million passengers and 750,000 tons of freight annually on the 244-mile system.

USSR

See map on pages 118-119.

USSR RAILWAYS
Novo Basmannaya 2,
Moscow 10714.

The railways of the Soviet Union form by far the largest single system in the world. Having 85,700 route miles, they are well over twice as large as any other and extend over 6000 miles from west to east and over 3000 from north to south. The first public railway in the land was opened in 1837 between St Petersburg (now Leningrad) and the royal resort of Tsarskoye Selo, fifteen miles. The first trunk line over the 400 miles separating St Petersburg and Moscow opened on 13 November 1851. This is the line where the Czar, asked to choose the route, sent for a ruler and drew a line; fortunately the country is flat!

The privately owned railway systems did not cope well with the demands of the Crimean War of 1877-78 and the government set about nationalizing them. One third had been acquired by 1900 and two thirds by 1914. The state also set up factories to make the USSR self-sufficient regarding locomotives and rolling stock. Standard designs were also adopted.

Much has been written of the crossing of other continents by rail but the construction of the 5900-mile trans-Siberian railway surely eclipses them all. The dates are rather complicated:

1891   The enterprise is approved. Tsarevitch Nicholas inaugurates construction at Vladivostok.

1903   The line is complete, except across Lake

Left: A traditional Soviet station, Rostov-on-Don.

Extreme left: The cab of a Soviet P36 class 4-8-4.

Above: A modern Soviet station, Sverdlovsk.

Top: Modern motive power in the USSR.

Extreme right, centre: The magnificent control station of Maiakovskaia on the Moscow Metro.

Below: Soviet FD class 2-10-2s double-head a freight, which can now be seen in China.

Extreme right, top: A Moscow Metro train at an outer terminus.

Right: Crowds throng the suburban platforms at the Kazan station in Moscow.

Baykal, where there is a ferry service. The journey also involved 800 miles (the Chinese Eastern Railway) laid in Manchuria, which was foreign territory.

1905 The loop round the shore of Lake Baykal is completed.

1915 The line north of the Chinese Border – the Amur River – is completed, giving a continuous railway on Russian soil from Moscow to Vladivostok.

When revolution came in 1917, half the present network had been completed, although the emphasis was much more in the European part of the USSR than in the Asian. The latter with two-thirds of the land area had less than one-fifth of the mileage.

The new regime made tremendous efforts, at considerable sacrifice, to improve and extend the system. All vehicles were fitted with air brakes and converted to automatic coupling before 1939. No doubt the fact that the Soviet gauge of 5ft 0in differed from that of all her neighbours except Finland, probably helped by minimizing the problems of interchange. Lines laid with weak track were strengthened and many new ones were built, particularly in Asia. Others, including the trans-Siberian from end to end, were doubled. Today the trans-Siberian line is having to be duplicated, on a new course further north.

The devastation in areas overrun by the Germans in World War II was on a colossal scale, but it was usually possible for most of the rolling stock and even workshop equipment to be evacuated in time. After the war, once the destruction had been made good, the strides made were even more remarkable. Thirty thousand miles of new route have been built, steam has been almost eliminated and

electrification of 25,000 miles of line has meant that over half of Soviet rail traffic is hauled electrically.

Civil Engineering

In addition to being the world's biggest system in the operational sense, the USSR has the biggest railway rolling stock, 17ft 2in in height and 11ft 2in wide. For many years these magnificent dimensions were not matched by track strong enough to carry a corresponding load. Locomotives with, say, a twenty-ton axle-load found themselves with a very limited territory in which to work.

Although the great rivers of the USSR intersect the railways at numerous points, no bridge is recorded as being longer than a mile. Similarly, there are no tunnels of world class in the USSR. The longest one is, as one might expect, in the Caucasus mountains. This is the Suram Tunnel, 2.5 miles long, on the Baku-Poti line.

Locomotive Landmarks

The first steam locomotive in the USSR ran on an industrial line in the Urals. M Cherepanov built it in 1833 following a visit to England. Locomotives for the first Soviet lines were imported from Britain and elsewhere, but indigenous production began in the early 1840s at St Petersburg under the supervision of Ross Winans of the Baltimore & Ohio Railroad in America.

The steam period in the USSR is remarkable mainly for the exceptional amount of standardization that was achieved both before and after the 1917 revolution, as well as for its extraordinary continuity across that watershed in history. The basic simplicity and, in later years, Soviet duplication of North American designs served

as recognition of what best suited Soviet conditions rather than inability to comprehend or design anything else; in the USSR, the academic foundation of and experimentation into possible improvements to the steam locomotive were carried further than anywhere else.

Two projects suffice to illustrate this point. In 1934, in order to provide a big pull on lightish rails, a fourteen coupled 4-14-4 locomotive was built, the longest non-articulated locomotive ever constructed. In the event, interaction between the track and the 33ft rigid wheel-base caused problems that were never surmounted.

A little later, attempts were made to develop a type of locomotive known as the Teplo-parovozy. This was a combined steam-diesel machine, which used steam for starting (remember that a diesel gives no push when stationary) and diesel plus steam for running; the steam was generated by waste heat from the diesel cylinders. Theoretically there is a promise of thermal efficiency better even than a diesel, as well as there being no need for the complications of electric or hydraulic transmission. Three attempts were made, two before and one after the 'Great Patriotic War' but in the end success remained elusive. Yet the promise remains.

Out on the line could be found the 'E' class 0-10-0, the most numerous locomotive class ever built. Thirteen thousand of them were made between 1912 and 1947. In the 1920s a batch was hurriedly ordered from Nohab of Sweden; they were loaded onto a Soviet ship which promptly unloaded gold bars on to the quayside in payment.

The standard passenger locomotive, the 'S' 2-6-2, the most numerous passenger class in the world, was built to the tune of 4000 or so, over an even longer period, from 1910 to 1951. Some 2-8-4s and finally 4-8-4s (the latter of a particularly handsome design) supplemented the 2-6-2s on the heaviest duties.

Freight movement was dominated by 13,000 2-10-0s and 2-10-2s of only three classes, supported by 2000 2-10-0s captured from the Germans. For light shunting, industrial and pilot duties the 'O' (for 'principal') 0-8-0, the first Soviet standard design of 1891, survived almost until the end of steam, an event which in 1978 has not yet been confirmed.

At its maximum in 1957, the steam fleet of 35,000 was easily the world's biggest. Ten classes accounted for over 30,000! In that year steam construction was halted without warning and Kaganovitch, the Commissar of Transportation who favoured continuance of steam, almost certainly liquidated.

The Soviet school of design had little effect on the world's locomotives outside the mother country – except in China, where it has been total.

In spite of the commendable efforts that were made, reliable diesel locomotives were not produced in the USSR before 1945 but, influenced by some American units that arrived during the war, production began in earnest afterwards. The earliest ones were conservatively rated at around 1000hp for each unit. A 2000hp unit was not out of the prototype stage in 1956 when the political decision to get rid of steam meant that the new design had prematurely to be put into mass production. The next step up, which led to 3000hp per unit was taken sensibly and slowly. In this way success was achieved. The size of the present fleet remains a state secret but is no doubt in the region of 10,000.

The USSR's electric locomotives are not specially remarkable, except that there are a lot of them and all are of the bogie type. A long series of designs with three-axle trucks were developed from some prototypes supplied by GEC of USA in 1929. Other prototypes have been supplied since the war by France, Germany and Sweden and production units from Czechoslovakia; the bulk, however, are homemade, both for 3000v DC and 25,000v AC. A common design is a permanently-coupled twin unit, with four two-axle trucks.

Train services

Freight dominates rail operations; the two million ton-miles produced annually by the railways is not only the greatest on any system in the world but is more than *ALL* the rest of the world's railway traffic put together. This is a figure so big as to be meaningless, but if one considers the overall tonnage handled per year (3600 million) one gets a figure perhaps of 250,000 loaded wagons dispatched each day. A typical freight train will weigh in the region of 3000 tons.

Passenger trains are in general timed to keep up with freight – but no more – and in consequence are not fast. The 'Russia' (the correct name for what is usually and incorrectly known as the 'Trans-Siberian Express'), for example, averages 30 mph on its 5900-mile journey from Moscow to Vladivostok. The standards of amenity and cleanliness are high; each coach has two attendants to keep it clean and heated, with the samovar on the boil. The premier Communist country can hardly have classes, so there are soft and hard cars. In spite of its taking second place to freight, the passenger count amounts to 3500 million each year, second in the world.

MOSCOW METRO
Moskovski Metropolitana Imeni V.I. Lenina, 5 Kolokolbnikov Street, Moscow 103045.

The first section of the Moscow Metro was one of the great show-pieces of the revolution although built using compulsory labour. The magnificent stations in the central area would more aptly be described as palaces. The first line opened in 1934. Since then further lines have been built (three transverse, three radial and one circular), making a 103-mile system. The gauge is the Soviet standard of 5ft and the current 825v DC with third rail. The Metro's annual traffic of 1800 million passengers is by far the heaviest traffic handled by any city underground railway.

USSR

R.S.F.S.R.
1. Daghestan A.S.S.R.
2. Kabardino–Balkar A.S.S.R.
3. Mari A.S.S.R.
4. Mordovian A.S.S.R.
5. North Ossetian A.S.S.R.
6. Tatar A.S.S.R.
7. Udmurt A.S.S.R.
8. Chuvash A.S.S.R.
9. Checheno–Ingush A.S.S.R.
AZERBAIJAN
10. Nakhichevan A.S.S.R.
GEORGIA
11. Abkhaz A.S.S.R.
12. Adzhar A.S.S.R.

Projection: Conical Orthomorphic with two standard parallels   East from Greenwich

YUGOSLAVIA

See map on pages 86–87.

YUGOSLAV RAILWAYS – JZ
Jugoslovenskih Zeleznica,
Nemanjina 6,
Belgrade.

Yugoslavia was another country created by the Allies in 1919, partly from the dismemberment of the Austro-Hungarian Empire, but including most of the territory of the former Kingdoms of Serbia and Montenegro. The first railway in what is now Yugoslavia was a section – between Maribor and Ljubljana – of the Austrian main line from Vienna to Trieste, then an Austrian port. It opened in 1849. Steady extension took place in the area controlled by Austria. In 1878 the Austrians invaded Bosnia and Herzogovinia (then under Turkish domination), and during this campaign laid narrow-gauge military railways. This system remained after the Turks were driven out; its main line connected Sarajevo, Mostar and Dubrovnik with the rest of the country and involved major engineering works as well as sections of rack-and-pinion operation.

The Kingdom of Serbia had both standard and narrow-gauge railways. Basically, the former applied on the plains and the latter in the mountains and the system penetrated to the Bulgarian and Turkish borders as well as to the Aegean Sea at Salonika. The narrow gauge

reached Uzice (now Titovo Uzice), twenty miles distant across the mountains from the Bosnian border.

Croatia was part of Hungary, and the Hungarian MAV system owned the trunk line from Budapest via Zagreb to Fiume (now Rijeka). All these areas became part of the new Kingdom of Yugoslavia after World War I.

There was great destruction of railways in World War I. The Serbian system (740 miles of standard gauge and 500 miles of narrow gauge) was almost totally destroyed.

After that war, the newly independent Kingdom of Yugoslavia restored the railway system, first bringing the Simplon-Orient Express route from Italy via Belgrade to Bulgaria up to international main-line standard. A new narrow-gauge link, involving some magnificent spirals in the mountains and the mile-long Sargan tunnel, was opened in 1925. It joined Visegrad to Uzice (now Titovo Uzice) and thus connected the Serbian and Bosnian systems. After a connecting line into Belgrade had been built in 1928, through running – of a dubious kind – was possible between the Serbian capital and the Adriatic at Dubrovnik. Before the war, Salonika was the main Serbian port.

In World War II, from all accounts, it was trains and the people in them which got destroyed, rather than the railways themselves. Four million out of sixteen million Yugoslavians died, but they took a proportionate number of the enemy with them. The survivors gained a strength of purpose from these sacrifices which enabled them not only to drive out

the Germans but to resist Soviet domination as well. Few visitors were allowed into the country in the first years after the war but Laurence Durrell (who served in the British Embassy then) writes a hilarious account of Yugoslavian rail travel in his book *Esprit de Corps* – in English in spite of its title – telling something of the happy-go-lucky air of those days, no doubt a reaction from the terrible years that had gone before.

The Communist government of Marshall Tito, in spite of many other calls on its meagre resources, then embarked on the greatest railway project to be constructed in Europe since the war. It was undertaken in order to provide Belgrade with an outlet to the sea, a mere 200 miles away across the mountains, but 470 miles by the meandering course of the narrow-gauge railway already discussed. The 26-hour journey, involving such fascinating but time-wasting delights as rack-and-pinion working south of Sarajevo, was definitely for enthusiasts only.

The new line, which was to run to the port of Bar rather than Dubrovnik, had been planned before the war. Construction started in 1952 and after a little go-stop-go in the early years, was opened throughout on 27 November 1975. It is 298 miles long; some idea of the work involved may be judged from the fact that 72 miles are in tunnel, the two longest, Sozina and Zlatibor, both being 3.9 miles in length. Two hundred and fifty others average 450 yards each; 234 bridges aggregate to nine miles and include the Mala Rijeka Bridge, 613ft high

1518ft long with a 460-ft central span. Electrification is in progress.

In the meantime, work had been initiated on the less spectacular task of transforming the original system, which had previously consisted of 4500 miles of standard gauge and over 2000 miles of narrow, into one of 6500 miles of standard gauge and a few stubs of narrow. The 65 miles of electrification (DC), inherited from the Italians in the north, have become 1650 miles; most of this is wired at 25,000v AC. Incidentally, the Bosnian-Herzegovinian 2ft-6in gauge mountain network, with 650 locomotives was, until conversion and abandonment took hold in the 1960s, the largest in the world laid to a gauge as narrow as this.

The locomotive power which Yugoslavia inherited came mostly from Austrian and Hungarian sources, but mechanical engineers in both these countries had a tendency towards complications as a means of solving difficult traction problems. It is significant that the new administration adopted straight-forward Serbian designs (2-6-2s, 2-8-0s and 2-6-0s) for stop-gap construction, following this with some very simple and handsome two cylinder 2-8-2s, 4-6-2s and 2-10-0s with interchangeable components for the main lines. The ruggedly basic Bosnian 0-8-2s went on being built for the narrow gauge. Such extravagances as 2-6-6-0s or 0-10-2s with flexible wheel-base (on the Klose system) and many other curiosities were not duplicated, although – to the regret of the mechanical department but to the pleasure of ferro-equinologists – had to con-

tinue in use for a long time because the country lacked the resources to replace them.

In traffic terms JZ is a busy railway, annually hauling eighty million tons of freight an average distance of 180 miles as well as carrying 130 million passengers. The amount of equipment is (unusually for a Communist country) given as 550 steam, 320 electric and 800 diesel locomotives, 3400 passenger cars and 52,000 wagons. The steam locomotives are mostly in reserve.

VATICAN CITY

VATICAN RAILWAY

The shortest railway system in any sovereign state is the final half mile of what is effectively an Italian State Railways siding leading into the Vatican City. Iron sliding doors shut off the rails in the Holy see from the secular ones outside. Provision is made for special passenger trains, although these have been almost non-existent in recent years.

Above: Until well into the 1970s sections of the once huge 2ft 6in gauge network in Yugoslavia continued to function – often by steam. This section of the Austria-Hungarian empire used 0-8-2 and 2-8-2 steam locomotives, ran buffet cars and had rack sections. Here is a typical train on the line from Hercegnovi to Uskoplje behind double-headed 83 class 0-8-2s complete with spark arresters on their chimneys.

Top left: The new Yugoslavian line from Sarajevo to Ploče is electrified.

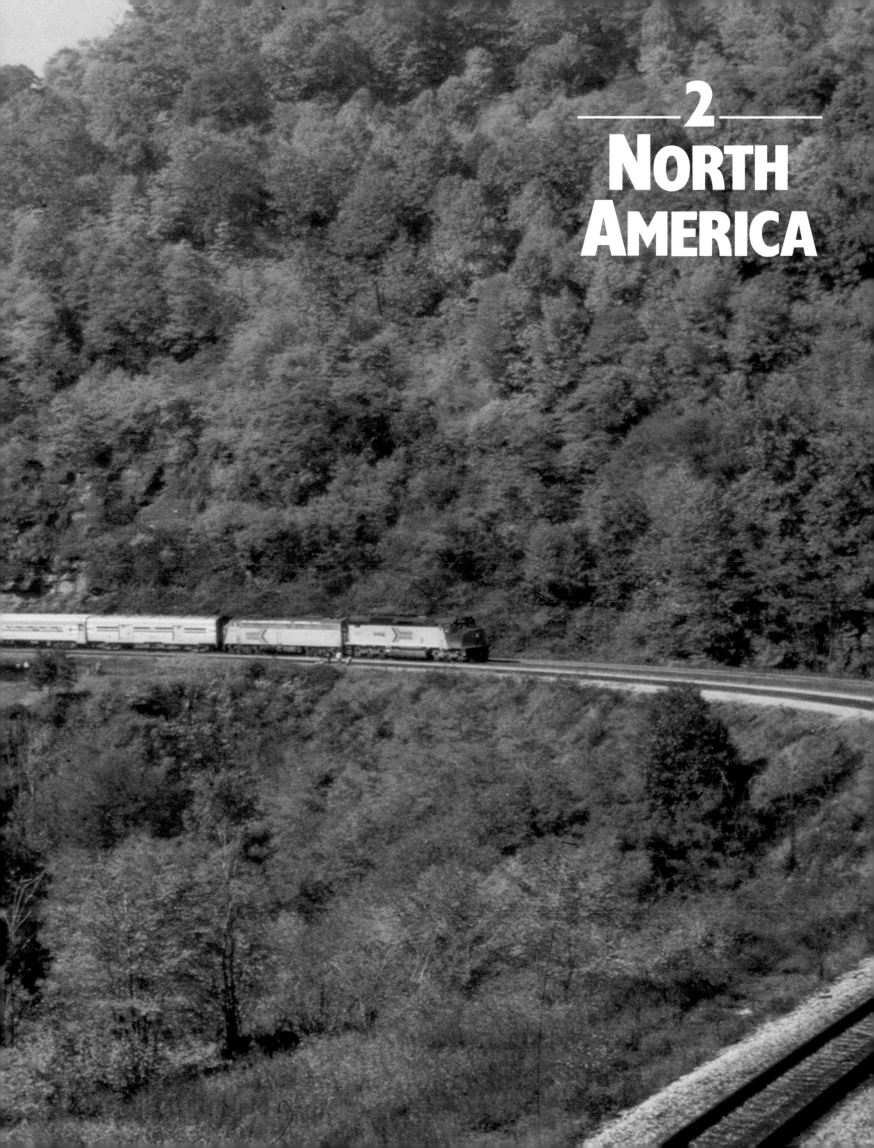

North America
The Official Guide

Canada
Canadian National Railways – CN
Canadian Pacific Limited – CP RAIL
Cartier Railway Company
Other Canadian Railways
   Algoma Central Railway
   British Columbia Railway
   Ontario Northland Railway
Quebec, North Shore & Labrador Railway
White Pass & Yukon Corporation Limited

Mexico
National Railways of Mexico

United States of America
The Pullman Company
Alaska Railroad
Amtrak – National Rail Passenger Corporation
Atchison, Topeka & Santa Fe Railway

Autotrain Corporation
Bay Area Rapid Transit – BART
Black Mesa & Lake Powell Railroad
Boston & Maine Corporation
Burlington Northern Inc.
Chessie System Inc.
Chicago, Milwaukee, St Paul & Pacific Railroad – The Milwaukee Road
Chicago & North Western Transportation Company
Chicago Transit Authority
   Chicago, South Shore & South Bend Railroad
Conrail – Consolidated Rail Corporation
Cumbres & Toltec Scenic Railroad
Delaware & Hudson Railway
Denver & Rio Grande Western Railroad
Detroit, Toledo & Ironton Railroad
Edaville Railroad
Florida East Coast Railway
Illinois Central Gulf Railroad
Long Island Rail Road
Maine Central Railroad

Other US Railroads
   Mount Washington Cog Railway
   New York City Transit Authority
   New York, Ontario & Western Railroad
   Norfolk & Western Railway
   Ponce & Guayama Railway (Puerto Rico)
   Port Authority Trans-Hudson Corporation – PATH
   Seaboard Coast Line Industries Inc
   Southern Pacific Transportation Company
   Southern Railway System
   Southwestern US Railroads
      Missouri Pacific Railroad – MoPAC
      Chicago, Rock Island & Pacific Railroad – Rock Island
      St Louis – San Francisco Railway System
      Missouri – Kansas – Texas Railroad – Katy
      Kansas City Southern Railway
   Strasburg Rail Road
   Union Pacific Railroad
   Western Pacific Railroad

Inevitably the railways in North America are dominated by those in the United States, but it is pleasing to note, that, in sharp contrast to those of other continents, railroad cars can and do circulate over virtually the whole of the mainland portion without any significant technical or political problems. Compatible couplers and brakes as well as an identical rail gauge (except where the spikes have worked loose) assist the former, commonsense and restraint – the rarest of all human qualities, especially among governments – the latter.

Having recently won independence from Great Britain, the USA, when railways first came to North America, chose to call *their* lines, rail*roads*, although some companies continued to use the British 'rail*ways*'. The term railway is fairly universal in Canada.

THE OFFICIAL GUIDE
424 West 33rd Street,
New York, New York.

No treatise on the North American railroad scene could avoid mention of one great institution – the once-monthly Official Guide of the Railways and Steam Navigation Lines of the United States, Porto Rico [sic], Canada and Cuba. Taking April 1949 as an example, we find a modest 1504 page volume, listing the services offered at 138,000 railway stations from Aaron, Georgia via (the writer is interested to see) Hollingsworth, Louisiana, to Zylonite, Massachusetts. The 730 railroads listed begin with the Aberdeen and Rockfish and end with the Yuma RR in Arizona. Vanished delights such as the 'California Zephyr', the 'Orange Blossom Special', not to mention the 'Twentieth Century Limited', abound in its pages. With the virtual extinction of passenger service in the USA on the part of individual railroads, *The Official Guide* has now become smaller but remains full of interest.

Above: Posed picture of Chesapeake & Ohio, Seaboard Air Line and Southern Railway trains crossing on a three-level bridge at St Louis, Missouri.

Top: The Great Hall – the interior of Union Station, Chicago, taken at a quiet period. This station effectively comprises two terminals back to back, sharing a common concourse. The scene today is much altered taking in Amtrak services and busy suburbans.

Above left: Completion of the Pacific Railroad Central Pacific 4-4-0 Reno and Union Pacific 4-4-0 No 119 in attendance at the driving of the last spike at Promonotory, Utah on 19 May 1869.

Left: This standard eight wheeler is a typical example of an early American locomotive type – the simple 4-4-0 woodburner – in this case Grand Trunk Railway No 255.

Above: A dramatized view of the 1937/38 'Burlington Zephyr' of the Chicago Burlington and Quincy Railroad.

Centre right: The inauguration ceremony for one of America's first post-World War II named trains, the 'City of St Louis', on 2 June 1946.

Page 122/123: Conrail's 'Broadway Limited' on the four-track Horseshoe Curve in Pennsylvania.

CANADA

1:15 000 000

100   50   0   100   200   300   400 miles
100   0   100   200   300   400   500   600 km

GREENLAND

ATLANTIC

Devon Island
Lancaster Sound
Bylot I.
Pond Inlet
Baffin Bay
Svartenhuk Peninsula
Angmagssalik

Brodeur Peninsula
Milne Inlet
Scott I.
Disko I.
Disko B.
Sondre Stromfjord
King Frederick VI Coast

Gulf of Boothia
C. Hewett
Davis Strait
Holsteinsborg
Sukkertoppen

Fury & Hecla Str.
Home B.
C. Dyer
Godthaab
Fiskenaesset

Melville Peninsula
Cumberland Peninsula
C. Mercy
Frederikshaab
Ivigtut

Prince Charles I.
Foxe Basin
Nettilling L.
Cumberland Sd.
Juliannehaab
Nanortalik
C. Farewell

Circle
Foxe
C. Dorchester
Amadjuak L.
Hoare B.
Sydproven

Rae Isthmus
Wager Bay
Wager I.
Amadjuak
Frobisher
Foxe Penin.
Frobisher Bay
Resolution I.

Southampton I.
Bell Pen.
Coats I.
Digges Is.
Saglouc (Sugluk)
C. Chidley
Akpatok

Chesterfield Inlet
Mansel I.
Ivugivik (Notre Dame d'Ivugivic)
Maricourt (Wakeham Bay)
Koartac (Notre Dame de Koartac)

Hudson Strait

C. Tatnam
Ungava
Payne (Bellin)
Payne Bay
Ungava Bay

HUDSON BAY
Ottawa Is.
Payne
Port Nouveau-Quebec (George R.)
Hebron

257
Portland Promontory
PENINSULA
Leaf
Ft. Chimo
Nain

Sleeper Is.
King George Is.
Inoucdjouac (Port Harrison)
L. Minto
Larch
George
Nutak

Belcher Is.
Clearwater L.
Lower Seal L.
Kaniapiskau
Whale
C. Harrison
Indian Harbour

Ft. Severn
C. Henrietta Maria
Gr. Whale R.
Poste de la Baleine (Great Whale River)
Lac Bienville
Scheffervile
Michikamau
North West R.
Hopedale
Rigolet
Cartwright

Severn
C. Jones
Ft. George
Petitsikapau L.
Churchill Falls
Churchill
Naskaupi
Cartwright 1128
Battle Harb.
Belle Isle

Winisk
D
Fort George
Kaniapiskau
Ashuanipi L.
Wabush City
St. Augustin
Str. of Belle Isle

Big Trout L.
James Bay
Akimiski I.
Nouveau Comptoir (Paint Hills)
1128
Gagnon
Moisie
Romaine
Twillingate
Lewisporte
Bonavista

Attawapiskat
East Main
Eastmain
Mistassini
Moisie
Natashquan
Grand Falls
Gander
Trinity B.
Carbonear

Ft. Albany
Charlton I.
Fort Rupert (Rupert House)
Rupert
L. Albanel
Mingan
Anticosti
Buchans
Harbour Grace
St. John's

TARIO
Albany
Moosonee
Nottaway
Chibougamau
Peribonca
Sept Iles
Port Cartier
Corner Brook
834
Placentia
C. Race

Albany
Missinaibi
Gouin Reservoir
L. St. Joseph
Harricanaw
Baie Comeau
Gaspé
Magdalen Is.
Cabot Str.
Port aux Basques
Trepassey

Armstrong
Nakina
Kenogami
Matagami
St. John
Saguenay
Rimouski
C. Gaspé
Gulf of St. Lawrence
Ray
C. North

Nipigon
Longlac
Hearst
Cochrane
Dolbeau
Roberval
Jonquiere
Chicoutimi
Gaspé Pen.
Campbellton
Bathurst
Cape Breton I.
Glace Bay

L. Nipigon
Heron Bay
Oba
Timmins
Noranda
Rouyn
La Tuque
Tadoussac
R. St. Lawrence
Chatham
Newcastle
Sydney

Thunder Bay
Franz
Matheson
Kirkland Lake
Senneterre
Doucet
Weymont
Shawinigan
Levis
NEW BRUNSWICK
Moncton
Port Hawkesbury
Mulgrave
C. Canso

Michipicoten Hr.
Haileybury
Cobalt
Temiskaming
Cabonga Reservoir
Trois Rivieres
Quebec
Thetford Mines
St. Leonard
Amherst
New Glasgow

Lake Superior
Sault Ste. Marie
Sudbury
North Bay
Joliette
Sorel
St. Hyacinthe
Sherbrooke
Woodstock
Fredericton
Truro
Windsor
Dartmouth

Calumet
Copper Cliff
Parry Sound
Pembroke
MONTREAL
Hull
Lachine
Saint John
Springhill
Bridgewater
Halifax

Laurium
Keweenaw
Cornwood
Georgian Bay
Arnprior
OTTAWA
Cornwall
L. Champlain
NOVA SCOTIA
Kentville
Liverpool
Sable I. (Nova Scotia)

Iron Mt.
Cheboygan
North Chan.
Sault Ste. Marie
Belleville
Kingston
VERMONT
Bangor
Digby
Shelburne

Rhinelander
Manistique
Lake Huron
Owen Sound
Peterboro
Watertown
Augusta
B. of Fundy
Yarmouth
Sable

WISCONSIN
Antigo
Menominee
Cadillac
Orillia
Oshawa
Glens
NEW HAMPSHIRE
Concord
Manchester
Portland

Wausau
Appleton
Green Bay
Manitowoc
TORONTO
Guelph
Niagara Falls
Rochester
Syracuse
Utica
Lowell
Boston
C. Cod

Madison
Sheboygan
Kitchener
London
Brantford
Hamilton
Elmira
Albany
Springfield
Worcester
Providence

Milwaukee
Racine
Grand Rapids
Muskegon
Saginaw
Sarnia
Buffalo
Binghamton
Waterbury
New Haven

Kenosha
Kalamazoo
South Bend
Windsor
NEW YORK
Scranton
Bridgeport
New York

Rockford
Gary
DETROIT
Toledo
Erie
Jamestown
Williamsport
Allentown
Jersey City

CHICAGO
Evanston
Cleveland
Akron
Youngstown
PENNSYLVANIA
Reading
Trenton

ILLINOIS
INDIANA
OHIO
Newark
NEW JERSEY

West from Greenwich
COPYRIGHT. GEORGE PHILIP & SON. LTD.
DHK

OCEAN

6309

CANADA

See map on pages 126-127.

Sharing a long border with a country as populous as the United States has meant that Canada is forced of necessity and not compulsion to adopt many US practices and policies. Canada's railways reflect this precisely especially regarding equipment; well-proven USA standards and practices prevail across the border. In this respect, the main Canadian railroads are just two more North American ones, interchanging cars and, in fact, owning a lot of trackage south of the border.

Although similarities exist, the Canadians have done a far better job than their neighbours in establishing a working relationship between railways and government. For example, the privately owned Canadian Pacific competes with the nationalized Canadian National for important flows of traffic keeping both parties honest. Furthermore in a sparsely populated country railway administrative problems came early – the bad period in Canada occurred sixty years ago, not now. With more than 190 miles of railway per thousand people, Canada has, on this basis, more railroad than any other country in the world, but because of the tracts of uninhabited territory, the country is low in the league on a 'per square mile' basis. Being at such extremes statistically, it is all the more creditable that the railway problem has been dealt with so well.

Passenger service, usually with sleeping and dining accommodation, is provided on most lines other than those purely of local interest. For some years, the Canadian government has subsidized the railroads concerned, for this loss-making activity. In 1978 the basis on which this happens was altered; an organization called Via Rail Canada has taken over the passenger trains – the name was previously used for joint CN/CP passenger marketing. Service, however, continues, but some rationalization has occurred. For example, duplicated CN and CP daily services across the continent have become integrated.

CANADIAN NATIONAL RAILWAYS – CN

935 Lagauchetière Street W,
Montreal, Quebec.

Canadian National Railways came formally into existence in January 1923, when all the government-owned lines in Canada were amalgamated. In fact, the name had been in use since 1918. The oldest of the constituents was the Grand Trunk Railway of Canada, incorporated in 1853. The GT's first component was the fourteen-mile line from Laprairie, Quebec to St John, New Brunswick opened on 24 July 1836. It connected the St Lawrence River with the Richelieu River, which flowed into the Hudson River. Hence, an all-steam service by water and by rail from Montreal to New York was available. The GT

developed into a large network in eastern Canada and also had lines across the border in Michigan, Indiana and the New England States. Its associated company, the Grand Trunk Pacific, began at Prince Rupert on the Pacific coast. The two lines came under government control in 1919-20.

The Canadian Northern was privately owned and also went sea to sea. Financial difficulties led to state control in 1916. Other lines, such as the Intercolonial Railway in New Brunswick and Nova Scotia, the Prince Edward Island Railway and the National Transcontinental Railway – from Quebec via a northern route direct to Winnipeg – were government-owned from the start.

The new child, Canadian National, had 24,000 miles of track at birth. Until the US mergers of the 1960s, it was the largest in North America. Among its tentacles was a line which went 1000 miles north from Winnipeg, through virtually uninhabited territory to polar-bear-infested Churchill on Hudson Bay. (For many years it was the most northerly of its branches.) Even today a sleeping and dining car train (you cannot call it an express – there are 77 stops) goes all the way and back three times a week. Grain exports were the line's *raison d'être*; Hudson Bay, although frozen up

each year for eight months or so, provides a much shorter route to Europe than the St Lawrence River.

At present, CN's most northerly point is the recently built line, running north from Edmonton, to reach mineral deposits near the Great Slave Lake. The most easterly point reached by CN is the far extremity of the 3ft-6in-gauge line of the ex-Newfoundland Railway. Normal freight cars can be consigned there – the bogies are changed after the ferry trip from the mainland – but no longer does the 'Newfie Bullet' (alias the 'Caribou') carry passengers the 547 miles from Port-au-Basques to St Johns.

These acquisitions less a few closures, have led to a net increase of 2000 miles in route mileage since the systems formation. Rare in the world nowadays are towns whose only means of land communication is the railway; motorcars used in the neighbourhood will have been hauled in on the train. There are a number of such places served by CN metals.

Canadian National's steel cantilever bridge over the St Lawrence River at Quebec has an 1810ft span, which is currently the longest in the world to be crossed by trains.

With an easier route across the Rockies than the other lines, CN did not need anything particularly exciting in the way of locomotive power. However, in one way, it was outstanding: the 4-8-4 was considered the ultimate in steam passenger power; if so, then CN was the ultimate railway for it had more of them (199) than any other. In general, the fleet was fairly standard North American, lent distinction in many cases by a big transverse cylindrical-feed water-heater mounted in front of the chimney. Dieselization was completed in 1960, but CN has also remained among the handful of lines in Canada and the US which continue to operate the steam locomotive, at present a much pampered 4-8-2, on regular tourist trips between Toronto and Niagara Falls. In addition, seventy other CN steam locomotives have survived to keep vivid steam's memory.

Notwithstanding, CN was the very first railroad in North America to operate successfully main-line diesel units in the 1000+hp category. This was in 1928, when two such units with Beardmore engines went into service. Ante-dating the present fleet of 2400 units by around thirty years, they anticipated the future by having both of the basic features of most present-day diesel power: electric transmission and multiple-unit operation.

There is a small amount of electrified operation in the Montreal area, with fourteen loco-

Bottom left: Sherbrooke, Quebec on a cold winter's night in 1955. Light Pacific No 5293 takes water in the snow.

Below: Canadian National's station at Vancouver is situated near Mount Pleasant opposite the end of False Creek.

Bottom: Canadian Pacific's 'Canadian' near Leanchoil, British Columbia with Mt Chancellor on the right. Note the vista-domed observation car.

Extreme right: A unit coal train of the Canadian Pacific Railroad returns empty to the mines in the Rockies.

Right: Canadian National's 'Super Continental' is about to leave Vancouver for Montreal.

Below: Canadian National's turbo-train for Montreal.

motives and some suburban multiple-unit trains.

A constituent of Canadian National, the Great Western Railway of Canada, later part of the Grand Trunk system, is credited with having introduced the world's first scheduled dining-car service in 1867. This concern to make passenger services attractive was reflected in CN's attitude to them; for example, during recent years when the rest of North America had given up trying, CN persevered with ultra-modern turbo-trains. It needed perseverence, too, because the new rolling stock had endless teething troubles. CN's

'Continental Limited' – later and currently the 'Super-Continental' – was the flag train across the continent via Edmonton, Jasper and the Yellowhead Pass. Under Via Rail Canada jurisdiction it will continue to operate. In 1975 there were 1365 passenger cars and 10.3 million passengers were carried.

Crossing the border from the US, one characteristic of a CN freight train is immediately obvious. Instead of being a kaleidoscope of different colours and owners' markings, most of the consist will be solid CN; this is because, unlike railroads in the USA, Canada has nation-wide railways and hence, much less interchange

of cars. CN has an immense car fleet of 120,000 units and keeps tabs on their movement by a sophisticated computerized system of US (Southern Pacific) origin known as TRACS (TOPS in the US). The installation of TRACS was aided by the fact that Canada's long-distance telecommunication services are a CN operation. More than 108 million tons of freight traffic were hauled an average distance of 675 miles in 1975; expenses are 105 percent of receipts.

CANADIAN PACIFIC LIMITED – CP RAIL
Montreal, Quebec,
H3C 3E4.

The building of the first Canadian trans-continental was not like its US equivalent. In the US, the government chose to build the transcontinental railroad to secure and protect California; in Canada, the building of the transcontinental railroad was an actual treaty clause struck in 1871 by the hard-headed people of British Columbia as their price for union. Construction of the line was to start

within two years, completion to be within ten.

When the time came for the government in the east to honour their bond, they were reluctant to do so but after deliberation and delay they eventually proceeded. The first sod was cut where Fort William now stands, on 1 June 1875, but it was not until 1882 that the Canadian Pacific Railway was incorporated by an Act of the British Parliament. The CP Company was to receive a $25 million subsidy, 25 million acres of land and 700 miles of rail-road on the line of route, already completed or under construction by the Dominion of Canada government.

The engineering problems were extremely difficult, particularly along the rough north shore of Lake Superior. In fact, the construction syndicate was on the point of going bankrupt when a certain Louis Riel, half French, half Indian, marched his followers against the Canadian authorities. The uncompleted CP railway was immediately put at the disposal of the military and the rebellion was crushed in four days. A grateful Government came up with some timely extra finance and, on 7 November 1885, the last spike (of plain iron) was driven with ceremony at Craigellachie, BC. The 2920-mile railway from Montreal to

Above: The 'Canadian' crosses Stoney Creek bridge, British Columbia.

Top right: CP's automated hump yard at Alyth, Calgary. Note cut of cars about to begin passing over the hump.

Centre right: White Pass & Yukon's narrow-gauge diesel braves the Yukon winter.

reduce cost as far as possible, the line was taken around or over obstacles rather than through them. The bridges were nearly all the familiar timber trestle. It was left to a later generation to build the five-mile Connaught Tunnel and the spiral tunnel in the Kicking Horse Pass, which reduced the grade there from a horrific 1 in $22\frac{1}{2}$ to an acceptable 1 in 45.

As well as boring tunnels to improve the route, improvements involving bridging were made. The steel viaduct at Lethbridge, Alberta, just over a mile long and 314ft above the Oldman River, avoided a series of sharp curves and timber bridges. Another remarkable wooden bridge replacement is the Stoney Creek bridge in British Columbia, a steel arch of 336ft span, 307ft high.

CP motive power was fairly conventional technically, but remarkable in various other ways. Its steam passenger locomotives were among the few on the North American continent to be painted a colour other than black – in this case it was a beautiful crimson lake. The red ones included the famous 'Selkirk' 2-10-4s for use over the Rockies – was there any other line which had streamlined coloured ten-coupled power? On the prairies ruled the 'Royal Hudson' 4-6-4s, complete with crowns on the sides and, for inter-city work, a batch of 4-4-4s was built in 1938 for a service of high-speed lightweight trains between Montreal and Toronto. Another feature, also rare in North America, was that secondary CP trains did not have to make do with elderly hand-me-downs. Some excellent little 4-6-2s were built for this work even after World War II. A 'Royal Hudson' 4-6-4 survives and is operational in tourist service at Vancouver. In 1978 it steamed east over the Kicking Horse Pass on a promotional tour.

Dieselization, which took place between 1948 and 1954, came first to the Rockies. Twenty years later, the mountains are being traversed by 10,000-ton block coal trains; eleven diesel units provide traction, eight at the head end and three slave units cut into the consist. Currently 1260 diesel units are owned together with 76,000 freight cars, used to haul 87 million tons of freight annually an average distance of 600 miles.

Passenger operations on CP have always been dominated by the daily Montreal–Vancouver transcontinental express, once called the 'Trans-Canada Limited', then the 'Dominion', but latterly the 'Canadian'. Characterized by excessive demand in summer and negligible patronage in winter, the entertainment which the long snakes of ageing but still comfortable stainless steel cars offered (and, hopefully, will continue to offer) was railway pleasure of the highest order, scenically, gastronomically and socially. Before 1972, as on Canadian National, travel tickets, unless specially requested otherwise, included food – twelve superb square meals, therefore, were included in the price for the full distance. CP's 302 passenger cars which ran on its transcontinental trip and supplied a very small number of other trains, are now the concern of the new Via Rail administration. The annual

Port Moody near Vancouver was complete. The whole railway, then as now, was laid to standard gauge.

Ninety years later CP had expanded to over 21,000 miles, extending to Halifax, Nova Scotia and into the northern US. The company constructed an alternative route over the Rockies, through the Crow's Nest Pass. Once its luxurious 'Empress' steamships crossed both the Atlantic and the Pacific. Today, CP Air serves many overseas destinations and CP Ships provide freight container service.

The construction problems were largely those of logistics. To speed the work and

OTHER CANADIAN RAILWAYS

ALGOMA CENTRAL RAILWAY
289 Bay Street,
Sault Ste Marie, Ontario,
P6A 5P6.

BRITISH COLUMBIA RAILWAY
1095 West Pender Street,
Vancouver, BC,
V6E 2N6.

ONTARIO NORTHLAND RAILWAY
North Bay, Ontario.

Adding another 1800 miles to the railway mileage of the country that already has more line (on a *per capita* basis) proportionately than any other are three medium-sized independent non-specialist Canadian railways.

The easternmost of the three lines is one owned by the Ontario government and called the Ontario Northland, which connects North Bay on Lake Huron with Hudson Bay at Moosonee, where an ocean port was intended but never happened. This railway was completed in 1932.

The absence of roads, however, means that the railway has an importance in the life of the community long vanished in many other places. Hence, both passenger and freight service, including an overnight sleeping car train (the 'Northland') through via CNR from Toronto to Cochrane, 480 miles from Toronto. You can continue the 186 miles to Hudson Bay by the 'Polar Bear', one of the very few mixed passenger and freight trains in the world to include a dining car. The southern section of the line is also serviced by a discarded luxury 'Trans-Europ Express' diesel set. The ONR also occasionally brings out its steam locomotive for enthusiasts.

The Algoma Central, also in Ontario, is a privately owned company whose railway runs northwards from Sault Ste Marie (between Lakes Superior and Huron) to Hearst. Its freight operations are to some extent connected with the needs of the Algoma Steel Corporation. The passenger train is also dignified by a dining car northwards as far as – surprisingly – Eton, a name no doubt explained by the fact that the ACR was financed in Britain. Again, very little ACR terrain is approachable by road and accordingly the railway plays a much wider community role than in most places.

passenger count was 4.7 millions.

The heroic operation of huge coal trains across the Rockies has been noted. No less impressive is the great wheat movement across the prairies from grain elevator to port, in trains which have on occasion reached 21,000 tons; that is, 2.5 miles long with 250 cars in the consist and hauled by seven diesel units.

CARTIER RAILWAY
Port Cartier,
Saguenay County, Quebec.
See Quebec, North Shore and Labrador Railway.

Other Canadian Railways – Statistics

	Ontario Northland	Algoma Central	British Columbia
length	600	325	870
locomotives (diesel)	34	34	107
carriages	34	40	10
freight cars	1000	2000	9000
passengers	226,000	189,000	45,000
freight, tons	5,800,000	4,000,000	6,400,000
expenses as a % of receipts	91%	76%	138%

Above: A Canadian Pacific freight approaches Port Moody on its way to Vancouver. The branch on the right goes to the north side of Burrard Inlet to Pleasantside.

The Pacific Great Eastern was a small railway which was saved from extinction by the British Columbia government which brought her back to Vancouver as the British Columbia Railway. It now extends 600 miles northwards to Fort Nelson, handling the minerals and timber of a rich but undeveloped region. A long branch from Prince George (where connection is made with CNR) northwest to Dease Lake is under construction.

Five stainless-steel-rail diesel cars work the passenger services which run only as far as Prince George (298 miles). A steam tourist service, using cars and a superbly restored 'Royal Hudson' 4-6-4 from the Canadian Pacific, makes daily excursions out of Vancouver in summer.

QUEBEC, NORTH SHORE & LABRADOR RAILWAY
1245 Sherbnooke Street West,
Montreal, Quebec,
H3G 1G8.

Two ports side by side on the St Lawrence in Quebec province provide the outlets for separate private railway networks serving iron-ore deposits on the borders of Quebec and Labrador. By serving separate mines and transporting ore for separate companies the two railways are complementary yet at the same time competitive and the friendly rivalry between them spurs them on to even greater heights than those already achieved.

The older of the two is the Quebec, North Shore & Labrador which opened in 1954 which carries ore for the Iron Ore Company of Canada from mines at Schefferville and Carol Lake (Labrador City) to the port at Sept-Iles. Trains of 260 wagons (carrying 23,400 tons of ore per train) cover the 360-mile route from Schefferville, while trains of 165 wagons traverse the 265-mile run from Carol Lake.

The Schefferville trains have additional locomotives marshalled in the middle of the train, to reduce the coupler forces which would otherwise be necessary. These extra locomotives are remotely controlled by radio from the front locomotives, using a system which allows different regulator settings between the two when necessary.

Branches to Wabush Lake near Labrador City and Pointe Noire near Sept-Iles enable the QNS&L to carry traffic for a separate ore company whose product has to be covered in transit. The problems of loading and discharging this on the move have been solved most ingeniously by borrowing parts from the car industry. On top of the wagons is a short vertical stub axle with a small rubber wheel on top. This engages with a ramp which opens a flap on top of the wagon for loading.

On each side of the wagons below the sole-bars is another similar wheel. At the discharge terminal the action of one wheel rolling along a ramp alongside the track opens the bottom doors to dump the load while the other wheel rolling along a similar ramp closes them again.

The mine at Carol Lake has a separate railway to transport ore from the mine face to the processing plant. This is electrified and is completely automatic, with no staff on the seven twenty-wagon trains continuously circulating over the internal system.

The younger of the two railways belongs to the Quebec Cartier Mining Company and opened in 1961 for the 190-mile line from Lac Jeannine to Port Cartier. Early in 1976 it was extended 85 miles to Mount Wright, where the most modern type of ore-loading equipment has been installed.

This permits a train of 156 wagons carrying 14,000 tons of ore to be loaded on the move in less than an hour, and consists of a chute fitting closely over the top of each wagon with a rapid-acting gate to control the flow of ore. The gate is opened and closed by micro-switches operated by a fixed ramp at each end of each wagon, while the sides of the loading chute regulate the quantity of ore in each wagon and spread it uniformly over the length of the wagon as it passes underneath. So far it has not been necessary to provide automatic control of the train speed during the loading process but this is currently being investigated.

The discharge equipment at the port is equally sophisticated and unloads the complete train in two hours. Rotary couplers between each pair of wagons enable them to be tippled without being separated from the train and a train positioner beside the dumper automatically moves the whole train forward two wagon lengths at a time.

With a combined capacity of over fifty million tons of ore per year these two railways are of vital importance in the exploitation of mineral resources from what would otherwise be an undeveloped area of this vast country.

WHITE PASS & YUKON CORPORATION LIMITED – WP&Y
Box 10140,
Pacific Centre, 701 West Georgia Street,
Vancouver, BC,
V7Y 1E6.

The White Pass and Yukon Railway opened for business on 21 July 1898; the 3ft gauge line had been laid in a great hurry to carry the traffic generated by the famous Klondike Gold Rush. It ran inland from the port of Skagway, Alaska. The first twenty miles were in US territory, the remainder in the Canadian Yukon Territory. It was completed to Whitehorse, 111 miles, in 1899, whence the company's stern-wheel paddle steamers took prospectors 460 miles further north up the Yukon River to Dawson City. It ran its own airline in 1937.

WP&Y was a pathfinder in containerization; in 1953 it acquired the world's first container ship and in this way overcame the joint handicaps of isolation from and incompatibility of gauge with its railway neighbours. Ten years later considerably more than half the WP&Y's traffic was handled in containers.

WP&Y passenger service is very much vintage North American with wooden coaches, parlour car and a sixty-minute meal halt (for a sourdough lunch) en route. Furthermore, one can bring one's own vehicle on board with one. The train is also one of the very few mixed freight and passenger trains still to run in North America. There are currently 21 diesel units, thirty passenger and 420 freight cars on the system. Financial problems are in need of solution if the line is to have an assured future.

Below: In days of long ago, a Fairlie articulated locomotive is seen to negotiate a spindly trestle bridge on its way from Vera Cruz to Mexico City.

MEXICO

See map on pages 190–191.

NATIONAL RAILWAYS OF MEXICO AND OTHER RAILWAYS
Ferrocarriles Nacionales de Mexico,
Avenida Central No 140,
Mexico 3.

President Porfirio Diaz of Mexico, who ruled the country for 35 years, is considered the Father of the railways there. From the time he took office in 1876 until he left in 1911 the rail mileage increased from 330 to 13,000.

The first railway in Mexico was a British-owned standard-gauge line, which followed Cortez's original 1519 route of conquest from the port of Vera Cruz to Mexico City. The distance is only 264 miles, but the problem lies in the fact that the capital is at 7350ft above sea-level and the line has to climb 1000ft higher to get there. The difficulties of driving the grade up into the mountains led to a 28-year construction period, from 1845 until 1873. The scenery is said to be unsurpassed on any railway route in the world; but having gradients of 1 in 22 and very sharp curves, the line was not so attractive (at least not until electrification fifty years after it was built) to the railway-men who had to work it. In the early days, a fleet of the unusual Fairlie-pattern articulated locomotives were responsible for traction. Now electrification has also faded into history, the diesel reigning supreme.

Diaz was not enthusiastic about foreign concessions, but accepted them on strict conditions: one such condition limited the use of expatriate staff on Mexican lines. In this way main lines were built fanning out from Mexico City to three points on the US border – Laredo, El Paso and Tucson. The last-named route along the Pacific Coast, completed as late as

1927, remained until quite recent years a subsidiary of the Southern Pacific Railroad of the USA. In 1908 the others became part of the National Railways of Mexico; US capital was involved in these but the US did not control them. Other independent railways existed, but all except two of the significant ones have now been brought under the wing of the National system. All these Mexican railways faced the same problem as the original Mexican Railway: a 6000+ft climb up to the central plateau. Consequently, steep grades and heavy engineering are commonplace.

Even if American dollars did not dominate the Mexican Railroads, US railroad practices and hardware were (and are) virtually universal. The mileage of the National Railways is 8900 of which sixty are laid to 3ft gauge. There are 1070 diesels, 1200 passenger and 33,000 freight cars; 22 million passengers are carried annually, as well as 55 million tons of freight, hauled an average of 327 miles. There are two other principal railways in Mexico, the 950-mile Ferrocarril Chihuahua al Pacifico and the 1360-mile Ferrocarril del Pacifico.

Bottom right: The Alaska Railroad's diesel-hauled 'Aurora Express' crosses Hurricane Gulch.

Right: A modern National Railways' train approaches Mexico City.

Below: A 3ft 0in gauge steam train crosses a bridge on the narrow-gauge section of Mexico's national network.

UNITED STATES OF AMERICA

See map on pages 142–143.

Although the railroads of the USA are now virtually unique in that they remain fragmented currently into 608 separate companies (with the majority still in the hands of private shareholders) nevertheless in many ways they form a homogenous single entity. Take, for example, rolling stock; 75+ percent of their motive power was built by two steam and two diesel locomotive builder's firms; most sleeping and dining cars were built and run by the legendary Pullman Car Company; freight cars, of course, circulate nationwide. Accordingly, US railroads are treated here first as a whole, describing their history and characteristics in general; then, subsequent entries emphasize the character of individual lines.

It may be said to have all begun when, on 9 August 1929, a certain Horatio Allen opened the throttle of a steam locomotive called *Stourbridge Lion* of the Delaware and Hudson Canal Company and was soon out of sight in the Pennsylvania woods. *Stourbridge Lion*, however, was considered too heavy for the light track and was shortly converted to stationary use. The first line in America to rely entirely on steam power was the South Carolina RR out of Charleston, now part of the Southern Railway. When completed in 1833, its 135-mile route to Hamburg (across the Savannah River from Augusta) was the longest in the world. The Baltimore and Ohio, although originally intended for horse traction, was the original inter-city line; its charter dated from 1827, but it did not reach its objective, the Ohio River, until 1851.

As in Europe, most of the early railways in eastern North America were built as connections and feeders to a canal and river transport system. Even here, the American tendency to do things in a big way stood out. One might cite the remarkable Portage Railroad, a system of rope-worked inclined planes across the Allegheny Mountains. This provided a link by which canal boats, designed to be divisible into two sections for the land portion of the journey, could be taken from Philadelphia, 115 miles to the Ohio River at Pittsburgh by a joint rail and water route. Once steam had come and been made reliable, railroad systems independent of waterways quickly developed and the settled portions of the continent in the East were soon served by a network of lines; in the first thirty years up to 1860, 30,000 miles were opened.

The next quarter century gave the world the most vivid illustration possible of the ways in which railways could play strategic, political and economic roles in a country's development. In 1861 came the Civil War. Although both sides were slow to realize the potential, in the end it was the first conflict in which the strategic value of railways was used to the full, particularly by the North. It is possible to speculate whether, if the South had seceded ten years earlier, before the rail network had been so fully developed, the offensives which finally defeated the Confederacy could have been mounted.

Settlement and civilization had not only come to the eastern seaboard and along the great rivers, but by the 1860s it had also come to California, ceded to the USA by Mexico in 1846. Communication involved a choice between, on the one hand, the perils of Cape Horn, and on the other, the hazards of covered-wagon travel in hostile territory. Because of this, Washington feared that independent government might develop in California and accordingly there was a favourable climate of opinion in which the then-fantastic idea of a Pacific Railroad could be planted.

Hence the Pacific Railroad Act was passed in 1862. The secession of the South had solved the main obstacle to a quick decision; the awkward choice between a northern route and an easier but now-unavailable southern one. Work began in 1963. The Union Pacific forged west from Omaha and the Central Pacific Company, now part of Southern Pacific, started east from Sacramento. More than 780 miles of railroad were laid during the next six years until finally on 10 May 1869 at 12.47 pm the telegrapher at Promontory, Utah sent the famous signal '*done, done, done*'. It was as notable an occasion as the moon landing a century later.

During the next twenty years, 70,000 more miles of railway were built west of the Missis-

The 'Aurora Express' about to leave Anchorage depot in Alaska.

sippi River. America may have built the railroads, but the railroads built America. Their extent in the USA seventy years ago represented a third of all railroading in the world and even today they comprise a fifth.

Investors were encouraged to risk their money laying down lines in country where traffic was non-existent, by the awarding of subsidies and the granting of free lands along the right of way. The immense sums of money involved and the vast power that came to the owners of this new means of transport bred a race of railroad robber barons, who all too often proved the truth of Lord Acton's saying that 'Power tends to corrupt and absolute power corrupts absolutely'.

Investors were not the only victims of the baron's business methods; they, after all, knowingly placed their cash at risk and could at least refuse to put up any more. Railroad users often had no such remedy; rates were dictated by the owners and the customers were at their mercy.

The tales told of the doings of the robber barons is part of the folklore of American railroads. However, there is a positive side to the coin. The brutal competitiveness and the principle of survival of the fittest led to a large and real reduction in the cost of transport – from an average of two cents a ton-mile in 1875 to less than one cent forty years later. This was a direct cause of US citizens later enjoying the highest standard of living ever known.

as well as to enforce better standards of safety. By the turn of the century the USA rail network was approaching completion and the scene seemed set for a golden age of railway progress and development. But clouds, as yet almost unnoticeable, appeared over the horizon. First, Henry Ford was beginning to mass-produce cheap automobiles; second, the brothers Wright flew an aeroplane for the first time.

Competition from other modes of transport was something new for the railroads; competition among themselves was something they understood, but this was different. The first lines to go were the local electric passenger railways, the inter-urbans as they were called. These had only entered the field in the 1890s but developed so quickly that by 1916 there were 25,000 miles of them. By 1925 only a handful were left.

Long-distance passenger operations were affected, but more slowly. Better roads and better motorcars made steady encroachment – except during World War II – until in the 1960s the jet airliner delivered the *coup de grâce*.

In 1977 the US government's expensive rail passenger holding operation known as AMTRAK carried only one out of every one hundred inter-city travellers – true revival must await the end of easily available motorcar fuel. The bus and aeroplane also remain minority carriers with five percent and eleven percent respectively; the vast majority of people travel in their own cars.

As a typical example of how passenger operations have declined, Union Station at St Louis had 276 arrivals and departures daily before World War I; 128 at the start of World War II; and a mere eight today. The greatest factor in this decline is the wealth and industrial strength which the railroads helped to create, permitting, in its turn, near-universal car ownership.

The typical American small town grew up around the railroad depot, the railroad track itself often forming a convenient line of demarcation between the areas where lived the 'haves' and 'have-nots' respectively – hence the expression 'the wrong side of the tracks'. Alas, this centre-of-town station is no longer used – in contrast to still well-used European ones built as an afterthought well outside a typical town.

Regarding freight, a titanic struggle against other modes of transport has ensued and is still being raged. The outcome is far from clear and it must be said that, while the railroads now carry over twice as much freight as they did fifty years ago, the trucks particularly have a proportionally much larger share of the market.

The normal tactics of commercial competition, such as labour-saving investment, the closing down of unprofitable operations, and price adjustments, are largely denied to the railroads because of government regulation and trade union pressure – hence, the poor financial record of the majority of lines. Mergers, on the other hand, have been allowed to take place; during the last fifteen years they have been on a scale unknown since the turn of the century.

However, profits also took precedence over safety. While no system of transport – walking included – can ever be entirely without risk, trains in the nineteenth century were not nearly as safe as they could and should have been. Brakes were inadequate and not fail-safe. Timber-built cars splintered to matchwood or went up in flames in accidents that occurred far too frequently.

In 1887 the Interstate Commerce Commission was set up to curb the rate-fixing and monopoly-forming tendencies of the railroads,

Accordingly many famous old railroad names have disappeared, as follows:

Alton – (to Gulf, Mobile & Ohio 1947) now Illinois Central Gulf

Akron, Canton & Youngstown – Norfolk & Western since 1964

Atlanta, Birmingham & Coast – (to Atlantic Coast Line 1945) now Seaboard Coast Line

Atlantic Coast Line – Seaboard Coast Line since 1967

Baltimore & Ohio – Chessie Systems since 1963

Central of Georgia – Southern Railway since 1962

Central of New Jersey – Conrail since 1976

Chesapeake & Ohio (Chessie) – Chessie Systems since 1963

Chicago & Eastern Illinois – divided between Louisville & Nashville and Missouri Pacific 1969

Chicago, Indianapolis & Louisville (Monon) – (to Louisville & Nashville 1971) now Seaboard Coast Line

Chicago, Burlington & Quincy ('Q') – Burlington Northern since 1970

Chicago Great Western (Corn Belt Route) – Chicago & North Western since 1968

Delaware, Lackawanna & Western (Lackawanna) – (to Erie-Lackawanna 1967) now Conrail

Erie – (to Erie-Lackawanna 1967) now Conrail

Great Northern – Burlington Northern since 1970

Gulf, Mobile & Ohio – Illinois Central Gulf since 1972

Illinois Central – Illinois Central Gulf since 1972

Lehigh Valley – Conrail since 1976

Louisville & Nashville – now Seaboard Coast Line

Minneapolis & St Louis – Chicago & North Western since 1960

Nashville, Chattanooga & St Louis (The Dixie Line) – (to Louisville & Nashville 1957) now Seaboard Coast Line

New York Central – (to Penn Central 1968) now Conrail

New York, Chicago & St Louis (Nickel Plate) – Norfolk & Western since 1964

New York, New Haven & Hartford (New Haven) – (to Penn Central 1972) now Conrail

New York, Ontario & Western – abandoned

Northern Pacific – Burlington Northern since 1970

Penn Central – Conrail since 1976

Pennsylvania (Pennsy) – (to Penn Central 1968) now Conrail

Pere Marquette – (to Chesapeake & Ohio 1947) now Chessie Systems

Reading – Conrail since 1976

Rutland – abandoned 1963 with some local take-overs

St Louis South Western (Cotton Belt) – now Southern Pacific

Seaboard Air Line – Seaboard Coast Line since 1967

Spokane International – Union Pacific since 1958

Spokane, Portland & Seattle – Burlington

Northern since 1970
Texas & Pacific now Missouri Pacific
Wabash – Norfolk & Western since 1964
Western Maryland – now Chessie Systems
Wheeling & Lake Erie – (to Nickel Plate 1947)
    now Norfolk & Western
Virginian – Norfolk & Western since 1959

Many further mergers are under negotiation.

In spite of poor financial performance, the railroads do an immense haulage job on their 210,000-mile network. Each day 90,000 railroad cars, carrying a mean 58 tons of cargo set out on a journey which averages 500 miles. The average train is 65 cars long and weighs 5000+ tons.

Regarded as one system, the US railroad network is easily the largest in the world.

Its agencies are as follows:

ASSOCIATION OF AMERICAN RAILROADS
1920 L Street NW,
Washington, DC 20036.

DEPARTMENT OF TRANSPORTATION
400 7th Street SW,
Washington, DC 20590.

INTERSTATE COMMERCE COMMISSION (ICC)
12th Constitution Avenue NW,
Washington, DC 20423.

Locomotive Landmarks
The first locomotive to run on rails in America was a demonstration model built to the design of a certain Colonel John Stevens – the Father of American Railroads – of Hoboken, New Jersey in 1826. *Stourbridge Lion* of the Delaware and Hudson came from Foster, Rastrick & Company of Stourbridge, England in 1829 and was the first attempt to use steam traction commercially. The first American-built steam locomotive of the basic form which we know today was the 2-2-0 *Old Ironsides* built by a mechanic called Mathias Baldwin in 1831 for the Philadelphia, Germantown & Norristown RR. Baldwin and the works he founded at Philadelphia went on to produce 60,000 more over the next 125 years. In 1836 the first 4-4-0 was built for the same railroad by another Philadelphia builder, James Brooks. The 4-4-0s were supplied by numerous builders to virtually all the US roads; 20,000 in all were made during the next sixty years. Not for nothing was the type known as American standard, being essentially simple, with the mechanism easily accessible, rugged and eminently suitable for the light rough tracks of a pioneering land. The military railway operations of the Civil War and the building of the first transcontinental lines were monopolized by these locomotives.

In the latter half of the century, other wheel arrangements such as 2-6-0, 2-8-0 and 4-6-0 became common, under the names *Mogul*, *Consolidation* and *Ten-wheeler*. The fact that these and other types are to this day known

worldwide by these American names reflects the influence which the US school of locomotive design had upon the world.

Around the turn of the century the American steam locomotive was brought rapidly to its final form, all the remaining elements being introduced in quick succession between 1895 and 1905. The typical 1895 locomotive had a narrow firebox of limited power-producing capacity between the wheels, slide-valve cylinders, Stephenson's valve gear also between the wheels and used unsuperheated steam.

Ten years and 40,000 locomotives later, the industry was producing wide-firebox superheated locomotives, with trailing trucks, piston-valve cylinders, and accessible Walschearts valve-gear in full view. Mechanical stoking was also introduced during this period. A whole series of new wheel arrangements resulted; 4-4-2, 4-6-2, 2-6-2, and 2-10-2. The 2-8-2 or *Mikado* type (so called because the original examples went to Japan) was, in the end, built in the largest numbers – 14,000 in America alone. The period was also notable for much experimentation with and the discarding of multi-cylindered compound designs.

The forty years that remained for steam development were largely devoted to perfection of detail and the building of ever-more powerful locomotives. Even by 1905, North America had steam locomotives more powerful than any built elsewhere in the world subsequently and in the end America had ones which led the world by at least fifty percent on all size and power counts.

Articulated locomotives – that is, those with a hinge in the middle – which also appeared during this turn-of-the-century period, eventually took weights up to 550 tons, grate areas to over 180 sq ft and tractive efforts above 175,000lb. Even straight two cylinder ones reached 400 tons, 122 sq ft and 97,000lb respectively.

Detail improvements were aimed mainly at reducing maintenance cost. Frames, cylinders and other detail were cast as a single monobloc casting; roller bearings replaced plain ones and so on.

In 120 years of steam in the USA, approximately 175,000 locomotives were built and of these the American Locomotive Company and its constituents built 78,000. Baldwins produced 59,000 and various US railroads 13,000 in their own shops. The remainder were built by smaller firms. Around 37,000 were exported and countless others (notably in the USSR and China, but in Germany, Great Britain and many other countries also) were built to US or US-like design.

In spite of early promise and no lack of know-how, electric locomotives were used very little in North America; the only two electrifications of any size were on the Chicago, Milwaukee, St Paul & Pacific and Pennsylvania railroads. On the other hand, the story of the diesel-electric locomotive (which in real truth is an electric locomotive which carries its own generating station) in the USA is also the story of the diesel locomotive in the world.

The US diesel locomotive is a proven, rugged

and relatively simple machine, whose weight and size allow it to go anywhere a freight car can. It also allows as many locomotive units as are required to provide power for any given haulage task to be plugged in together and the whole handled and controlled as a single locomotive. The only limit is the strength of the couplings and even this can be overcome by having radio-controlled slave units cut into the *middle* of the train, instead of the head.

Most of the credit is due to the conglomerate, General Motors, who, through their subsidiary Electromotive Diesels (EMD), offered a production unit for passenger service as early as 1938. Electromotive had cut its teeth on gas- and diesel-electric cars and trains, but it is a long stride from such things to work-horse locomotives.

Operations and Services
Pullman sleepers, in the days when trains were the only way to travel, were not for the majority of Americans. They had to make do with plain sit-up coaches, but most of the 200,000+ miles of railroad had passenger service, even if it was only a rickety combine car at the end of the daily freight. Fifty years ago the railroad carried 600 million passengers a year – now this figure has fallen to 270 million, mostly commuters in and out of New York City and Chicago: passenger trains now only serve a mere 30,000 miles of route, with 5400 cars in use.

Viewed as an entity, the US railroads, in spite of all that is wrong, haul vast amounts of freight: in specific terms 450 million tons a year, hauled an average distance of 530 miles in trains with an average pay-load of 1400 tons. There are over 500,000 freight cars. Although still a very small proportion of the total, two types of freight movement are growing. The first one is known as TOFC/COFC (Trailer On Freight Car/Container On Freight Car); in this way the economy of road transport for local collection and delivery can be combined with the economy of rail for the long haul. The second growth area is in the use of what are called unit trains, carrying bulk materials from one source to one destination – a flow of coal from a mine to one large consumer is an example. In extreme cases – for example, with the aid of automatic loading and unloading – the utilization of expensive gondola or hopper cars is improved from so many days per trip to so many trips per day. The current fleet of 27,000 diesel and 150 electric locomotives are almost wholly engaged in freight-train operation; the twelve steam locomotives still on the books are confined exclusively to pleasure use.

The traditional US method of ensuring safety of operation, which has spread widely around the world, is based on the timetable, employees' watches and the superiority or inferiority of particular trains. One train can be inferior to another by direction, or class, or both; it is the duty of an inferior train to keep clear of a superior one when it is due, by entering a siding. A gentleman called the dispatcher (in whose infallibility it is necessary to have an almost religious faith) is in charge of each section of the railroad and he is empowered to issue orders, normally by telegraph or telephone, which vary the timetable and the rights of one train over another.

Although many miles of lines worked this way still remain, the normal thing now for any route of importance is for all movements to be fully signalled, all switches to be interlocked and the presence of trains detected by continuous track circuiting. Control of a whole route can be concentrated in what under the traditional system would have been the dispatcher's office. In this way signalling practice approaches worldwide standardization.

THE PULLMAN COMPANY
165 North Canal Street,
Chicago, Illinois 60606.

Born in 1831, George Mortimer Pullman produced his first sleeping car, by converting a Chicago & Alton RR day coach, in 1859. His first luxury sleeper was the *Pioneer* of 1864. Recognition came when *Pioneer* was used to convey President Lincoln's funeral party from Chicago to Springfield, Illinois. In 1867 the Pullman Palace Car Company was formed, with the intention of providing hotel comforts for railway travellers. His first dining car, the *Delmonico*, entered service in 1868. By the turn of the century, most of his competitors had been taken over or put out of business. At its peak before the crash of 1929, Pullman had 9000 sleeping cars, parlour cars and diners in operation on the majority of the railroads in North America. Pullman day coaches, known as parlour cars, ran on short runs and it was the parlour car which became known as a Pullman in Europe.

In contrast to Europe, where transverse beds prevailed, the standard arrangement of Pullman sleeping berths was longitudinal, with wide lower and narrower upper berths in each section. Privacy was assured by heavy curtains, drawn at night along either side of the central aisle.

Later came Pullman cars with rooms or compartments, some of which had transverse berths. The luxuries and the comforts of most of those world-famous trains upon which individual railroads so prided themselves were almost all provided by Pullman.

Every imaginable frill could be found on the cars of the fleet. Observation cars of course, club cars, bars and lounges, master bedrooms, even a choice of fresh- or salt-water baths, library cars, radio and telephone rooms and so on. But even the humblest sleeper had a name. Pullman names ranged from *Eva*, through conventional *Hickory Creek* and *George Washington*, to exotic *Quantzintecomatzin*.

Pullman cars were built and overhauled in an immense works in the company town of Pullman near Calumet, Michigan and there was also a nationwide organization to maintain and run them. 'Pullman' deserved its reputation – success was due to applying the highest possible standards in all things.

With the usual 'un-wisdom' of political organizations, in 1940 the US government brought an anti-trust suit against Pullman.

Top: This Alaska Railroad steam engine is no longer in active service but does provide an educational 'toy'.

Above: Wagons are unloaded from SS Alaska at Whittier, Alaska.

Seven years later, after protracted legal proceedings, the company was forced to dispose of the operating side of its business to a consortium of 59 user railroads. The construction side still trades as a railcar builder under the name of Pullman Standard.

AKRON, CANTON & YOUNGSTOWN RAILROAD
See Other US Railroads

ALASKA RAILROAD
Federal Railroad Administration,
Anchorage, Alaska 99510.

See map on pages 126-127.

The Alaska Railroad began in 1903 as the privately financed Alaska Central Railway, to run from the port of Seward to the gold fields at Fairbanks. It was a financial disaster and only one sixth of the distance was completed when construction ceased *circa* 1910. The US government then took over and in 1914 passed an Act authorizing construction using Federal funds. The line was completed in 1923, but since the combined population of the three towns the railroad served was under 6000, it is not surprising that heavy losses were incurred. World War II caused an explosion in traffic demand, and since that time the railroad has succeeded in balancing its books.

Fifty-four locomotives, 1606 freight cars and 38 passenger cars are used to haul 800,000 passengers and 1.9 million tons of freight annually over the 525-mile line which includes spectacular scenery and some quite heavy engineering works.

UNITED STATES OF AMERICA

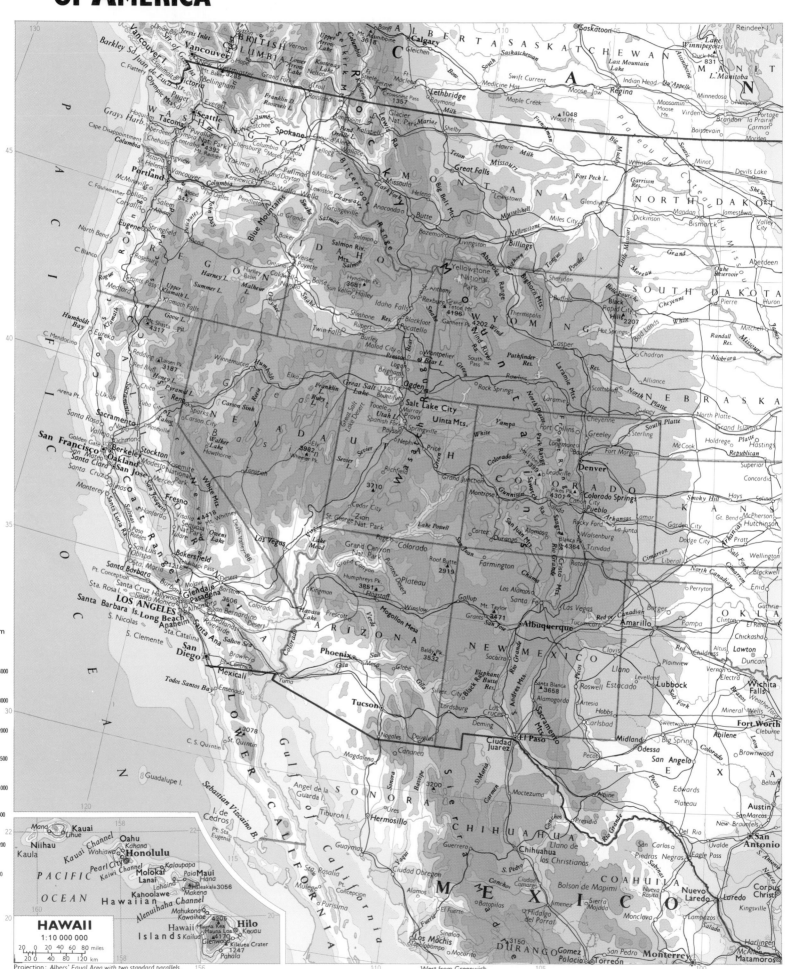

HAWAII
1:10 000 000

Projection: Albers' Equal Area with two standard parallels

West from Greenwich

142

1:12 000 000

COPYRIGHT. GEORGE PHILIP & SON. LTD.

Left: Typical of the new equipment that dominates Amtrak's Washington to Boston Northeast Corridor is this Amfleet-equipped train at Elkton, Maryland.

Below left: Track crews and highly specialized equipment have begun the major task of upgrading Amtrak's Washington to Boston Northeast Corridor. The $1.75 billion programme will result in 120 mph speeds throughout the corridor by 1981.

AMTRAK – NATIONAL RAIL PASSENGER CORPORATION
400 N Capital Street NW, Washington, DC 20001.

The National Rail Passenger Corporation (Amtrak for short) was formed by Act of Congress in 1970 in order to provide long-distance inter-city passenger transport in the USA. For some time this had been a loss-making operation for the railroads and, while the government had powers to compel them to continue running passenger trains, the service given under such forced circumstances was not all that could be desired – with a few honourable exceptions. It was a voluntary deal (certain roads opted out) which involved handing over passenger equipment to Amtrak in return for no longer having to bear passenger-train losses.

The 26,000 miles of route served by Amtrak trains are only sixty percent of those operating just before the take-over and serve a mere thirteen percent of US mileage as a whole. Most Amtrak trains are now hauled by Amtrak's own 370-strong locomotive fleet and a high proportion are equipped with new (post-1970) 'Amfleet' cars. Since the Penn Central debacle and the formation of Conrail, Amtrak has completely taken over the Washington–New York–Boston 'northeast corridor' tracks – this was the only predominantly passenger inter-city line in the country. Overall expenses are currently over twice the receipts and it is necessary to go cap-in-hand to the government each year to make up the losses; all this in aid of one percent of inter-city travel. There are 2015 passenger cars; almost twenty million passengers are carried annually.

The service which Amtrak offers its customers is on the plain and simple side and should not be confused with the service provided by the now-legendary luxury trains of the past. One of the selling points to Congress for the Amtrak operation was low vulnerability of rail travel to interruption in bad weather. Alas, experience, particularly in the bad winter of 1976–77, has shown Amtrak to perform poorly in these circumstances; it almost had to close down in February 1977.

Most of these shortcoming are not fundamental to rail but arise directly or indirectly from a shortage of funds; there is little doubt that it is sound national policy to keep a vestigial rail passenger service in being until, as anticipated, it becomes the major mode of travel of the early 2000s. Outside the Boston–New York–Washington 'corridor', on which a frequent service is maintained, the principal long-distance passenger trains are listed on the following page.

Right and below right: Two views of piggy-back trains hauled by a three-unit diesel through the Cajon Pass, California.

Below: Amtrak's 'Broadway Limited', en route from New York and Washington to Chicago, rounds Pennsylvania's Horseshoe Curve, a section of track cutting through the Appalachian Mountains.

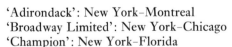

'Adirondack': New York–Montreal
'Broadway Limited': New York–Chicago
'Champion': New York–Florida
'Coast Starlight': Los Angeles–Seattle
'Empire Builder': Chicago–Seattle
'Floridian': Chicago–Florida
'Inter-American': Chicago–Laredo (for Mexico)
'Lake Shore Limited': New York–Chicago
'Lone Star': Chicago–Houston
'Montrealer': Washington–Montreal
'Mountaineer': Chicago–Norfolk
'National Limited': New York–Kansas City
'North Coast Hiawatha': Chicago–Seattle
'Panama Limited': Chicago–New Orleans
'Pioneer': Salt Lake City–Seattle
'San Francisco Zephyr': Chicago–Oakland
'Silver Meteor': New York–Florida
'Silver Star': New York–Florida
'South West Limited' (the erstwhile 'Super Chief'): Chicago–Los Angeles

'Sunset Limited': Los Angeles–New Orleans – (New York)

ANN ARBOR RAILROAD
See Other US Railroads

ATCHISON, TOPEKA & SANTA FE RAILWAY – Santa Fe
80 East Jackson Boulevard, Chicago, Illinois 60604.

It is fitting that the first major railway in the North American section of this Atlas is also one of the greatest; it even has the rare distinction of being immortalized in song. It is the only line whose metals run all the way from Chicago to California and is currently among the few US railroads in excellent physical and financial shape. To this, a remarkably high average length of haul for freight (655 miles), a passenger-carrying count of zero and a certain diversification into non-railway activities, combine to contribute.

The first sod was turned by Colonel Cyrus K Holliday at Topeka, Kansas in 1872 and by 1887 Los Angeles had been reached. A quirk of its development was that the name-towns of this huge transcontinental concern are three places of relatively modest importance and not very far apart in the southwestern USA; only two are on the present main line. In the west the route followed the approximate line of the old Santa Fe covered-wagon trail.

Later on, tentacles of the system reached Oakland on San Francisco Bay and the Gulf of Mexico at Galveston, Texas, but the spread was always oriented towards what railways best provide, *viz*, mass long-distance transportation – hence, prosperity in good times and survival in bad ones, such as the present.

Extreme right, top: An Atchison, Topeka & Santa Fe switch engine at Stockton, California.

Extreme right, bottom: An aerial view of Santa Fe Railroad's computerized classification yard at Barstow, California.

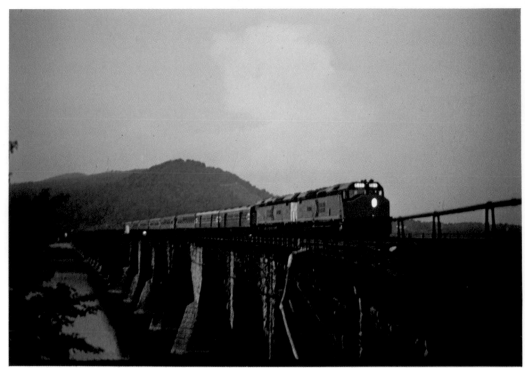

Right: Amtrak's 'Broadway Limited', en route from New York to Chicago.

Bottom: Amtrak's 'North Coast Hiawatha' which runs from Chicago to Seattle.

Below: Amtrak's Los Angeles–San Diego train shows Amfleet cars running alongside the Pacific Ocean.

A brief marriage with and divorce from what is now the Frisco (St Louis and San Francisco RR) in the early years of the century caused a 'hiccup' in this continuing satisfactory state of affairs; but in general Santa Fe has managed to please both its patrons and its stockholders.

At the present time Santa Fe's 1686 blue and yellow diesel locomotives haul 77 million tons of freight annually an average distance of 655 miles. The annual expenses of 1.1 million dollars are 81 percent of the receipts from railway operations on the 12,000-mile system.

The Santa Fe chose a fairly easy route across the US, but two notable river crossings were unavoidable, namely that across the Mississippi at Fort Madison and across the Missouri at at Sibley. The Fort Madison bridge is 3347ft long with 24 spans including one of 525ft which opens to river traffic; at Sibley the structure is 4034ft long and has 39 spans. There is a 225ft high bridge across the Canyon Diabolo (Devil's Gulch) in Arizona. The summit of the system is the 7590ft Raton pass in Colorado, approached by long 1 in 33 gradients. The longest tunnel, situated in Pittsburg, California, is only just over a mile long.

The quality of Santa Fe's permanent way (as well as the state of its finances) is reflected in a permitted speed as high as 90 mph and the use of rail up to 136 lb/yd, carrying axle-loads as high as thirty tons. Such a combination is not paralleled elsewhere in the railway world.

Among the particular characteristics of the Santa Fe's steam motive power fleet (the majority of which came from Baldwin's) was early experimentation – and early disenchantment – with Mallet articulateds, including some amazing 2-10-10-2s with (believe it or not) a hinge in the boiler. The road gave its name to the 2-10-2 type, introduced in 1902, but it is better known perhaps for 4-8-4s, coal-fired like most AT&SF steam power, that ran without change from Kansas City to Los Angeles, a distance of 1780 miles. Sixteen wheel tenders, holding 19,600 gallons of water and 5600 gallons of oil were provided on these locomotives and on their freight equivalents – magnificent 2-10-4s with big 74in driving wheels. Extensible chimneys were a feature, erected for running over the many miles of overbridge-free territory in order to keep smoke clear of the cabs. The last steam locomotive was retired in 1959.

Santa Fe was a pioneer of dieselization, purchasing its first units (for the 'Super Chief') from General Motors as early as 1935. Freight diesels came in 1941. During the war the government controlled and rationed the supply of diesel locomotives. However, because of the need to haul in water to the desert areas in the southwest for steam operation, Santa Fe was able to obtain priority and, accordingly, pioneered the dieselization of two complete divisions in 1943.

Throughout its 85-year period as a transcontinental passenger carrier, the standards set by Santa Fe were a byword for excellence. For example, the classic Chicago-Los Angeles 39½-hour 'Super Chief' became a legend. The 'Super Chief's' predecessors, the all-Pullman 'Chief' of 1923, the 'De-Luxe' (limited to sixty passengers, extra fare $25 in the dollars of 1910) and the 'California Limited' of 1897 were equally notable. Coach-class passengers were not neglected and they had their own Chicago-Los Angeles streamliner 'El Capitan' from 1938 onwards.

A superb standard of meal service both in the stations and on the trains was also a feature; in the early days in the pioneer West, it was of unheard-of quality. Surprisingly, an Englishman called Fred Harvey was responsible, obtaining the catering concession from the Santa Fe in 1869. Not only were his food and his restaurants respectable but also his waitresses. Until then and elsewhere the ladies who served in the eating houses of the West had a certain 'reputation'. The Harvey girls' respectability was, however, not at the expense of their charm, because among the good things that Fred Harvey offered his customers should be the thousands of his girls who married and settled in Santa Fe territory.

The present Santa Fe, of course, answers a laconic 'none' when asked how many passengers it carries. Freight is the lifeblood and its flow at say, Winslow, Arizona is as remarkable a sight as that of the nearby Grand Canyon of the Colorado River. The procession of mile-long 80 mph trains on the double track main is a tonic to any observer suffering from the pessimism which inevitably follows a close study of the railroad problem in many other parts of the USA.

ATLANTA AND WEST POINT RAILROAD
See Other US Railroads

AUTOTRAIN CORPORATION
1801 K Street NW,
Washington, DC 20006.

'Depend upon it, sir, when a man knows he is to be hanged in a fortnight, it concentrates his mind wonderfully.' Dr Johnson's saying is appropriate to the US organization Autotrain, the only long-distance passenger rail service on the American continent to be run commercially, that is, if it does not make a profit, it does not run. Autotrain covers the 856-mile route from Lorton, fifteen miles south of Washington, to Sanford in Florida and provides a superior version but the *only* example in North America of a kind of service that has developed extensively into a network of 135 routes in Europe. Travellers who sample Autotrain's standard of service report favourably on the effect of its unsubsidized condition. Extension is, alas, precluded by Amtrak's monopoly of passenger movement on most rail routes in the USA.

Autotrain have a fleet of twelve diesel locomotives, 182 passenger and 315 auto-carrying cars. About 250,000 passengers are carried annually.

BANGOR & AROOSTOOK RAILROAD
See Other US Railroads

BAY AREA RAPID TRANSIT – BART
800 Madison Street,
Oakland, California 94607.

No more vivid illustration of the current move back to railways – and also of the extravagance of ever having moved away – exists than that of the San Francisco Bay Area Rapid Transit. A comprehensive electric railway system was dismantled in the 1930s and effectively replaced by the private car. Soon hideous road congestion, in spite of a vast motorway construction programme, made the citizens return to thoughts of a railroad.

Immediately after World War II, proposals were made to build a new electric railway network. Serious studies began in 1957 and ground was finally broken – by President Lyndon Johnson – on 19 June 1964 for a three-pronged 72-mile system; the shank of the trident was to cross the bay by means of a tunnel formed of prefabricated sections lowered onto and buried in the sea-bed. In spite of the advanced technology used, the legal obstacles put in the BART Authority's way far exceeded any engineering ones, but finally on 16 September 1976, trains began running under the bay, almost thirty years after the project was mooted. Thirty-four stations are now served by a fleet of 450 cars, characterized by a remarkably high running speed of 80 mph and an average one of 50 mph. Extensions are planned.

Equally remarkable and equally a *stupor mundi* is the cable worked San Francisco municipal tramway system connecting with BART at the Powell St station and running up and over the hill to two termini in the Fisherman's Wharf area. The vintage cable cars manage only one-eighth the speed but offer eight times the thrill.

BESSEMER & LAKE ERIE RAILROAD
See Other US Railroads

BLACK MESA & LAKE POWELL RAILROAD
Page, Arizona.

In the world at large, electric traction is regarded as the only possible long-term solution to the railway problem. This is not the case in the USA where it has been one of the greatest non-events of railroad history. Brand-new American railroads have also been rare recently. On both counts, therefore, the brand-new (1973), all-electric Black Mesa & Lake Powell RR deserves notice – although it is not a common-carrier, is not 100 miles long and has only one train, hauled by a single three-unit electric locomotive.

The isolated BM&LP was built to carry coal dug in northern Arizona to a power station which needed to be situated eighty miles away, near Lake Powell's supplies of Columbia River cooling water. It is equally remarkable as it is free of both ICC regulation and trade union featherbedding. Each time the train makes a loaded trip it conveys 9000 tons of coal – the hopper cars are loaded and unloaded automatically. The original proposal was for train movement also to be handled automatically but this seems to have foundered. Even so, only two operators are needed as opposed to a minimum of five for a similar unit train movement on a common-carrier US railroad; this modest amount of staff and equipment carries almost three million tons of freight per year. Hopefully, it is a signpost to the future.

BOSTON & MAINE CORPORATION
150 Causeway Street,
Boston, Massachusetts 02114.

The Boston & Maine Railroad is the largest of the New England Railroads, serving Maine, New Hampshire, Vermont, Massachusetts and New York. It was formed by mergers over the years of nearly one hundred other railroads, the earliest of which was the Andover and Wilmington which was chartered in 1833 and commenced operation in 1836 between Massachusetts and Maine. The peak year for miles-of-line-in-operation was 1922 when Troy in New York, Bellows Falls and White River Junction in Vermont, Groteton, Berlin, Intervale, and Lincoln in New Hampshire, and Portland, Maine were all on B&M track. This covered 2248 miles of route and with trackage rights on other railroads you could ride on a B&M train to Montreal, Quebec or Bar Harbor in Maine. From that peak there has been a slow decline in mileage until today the railroad covers about 1700 miles.

Although small when compared to the vast railroads in the west, the B&M still holds an important place in American railroad history. It has several notable items in its past, in its plant, in its motive power, and in its services. For example, in western Massachusetts there

was a need for a rail route between Greenfield and the large cities in upstate New York. The Berkshire mountain chain stood squarely across the path of this extension, so in the 1850s a start was made on what was to become the Hoosac Tunnel. Completed in 1876 this was the longest tunnel in North America. It was 4.75 miles in length, bored through solid granite for its entire length and still handles all B&M traffic to the west. Until the end of the steam era electric locomotives were used to pilot trains through this bore. A train arriving at either portal would have its fire banked, the electric engine would couple on ahead and take the whole train, steam engine and all, through to the other side of the mountain. Once through, the steam engine would again assume control.

Bottom left: A BART train approaches Rockridge Station with the Bay Bridge, San Francisco skyline and Mount Sutro in the background.

Bottom: Boston & Maine Railroad's sorting yard at East Deerfield, Massachusetts.

Below: A Boston & Maine RR's Portsmouth to Boston passenger train in the street of Salem, Massachusetts.

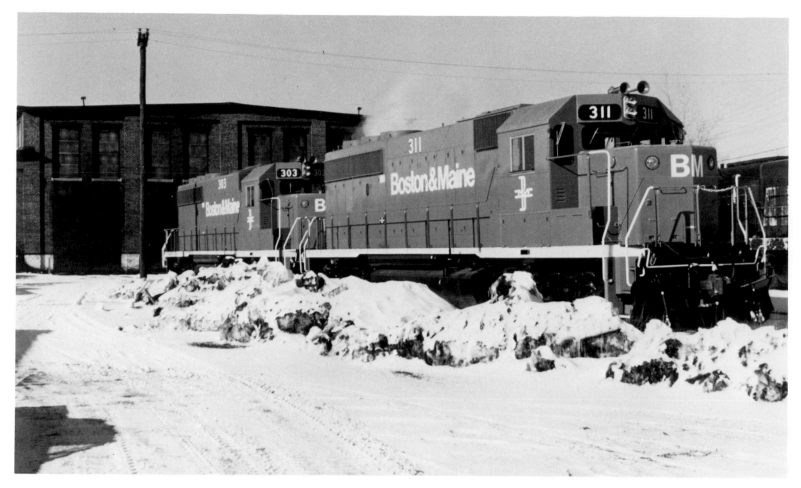

As to rolling stock, the B&M was a conventional New England railroad in large part but they did possess some unusual equipment. In recent times they were the first railroad east of the Mississippi River to try a lightweight diesel-electric articulated train. This was called the 'Flying Yankee' and its arrival on the property in 1934 was a bold and innovative step. It was a three-car single-ended streamline train, built of stainless steel by The Budd Company.

The B&M even owned a narrow-gauge line for a short period of time. This was a 3ft gauge branch line which was located in the Franconia Notch region of New Hampshire and served the resort hotels in this scenic mountain area.

As to standard gauge stock, there were in later years two or three notable classes of steam locomotives. One was the T-1 class Berkshire 2-8-4 freight locomotives with their unique Coffin feedwater heater mounted outside the smokebox front, which gave these locomotives a formidable and unmistakable countenance. These were among the first super power classes of freight locomotive built by Lima in 1929.

The last and largest steam power purchased was the R1 class of Mountain 4-8-2s. These dual purpose engines, with fourteen-wheeled centipede tenders, were the last word in modern steam power when delivered by Baldwin Locomotive Works between 1935-41. The handsome appearance of these eighteen engines was enhanced by each one of the class carrying a large name-plate on each side of the running board. The names were chosen from ones submitted by school children and lent a 'touch of class' not often seen on American railroads.

Some of these name-plates are now in museums but none of these locomotives was preserved. There are however, three steam engines still extant: at Edaville tourist railroad along with the 'Flying Yankee' is a 2-6-0; at Science Park in Boston is a latter-day 4-6-2; and at a city park near White River Junction in Vermont is a 4-4-0, built in 1892 by the Manchester Locomotive Works.

In its heyday B&M had an impressive roster of passenger services with named trains such as the 'Bar Harbor Express', the 'East Wind', and the 'Pine Tree Limited' with parlour, sleeper, and dining cars from Boston serving Portland, Maine; Montreal, Quebec; and Bar Harbor, also in Maine. In addition, Boston & Maine participated in through-services between New York and Canada's Maritime Provinces.

The railroad's major passenger terminal was North Station in Boston, which now handles only commuter trains each day, but in the 1930s its 24 tracks were in constant use accommodating the many local trains for eastern Massachusetts as well as the named trains which were arriving and departing for Portland, Halifax, Montreal, Troy and Albany New York, and the west.

The B&M in 1978 is still an independent railroad, not part of the Conrail system, nor a subsidiary of some larger corporation. Its business is now freight only, but it does operate the rail commuter lines for the Massachusetts Bay Transportation Authority. Although not the most prosperous road in the country, it still does the job that was started by the Andover and Wilmington Railroad 140 years ago.

BURLINGTON NORTHERN INC – BN
BN Building, 176 East Fifth Street,
St Paul, Minnesota 55101.

The first section of what is now the Burlington Northern received its charter in 1849 and was completed the following year. It connected the town of Aurora – a suburb of Chicago – with another line leading into that city. The present BN was formed as recently as 1970 (at which time it was the longest railroad in North America) by the merger of three major lines: first, the Chicago, Burlington and Quincy, which served the area west of Chicago ('Everywhere West' was its slogan) and reached out to Denver, Omaha, Kansas City and in particular the seven cities, St Paul-Minneapolis; second, the Northern Pacific (NP); and third, the Great Northern (GN). Both NP and GN connected the twin cities with the Pacific north-west.

NP received its charter by act of Congress over President Lincoln's signature in 1864, only two years after the Union Pacific's (with whom the CB&Q also connected) was granted. The usual land grants and subsidies were offered for a line to follow the route originally explored in 1804 by the famous pioneer travellers, Rogers and Clark. Even so, progress was slow and the financial crash of 1873 brought construction to a halt for six years. Movement of troops to put down the Sioux rising of 1876 was greatly aided by the existence of the railroad, while the NP people found, rather to their surprise, that, with the spur of military expediency, it was quite possible to operate in 45°F below zero temperatures and several feet

Top left: A pair of new diesel locomotives for the Boston & Maine RR.

Top: A Burlington Northern train on the Gasman Coulee Bridge in North Dakota.

Centre left: A Burlington Northern coal train at Cordero Mine, Wyoming.

Centre right: A typical Burlington Northern freight train hauled by a four-unit diesel.

Left: The Great Northern Railway's 5000 hp electric locomotive, takes a freight train through the Cascade Mountains near Leavenworth, Washington. Although this was a modern electric locomotive, the need for this relatively short electrified section came to an end with the advent of powerful diesel traction.

of snow. The settlement induced by the pacification of the country and the existence of rail transport led, in 1879, to an upsurge in confidence and a resumption of progress. The golden spike was driven in the presence of President Ulysses Grant on 21 April 1883. The second transcontinental line was complete.

The GN was a very different and more personal affair. Its driving force was a certain James Jerome Hill. Without government assistance and in the face of universal prognostication of disaster he built his Great Northern Railway through to the Pacific in three years. The last spike (an iron one this time) was driven without ceremony on 18 September 1893 – even Hill himself was not present. No doubt he had set his sights on a great day a short ten years ahead when his steamship *Minnesota* would carry the GN flag on to China, connecting with his all-Pullman 'Oriental Limited' from Chicago.

The route taken by the GN was well to the north of the NP, in fact close to the Canadian border. The line was well-engineered and soundly constructed; very little rebuilding has been necessary since. JJ avoided financial disaster by making immense efforts to develop agriculture in the lands opened up by his line and appeared, unlike most of his contemporaries, to put the long-term benefits to his

Above: Burlington Northern's daily fast freight from Galveston, Texas, heads for its Seattle terminus headed by three 3600 hp diesel electric locomotives. This train, shown in the spectacular Wind River Canyon, Texas, moves shipments from the Gulf Coast to the Pacific northwest.

Right: A caboose brings up the rear of a long coal train on the Burlington Northern. Wagons used in modern American railroad service are huge and the caboose sports comforts scarcely dreamed of in the heyday of railroads.

Below: A Chicago Burlington & Quincy Railroad 4000 hp passenger locomotive.

homeland ahead of short-term money-making for himself – not that he was by any means poverty stricken when he died in 1909 leaving 53 million dollars.

The CB&Q – called for short 'the Burlington' or even 'the Q' – laid its rails over the flat wheatlands of the midwest – it is said nowadays to be never out of sight of a grain elevator. This country would have presented few problems in construction were it not for three rivers – the Mississippi, the Ohio and the Missouri – which crossed the Q's path. The bridge at Metropolis, Illinois over the Ohio includes the longest single girder span ever made – 720ft – in a total length of 7700ft. Subsidiary lines – like the famed narrow-gauge Denver, South Park and Pacific (later Colorado & Southern) – were built over less easy terrain.

The GN and the NP had to cross both the Rockies and the Cascades: GN's 7.75-mile Cascade Tunnel is the longest in the US. The 134-mile division in which it lay was electrified on the 25-cycle AC system, from 1912 until 1956 when diesel traction took over. The longest bridge on the system is the Young's Bay bridge at Astoria, Oregon, which is a 8184ft timber trestle of 592 spans. The highest is at Opal City, Oregon, which has a 340ft span arch 320ft high.

Burlington was notable as one of the handful of American railroads that constructed many of its own steam locomotives: excellent, sensible but not specially notable machines – many oilburning – emerged from the West Burlington shops. The railroad has its place forever as, after Germany, the pioneering pathfinder of diesel-electric traction. The first of the famous streamline 'Zephyrs' went into service on 10 January 1934 between Chicago and St Paul-Minneapolis. Others followed including the overnight 'Denver Zephyr' with sleeping accommodation.

The other two partners reacted to the more severe nature of their terrain. When other roads were using 4-4-0s and 4-6-0s, both NP and GN were noted for using 4-8-0s or Mastodons – a type very rare elsewhere in North America, then or since. (One supplied to the GN in 1898 was noted as the heaviest locomotive in the world.) Both lines in the later years of steam had articulated power that was greater than Union Pacific's 'Big Boy' on particular counts. In fact, GN is reckoned to have had the first successful Mallet articulated in the USA, a 2-6-6-2 which came from Baldwins in 1906. In 1936, GN's own Hillyard shops turned out a 2-8-8-2 which had the largest heating surface ever successfully applied to any locomotive boiler. NP in 1938 obtained a 'Yellowstone' 2-8-8-4 from Baldwins which had the largest grate or fire area (182 sq ft) ever known. The reason for this was the local lignite coal used on NP. (It gave the British 4-6-2 *Flying Scotsman* [renowned for being unchoosy about the quality of its diet] severe indigestion and the indignity of diesel assistance when owner Alan Pegler went west – figuratively as well as literally – with it over NP in 1972.)

The same lignite put NP among the honourable handful of lines who have given their

name to a widely used locomotive type. The need for a big firebox meant a four-wheel instead of a two-wheel trailing truck under what would otherwise have been some 4-8-2s supplied by Baldwins in 1926; hence, the 4-8-4 or Northern which later became the standard passenger power on more than thirty US railroads. It was rightly felt that what was good for lignite burning would be even better for high quality coal. Later NP Northerns took the eighteen-car 'North Coast Limited' the first 1008 miles westward from St Paul without engine change, a world record for coal-firing locomotives.

As regards the new megalith, Burlington Northern, the welding of the parts into the whole was made easier by many years of close association, when most GN as well as most NP trains were handed over at St Paul to the Burlington for onward transit to Chicago and vice versa. One measure taken was the installation of Southern Pacific's computer-based railroad management system – called TOPS on SP but named COMPASS on BN. COMPASS was fully cut over in 1972.

As might be expected BN's combination of many a-few-cars-a-day branches in the farm belt with some prodigious transcontinental hauls has not made it terribly prosperous, but it has not yet fallen into a disaster situation either, although expenses of 1740 million dollars are 97 percent of receipts. Consolidation of duplicate lines and the like have permitted a reduction of BN route mileage from 31,725 in 1970 to 24,600 today. Currently, BN's 2500 locomotives annually haul 125 million tons of freight an average distance of 558 miles and, additionally, transport twelve million commuters in 119 passenger cars.

Left: Diesels-in-multiple head a climbing eastbound train towards the summit of Marias Pass on the Burlington Northern Railroad.

Below: A posed photograph of a Baltimore and Ohio train with 'President' class 4-6-2 in the 1930s.

CHESSIE SYSTEM INC
Terminal Tower,
Cleveland, Ohio 44101

Chessie's corporate history goes back to 1785 when the James River Company received its charter. As president of the Company we find no less a figure than George Washington and no railway in the world can claim a more distinguished father-figure than that. Chessie's oldest railway constituent was the fabled Baltimore & Ohio Railroad, incorporated in 1827, opened (with horse traction) in 1830. It thus became the first common-carrier railroad in the USA or, for that matter, on the American continent. Regular steam operation began the following year.

B&O remained in the forefront of progressive railroads – actually taking delivery in 1935 of the first production model diesel-electric locomotive units – until 1973, when financial problems allowed coal-hauler Chesapeake & Ohio to take over the company. B&O reached its declared objective, the Ohio River, in 1852. Other constituents (absorbed later) took trains to St Louis, Chicago and – via running rights over Central of New Jersey – to a passenger terminal on the west bank of the Hudson River opposite New York City.

At Baltimore in 1895, through the 1.5-mile Howard Street tunnel, B&O installed the first main-line electrification in the United States. Low-voltage DC was used; originally the conductors were overhead, but in 1901 the system was changed to third-rail. This was the longest tunnel on the line. The oldest railway viaduct in the world is also claimed: the Thomas Viaduct on the original line out of Baltimore. Other notable bridges include the

$1\frac{1}{4}$-mile bridge over the Susquehanna River at Havre de Grace, Maryland (the longest on the system) and a remarkable lifting bridge of 558ft span, which carries the connection to subsidiary Staten Island Rapid Transit across a stretch of water called Arthur Kill, in the New York area. This is thought to be the largest span of any moveable bridge in the world.

The 'Capitol Limited' was B&O's all-Pullman 'flag train' from Baltimore and Wash-ington to Chicago and in quality of service it rivalled its competitors' 'Broadway Limited' and 'Twentieth Century Limited'. Through cars were provided to and from New York.

Chesapeake & Ohio as a company did not appear until 1868, but *its* earliest railway con-stituent, the Louisa Railroad Company of Virginia, dated back to 1836. Expansion through amalgamation, purchase and new construction took C&O from its main base in the coal-fields of Virginia to the Atlantic Ocean at Newport News, as well as to Chicago, Washington, Detroit, Buffalo and into Canada along the northern shore of Lake Erie. Mil-waukee was served by car-ferry across Lake Michigan. The latest C&O take-overs before Baltimore & Ohio were the Pere Marquette RR (in Michigan) and the Western Maryland. Incidentally, the B&O absorption had been preceded by an 'affiliation' ten years earlier.

The peak of C&O steam power was a world peak in that some amazing 2-6-6-6 steam locomotives built in 1941 recorded the largest power output in service of any steam locomotive ever made. Their wheel arrangement was also unique and, like the rest of the fleet, two great air-pumps mounted on the smokebox front gave a ferocious appearance in keeping with their capabilities.

Inevitably, C&O's Number One train was called 'The George Washington'. It ran from Washington to Cincinnati with through cars serving New York, Chicago, St Louis and Detroit. In 1932 a re-equipment earned it the title of the first fully air-conditioned sleeping-car train in the world. Very little passenger traffic is now handled – there are only 25 passenger cars on the combined Chessie system – but one notes with pleasure that trains for steam lovers are included.

The longest bridge on the 11,190-mile combined system is 2.75 miles long at Richmond, Virginia, and the longest tunnel the 1.75-mile Big Bend tunnel, also in that State. A recorded 220 million tons of traffic each year are hauled an average distance of 250 miles, using a fleet of 2008 diesel locomotives and 205,000 cars. Expenses are currently 93 percent of receipts.

CHICAGO & ILLINOIS MIDLAND RAILWAY
See Other US Railroads

Top left: The Chesapeake & Ohio 'George Washington' express at Romulus, Michigan.

Extreme left: A Baltimore & Ohio M-1 class 2-8-8-4 on the Cranberry Grade, West Virginia, with coal for Terra Alta.

Left: A Chesapeake & Ohio coal train heads up the grade led by a 2-6-6-6 Mallet.

Right top: A Baltimore & Ohio train at Monroe, Michigan.

Right centre: A Chicago, Milwaukee, St Paul & Pacific double-deck push-pull train arrives at Chicago's Union Station.

Right bottom: A Chicago, Milwaukee, St Paul & Pacific road-switcher and local freight at Seattle.

CHICAGO, MILWAUKEE, ST PAUL & PACIFIC RAILROAD COMPANY –
The Milwaukee Road
Union Station,
Chicago, Illinois 60606.

The Chicago, Milwaukee, St Paul & Pacific is another railroad that remains as yet unaffected by the present merger mania.

The first section opened was the Milwaukee & Waukesha RR of 1851 and by 1863 the Milwaukee & St Paul Railway was operating 830 miles of road. It was extended to Chicago in 1873 (the next year saw Chicago added to the Railway's name) and by 1900, 6000 miles of line – tentacles went out as far afield as Kansas City – were operated. It became the anti-penultimate transcontinental when the Pacific was reached in 1909; the present title was adopted in 1913, making three (or four, if you count Union Pacific's sidelong approach) routes from Chicago to the Pacific northwest. Alas, it is now the exception that proves the rule that the big long-distance western railroads are financially viable. Its two main competitors – Great Northern and Northern Pacific – amalgamated in 1960 (see the Burlington Northern entry) and their combined strength has been too much for the Milwaukee RR. Bankruptcy could not be staved off, even by a reduction in expenditure that has involved 33 percent of the line's mileage being subject to slow orders. So many locomotives are laid up awaiting overhaul that others are having to be hired to cover day-to-day demands.

It is sad to see a once successful and inspiring concern in danger of losing its corporate identity. The Milwaukee is best known for two things: it was the only railroad in America where it was possible to make a journey of more than 400 miles entirely by electric traction and the only railroad in the world to run steam trains which needed to reach 100 mph to keep time. Begun in 1914, completed in 1920 and entirely justified by its economics, the electrification covered the mountain sections of the transcontinental route, where it crossed the Bitter Root and Cascade ranges respectively. The former covered the 440-mile section from Harlowtown, Montana, to Avery, Idaho, and the latter, the 207 miles from Othello to Tacoma, Washington. An extention to Seattle came in 1927. A 220-mile gap separated the two electric sections and this was never filled. Of the very powerful electric locomotives used, one might single out for mention the famous 'bi-polars' with 24 driving wheels or the triple-unit 'box cab' freight units of the 2-B-B + B-B + B-B-2 wheel arrangement. The line used 3000v DC current, generated by water power. It was the first of only two major mainline electrifications in the USA. In 1974 the wires were taken down after straight electric traction was abandoned and diesel-electric locomotives ran through over the previously electrified sections.

'Swift of foot was Hiawatha' – certainly the steam-hauled streamlined luxury expresses that were introduced by the Milwaukee Road in 1935 between Chicago, Milwaukee and St Paul-Minneapolis were appropriately named. Specially built oilburning 4-4-2s were used and handled up to nine cars on a 6½ hour timing for the 425 miles, including eight stops. (The best Amtrak time today is 8¾ hours.) The trains were immensely successful and soon enough it was a question of 4-6-4s handling fourteen cars and it is thought that the run of 78.3 miles timetabled at 58 minutes between Sparta and Portage (81 mph) represented the fastest timing with steam power regularly scheduled anywhere in the world at any time. Other 'Hiawatha' trains served other Milwaukee Road destinations, including the 'Olympian Hiawatha', a luxury train from Chicago to Seattle, which was introduced after diesels had taken over from steam on the non-electrified sections.

CHICAGO & NORTH WESTERN TRANSPORTATION COMPANY – C&NW
400 West Madison Street,
Chicago, Illinois 60606.

A constituent of the Chicago & North Western Railway was the first railroad west of Chicago. This was the Galena & Chicago Union RR, on which the first train ran in October 1848. The C&NW was formed in 1859 and hence is one of the oldest surviving names in US railroading. By the turn of the century the system had extended to 8300 miles; currently it is almost 10,000. Unlike so many railways, it serves the exact area specified in its title, reaching Minneapolis, Duluth and connecting with the Union Pacific at Omaha.

For many years, although at least four other railroads provided a reasonable alternative, the C&NW carried the expresses of the Overland Route between Chicago and the interchange with Union Pacific at Omaha. This included the first transcontinental streamliner, 'City of Portland'. It also was well up in the three-way competition for the lucrative daytime passenger business between Chicago and St Paul-Minneapolis, although it is perhaps characteristic of the line that its '400' expresses (400 miles in 400 minutes) were good in a solid conventional way and had little of the flashiness associated

Extreme left: A Chesapeake & Ohio 4-6-2 pulls a local passenger train through Athens, Ohio. Baltimore & Ohio's 'Cincinnatian' takes water alongside.

Left: Milwaukee Road's No E4 is one of the famous 1-B-D+D-B-1 'bi-polar' electric locomotives of the early 1920s.

Below: A Chicago–Milwaukee train climbs through the Rocky Mountain forests during the snowy winter of 1935.

Top right and above: The Milwaukee Road's famous 'Hiawatha'. Pictured top right is the original high-speed train from Chicago to the twin cities of St Paul and Minneapolis, with oil-fired 4-4-2 locomotive in 1935. Above is a 1950 picture of the same train.

Left: An eight-coach elevated railway train crosses the Chicago River on the Lake Street two-tier opening bridge. The tower on the river bank is a lookout position for the bridge controller watching for river traffic.

with the 'Hiawatha' and 'Zephyr' creations of its rivals.

History was made when, in 1965, in an attempt to resolve a situation where no profits could be made from railroad operations, the company made over its railway interests to its employees. The operation of the system has continued in this way ever since.

Current statistics are:

locomotives	950
passenger cars	282
freight cars	34,000
passenger traffic	2.6 million
(in commuter service)	
freight carried	76 million tons
average length of haul	300 miles
expenses as % of receipts	96%

CHICAGO, ROCK ISLAND & PACIFIC RAILROAD COMPANY
See Southwestern US Railroads

Right: Chicago & North Western Railway's double-deck local train in the Chicago area, 1977.

Right below: The post-World War II inauguration of diesel traction on the 'Twin Cities 400' trains of Chicago and North Western Railway.

Right, bottom: The '400' express is a diesel-hauled C&NW train which runs the '400' miles between Chicago and the Twin Cities in '400' minutes.

CHICAGO TRANSIT AUTHORITY
Merchandise Mart Plaza,
Chicago, Illinois 60654.

CHICAGO, SOUTH SHORE & SOUTH BEND RAILROAD
North Carroll Avenue,
Michigan City, Indiana 46360.

The Chicago Transit Authority operates one of the only two 100+ mile (in fact the CTA operates almost 200 miles) city transport railways in the world which are situated other than in a national capital. Unlike other US cities, where the unsightly 'L' or elevated railways have now gone underground, the CTA has still only ten miles of subway. The central loop line down the centre of the streets in downtown Chicago gives its name to the main business district, the Loop, which it surrounds. The system has been fully electrified (all except five miles is equipped on the DC third-rail system) since the turn of the century, after a few no doubt rather traumatic years with Forney-type steam bogie tank locomotives. These were of a design suitable for traversing 90ft radius curves at street junctions. Eleven hundred cars provide service for ninety million passengers carried each year.

What seems to be in process of becoming *de facto* part of the Chicago Transit system is the Chicago, South Shore & South Bend Railroad. This concern operates – at a considerable loss –

the last seventy-mile remnant of the huge 25,000-mile network of electric inter-urban lines that, during the first quarter of the present century, briefly provided local passenger transport in the USA. Currently a fleet of sixty electric cars handles 1.8 million passengers annually at average speeds well over double that of the CTA.

Chicago also had a remarkable underground narrow-gauge (2ft) freight railway system which operated in 62 miles of tunnel under the principal areas of the city: the tunnels were shared with cables and pipes. There were 150 electric locomotives and 3500 freight cars. Many large warehouse, factories and, of course, depots of the main line railroads, were directly served by conveyors and elevators.

CONRAIL – CONSOLIDATED RAIL CORPORATION

Transportation Center, Six Penn Centre Plaza, Philadelphia, Pennsylvania 19104.

There is little doubt that the two greatest names there have ever been in railroading, financially, technically and operationally, were the New York Central and the Pennsylvania. Grand Central Station, New York and the 'Twentieth Century Limited', which left from it, were, respectively, the most famous station and the most famous train in the world. Penn's nickname 'Standard Railroad of the World' was no figure of speech. Even in 1955 it would have been unthinkable to suggest that twenty years later both would have been brought down into single ignominious bankruptcy, subjected to a thinly disguised form of government con-

fiscation and finally swept up into what pessimists regard as a kind of old people's home for the last days of destitute and dying railroads. Optimists say that the conditions under which the Consolidated Rail Corporation will do business are such that there is a reasonable prospect of success, but only time will tell.

The oldest proper section of New York Central (and of Conrail) was the Mohawk and Hudson Railroad between Albany and Schenectady, incorporated in 1826 and opened in 1831. The name New York Central appeared first in 1853 as a consolidation of railroads connecting Albany with Buffalo. The NYC in its final form was created by a further amalgamation of lines in 1914, including the New York Central & Hudson River Railroad and

Above: Forty-four new diesel locomotives were delivered to Conrail (Consolidated Rail Corporation) as a part of a 217-locomotive, 113 million dollar order received in 1978. With completion of this order, Conrail has more than 4500 diesel locomotives in its fleet, nearly 400 of which have been acquired (new) since Conrail began operations on 1 April 1976.

Left: Pennsylvania Railroad's 'Congressonial' express hauled by a GG1 electric locomotive at Eddystone, Pennsylvania.

the Lake Shore & Michigan Southern Railway. The main line of the NYC – much of which was quadruple track until recent years – was the so-called Water Level Route between New York and Chicago; centres such as Montreal, Cincinnati, Columbus, Indianapolis and St Louis were also served. Through running between New York and Chicago was possible from 1866 onwards after completion of a bridge across the Hudson River at Albany.

The first section of what was to become the Pennsylvania Railroad also began operation in 1831, but later in the year. This was the Camden and Amboy Railroad in New Jersey; on 12 November that year, the locomotive *John Bull*, built in England, hauled its first passengers. The 'Pennsy' proper got its charter in

1846 for a line from Philadelphia to Pittsburgh; by 1874 it was a 10,000+ mile system, the largest in the country. The line's Keystone herald very fairly indicated the position it occupied in the economy of the eastern US. It served eight out of the ten largest cities in the USA.

The other lines which have been merged into Conrail had been in trouble longer. The Erie Railroad commenced operations from Pierpont, New York in 1841 and reached Lake Erie at Dunkirk in 1851. It was then the longest railroad in the country with 450 route miles laid to the widest gauge – 6ft – ever used in America. In 1878 conversion to standard gauge took place. There followed a period of wheeling and dealing in its shares which earned the Erie the title 'Scarlet Woman of Wall Street', the effects of which were still noticeable when the 2338-mile road amalgamated with the 968-mile Lackawanna in 1960.

Another lady, dressed in white this time, was Phoebe Snow of the Delaware, Lackawanna & Western Railroad, who made sales talk such as

'Phoebe says and Phoebe knows
   That smoke and cinders ruin clothes
So 'tis a pleasure and delight
   To take that road of anthracite'

to woo passengers to a line that used this clean-burning fuel. The Lackwanna also offered through cars to Chicago from the New Jersey shore; so did Lehigh Valley and Central of New Jersey, although in the last-named case it was just a matter of accommodating the Baltimore & Ohio service. All these lines and the Reading RR as well, served the area between the trunk routes of the New York Central and the Pennsy, providing – until Conrail took them all over – severe competition at any and all intermediate places.

The oldest constituent of the New York, New Haven & Hartford Railroad as well as the oldest of Conrail was the Granite Railway of Boston, built to bring in material for the Boston Bunker Hill monument in 1826. Of course, it was neither steam nor common-carrier. The New Haven was an amalgam of over 200 smaller lines; its trains were accommodated in the Pennsylvania Station in New York and served the New England area. They included the last all-parlour-car train to run in the USA, the 'Merchants Limited', between New York and Boston.

In respect of motive power, it almost suffices to say that New York Central was the owner of high-stepping 4-4-0 No 999, credited (rather dubiously) in 1893 with a world-speed record of 112 mph, while handling the crack 'Empire State Express', predecessor of the 'Twentieth Century Limited'. Right up until steam gave way to diesel, NYC remained in the forefront of locomotive development. Even then it did not give up without a fight, for the 'Niagara' 4-8-4s of 1946 went on and on, putting up figures for performance and overall economics that diesels could only match, not improve upon. Eventually, problems with coal supplies

gave diesel salesmen their chance.

There was a period in the early years of the century when scientific work at its famous Altoona test plant made Pennsy a much acclaimed world leader in steam design. By the 1940s, electrification of the main lines to Washington and Harrisburg had led to steam development taking second place. The picture then was of a fleet of modest-sized locomotives – the legendary K4 4-6-2s were a case in point. As with the diesels which replaced them, when more power was wanted one simply put two (or more) together. After World War II, Pennsy unwisely went away from the simple 'World Standard' concept of steam locomotive and

adopted the more complicated so-called 'Duplex' designs which were, in effect, two engines in the same set of frames. The 'Duplexes' were not successful and again General Motors' salesmen moved in.

Central of New Jersey, Lehigh Valley and Reading were famous for the steam locomotives known as 'camel-backs'. The driver's cab was mounted on top of the boiler half-way along; the fireman, of course, had to work in another cab in the conventional position, but the idea was to give better visibility in either direction. The identical principle has given rise to the 'hood-unit' layout of most modern diesels.

CNJ and LV were the only constituents of

Conrail not to have some electrification. The Pennsylvania had by far the largest installation (670 miles at 11,000v AC, 25 cycles) still surviving in America, but much of this is now in Amtrak's hands as owners of the Boston–New York–Washington passenger corridor. Dieselization of all non-electric Conrail operations has, of course, been complete for many years; at present there are nearly 5000 units in service, the largest fleet in North America.

As regards passenger services, the erstwhile 'Twentieth Century Limited' still remains the standard by which other trains are judged, while Pennsy's 'Broadway Limited', still surviving in Amtrak hands, was as good. Conrail

still carries 112 million commuter passengers, annually using 893 cars, on services provided under contract to various state and local government authorities. Grand Central Station, New York, where a great deal of this traffic is handled, is the largest station in the world, with 44 platforms on a 48-acre site.

Conrail ranks first among US railroads on most other counts, including the amount of annual deficit, $626,133 in 1977. There are 145,000 freight cars, in which 269 million tons of freight are carried annually an average distance of 344 miles. Expenses are 120 percent of receipts. In 1979, 16,826 miles of track were controlled by Conrail.

Above: New York Central's New York to Chicago Train of Trains – the 'Twentieth Century Limited' at the peak of its luxury in 1938.

Left: Four GE diesel electric locomotives head a massive Erie Railroad freight train.

Extreme left, top: Conrail's famous Horseshoe Curve on the busy mainline west of Altoona, in central Pennsylvania's Allegheny Mountains.

Extreme left, centre: In the early 1950s even the coal-carrying Erie RR had gone diesel as shown by this posed picture of its then-most-modern three-unit locomotive.

Extreme left, bottom: The 'Empire State Express' near Albany on the New York Central main line.

Top centre: American railroads generally made little use of water troughs between the rails. However, New York Central's No 3130 makes a brave show at the head of a fast freight in July 1945.

Top right: New York, New Haven & Hartford Railroad's streamlined 4-6-4 No 1409 with standard heavyweight cars near Branford, Connecticut in 1938.

CUMBRES & TOLTEC SCENIC RAILROAD – CATS
PO Box 789, Chama,
New Mexico 87520.

If one takes a view of railways as an art form, then one of the greatest masterpieces among recent survivors was the 200-mile narrow-gauge main line of the Denver & Rio Grande Western RR between Alamosa and Durango on the border between New Mexico and Colorado. It was definitely a railroad on which, when trouble comes, one would expect John Wayne to ride up to the rescue. Indeed he and his successors have done just that on many occasions when films were made using its evocative rolling stock and superb scenery. Such features as steam power driven wide open on four percent grades, rotary steam snow ploughs and whistles which scare the eagles off their nests for miles around, combined to make it something very special.

Carried away by the enthusiasm of the *aficionados*, the States of Colorado and New Mexico were inveigled into buying the 64-mile stretch between Antonito, Colorado and Chama, New Mexico including twelve 2-8-2 steam locomotives and a hundred or so cars. They thus obtained for themselves the dubious privilege of owning the longest museum railway in the world. Regular summer operation is supplemented by an occasional winter happening when the operable steam rotary plough puts on a show unparalleled in the steam-for-pleasure world.

DELAWARE & HUDSON RAILWAY D&H
D&H Building,
Albany, New York 12207.

The first US railroad to employ steam locomotives finds itself 150 years later with the same title – only having dropped the word 'canal' – but with a quite different transportation role. It is now a 'bridge route' connecting eastern Canada with the eastern USA rather than a local canal feeder and mine-run line. By managing to keep its identity although not its independence, D&H has illustrated that bridge routes are more viable propositions than many other types of railroads. (D&H is owned by, but has not merged with, conglomerate Norfolk and Western.)

D&H steam locomotive history is full of distinction. It was made notable for steam locomotives with smooth, almost English outlines, but of American dimensions, from 2-8-0s to 4-8-4s and 2-8-8-2s. Pipework and accessories were mounted chastely out of sight.

It was also notable for a sustained and technically successful effort to improve thermal efficiency by increasing the temperature and pressure of the steam. *Horatio Allen* was the appropriate name for the first 1924 attempt, which was a 2-8-0 with a special boiler permitting 350 lb/sq in pressure. There are great difficulties in designing locomotive boilers of normal pattern for pressures higher than 300 lb, but this one had a water-tube firebox of un-

orthodox type which could resist this modest increase of pressure. Three subsequent experiments in 1927, 1932 and 1935 respectively enabled D&H, who so sensibly decided to learn to walk before they could run, to take the steps up to a triple-expansion 600 lb/sq in 4-8-0 with tender booster. This was the only technically successful application of the triple-expansion principle (standard in marine practice) to a single-chassis locomotive. Alas this technical *tour de force* did not stand up to examination of its overall economics.

At present eleven million tons of traffic are carried annually an average distance of 340 miles, using a diesel locomotive fleet of 175 units and 6000 freight cars. About 1650 miles of railroad are operated for freight, but no passenger service is given.

Above: Two Delaware & Hudson Railway Baldwin diesels make fuel stops at Whitehall, NY in December 1950.

Top: A British-looking 4-8-4 of the Delaware & Hudson Railway in 1950.

Top right: Denver & Rio Grande Western Railroad runs this Durango to Silverton steam narrow-gauge tourist train, seen here in Lost Souls canyon.

Right bottom: Rio Grande freights head up the Wasatch Mountains out of Helper, Utah. The coal cars in the foreground are symbolic of the Carbon County coal fields of northern Utah which generate considerable railroad traffic.

DENVER & RIO GRANDE WESTERN RAILROAD – Rio Grande

*No 1 Park Central, 1515 Arapahoe St,
Denver, Colorado 80217.*

To anyone who is ignorant of the topography and history of Colorado the 500-mile bridge route connecting Denver to Salt Lake City would seem unremarkable. Yet this outwardly rather conventional line is the result of one of the most exciting and romantic stories in the history of railroading – the truth being a good deal more spectacular than the plots of countless Western films which have located their train scenes on its metals. (An oft-used stage setting is the Canyon of the Lost Souls where one can look down a vertical rock face to the river 300ft below.)

In 1872 General William Jackson Palmer sent his construction crews south from Denver with the intention of reaching El Paso, Texas via the Rio Grande Valley. However, the Santa Fe people got rails down first on the Raton Pass, the only practical route. Undaunted, Palmer then turned west and after a pitched battle with the rival road's gangs, won and held the Royal Gorge of the Arkansas for his railroad. The terrain to be served was as mountainous as any in the US and, moreover, was in the throes of a silver-mining boom. The economics of laying the rails close together seemed attractive and, accordingly, the narrow gauge of 3ft was chosen. The Rio Grande was the only *major* railroad in the USA to be laid in the narrow gauge.

By 1888 the Denver & Rio Grande and its companion the Denver and Rio Grande Western had covered Colorado, Utah and much of New Mexico with a network of 1670 miles of slim gauge lines reaching all the mining areas and extending as far west as Salt Lake City, Utah and south to Santa Fe, New Mexico. The devaluation of silver in 1892 led to bankruptcy and re-incorporation (the first of several) and the end of expansion. There was also complex financial juggling between the two companion roads before consolidation in 1908. The limited speed possible on the narrow gauge was a severe handicap to a long-distance carrier and, accordingly, the conversion of the main line

from Denver to Salt Lake City had been completed in 1890.

General Palmer's second thoughts on destination for his railroad had made its route a circuitous one. Some rerouting was done in connection with the regauging – to avoid the Marshall Pass with its four percent grades as well as the vulnerable trackage in the Black Canyon of the Gunnison River – but in 1934 a new line in the mountains, including the six-mile Moffatt Tunnel, gave the Rio Grande a direct route west from Denver, saving 175 miles on the journey to Salt lake City.

The same period saw the beginning of the end for the narrow gauge, although freight movement on the last section – the 250 miles from Alamosa to Farmington via Durango did not finally cease until 1967. This was the last 'normal' narrow gauge as well as the last steam freight common carrier operation in the USA. Passengers are, however, still carried (for pleasure) the 45 spectacular miles up the Lost Souls Canyon and back by steam. The 'Silverton Train' as it is called, is based in Durango and runs daily in summer; it has the highest earnings per mile of any passenger train in the US, has the status of a National Monument and is mentioned in many guide books alongside the Grand Canyon and Niagara Falls.

Book well ahead.

All the devices of the railway engineer were used to overcome the problems of the terrain at minimum cost. The narrow gauge permitted curves as sharp as 24° (243ft radius) while four percent (1 in 25) grades were normal and $4\frac{1}{2}$ percent ones existed. Zig-zag reverses, spirals and long return loops were used to gain altitude and many were the places where the trains crept along high up the walls of canyons on narrow ledges or teetered over high trestle bridges. Steam locomotive power also reflected the terrain. Air brakes were fitted long before they became compulsory, for example. In the early days, very few locomotives had less than eight coupled wheels because of the gradients and, later very few had more because of the curvature. A series of 2-8-0 'mountain ponies' supplied in their hundred became as much a classic for the narrow gauge as the American standard 4-4-0 was on standard gauge. Notable also in the early period were conversions of locomotives from narrow gauge to standard and, in the 1920s, the reverse operation. The latter produced some 2-8-2s that were very large for the narrow gauge; a weight of 27 tons, grate area 45 sq ft and 37,350 lb tractive effort was exceptional for 3ft between the rails. The later and bigger standard-gauge steam loco-

Extreme left: Rio Grande freight in Glenwood Canyon on the Colorado River.

Left: A Rio Grande 'rattler' (hobo slang for freight train) heads out of Salt Lake Valley, Utah.

Below: The only section of the Rio Grande's once great network of 3ft 0in gauge track still to operate under its banner is the 45-mile Silverton branch out of Durango. Here one of the branch's Sports Models, 2-8-2 No 473 runs, decked out in fancy dress for a movie, alongside the Animas River.

Above: The other section of Rio Grande's narrow gauge still running is the now state-owned Cumbres & Toltec RR – a section of the one-time Alamoso-Durango main line over the Cumbres Pass. Never an easy line to work because of the steep gradients, it is today a spectacular tourist attraction during the summer season.

motives had additional linkage added to their Walschearts valve gear to give variable lead – very much akin to advancing and retarding the ignition on a motor car – as an aid to slogging up long mountain grades.

Standard-gauge steam came to an end in 1952 – the natural affinity of diesel locomotive characteristics to steep gradients has meant little in the way of specialities among the road's fleet of 260 modern diesel units.

When Amtrak was formed in 1970, the Rio Grande was one of the very few roads which opted out and it still runs its own 'Rio Grande Zephyr' three days a week on the spectacular run from Denver to Salt Lake City. This train is in fact a vestigial remnant of the remarkable 'California Zephyr' which, although now defunct, brought new thinking to passenger operation (see Western Pacific). A fleet of 40 passenger cars protects the 'Zephyr' and 'Silverton' trains.

In respect of freight operation Rio Grande has tended towards short, fast and frequent trains rather than the immense drags typical of most US operations. Currently the Rio Grande handles 310,000 passengers and 30 million tons of freight annually, hauling the latter an average of 307 miles. Annual expenses are 92 percent of receipts.

DETROIT & MACKINAC RAILWAY
See Other US Railroads

DETROIT, TOLEDO & IRONTON RAILROAD
One Parklane Boulevard,
Dearborn, Michigan 48126.

The Detroit, Toledo & Ironton Railroad was formed in the early years of the century from a collection of short lines in the neighbourhood of Detroit. In 1920, when it had become badly run down and was in dire financial straits, it was bought by car magnate, Henry Ford. (For some time he had been in the habit of going into print with articles such as 'If I Ran The Railroads'.) Strangely enough and unlike other amateur railwaymen, he was quite successful; in spite of a huge expenditure on reconstruction, the line became profitable. Moreover, Ford electrified part of the line on the high-voltage AC system, but used locomotives which converted it to direct current for traction. In fact he did what the rest of the world (except Hungary) did not do until forty years later. A feature of the electrification was the use of reinforced concrete arched portals to hold up the overhead wires – some are still there today.

In the late 1920s Ford lost interest in playing

trains (it is said that he became fed up with the bureaucratic problems of running a public railway) and sold the DT&I, abandoning the electrification. The 480-mile railroad is still, however, in independent existence, carrying 13 million tons of traffic annually with a fleet of seventy diesel units and 4300 freight cars. Expenses are eighty percent of receipts. One feature is that its maximum permitted axle-load is as high as 38 tons.

DULUTH, MISSABE & IRON RANGE RAILWAY
See Other US Railroads

EDAVILLE RAILROAD
Box 7,
South Carver, Massachusetts 02566.

The present cult of preserving old-time steam railways is considered to have begun on 7 April 1947. On that day a little train, recovered and restored from abandoned 2ft-gauge railroads in the State of Maine, began a five-mile circuit of line which farmer Ellis D Attwood (hence the name EDAville) had laid down on his cranberry farm. Thirty years later, it is a major tourist attraction in an area which includes Cape Cod and Plymouth Rock.

ELGIN, JOLIET & EASTERN RAILWAY
See Other US Railroads

Above: Today steam has vanished from the regular American railroad scene and narrow-gauge tracks too are virtually extinct. Steam can, however, be seen on many preserved or tourist lines, the pioneer of which is the Edaville Railroad at South Carver, Massachusetts. This 2ft 0in gauge line is one of New England's premier tourist attractions and this Baldwin 2-4-4T from the Bridgton & Harrison Railroad is a wonderful working museum-piece.

Bottom right: The 'Panama Limited' begins its 920-mile journey from Chicago to New Orleans circa 1960. This all-Pullman train was the Illinois Central Railroad's finest train.

Below: Florida East Coast Railway's General Motors diesel for the 'Florida Special'.

FLORIDA EAST COAST RAILWAY – FEC
St Augustine, Florida.

The story of the Florida East Coast Railway has all the qualities – and most of the ingredients – of a fairy tale. There is even a happy ending.

In 1883 a middle-aged oil millionaire called Henry Flagler, spent a holiday at a then-new beauty spot in Florida called St Augustine. To get there he had to cross the St Johns River by boat and trundle down the peninsula on a ramshackle narrow-gauge line called the Jacksonville, St Augustine & Halifax Railroad. Some might have shrugged off the inconvenience but not Flagler – he bought the railroad, bridged the river and, so that he could in future go all the way in his own train, brought the line up to main-line standard. He enjoyed railroad building so much that, with no prospect of financial return in what was then a wilderness, he extended the line right to the tip of the peninsula. An unknown place called Palm Beach was reached in 1894, another one called Miami in 1896. Even this did not satisfy his craving to play trains and, incredible to record, he took his line a further 57 miles, island-hopping across the sea to the very last fragment of Florida, an island called Key West. Of all the follies perpetrated in the history of railways, the Florida East Coast's extension to Key West, with its 17 miles of bridging across open water stands alone. The only traffic objective was a modest speeding up of the journey by train and boat to Cuba, for which an expenditure of $20 million of the dollars of those days was hardly justified. Flagler was just able to enjoy the opening ceremony a few months before he died, aged 85, in 1912.

Although dividends were never paid, the FEC pursued a fairly lordly existence for a decade or so, until it was hit by the amazing Florida boom of the mid-1920s. Traffic multiplied several times over in three years and the railroad responded with a colossal re-equipment programme. Just as the up-dating was completed and needed to be paid for, came the 1929 crash. Inevitably, bankruptcy ensued; worse was to follow, for in 1935 the Key West extension was destroyed in a hurricane (it was later reconstructed as a highway).

Even though the road was bankrupt, trains such as the 'Florida Special' continued to run. This was an all-Pullman train from New York, the first train in America to be lit by electric light and to have enclosed vestibule connections between the cars. George M Pullman conducted the first run in person. During the 1930s' winters, in spite of the economic situation the train frequently ran in multiple; as many as seven parts were noted in one day in 1937. It shared with the 'Twentieth Century Limited' alone the *cachet* of regular red-carpet treatment – this at the Miami end.

The 'Florida Special' had just celebrated its 75th anniversary when the railroad brotherhoods declared a strike over a wage issue. Eleven days later – on 3 February 1962 – the little FEC, showing considerable courage, began running trains again, using supervisory staff in operating positions. Extreme measures, from the dynamiting of trains to political pressure from the White House, were used to force FEC to settle on the unions' terms; in the end, the FEC management won back its 'prerogative to operate the railroad', as they put it.

The position now is that, alone among the common-carrier railroads of the USA, the FEC does not have to abide by the steam-age work rules, those featherbeds of operations elsewhere. Before 1962, for example, there had to be five men on each FEC train and, because each crew could only work over one short designated division, three crews were needed for the run from Jacksonville to Miami. Now one two-man crew does the journey without change. Both ride on the locomotive; the caboose at the rear is eliminated having been replaced by a radio transmitting box fixed to the rear coupler, as a check that the train is complete and the brakes working. There were many other similar changes; in effect, one-half the employees now handle twice the workload of traffic. At present this amounts to nine million tons hauled an average distance of 210 miles, using a 1300-strong car fleet hauled by 59 diesel locomotive units.

The financial gains enabled a thorough rehabilitation of the physical plant to be put in hand. FEC's track, now welded rail on concrete sleepers, laid on a mountain of sharp stone ballast, comes closer to being truly a permanent track than most others. There were also funds to install the latest electronic systems of trackside safety surveillance.

The financial improvement (expenses have averaged sixty percent of receipts in recent years) of the 535-mile system has given employees job security, and the physical improvements have given them personal security and safety while on the job. The tragedy – for railroad employees as well as shareholders and the nation at large – is that the unofficial role of railroads elsewhere in the USA as sources of unemployment pay, precludes an FEC-type solution being applied nationally.

FRISCO
See Southwestern US Railroads

GEORGIA & FLORIDA RAILROAD
See Other US Railroads

GREEN BAY & WESTERN RAILROAD
See Other US Railroads

HAWAII
See Australasia, Oceania

ILLINOIS CENTRAL GULF RAILROAD
*233 North Michigan Avenue,
Chicago, Illinois 60601.*

When the Illinois Central Railroad received its charter on 10 February 1851, it was the longest railroad which had been promoted up till then. It was also the first of many to receive a grant of lands as a subsidy on completion, in this case within seven years. In September 1856 the 705-mile line, which ran southwards from Chicago to the confluence of the Mississippi and Ohio Rivers at Cairo, was opened, thereby earning the land grant of 2,500,000 acres. Such non-railroad acquisitions have stood the company in good stead ever since and never more so than today, when railway operations are barely profitable.

Southwards from Cairo, freight and passengers could travel on by the famous Mississippi river steamers – such as the fabled *Robert E Lee* – to Memphis and New Orleans. Soon afterwards, the river part of the journey was confined to a ferry trip across the river and even this came to an end when the great four-mile bridge across the Mississippi at Cairo was inaugurated in 1889. Eight years before, 550 miles of the main line south of this point had been converted from 5ft gauge to 4ft 8½in in a single day, as preparation for through running.

While it was expanding, IC absorbed over one hundred smaller railroads, reaching out to Kansas City and Omaha to the west and Indianopolis and Louisville to the east. One of those absorbed was the first railroad in the southern states, the 26-mile West Feliciana RR, on the border between Mississippi and Louisiana, which was completed in 1842.

In 1972 IC merged with Gulf, Mobile & Ohio, which since 1947 (when the Chicago & Alton was acquired), had also provided through service from Chicago to places on the Gulf of Mexico. Thus Illinois Central became the Illinois Central Gulf, a 9250-mile railroad, having 1060 diesel units, 47,000 freight cars and hauling 95 million tons an average distance of 315 miles each year.

IC's 'Panama Limited' from Chicago to New Orleans was one of two last all-Pullman luxury trains in the USA to run – it still operates less exclusively under Amtrak's banner. Such luxuries as the 'King's Dinner' of five courses were available to the end of IC working. Even today, IC is not out of the passenger business, since there is an electrified commuter service out of Chicago. Fourteen million passengers are carried annually, using a fleet of 162 cars.

IC's steam operations are rather overshadowed by the immortal song and tale of Casey Jones, 'Who mounted to the cabin with his orders in his hand, On his farewell trip to the promised land' . . . because of course, J L Jones was an actual Illinois Central engineer, who came to grief after a particularly flagrant disregard for regulations. His 4-6-0 was very

typical of its day and this remark perhaps can be applied to virtually all IC motive power. It was a little unusual in that the few new locomotives built in the latter years of steam were homemade in the line's own Paducah shops; furthermore, rather than purchase new power during the lean years of the 1930s, these new shops undertook the major surgery involved in such operations as rebuilding old 2-8-2s into 2-10-2s.

ILLINOIS TERMINAL RAILROAD
See Other US Railroads

KANSAS CITY SOUTHERN RAILWAY COMPANY – KCS
See Southwestern US Railroads

KATY
See Southwestern US Railroads

LONG ISLAND RAIL ROAD
Jamaica Station,
Jamaica, New York 11435.

The Long Island Railroad received its charter in 1834 and is therefore among that select fraction of the world's railways who have carried on under one name since the 1830s. It is definitely not, however, among the four or five in the world who have remained in the same

ownership. In its early days the LIRR was the main line to Boston; travellers went from Brooklyn terminus to Greenport, thence by ferry across Long Island Sound and then took the Old Colony Line. An all land route was opened in 1850 and the LIRR then settled down to a peaceful country branch-line existence for half a century. In 1900 it was purchased by the Pennsylvania Railroad and started a new phase of existence as a New York commuter line. Electrification (third rail DC) was begun in 1904 and in 1910 LI trains began using the then-new Pennsylvania Station.

Political interference in the form of a thirty-year fare freeze, from 1918 to 1948, led to bankruptcy in 1949 in spite of financial aid from Pennsy. Eventually the line, by then a byword for all that was disreputable in the industry, was bought in 1964 by the New York State Metropolitan Transit Authority. Modernization and renewal was then put in hand, but political pressure to speed the work led to a hurried design. Following some tedious modification, the new trains, consisting of 620 cars and capable of 100 mph began running and in the end greatly improved the service. Currently some 250,000 'daily bread' riders are carried into and out of New York each working day. Some freight is also handled.

Extreme left: The 'City of Miami' makes its way out of snowy downtown Chicago heading for Miami circa 1960. The clock tower in the centre of the picture marks the company's Central Station; the sidings behind the train comprise the Weldon coach yard.

Left: The power of the seventies is revealed by this Illinois Central Gulf locomotive.

Left below: Maine Central Railway locomotives are serviced at the company roundhouse yard after arriving at Bangor from Boston with a heavy freight in August 1978.

line climbs the mountain at a maximum inclination of one in $2\frac{2}{3}$.

NATIONAL RAIL PASSENGER CORPORATION
See Amtrak

NEVADA NORTHERN RAILROAD
See Other US Railroads

NEW YORK CITY TRANSIT AUTHORITY – NYCTA
370 Jay Street,
Brooklyn 1, New York.

With 137 miles of route in tunnel, the New York City Transit Authority is by far the largest underground railway system in the world. It began as a famous elevated railway back in the 1870s using steam traction, but from 1904 on, the 'L' has been gradually replaced by an underground system; the only

MAINE CENTRAL RAILROAD COMPANY
242 St John Street,
Portland, Maine 04102.

Once upon a time the little Maine Central ran all-Pullman trains whose passenger lists rivalled the 'Twentieth Century Limited' in including the best-known names in America. All summer the 'Bar Harbor Express' and other trains rolled east to the Atlantic coast via Portland from Boston, New York and Washington. Another unexpected extravagance in the history of what is now a small down-to-earth freight-only road was the ownership – unique among Class I railroads – of a large 2ft gauge system. This was the fabled Sandy River & Rangely Lakes Railroad, relics of which survive at Edaville including a tiny parlour car.

It is said that Maine has two seasons, July and winter; no doubt the advantage which flanged wheels and steel rails possess over unploughed roads and slippery snow are one reason for the MEC's independent survival.

The line currently operates 900 miles of route with 65 locomotives (all diesel) and 4000 freight cars. Eight million tons of freight are hauled by the Maine Central Railroad an average distance of 110 miles. Expenses are ninety percent of receipts.

MILWAUKEE ROAD
See Chicago, Milwaukee, St Paul & Pacific

MISSOURI – KANSAS – TEXAS RAILROAD COMPANY
See Southwestern US Railroads

MISSOURI PACIFIC RAILROAD COMPANY
See Southwestern US Railroads

MONONGAHELA RAILWAY
See Other US Railroads

MoPAC
See Southwestern US Railroads

MOUNT WASHINGTON COG RAILWAY
See also Norfolk & Western Railway Company
Mount Washington,
New York.

The very first cog railway in the world was built up New Hampshire's 6290ft Mount Washington and opened in 1869. It still runs, using eight steam locomotives of the same original 1875 design, plus one repeat order delivered in 1975, thereby having both the oldest and the newest standard-gauge steam locomotives running in the USA. The 3.5-mile

Constructed in 1869 the Mount Washington Cog Railway is the world's oldest cog railway. Today the railway is still a great tourist attraction and its ancient engines battle their way to the cloudy summit crewed during peak periods by students on vacation.

elevated sections now left are a few in outlying areas as extensions of the subways. Electrification (third rail DC) took over from around the turn of the century. Many of the thirty routes have parallel fast and slow lines, the fast trains only serving the principal stops. There are 6800 cars which carry over one thousand million passengers each year.

NEW YORK, ONTARIO & WESTERN RAILROAD – NY&OW

The 546-mile New York, Ontario & Western Railroad had the dubious honour of being the largest railroad to have been completely abandoned. At one time its 'Mountaineer Express', complete with steam locomotive styled by the famous Otto Kuhler traversed the 334-mile main line from Weehawken (across the Hudson River from New York) to Oswego (across the lake from Ontario). Early dieselization made no difference to its fundamental weaknesses – the 'Old Woman' being just one

Top: A three-unit Bo-Bo diesel-hauled Maine Central Railroad freight train passes the Penobscot River as it approaches Bangor, Maine.

Above: A New York, Ontario & Western Railroad diesel-hauled freight train in the days before abandonment.

Above: New York's Third Avenue EL prior to electrification. This was, in fact, the last elevated railway to run in Manhattan proper. It closed as recently as 1950. The drawing of the locomotive (a Forney type 0-4-4T) is not totally accurate; its date is January 1879.

Below: Being a coal carrier, the N & W was one of the last of the big American roads to use steam. A streamline 4-8-4 makes light weight of her train along the New River of Virginia at the end of 1950.

of too many railroads in the area – and operations were discontinued in 1956.

NORFOLK SOUTHERN RAILWAY
See Other US Railroads

NORFOLK & WESTERN RAILWAY
Roanoke, Virginia 24042.

The Norfolk & Western Railway is another 1830s line – its first constituent, the City Point Rail Road out of Petersburg, Virginia, opened on 7 September 1838. In the 1850s came the Norfolk & Petersburg Railway, the South Side RR from Petersburg to Lynchburg, the Virginia & Tennessee RR from Lynchburg on to Bristol and so on. In 1870 there was a consolidation under the wide-ranging name of the Atlantic, Mississippi and Ohio Railroad. In 1881 the concern was re-organized under the humbler title of the Norfolk & Western Railroad; in 1896 a further re-organization made it the N & W *Railway*.

The Ohio River was, in fact, reached at Kenova and Cincinnati and the line went on to Columbus beyond. But the main source of traffic for the next seventy years was to result from the immense coal output of the West Virginian coal fields, either to tidewater at Norfolk or direct to industry. During the whole of this time the company remained among the world's most prosperous railroads; this was not surprising, because its traffic of minerals in bulk was the kind that railways handle best. But first-class management and high standards in all things also contributed.

It was against this background that during the 1940s and 1950s, the N&W management wrote the last and final – as well as one of the greatest – chapters of the story of the steam locomotive in the USA. The superbly built and superbly run Norfolk and Western steam fleet held out alone against the diesel locomotive for a full decade, entirely on its merits as the most economic way of fulfilling the road's demands for haulage.

First, N&W built its locomotives to its own specifications in its own shops. Second, it provided maintenance and servicing forces with the tools for the job; an almost hospital-like atmosphere prevailed in the lubritoriums and repair shops. Such convenient and well-equipped facilities were almost unknown elsewhere in the steam world. Third, being quite open-minded about diesel traction, on several occasions demonstration units from General Motors and others were tried and found efficient, but for a long time they never quite succeeded in making a case for displacing steam.

N&W had some lovely steam locomotives. In charge of the coal drags and mainstay of the fleet were 105 2-8-8-2 compound articulated Mallets, the newest (class Y6b) dating from 1952 and the last big steam built in America. For their hot-shot freights there were some fine 2-6-6-2 articulateds (the 'A' class) and protecting the 'Pocahontas Express' on its runs between Norfolk and Cincinnati were a handful of magnificent 'J' class 4-8-4s. Even the switch-

Above: Along with other major US railroads, the Norfolk & Western constructed its own electronically controlled classification yards. Pictured above are the facilities at Bellevue, Ohio in 1967.

Top left: Because of the huge freight hauls, large and powerful locomotives were very necessary on the N & W roster. Mallets such as this continued to run until the end of steam in 1960.

Top centre: Norfolk & Western's short length of electrification was not able to match the economy and efficiency of the Road's magnificent steam locomotives.

Extreme right, both: Today, with steam gone and the availability of multiple unit power, Norfolk & Western's trains reach undreamed-of length. Four or even five diesel locomotives coupled together and worked by one crew not only present a great and powerful traction force but a considerable saving in labour as well.

ers were modern; in fact, little 0-8-0 No 244 was the last locomotive built by N&W and the last new steam engine for any US main-line railroad, when it was put into service in 1953.

The indices of performance of these modern units of motive power (such as like ton-miles per locomotive-hour) continued to be diesels or no diesels, well in the forefront nationwide on this highly profitable road. N&W locomotive depots could service a Mallet in under an hour: that is, a complete lubrication job, empty the ashpan and smokebox, refill the tender with twenty tons of coal and 15,000 gallons of water. So often brand new diesels, serviced in brand new depots, were compared with run-down steam power maintained in appalling conditions, but on the N&W they had for once to compete on even terms; the results showed that steam could still stay in the game. In the end, however, the problems of being the only major continuing steam user began to tell. Suppliers of components one by one went out of business, shareholders began to criticize and the price of coal rose – temporarily as it turned out – compared with oil. In 1960 these factors in combination justified the replacement of steam. The deed was done quickly and cleanly; the last fire was dropped when a Y6b 2-6-6-2 came in from a mine run on 4 April. So ended an epoch.

An epoch ended in another way too. Norfolk & Western decided to become a big railroad as well as a great one. The rival Virginian RR was absorbed in 1959 and in 1964 the New York Chicago and St Louis (better known as the 'Nickel Plate'), the Wabash and the Pittsburg & West Virginia came into the fold. The metamorphosis is best explained using the table below.

Historic Delaware & Hudson was acquired, but remained separately operated. All this expansion took N&W to such places as Chicago, St Louis, Detroit and even Montreal, but whether such a stake in the problem areas of a problem industry is one which the management is wholly glad to have taken is a question better left unanswered.

Of the absorbed constituents, the Virginian RR was remarkable for having both the strongest (that is, with the highest tractive effort) steam and the strongest electric locomotives ever successfully used. The compound 2-10-10-2s were rated at 176,000 lb, when working, simple at starting, and the maximum tractive effort of the 1-B-B-1+1-B-B-1+ 1-B-B-1 electrics was 277,500 lb. Electric traction was in operation on one heavily worked and heavily graded 134-mile division, the low-frequency high-voltage AC system being used.

The Wabash Railroad also dates from 1838, for it was on 8 November that year that the Northern Cross RR ran its first train from Meredosia to Springfield, Illinois. The Wabash's lines have brought the N&W flag – the Wabash actually used a flag as its emblem – to fly in Kansas City and Omaha. Incidentally, the Wabash was at one time to have been the central section of the coast-to-coast railroad planned by railway baron Jay Gould.

OTHER US RAILROADS

In spite of the current merger fever, there are still well above 500 medium and small independent un-merged railroads in the US. Nineteen, which lie in the 100-500-mile range (and, hence, elegible to receive individual mention here) are listed opposite.

Growth of Norfolk & Western	1955	1975
Length, miles	2100	7600
Locomotives	425 (steam)	1600 (diesel)
Passenger cars	360	23
Freight cars	56,000	97,000
Passenger traffic	482,000	—
Freight traffic, tons	70 million	95 million
Length of haul, miles	283	316
Expenses as % of receipts	66%	72%

This list of names – like the hundreds of others not mentioned individually – conceals individual roles at extreme ends of the railroad spectrum. They include several which are Class I railroads – that is, with annual revenues greater than $50 million. One of these, the Duluth, Missabe & Iron Range, is an iron-ore carrier, whose 2-8-8-4s once worked the heaviest steam trains ever run. These locomotives were also the heaviest ever built; weighing, with tender, 508 tons, over five tons more than the famous 'Big Boys' of Union Pacific.

Another notable 'little' railroad is the Richmond Fredericksburg & Potomac, which once rolled nightly strings of the plushest limiteds in the land over its short 100-mile link, on their way from New York and Washington to Florida. It still does reasonably well with fast freights and the occasional Amtrak passenger train.

Lucky RF&P not to be concerned with the loss-making business of collecting and delivering cars in penny numbers; yet it is possible to scrape a living at this thankless chore. The Illinois Terminal does a great deal of it, while Elgin, Joliet & Eastern does a general distri-

Other US Railroads	Route mileage	Number of locomotives	Number of freight cars	Annual freight tonnage in millions	Notes & location
Akron, Canton & Youngstown RR	171	18	1700	3.4	Ohio
Ann Arbor RR	299	17	390	4.8	Taken over by the state of Michigan
Atlanta & West Point RR	225	24	1350	6.1	Georgia
Bangor & Aroostook RR	500	45	4800	4.1	Maine
Bessemer & Lake Erie RR	221	66	8600	28.6	Albion, Pennsylvania
Chicago & Illinois Midland Rly	121	21	800	9.0	Springfield, Illinois
Detroit & Mackinac Rly.	232	8	980	2.1	Tawas City, Michigan
Duluth, Missabe & Iron Range Rly	462	98	9740	27.5	Minnesota
Elgin, Joliet & Eastern Rly	205	106	10400	26.5	Chicago area
Georgia & Honda RR	321	13	500	2.5	Augusta, Georgia
Green Bay & Western RR	255	17	1400	—	Wisconsin
Illinois Terminal RR	387	32	2500	6.4	St. Louis, Missouri
Monongahela Rly	171	18	—	6.7	Brownsville, Pennsylvania
Nevada Northern RR	162	3	23	0.4	Eastely, Nevada
Norfolk Southern Rly	492	37	2350	5.1	Raleigh, North Carolina
Piedmont & Northern Rly	150	18	16		Charlotte, North Carolina
Richmond, Fredericksburg & Potomac RR	113	41	1650	9.6	Richmond, Virginia
Sacramento Northern Rly	349	13	230	0.9	California
Spokane International RR	150	10	81	2.5	Washington State

bution job between the many roads leading into and out of Chicago, with which it connects. The latter owns one locomotive for every two miles of route, reflecting the busy nature of its operations.

At the other end of the spectrum, and owning one locomotive for about fifty miles of route, is miles-away-from-anywhere Nevada Northern, whose survival is very hard to credit, unless one has seen it with one's own eyes.

Of the hundreds of smaller fry, three groups are on the increase. First, big organizations find it hard to learn the 'baling wire and string' techniques necessary to keep a short line running. Accordingly, local people have been taking over local branches from the big companies and operating them themselves as independent short lines.

Second, the railroad industry as a whole offers such a bad return on investment that new capital is hard to raise; hence, a preference for leasing rather than buying new freight cars. Although any finance company can buy and lease cars, another railroad can lend freight cars to other railroads under rather better terms and conditions. The terms, known (in American Railroad Latin) as the *per diem* payments, are levied on all cars which are situated on one railroad while owned by another. It follows that car leasing companies have been often doing business under the flag of a moribund (and thus cheaply acquired) short line.

Third, railroads for pleasure are a growth industry and many of these (but, strangely, not all) are formally constituted as short lines. Eighty-four are currently recorded in the author's recent book *Steam for Pleasure*, jointly written with J B Snell and P B Whitehouse and published by Routledge and Kegan Paul of London and Boston.

PIEDMONT & NORTHERN RAILWAY
See Other US Railroads

PONCE & GUAYAMA RAILWAY
Corporacion Azucarera de Puerto Rico,
Aguirre, Puerto Rico 00608.

This sixty-mile railroad, operated by the sugar corporation of Puerto Rico, is now all that is left of a public common-carrier system six times the length. It was known as the Puerto Rico Railroad. The only un-American thing about the line was that it was laid to metre gauge; it is not known whether it was in existence before the US took over the island after the Spanish-American war of 1898. Currently twenty diesel locomotives and 1200 freight vehicles carry half a million tons annually an average distance of 25 miles.

Above: Abandoned as late as 1960, Southern Pacific's narrow-gauge (3ft 0in) line ran for some seventy miles from a junction with the standard gauge Owenyo in California, to Laws. Years before the railway ran far up into the mountains of Nevada for 300 miles as the Carson & Colorado Railway. Before the end, narrow-gauge diesels superseded steam.

Top left: A Bangor & Aroostook train in the elegant livery of the line.

Top right: Rock Island Railroad's double-deck commuter coach at La Salle Street station, Chicago.

Left: A Southern Pacific suburban train at 3rd and Townsend station, San Francisco.

PORT AUTHORITY TRANS-HUDSON CORPORATION – PATH
One World Trade Center,
New York, New York 10048.

The PATH system is independent from the New York City Transit Authority and dates from 1909; it carries around 35 million passengers annually (with 300 cars) from Manhattan under the Hudson River to Jersey City and Newark. It is intended to integrate certain electric suburban services of the old Erie and Lackawanna sections of Conrail into the PATH system.

RICHMOND, FREDERICKSBURG POTOMAC RAILROAD
See Other US Railroads

ROCK ISLAND RAILROAD
See Southwestern US Railroads

SACRAMENTO NORTHERN RAILWAY
See Other US Railroads

ST LOUIS – SAN FRANCISCO RAILWAY SYSTEM
See Southwestern US Railroads

SEABOARD COAST LINE INDUSTRIES INC 'THE FAMILY LINES'
500 Water Street,
Jacksonville, Florida 32202.

'The Family Lines' are a great conglomeration of 16,500 miles of railroads connecting such places of world renown as Chicago, Miami, Washington, St Louis, New Orleans, and so on. The core of the system is a merger of two important railways of the southeast, Seaboard Air Line and Atlantic Coast Line, which took place in 1968. Other lines are wholly owned but to some extent separately operated. The principal among these is the Louisville and Nashville, the acquisition of which in 1971 gave Family Lines access to St Louis, Cincinnati and New Orleans. The L&N itself, also in 1971, absorbed the Chicago, Indianopolis & Louisville familiarly known as the Monon. Hence, the system obtained access to Chicago.

Both SAL and ACL have their ancient roots in Virginia, their earliest constituents receiving charters in 1832 (for the Portsmouth & Roanoke RR) and 1830 (for the St Petersburg RR) respectively. The Monon was next in the field, via the New Albany and Salam RR of 1847. The Louisville & Nashville (which held on to its old name in spite of eventually covering a vast area of the central southern US) was completed between the two places of its name in 1859, just in time to be in the front line of the Civil War, during which it was destroyed and rebuilt more than once.

None of these railroads stands among the 'great innovators' in motive power, although some 4-4-2s for the Atlantic Coast Line in 1894 gave that wheel arrangement its worldwide name. Seaboard wandered early into dieselization – for its legendary New York to Florida 'Orange Blossom Special' – while ACL countered with some lovely 4-8-4s, which, in the end, proved too damaging to the track.

Although the lines had a great tradition of providing the best in passenger services from the north to sunny Florida, all is now over. Amtrak provides passenger service, using Seaboard's old names such as 'Silver Meteor' and 'Silver Star'. Leased subsidiary Clinchfield Railroad returns a vestigial passenger count (15,000 annually) and this includes excursions behind a veteran 4-6-0 with vintage diesel booster unit controlled from the steam locomotive's cab – an arrangement thought to be unique.

'Family Lines' business is freight, currently to the tune of 308 million tons a year, hauled an average distance of 250 miles using the 69,000-strong car fleet.

SOUTHERN PACIFIC TRANSPORTATION COMPANY – SP
1 Market Street,
San Francisco, California 94105.

The best address in the USA (and arguably in the whole world) befits an organization that is still one of the great institutions of North America. Constituent Central Pacific (leased in 1885, finally absorbed in 1955) participated in the building of the first transcontinental railroad, and the CP's constituent, the Sacramento Valley RR was begun on 9 August 1855. The name Southern Pacific first appeared in 1865. (Eight incorporations and a century later, it has become the Southern Pacific Transportation Company.) The rails from Portland, Oregon to New Orleans – a distance of 2824 miles –

Right: One of the first diesel-powered streamliners in America was the 'City of San Francisco', seen here on Southern Pacific's Lucin Trestle over the Great Salt Lake in 1939.

Extreme right, top: A Southern Railway double-headed freight leaves Atlanta. A black 2-8-2 leads a green and gold 4-8-2.

Extreme right, centre: A Southern Railway three-unit diesel locomotive hauls a 215-car freight train up White Oak Mountain in North Carolina.

Extreme right, bottom: A long MoPAC freight train passes through White County in Arkansas.

Below: Southern Pacific's unit steel train heads east through the high desert west of Palm Springs.

were finally joined in 1887. SP's own steamers at one time connected New Orleans with New York.

Common ownership with the Union Pacific in 1901 under E H Harriman was vetoed by the ICC after his death in 1909, but many other smaller concerns were swept into the SP organization, including over 1000 miles of electric inter-urban railways. At one time the system had over 16,000 route miles (the current total is 13,468) and was notable also for extensive ferry operations in the San Francisco Bay area. Southern Pacific of Mexico operated almost 1000 miles of track in Mexico until it was nationalized in 1951.

The engineering achievement involved in building the original Central Pacific and Southern Pacific lines lay more in the size of the undertakings and climatic obstacles than in any specific artifacts. In fact, most notable were ancilliary feats like the construction of 31 miles of snow-sheds on the line across the Sierras and the laying of ten miles of track end-on in one day near Promontory on 11 April 1969, just before the completion of the line. It is said that the CP waited until the UP were within ten miles of the last spike site, so that the CP's record should stand for all time.

Later improvements to the line led SP to build (in 1905) the world's longest railway bridge – the thirteen miles of timber trestle across the Great Salt Lake in Utah, which replaced a circuitous route round the north end of the lake, and thereby saved 44 miles. The bridge is now replaced by an embankment. As a user of the five-mile 1935 Huey P Long bridge over the Mississippi at New Orleans, SP still retains some claim to this particular record.

Another remarkable bridge also replaced a train ferry in this period: the 5600ft long bridge (with a 325ft lifting span) across the straits of Carquinez, an arm of San Francisco Bay. Not until then was the Overland Route completed between Chicago and Oakland. At one time SP electric trains traversed the San Francisco Bay bridge; its two suspension spans of 2310ft were by far the greatest on which railway trains have ever run.

Southern Pacific mechanical engineering has always tended towards the well-proven and

reliable rather than the innovative, but some achievements are worthy of note. Following the success of some 4-8-0s designed for the ascent of the Sierras, the remarkable and unique 4-10-0 *El Gobernador* was completed in the road's own Sacramento shops. Alas, the huge machine was a little too advanced for the year 1884 and 33 years were to elapse before ten coupled locomotives were seen again on SP.

In 1895 after the discovery of oil in California, SP converted a 4-4-0 to burn oil and the success of this venture led to a general change-over from coal to oil. The type of burner, called the Van Boden burner after SP's own superintendent of motive power, was used in most oilburning locomotives built in the world up to the end of the age of steam.

The introduction of oilburning made possible a strange looking back-to-front type of locomotive peculiar to SP – the 195 big articulated 4-8-8-2s known as the 'cab-in-fronts'

with the cab at the front and the tender trailing behind at the smokebox end; crews got a superior view as well as being less likely to be asphyxiated in tunnels and snow-sheds.

Colourful steam locomotives were rare in the USA after the 1870s. SP's were in general no exception and accordingly mention must be made of the streamlined orange and silver 'GS' or 'Daylight' class 4-8-4s introduced in 1937 for working the daytime San Francisco to Los Angeles streamline trains of that name. They have often been described as the most beautiful locomotives in the world. The initials GS were intended to stand for 'Golden State', but when, during the war, more were needed, SP told the War Production Board that GS stood for 'General Service' so that their construction could be authorized in wartime conditions.

Dieselization began in 1934 with the joint SP/Union Pacific/Chicago & North Western luxury 'City of San Francisco' express; a

The present Southern Railway company was formed in 1894 and has since grown to its present size of 10,100 miles partly by absorption and partly by gaining voting control of other railroads in its area. Currently it earns a good living hauling 150 million tons annually an average distance of 300 miles, using a fleet of 1350 diesels and 75,000 freight cars. However, the carriage of around 200,000 passengers in 144 passenger cars was found to be such a loss-making activity that the management decided to stop all passenger service. Hopefully the high quality Washington–New Orleans 'Southern Crescent', which carries a through-sleeping car from New York to Los Angeles, will continue to operate under Amtrak auspices.

More than 120 years of steam operation (in the normal sense) came to an end in 1953. But to the SR's catalogue of merit should be added a sixth item, the fact that it is one of about four US railroads which indulges the lovers of steam by regularly running museum-piece locomotives for them (and at the same time makes the odd dollar or so by doing it).

SOUTHWESTERN US RAILROADS

A group of five railroads share the same problems as well as the same slice of territory in Missouri, Kansas, Texas and neighbouring southwestern states. In descending order of magnitude they are:

MISSOURI PACIFIC RAILROAD – MoPAC
St Louis, Missouri 63103.

CHICAGO, ROCK ISLAND & PACIFIC RAILROAD – Rock Island
139 West Buren Street,
Chicago, Illinois 60605.

ST LOUIS–SAN FRANCISCO RAILWAY SYSTEM – Frisco
906 Olive Street,
St Louis, Missouri 63101.

general change-over proceeded in earnest after the war. Steam came to an end in 1959 – on the narrow-gauge Owen's Valley branch – and, presently, the current fleet of 2150 diesel units in SP's dignified dark grey livery, are connected up as many as six together to power the system's freight trains.

In regard to freight, SP handles 117 million tons annually, the average length of haul being 562 miles. SP's own computer-based freight movement control and management system (known as TOPS or Total Operations Processing System) has contributed greatly to the efficiency with which car and train movement is handled. Annual expenditure at $1.5 million is 96 percent of receipts. SP operates 13,468 miles of track.

SOUTHERN RAILWAY SYSTEM – SR
920 15th Street NW,
Washington, DC 20005.

The Southern Railway, whose main lines extend from Washington and Cincinnati to New Orleans, has five major claims to fame. First its earliest constituent operated the first scheduled rail service in the USA, on Christmas Day 1830; this was on the South Carolina RR out of Charleston. Second, the SR operates the steepest grade on any Class I US line – the 1 in $21\frac{1}{4}$ Saluda Hill. Third, in spite of being an ordinary railroad instead of a specialist (such as a transcontinental bridge road), it turns in some of the best financial results of any major system. Fourth, it is a road which preferred to reject Amtrak and the only one in the US which lately operated an overnight passenger train with the usual amenities. Fifth, the SR was one of that tiny fraction of lines in America which painted its locomotives in steam days a colour other than black – in this case it was a vivid emerald green with elegant gold lining and lettering.

MISSOURI–KANSAS–TEXAS RAILROAD COMPANY – Katy
Katy Building,
Dallas, Texas 75202.

KANSAS CITY SOUTHERN RAILWAY – KCS
114 West 11th Street,
Kansas City, Missouri 64105.

Their individual statistics are presented below:

Southwestern US Railroads - Statistics

	MoPAC	Rock Island	Frisco	Katy	KCS
Locomotives	1176	642	427	165	243
Passenger Cars	—	106	—	—	—
Freight Cars	55,000	23,000	19,000	8000	8000
Passengers, annual count	—	106,000	—	—	—
Freight, millions of tons annually	117	41	40	16	28
Average length of haul, miles	410	360	370	320	270
Expenses as % of receipts	74	88	79	80	81
Length, miles	11,200	7170	4580	2220	1669

Set out like this, the margins of receipts over expenditure might seem satisfactory. However, it must be remembered that several of them are debt-ridden and so have barely sufficient net income to cover the fixed payments on money owed. The problem faced by these railroads is the simple basic one that there are too many of them: hence, the present game of musical chairs. The question is, when will the music stop?

Although it could be said with a certain truth that none of the five is ever out of sight of a grain elevator and therefore, traffic, it is also true that few important places in the area are served by less than five competing lines. Efforts made to remedy this state of affairs have resulted in vicious bureaucratic harassment; for example, a merger which might have solved some of the problems was disallowed after sixty million words of testimony and six years of delay.

But none of these sad things was envisioned on 4 July 1851, when the first sod of what was intended to be the Pacific Railroad was cut at St Louis. It was the first steam railroad west of the Mississippi River and was laid to the 5ft 6in gauge. The Pacific was never reached and western and southwestern shoots became respectively the Missouri Pacific and St Louis & San Francisco railroads (the Frisco changed the ampersand for a dash when reorganized later), but neither of these reached the Pacific either! The name Missouri Pacific dates from 1872, when the Pacific RR went bankrupt (its gauge had been changed to standard in 1869). The present system extends from St Louis to the Mexican border at El Paso and Laredo, to Pueblo, Colorado and to Omaha, Nebraska.

The Chicago, Rock Island & Pacific, which was opened between Chicago and Joliet (forty miles) on 10 October, 1952 as the Chicago & Rock Island, in fact came nearest to getting there. Rather distinguished trains, such as the 'Golden State Limited' ran through from Chicago to Los Angeles using Rock Island

metals between Chicago and Tucumcari, thence via Southern Pacific. In fact, a super edition of one of The Rock's famous 'Rocket' trains (called the 'Golden Rocket') was built for this service in 1947, but SP vetoed the scheme just before inauguration.

The Missouri–Kansas–Texas, affectionately known as the 'Katy' was promoted and begun as the Union Pacific Southern Branch in 1868 out of Junction City, Kansas. Texas was entered in 1872, Dallas reached in 1886, St Louis in 1885 and Houston in 1893. Serving much the same territory as the Frisco, the two lines co-operated to a certain extent, working such well-known trains as the 'Texas Special' (St Louis–Dallas–Fort Worth–San Antonio) and 'Bluebonnet' (from Kansas City to the same destinations) jointly.

The Kansas City Southern was the baby of the group and had a very humble origin as a switching line called the Kansas City Suburban Belt Railroad. A few years later the owners, one of whom was a man called Arthur Stilwell, decided they would have their own line to the Gulf of Mexico and changed the name of the line to the Kansas City, Pittsburg & Gulf RR. The Gulf at the new Port Arthur (named after Mr Stilwell) was reached in 1897; Pittsburg was abandoned as a goal and the present name adopted in 1900. KCS was well known for having a train with the original but unromantic name of 'Flying Crow', but, like all the others of this group except Rock Island, no longer deals with passenger traffic. The Rock never made the deal with Amtrak and accordingly is still obliged to provide long-distance passenger service on a small scale, principally on the Chicago–Rock Island and Chicago–Peoria runs.

SPOKANE INTERNATIONAL RAILROAD
See Other US Railroads

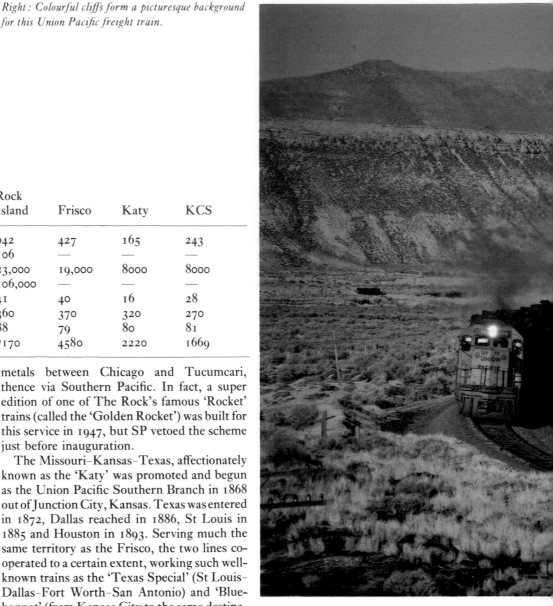

Right: Colourful cliffs form a picturesque background for this Union Pacific freight train.

Above: This diesel-hauled streamliner is known as the Rock Island Rocket.

STRASBURG RAIL ROAD
PO Box 96,
Strasburg, Pennsylvania 17579.

The oldest railway company in America still running trains is the little 4.5-mile Strasburg Rail Road, whose charter dates from 9 June 1832. It misses the world title by a mere two weeks – the Festiniog Railway in Wales received its Act on 25 May. However, as the Strasburg RR is much shorter, it no doubt was finished first and accordingly will be the company which has run a railway the longest.

It is a perfect example of the American short Short Line, un-typical only in that it moved with the times more quickly than most. Until 1958 its object in life was to connect the town of Strasburg with the rest of the world and in particular with the Pennsylvania RR's New York – Chicago main line at Leaman Place. It got out of the passenger business and 'dieselized' (using a gas-engined shunter) in the 1920s and in 1959 became the first standard-gauge museum line in the world.

Twenty years later using five restored steam locomotives of its own, plus others borrowed from the superb Pennsylvania RR Museum nearby, it is carrying half a million passengers a year and is prosperous enough (expenses are 71 percent of receipts) to order custom-built Victorian passenger cars for its traffic.

The Strasburg example inspired many others to do likewise.

UNION PACIFIC RAILROAD – UP
345 Park Avenue,
New York, New York 10022.

'Along the Roaring UP Trail' wrote Zane Gray and indeed the words Union Pacific epitomize the conquest of the USA by rail,

Right: A Western Pacific Bo-Bo road switcher approaches a level crossing at Sacramento, California, in 1977.

179

Extreme right, top: Western Pacific's diesel-hauled 'Exposition Flyer' crosses Niles Canyon, California.

Below: Working over the tremendous grades of the Union Pacific between Cheyenne and Laramie with loads in excess of 5000 tons, the Big Boys jointly earned their reputation. These huge 4-8-8-4 locomotives were built in 1941 and lasted until 1960.

Extreme right, below: A Western Pacific freight train in steam days.

Right: One of Union Pacific's famous 'City' streamliners which features two dome cars.

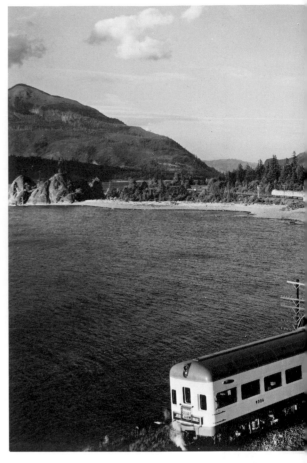

although, in fact, UP rails only span 990 of the 2260 miles between Chicago and San Francisco Bay. UP is perhaps the immortalized company because traffic on the eastern section as far as Omaha was shared between five separate roads (there are still four) and the western section was built by the Central Pacific, a company which soon lost its corporate identity. Further, whereas CP had its deserts and mountains to cross, UP had the more exciting Indian problems.

To compensate for going only part way to San Francisco, the UP goes all the way to both Los Angeles and to Portland, Oregon. An eastern tentacle serves Kansas City. It should be noted that UP is still viably in business using the same name and carrying the same traffic as it did when the first rail was laid near Omaha on 10 July 1865.

Bankruptcy in 1893 – the result of too rapid an expansion – was followed by a take-over on the part of magnate E H Harriman, who also controlled Southern Pacific and other roads. He was responsible for major improvements, track strengthening and re-alignment, standardization of locomotives and so on. Since then standards of operation have remained consistently high. Double track on the original Overland Route between Omaha and Ogden was completed in 1923.

At present UP operates 9750 miles of route; the principal lines have a maximum permitted speed of 70 mph, with axle-loads up to thirty tons. The system is one of that handful of US railroads whose physical plant is in top condition.

Ever since the Harriman regime, during which locomotive policy tended towards the

well-tried, solid and reliable, (previous policy had tended just towards the well-tried) UP has been a pathfinder for the rest of the US in the search for more powerful motive power. The ever-increasing demands for moving tonnage across the Overland Route with its 8250ft Sherman Summit has resulted in some remarkable machinery.

As a start one might note one of the very few twelve-coupled steam locomotive types run in the world – the three-cylinder 2100 class 4-12-2s; fifteen were built between 1923 and 1928. In 1936 UP purchased a type of articulated (Mallet) locomotive which broke new ground in that unlike previous articulateds, it was stable enough to be used in fast passenger or fast freight service. The 105 'Challenger' 4-6-6-4s were very successful machines and were widely imitated.

Then in 1941 came the world ultimate in steam, the 25 'Big Boy' 4-8-8-4s, generally thought of as the biggest and most powerful locomotives ever built, although in fact on particular counts other US examples exceeded them marginally. With tenders full of thirty tons of coal and 24,000 gallons of water they would set out to conquer the Sherman Hill out of Cheyenne hauling ninety cars weighing 7000 tons. Thirty miles and 1½ hours later this enormous tender would need refilling, but the tonnage moved over the road.

The last 'normal' steam run on UP was in 1958, but for the past twenty years the road has maintained its last-built steam locomotive (4-8-4 No 844 of 1944) in running order for occasional celebratory or steam-enthusiast use.

In moving on to internal combustion traction, UP has not been content just to buy diesels off

the shelf or indeed, confine itself to diesels. Its very first venture, before a satisfactory American diesel engine for rail traction had been developed, was the remarkable four-car streamline lightweight diesel train M-10000 later 'City of Salina' which in May 1932 was run through from Chicago to Los Angeles, covering 3100 miles in 36½ hours, without ever shutting off its spark-plug engine. This was the pioneer streamliner, the forerunner of those for which there was such a vogue in the late 1930s.

UP was right in the van with such trains as diesel-powered streamliners, 'City of Portland' (1934), 'City of Los Angeles' (1936) and 'City of San Francisco' (1937). The earliest versions were self-contained in the sense that they had power cars rather than separate locomotives.

Diesel locomotives for general service were purchased soon after World War II, but a sustained effort was then made to introduce gas-turbine locomotives. Twenty years ago as many as forty were in use (no other railway in the world ever got beyond one or two experimental models) and these included some twin units of 8500hp – probably the most powerful locomotives ever made. In the end, however, the convenience of being able to buy motive power off the shelf from General Motors' or General Electric's locomotive supermarkets triumphed. But even here UP was able to have put together a speciality in the form of its 6200hp single-unit 'Centennial' diesel design. This would at last match the power of a 'Big Boy' but, of course, diesel units are building blocks from which locomotives of any desired power can be assembled. The UP diesel fleet currently numbers 1400 and there are 64,000 freight and a handful of passenger cars.

Aside from the Union Pacific's position as a pioneer of luxury streamlined trains, its passenger trains were always of good standard. It is however a sign of the times that the 'Overland Mail', once the 'flag' passenger train of the route, is now a fast freight with a timing of fifty hours between Chicago and Oakland, barely slower than Amtrak's passenger train between the same two points.

Now as always, the lifeblood of the system is the immense flow of ordinary freight tonnage – currently amounting to ninety million tons annually, which UP hauls an average distance of 660 miles, earning $1.3 million gross and $150,000 net in the process, the largest net revenue in the industry.

WESTERN PACIFIC RAILROAD – WP
Western Pacific Building, 526 Mission Street, San Francisco, California 94105.

Around the turn of the century, railroad tycoon George J Gould, son of empire builder Jay Gould, planned the first true US transcontinental, that is, one road connecting the Atlantic to the Pacific. Towards this end, as a result of his famous father's efforts he already controlled the Wabash, Missouri Pacific and Denver & Rio Grande roads, but control of an existing line from Salt Lake City to the Pacific was denied him. Accordingly he set out to build his own, a duplicate of the original Overland Route across Utah, Nevada and California to San Francisco Bay. The final spike was driven without ceremony on 1 November 1909, the last one to be driven on a line crossing the American West.

Gould never achieved an ocean-to-ocean railway, in fact the financial burdens of building WP were such that he and his family lost control of his railway empire. His line, however, soldiered on through various financial vicissitudes, wheeling and dealing. There was a dubious bankruptcy in 1915 and a more genuine one in 1935. Today the 1340-mile railroad is in reasonable financial health with expenses running at 86 percent of receipts.

The route chosen took the main line south of the Great Salt Lake, at that time fairly close to rivals Southern Pacific (then still Central Pacific) across the Nevada Desert. Since 1924 the usage of the two tracks over a 180-mile stretch have been pooled. Instead of the SP's notorious climb over the Sierras, WP crosses the range at 2000ft less elevation, through the Feather River Canyon to the north. It offers a one percent grade instead of SP's 2.2 percent, at the cost of an additional 150 miles distance. The easier line was and is a great advantage in moving freight economically, which WP (the 'Wobbly') does nowadays to the tune of 9.5 million tons a year, with an average 525-mile haul, using a fleet of 140 diesel units and 6500 cars.

WP is now out of the passenger business completely; it does not run passenger trains and does not allow passenger trains to run on it except occasionally when the SP route is blocked by a wreck or landslide. However, from 1949 to 1970, WP was a partner in one of the most remarkable and well-liked trains ever to cross the continent. This was the brand-new 'California Zephyr', run in conjunction with the Rio Grande and Burlington lines. With its 53-hour Chicago-Oakland timing, the train hardly competed with rival railways, let alone aircraft. What it did offer, though, was an unexcelled scenic ride, with ample vista-dome viewing space as well as an observation car, excellent food, and timings so that the best scenery was seen in daylight. For night-time, excellent beds were not only offered, but taken; there were capacity loads run after run, with a clientele who came for the pleasure of the journey rather than for whatever lay at its end. Five train sets provided daily service. Even so, the end for the 'California Zephyr' came after twenty years when its equipment was beginning to age, and when rising losses began to overtake reason.

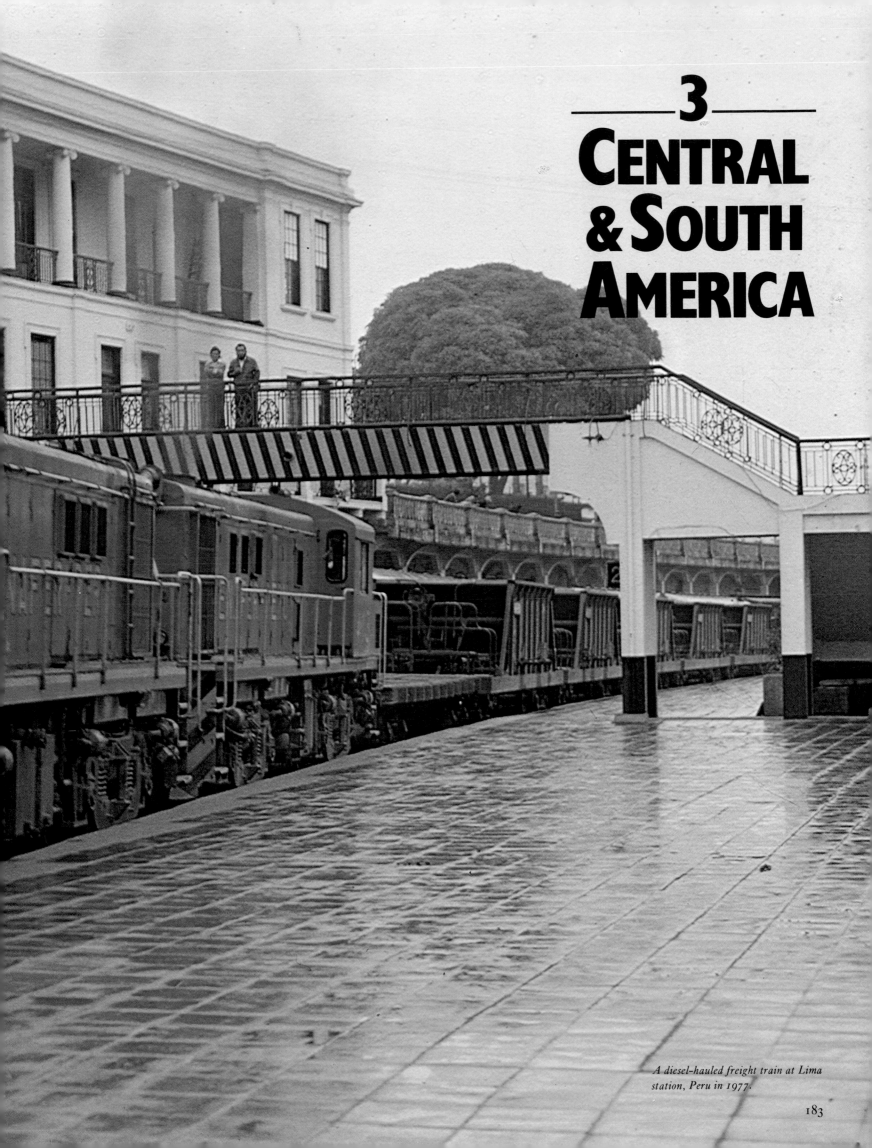

3
CENTRAL & SOUTH AMERICA

A diesel-hauled freight train at Lima station, Peru in 1977.

Argentina Argentine Railways Rio callegos – Rio Turbio Industrial Railway	**Cuba** Cuban National Railways	**Paraguay** President Carlos Antonio Lopez Railway
Belize	**Ecuador** Ecuador State Railways	**Peru** Peruvian National Railways
Bermuda	**Falkland Islands**	**Salvador, El** National Railways of El Salvador
Bolivia Bolivian National Railways	**Guatemala** Guatemala Railway	**Surinam** Surinam Government Railway
Brazil Brazilian Federal Railways Vitória a Minas Railway	**Guyana**	**Uruguay** Uruguayan State Railways
Chile Chilean State Railways	**Honduras**	**Venezuela** Venezuela National Railways
Colombia National Railways of Colombia	**Jamaica** Jamaica Railway Corporation	**West Indies: The Smaller Islands**
Costa Rica National Atlantic Railroad Pacific Electric Railroad	**Nicaragua** Pacific Railway of Nicaragua	
	Panama Panama Railroad	

ANTIGUA
See West Indies: the Smaller Islands

ARGENTINA

See map on pages 186–187.

ARGENTINE RAILWAYS – FA
Ferrocarriles Argentinos,
Avenida Ramos Mejia 1302,
1104 Buenos Aires.

It is a happy quirk of nomenclature that the South American country with by far the largest and most highly developed railway system is the first to be described.

Railways first came to this vast food-producing country in 1857, when a short 5ft-6in-gauge line from Buenos Aires to Flores was opened. (The reason for the gauge chosen is understood to be that some equipment ordered for India was acquired by Argentina.) This signalled the start of an explosion of railway construction which in its turn led to a great increase in prosperity. The Flores line was the start of what became the 7400-mile Buenos Aires Western. The 4000-mile Central Argentine Railway's first component was opened in 1862 and in 1865 the first section of the largest South American privately financed railroad, the 5300-mile Buenos Aires Great Southern, was opened. The 3200-mile Buenos Aires & Pacific (which in good American tradition, never got there) began operations in 1888. These four systems still preserve a measure of independence as separate divisions of the national network. They use names of four past national heroes – respectively, Domingo F Sarmiento, General Mitre, General Roca and General Martin.

A disconnected 2000-mile standard-gauge system grew up in the north-eastern corner of the country, between the River Parana and the river Uruguay, (the latter forms the frontier). Neither river has yet been bridged, so inconvenience of break of gauge is not yet a problem. The two associated companies were called, appropriately enough, the Entre Rios ('between rivers'), and the Argentine North Eastern; they are now called the General Urquiza Railway.

There were also a number of metre-gauge railways, totalling over 8000 miles in extent, in outlying areas. The biggest concentration of these railways is in the mountainous but sparsely populated north-western area of the country. The rewards to be gleaned from this area were sparse also, so British-owned companies were less eager, allowing the state, a provincial government and a French company opportunities for railway ownership. These lines are now known as the General Belgrano Railway.

The honeymoon stage of this marriage to foreign capital really lasted a surprisingly long time. British investors made money for themselves, it is true, but the companies were good employers and the services they offered brought prosperity to the country. At the same time they invested heavily in up-to-date equipment and took a long-term and responsible view of their future. But, like other marriages on not too solid a foundation, bliss did not survive hard times. These came in full measure during the 1930s when for a number of years none of

Left: Buenos Aires' suburban Escalada station, looking towards Plaza Constitucion Terminus.

Extreme left: A British-built 4-8-0 and local train at Tandil, Argentina. Note the semaphore signals.

Centre left: A vintage San Martin Railway 4-6-0 pulls a mixed train at Rufino, a small pampas town 270 miles west of Buenos Aires.

Bottom left: An essentially British signal gantry at the west end of Rufino station.

Bottom right: The magnificent overall station roof at La Plata, Argentina.

the British companies could pay any sort of dividend. Of course, similar problems applied to railways everywhere, due to road competition and the worldwide slump. The result was that in 1948 the state, using sterling balances accumulated during the war, was able to enforce the purchase of the foreign-owned railways. It is no pleasure to write that politicians' control has not yet led to a railway system of which Argentina can be proud, although better-advised efforts are now at last being made.

The majority of Argentina's 25,000 miles of railway are laid in easy farming country – a stretch of dead straight and dead level track 205 miles long on the BA & Pacific line tells its own tale. However, the lines approaching the crossings of the Andes are a very different story.

The first and most famous of these, the Trans-Andean Railway, made a direct route between Buenos Aires and Valparaiso in Chile. It was built with British capital and opened just before World War I. The mechanical solution to mountain climbing, that is, rack-and-pinion working, was adopted, together

–SOUTH AMERICA–

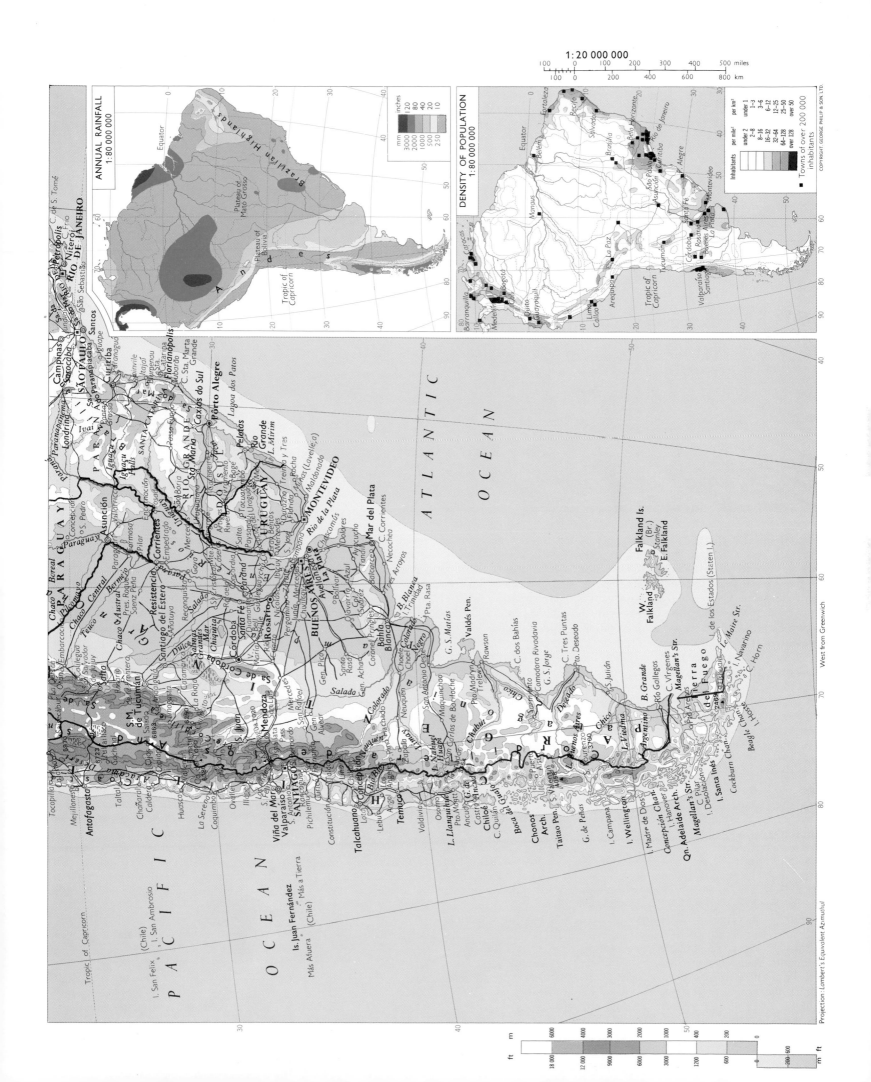

ANNUAL RAINFALL
1:80 000 000

mm	inches
3000	120
2000	80
1000	40
500	20
250	10

DENSITY OF POPULATION
1:80 000 000

per mile²	per km²
under 2	under 1
2–8	1–3
8–16	3–6
16–32	6–12
32–64	12–25
64–128	25–50
over 128	over 50

■ Towns of over 200 000 inhabitants

COPYRIGHT GEORGE PHILIP & SON, LTD.

1:20 000 000

Projection: Lambert's Equivalent Azimuthal

West from Greenwich

with one-in-eight grades and the metre gauge. The rack was a special version of the Abt system, bit with three rows of teeth instead of the more usual two. Traffic is not helped by there being three changes of train – two breaks-of-gauge in the foothills and a change from an Argentine to a Chilean train near the summit, at just over 10,000ft altitude.

A lesser known but much more useful line crosses the Andes 650 miles further north from Salta to Socomba; here, the solution adopted was the civil engineering one of using zig-zag and loops to extend the distance and thereby reduce the grades to something which ordinary locomotives can cope with. This was done even though the summit level here is as high as 14,680ft. The line is above 12,000ft for 250 miles. Construction had taken more than twenty years when the line was opened in 1948. Through trains are not operated although the connecting railways on either side being of similar metre gauge.

Another route by which it is possible to cross the Andes by rail leads out of Argentina into Bolivia. This also has rack assistance for a 1 in 16.5 grade.

With so many companies operating, each with their own locomotive practices, one can only say that most Argentine steam locomotives were more British looking than those that ran in Britain. Other nations' products can also be found; the Northern Transandine had, for example, a big fleet of modern German- and American-built 2-10-2s. The German-built

0-12-2Ts that worked the rack line leading to Bolivia are thought to represent a wheel arrangement not duplicated elsewhere.

With Argentine coal of poor quality and Welsh coal prohibitively expensive when landed in the country, there was every reason to adopt diesel traction. To the BAGS railway goes the credit for taking diesel-electric traction in Argentina out of the experimental stage into practical use; their mobile power houses were working the Buenos Aires Suburban services as early as 1936. A main-line diesel locomotive of 1200hp was also in operation. After the war, this hard-won experience was not, however, used as a basis for a gradual change to the new form of traction; instead, the new management has to relearn the hard way that there is a good deal more to dieselization than just buying some new shiny locomotives. Because of the problems encountered a big effort had to be put into improving existing steam power and some success achieved. However, solutions are now to hand and some of the 490 steam locomotives shown on the books will not steam again. Other particulars are as follows:

In addition there are a fleet of diesel railcars for branch-line use and electric trains for certain Buenos Aires suburban services.

With this equipment in 1976, eighteen million tons of freight were transported an average distance of 400 miles; 450 million passengers were carried. British standards and methods of signalling and operation in general continue to apply.

RIO GALLEGOS – RIO TURBIO INDUSTRIAL RAILWAY – RFIRT
Ferrocarril Industrial de Rio Gallegos a Rio Turbio,
State Coalfields Board, Railway Department, Rio Gallegos.

Rio Gallegos where the RFIRT is situated is in Patagonia not far from Cape Horn, and is the location of the world's present most southerly working railway.

The line is 2ft 6in gauge, wholly steam-operated and its function is to transport coal from mines 162 miles inland; a journey on it in high summer was described thus . . . 'Bitterly

Argentine Railways	5ft 6in gauge lines	4ft 8½in gauge lines	Metre gauge lines	Total
Mileage	14,550	1950	8400	24,900
Locomotives, diesel	890	50	310	1250
Carriages	2450	350	1200	4000
Wagons	39,000	3500	19,500	62,000

cold and strong winds howled through . . . the broken windows (and) badly fitting doors. The only source of welcome warmth was a red hot coal stove around which sat four shivering travellers huddled on comfortless wooden benches.' The journey in a passenger car specially attached to a coal train, took nine hours; passenger travel is a bit of an acquired taste at the 52°S parallel of latitude!

Much of the permanent track and some equipment came from a closed line which once served Port Madryn and the Welsh colony in Patagonia, for the RFIRT was built as recently as 1951. Trains up to 1700 tons in weight and two-thirds of a mile in length are worked by a series of 25 specially built 2-10-2s through a bleak and inhospitable landscape with surprising ease and economy.

One reason is that some of these locomotives have had their fireboxes, mechanical stokers and the very manner in which their fuel is burnt altered in a unique way that might have made history, even halted the advance of the diesel in coal-producing countries, had it come a little earlier. The majority of the air needed for combustion is not drawn through the fire, but introduced above it. The coal is burnt at a lower temperature in a manner that produces very little smoke or waste. The arrangement is the brain-child of Senor Porta, an officer of the Argentine Railways who, almost alone among the present railway mechanical engineers of the world, has the courage to advocate the retention and development of the steam loco-motive. (Courage is the right word, for Joseph

Stalin liquidated Porta's Soviet equivalent for doing just that.) In the meantime one of the world's very few exclusively steam railways soldiers on with economy and efficiency. In fact it is said that some 2-10-10-2 steam-articulateds are being considered.

BARBADOS
See West Indies

BELIZE

See map on pages 190-191.

British Honduras, now known as Belize (but, oddly enough, still rather reluctantly possessed by Britain) had at one time a 25-mile railway with four steam and two gasoline locomotives, 65 trucks and one solitary passenger carriage. This great national system was known as the Stann Creek Railway and had closed by the 1950s.

BERMUDA

See map on pages 190-191.

From 1931 to 1947 a fourteen-mile line of standard gauge operated in Bermuda. It ran from Somerset via Hamilton to St George's and gasoline railcars provided traction. To

Left: A General Roca Railway 2-6-2T leaves Plaza Constitucion Terminus, Buenos Aires.

Bottom: A 2-10-2 takes water at La Sofia on the 2ft 5½in gauge Rio Turbio Industrial Railway.

Below: A Baldwin 2-8-2 heads a northbound narrow-gauge freight at Fatalancao on the Esquel Branch in Patagonia.

CENTRAL AMERICA

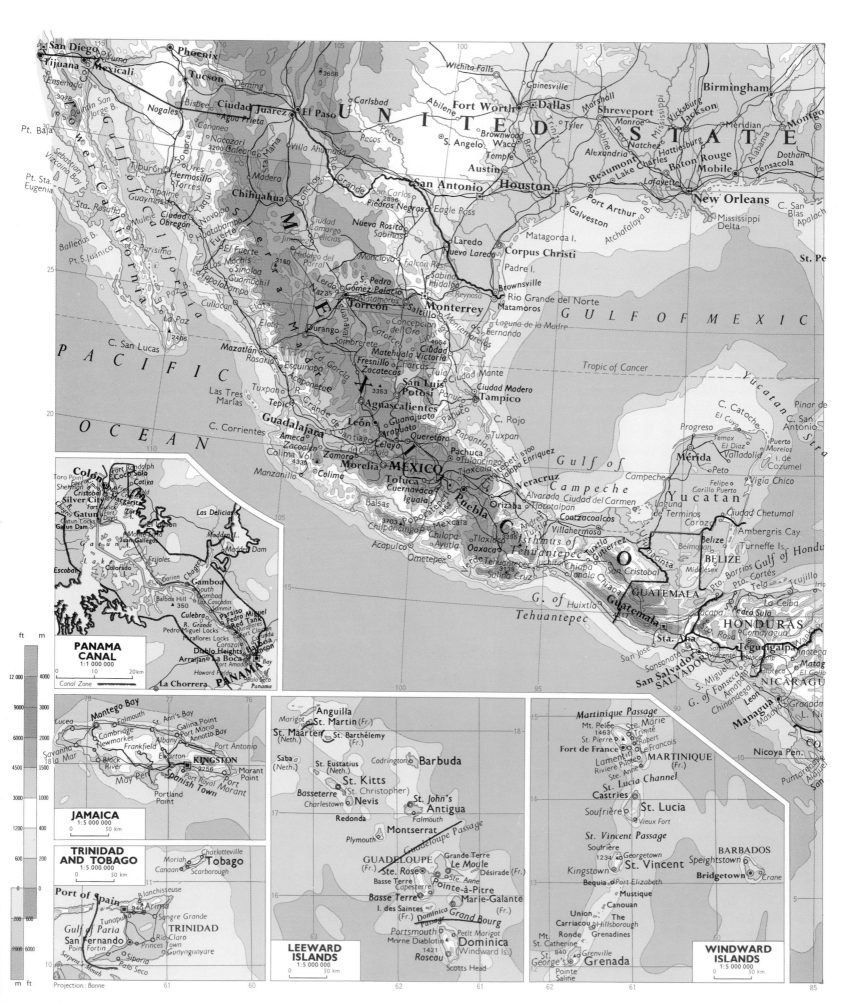

PANAMA CANAL
1:1 000 000
0   10   20km
Canal Zone

JAMAICA
1:5 000 000
0   50 km

TRINIDAD AND TOBAGO
1:5 000 000
0   50 km

LEEWARD ISLANDS
1:5 000 000
0   50 km

WINDWARD ISLANDS
1:5 000 000
0   50 km

Projection: Bonne

BERMUDA
1:750 000
0   5   10 km

St. George   St. George's I.
St. David's I.
Spanish Pt.   Castle Harb.
The   Tucker's Town
Flatts   North Village
Ireland I.
Somerset   Hamilton
Somerset I.

NORTH AMERICA
ANNUAL RAINFALL
1:80 000 000

REFERENCE TO COLOURING
mm   inches
3000   120
2000   80
1000   40
500   20
250   10

1:15 000 000
100   0   100   200   300   400 miles
100   0   100 200 300 400 500 600 km

Columbia
Atlanta
Macon   Augusta
Columbus   Charleston
Savannah
Albany   Altamaha
Tallahassee
Jacksonville
Daytona Beach
Orlando
Tampa   Lakeland
tersburg   Sarasota   L. Okeechobee
West Palm Beach
Grand Bahama I.
Freeport
Miami   Fort Lauderdale
Gt. Abaco I.
C. Sable
Key West   New Providence I.   Gt. Abaco I.

BAHAMAS
Andros I.
Nassau
Eleuthera I.
Cat I.
S. Salvador or Watlings I.
Long I.
Tropic of Cancer
Mayaguana

Havana
Marianao
G. of Batabanó
I. of Pines
Matanzas   Cárdenas
Sta. Clara
Cienfuegos   Sancti Spiritus
Trinidad
Grand Cayman (Br.)

Acklins   Caicos I. (Br.)
Gt. Inagua   Turks Is. (Br.)
Camagüey   Nuevitas
Holguin
Antilla
Guantánamo
Santiago de Cuba
Port de Paix
Cap Haitien
Monte Cristi
Pto. Plata
Santiago
Sanchez
S. Francisco de Macoris
Mona Passage
PUERTO RICO (U.S.A.)
St. Thomas (U.S.A.)
San Juan
Charlotte Amalie
Virgin Is. (Br.)
Anguilla
St. Martin (Fr. & Neth.)
Sombrero (Br.)
St. Kitts (St. Christopher)
Barbuda
St. Croix (U.S.A.)
Basseterre   Nevis
Antigua   St. John's

Montego Bay
St. Ann's Bay
Savanna la Mar
JAMAICA
Kingston
Spanish Town
Les Cayes
Port au Prince
Jérémie   Leogane
Gonaïves   St. Marc
La Vega
DOMINICAN REP.
Santo Domingo
Barahona
Pedro de Macoris
La Romana
Hispaniola
Mayagüez
Ponce
Guayama   Christiansted
Charlestown   Montserrat
Plymouth
Guadeloupe (Fr.)
Pointe à Pitre
Marie Galante (Fr.)
Dominica
Roseau
Martinique (Fr.)
Fort de France
Castries
St. Lucia
Barbados
St. Vincent   Bridgetown
Kingstown
The Grenadines
Grenada
St. George's

GREATER ANTILLES
LESSER ANTILLES
Leeward Islands
Windward Islands

Caratasca Lagoon
C. Gracias á Dios
Puerto Cabezas
Providencia (Col.)
San Andrés (Col.)
Bluefields

CARIBBEAN SEA

Pta. Gallinas
Pen. de la Guajira
Gulf of Venezuela
Aruba (Neth.)
Curacao (Neth.)
Willemstad
Bonaire (Neth.)
La Blanquilla (Ven.)
Margarita
La Asunción
Tobago
Port of Spain
Trinidad
San Fernando

Barranquilla
Santa Marta
Riohacha
Pen. de Paraguaná
Coro
Dabajuro
Pto. Cabello
Maiquetia
La Tortuga (Ven.)
Cumaná
Carúpano
G. of Paria
Delta of the Orinoco

Cartagena
G. of Darién
Soledad
Calamar
Sierra Nevada de Santa Marta   5800
Plato
Ciénaga
Maracaibo
L. de Maracaibo
Trujillo
Valera
Caracas
Maracay
Valencia
Barcelona
Cotipero
El Tigre
Tucupita
Maturín
Barquisimeto
San Felipe
Las Mercedes
Ciudad Guayana
Ciudad Bolívar
Georgetown
New Amsterdam
Wismar

Panama
Colón
Panama Canal Zone
G. of Darién
Turbo
Pearl Is.
Chitré   La Palma
Azuero Pen.
G. of Panama
Coiba
G. of Cupica
Quibdó
Medellín

Cúcuta
Pamplona
San Cristóbal
Bucaramanga
Cord. de Mérida   5007
Barrancabermeja
Pto. Berrio
Pto. Wilches
Arauca
Apure
San Fernando de Apure
Pto. Páez
Meta
Pto. Carreño   2288
Pto. Ayacucho
Caicara
El Callao
Tumeremo   2560
Roraima   2810
Sierra Pacaraima
1280

VENEZUELA
GUYANA
SURINAM

Manizales
Pereira
Cartago   4750
Buga
Palmira
Cali
Buenaventura
Pta. Charambirá
Armenia
Girardot   5215
Bogotá
Honda
Neiva
Ibagué
Popayán   4646

COLOMBIA
Guaviare
Guainía
Casiquiare

BRAZIL

West from Greenwich   80   75   70   65

COPYRIGHT. GEORGE PHILIP & SON. LTD.

191

maintain the island's original charm, mechanical road transport was forbidden in Bermuda until US forces arrived, early in World War II. After the war was over and small engined cars and mopeds were allowed, such a short line had no function to perform and accordingly closed.

BOLIVIA

See map on pages 186-187.

BOLIVIAN NATIONAL RAILWAYS – ENFER

Empresa Nacional de Ferrocarriles,
Estacion Central, Casilla 428,
La Paz.

Bolivia's railways were developed piecemeal, mostly by foreigners. The first railway in Bolivia was opened in 1873 out of the port of Antofagasta (it was 2ft 6in gauge and called the Antofagasta Nitrate & Railway Company) in territory that was taken by Chile as the spoils of victory in the war of 1879-82. The effect of the war was to make Bolivia land-locked, depriving her of ports on the Pacific coast.

This same railway, by now appropriately renamed the Antofagasta (Chile) & Bolivia Railway (FCAB) was extended into Bolivia and reached the tin-mining centre of Oruro in 1892. In 1903 Bolivia sold some disputed territory in the north-east to Brazil for a sum sufficient to enable further extensions (this time on the metre gauge) to be financed and leased for operation to the FCAB. The FCAB thus became a two-gauge railway. Bolivia laid the foundations of a national system and also gained (at Condor on the Potosi branch) what is currently the highest altitude (15,705ft) at which passenger trains are run.

These extensions gave rail access to the capital, La Paz, in 1908; the final stretch from Viacha was over the metals of a third administration, the Guaqui-La Paz Railway, also com-

pleted that year. Guaqui was on Lake Titicaca an inland sea (at 12,500ft altitude). Steamers crossed the lake to connect with the Peruvian Southern Railway and hence the Pacific again. The last steep section descending from the Andean Plateau into La Paz at 1 in 14 was electrified from the outset, the first electrification in South America.

In 1913 La Paz got its third and shortest outlet to the Pacific, the Arica-La Paz Railway, promoted by Chile. La Paz was later connected to the Argentine system and hence the Atlantic, while separate lines in the eastern lowlands of the country have, in addition to a further Argentine connection, an outlet to Brazil.

All the significant railways have now come under the National Railway Administration, ENFER, which was set up in 1964. The system is now being extended towards the heretofore 'railwayless' North. A connection between the two distinct west and east systems is also proposed.

Currently the system is 2270 miles in extent, of which six miles are electrified; on it run thirty diesel, five electric and (nominally) 120 steam locomotives, 170 carriages and 1800 freight cars. About 1.3 million passengers and 1.1 million tons of freight are carried, the latter an average distance of 260 miles.

Right: A Japanese-built 2-8-2 at Vila-Vila, Bolivia on the Potosi to Sucre line with the weekly mixed train.

Extreme right, centre: An electrically hauled train approaches La Paz.

Extreme right, bottom: A freight train at Potosi, hauled by Japanese-built 2-8-2.

Extreme left and left: The railway side and the decorative, imposing front façade of the main station at La Paz, Bolivia.

Below: A train leaves Potosi for Rio Mulato via Condor summit.

BRAZIL

See map on pages 186-187.

BRAZILIAN FEDERAL RAILWAYS – RFFSA
Rêde Ferroviaria Federal SA,
86 Praca De Caxias, Rio de Janeiro.

Brazil has a land area slightly smaller than the USA, has one half of the US population but a rail mileage of only one tenth. The history of the railways is complicated, including every sort of arrangement that could be imagined. There were, fifty years ago, central government (federal) railways, provincial government (state) railways, privately-owned railways, financed both locally and abroad (mostly in London), both with and without guarantee. There were other complex combinations such as railways built by either the central or the state government and leased to home or foreign private operators. There were even lines built by the federal government and leased by the provinces and vice versa. There were some pit-to-port lines financed by the industries which used them, as well as miles of very narrow gauge line serving and owned by local sugar plantations.

The first railway in Brazil, a short line in the neighbourhood of Rio de Janeiro, opened on 30 April 1854. The 2-2-2 locomotive *Baroneza* which hauled the train is on view in the railway museum at São Paulo. By 1939 there were 23,000 miles of railway, all metre gauge except for 2100 miles of broad and 900 miles of narrow. The system was divided amongst fourteen major and 33 minor administrations. The lines formed several separate networks and although Brazil has a frontier with every South American country except Equador and Chile, eleven in all, Brazil's railways were connected only to one other national system, that of Uruguay. No major line was exclusively broad gauge.

After World War II, the government began patiently acquiring the privately owned railways. There was no dramatic gesture of confiscation or nationalization – remember, Brazil is basically Portuguese not Spanish – but one 69-year concession would expire, another company would be bought out, and so on. For some time the old names like Leopoldina, Mogyana, Great Western of Brazil (which had the easternmost lines!) remained, but in 1975 most railways in the country were unified, the old com-

panies forming the divisions of the new administration.

Alas, their situation is not good. The Federal Railways expend 207 cruzieros for every 100 they take in receipts, the worst operating ratio of any of the world's major railway systems. Worse, the transport market share of rail fell, during the twenty years between 1953 and 1973, from 29 percent to 16 percent in the case of freight, and from 30 percent to 8 percent for passengers. Symptomatic of this is the fact that the new central capital of Brazil, Brasilia, can

Division of Railways (1978)

	5ft 3in	4ft 8½in	Metre	2ft 6in	Total
Federal Railway System	1041	—	13,873	126	15,040
São Paulo State (Provincial) Railway	1029	—	2288	—	3317
Vitória a Minas Railway	—	—	489	—	489
Amapa Railway	—	121	—	—	121
Campos do Jordão Tourist Railway	—	—	29	—	29
Totals	2070	121	16,679	126	18,996 miles

Left: The narrow gauge at Sao João del Rei, Brazil, north of Rio de Janeiro.

Extreme left, below: A train, consisting of new stainless steel coaches, ascends the rope-worked inclines en route from Santos to São Paulo, Brazil.

Bottom: An Argentinian express train destined for Buenos Aires at Rosario (North). Note British-style platforms, footbridge and signals.

Below: A Rio de Janeiro suburban station.

only be reached by four trains a week. The journey from Rio involves three changes.

However, this situation of disaster is being taken as an inspiration rather than a source of despair. Divine discontent is motivating the Brazilian government and railway administration to set out on a course of basic modernization and improvement based on a realistic market plan. The previous efforts at modernization were aimed at relatively superficial matters – new diesels, for example, were sorely handicapped by a poor infrastructure and inferior standards of operation. This plan to bring Brazil's railways back from the brink of the grave deserves to succeed.

Civil Engineering

One unusual and successful bit of railway engineering exists on a line which, although very low down in the mileage league, had been certainly in the premier one financially – the 5ft 3in São Paulo Railway connecting the city of that name with the port of Santos. The problem was the coastal escarpment, called the Sierra do Mar, which rose nearly 3000ft a few miles from the shore. A young British engineer called David Fox recommended in 1858 that, instead of a long and expensive diversion – at

*Extreme right, top: Until comparatively recently
South America was a Mecca for those seeking
railway variety. One of the most interesting was the
'Fell' section of the metre-gauge Leopoldina Railway.
This ran for eight miles up the coastal escarpment
near Rio de Janeiro and had the Fell centre rail for
traction and braking. The maximum gradient was
1 in 12.5 and trains were limited to two coaches. This
picture shows what may well be the most modern Fell
locomotive to be built – a North British 0-6-0 of
1946. The line closed in 1965.*

*Extreme right, centre: This Brazilian coal train on
the Dona Teresa Chistina Railway is hauled by a
Baldwin 2-10-2.*

*Below: A pair of American-built diesel-electric
locomotives head a heavy iron-ore train from the
Aguas Claras mine to Sepetiba.*

*Right: A very clean example of North American
influence in South American railroading. This is the
yard at São Paulo – note the US-built diesel-electric
locomotive and typical American type boxcars.*

*Extreme right, bottom: Rio, like most capital cities,
has its show-piece station modernized as far as money
will permit. There is a view from the platform
showing a brand new Japanese-built train on the
Grande Rio suburban system.*

1 in 40 it would be 24 miles long – a system of four one-in-ten rope-worked inclines, using using stationary steam winding engines, would solve the problem. His solution has ever since remained one of the railway wonders of the world. The original inclines had to be duplicated with a second system of five one-in-twelve ones in 1905; in 1974, a modern electrically worked rack-and-pinion incline was built, but the later set of rope inclines still 'temporarily' continues to function. Nowhere else in the world has cable traction been integrated successfully – and other than briefly – into working all traffic on a heavily worked main-line railway. It is said that four-fifths of the world's coffee moves on the line. Both the rack and the ropes are now to be by-passed by a much longer line with a one-in-100 grade, for the import of iron ore.

The British-owned and charmingly named metre-gauge Leopoldina Railway – the longest in Brazil – had problems with this same ridge further north, on lines radiating from Rio de Janeiro. One line had the Fell centre rail and the other had a Riggenbach rack, but both have recently ceased operation.

A glance at the map shows an enormous rail-less area away from Brazil's coastal belt. You can be as much as 1500 miles away from the nearest Brazilian railway and still be in Brazil. Until recently this figure was a mere 750 miles, before the notorious Madiera–Mamore ('a skull under every tie') railroad was closed. The grim phrase quoted in the preceding sentence referred to the abortive 1882 attempt to construct the 225-mile line; only a few thousand sleepers were laid when work was stopped because of the terrible toll taken by disease in the jungle. The line was successfully completed thirty years later, when the precautions necessary to keep the workforce healthy were better understood. Such is railroad construction in the central areas of Brazil. In the case of the 'Mad Mary', the objective was to by-pass an unnavigable stretch of the River Madiera, a tributary of the Amazon.

Steam operation in Brazil is now confined to a few pockets; one is the Lady Teresa Cristina Railway (a coal-hauling line within the state system) at Tubarão, where some excellent and excellently maintained examples of Baldwin 2-10-2s and other types, all in the very best US design tradition, perform on heavy coal trains.

The current statistics of the Brazilian railway system are as follows: mileage 20,625; electrified mileage 870; locomotives – steam 40, electric 230, diesel 1620; carriages – 3744 (340 are formed in electric trains); wagons – 57,635.

VITORIA A MINAS RAILWAY
*Caixa Postal 155,
29000 Vitória,
Espirito Santo.*

The extensive iron-ore deposits in the region around Belo Horizonte are served by the state railway line to Rio de Janeiro. It was proposed that the congestion could be relieved by construction of the new Ferro de Aco, and also by the Vitória a Minas line with its outlet on the coast further to the north.

Whereas the RFFSA broad-gauge central line passes through the most difficult mountainous terrain necessitating the provision of additional locomotives at various points to assist trains over the most steeply graded sections, the Vitória a Minas metre-gauge route follows the Rio Doce for virtually the whole of its alignment. This enables it to have very few adverse gradients for loaded trains and to operate very long trains with a small

196

number of locomotives despite its narrow gauge and sharp curvature.

During its history a number of re-alignments have been made to avoid the sharpest curves usually by the construction of cut-offs across the end of side-valleys, but more recently the line has been completely doubled and re-signalled to increase its capacity to about 120 million tons of iron ore/year in addition to its passenger and general freight traffic. The system of signalling adopted uses cab signalling operated by alternating currents of different frequencies fed through the running rails and is unusual in that no lineside signals are provided other than stop boards at the end of each block section. Double crossovers are provided every four miles and the whole system is controlled from a new CTC building at Tubarão north of Vitória. Tubarão is also the site of a new ore discharge terminal replacing the cramped facilities in the centre of Vitória. This terminal has the most modern rotary dumpers and train positioning equipment. The wagons have rotating couplers enabling them to be emptied without being uncoupled from the train. The train positioner moves the whole train forward two car lengths at a time using a machine running on a separate track parallel to the train and a cantilever arm which hooks over the automatic coupler between each pair of wagons. With trains of 156 wagons it is impossible to position wagons precisely enough within the dumper by using locomotives at either end. The wagons are examined immediately after they have been discharged and those needing repair have to be separated from the train. With trains of such length the shunting movements involved are cumbersome and difficult to control. At Tubarão the rather unusual solution has been to provide a complete hump yard with automatic route setting and retarders. As each train passes over the hump it is cut into the maximum lengths that can be handled safely through the retarders and faulty wagons are switched out to the maintenance sidings. A complete train is then re-formed using the original wagons in good order and replacements which have already been repaired.

BRITISH GUIANA
See Guyana

BRITISH HONDURAS
See Belize

Top: A mineral train from the Aguas Claras mines in Brazil.

Right, top: The La Paz Express of the Antofagasta & Bolivia Railway in prewar days hauled by an oilburning 1-8-4T.

Right, centre: The daily mixed train for Cunco leaves Temuco headed by a 2-6-0 locomotive.

Above: The 5ft 6in gauge railways of Chile are now heavily dieselized and fast modern expresses carrying dining and sleeping car passengers (on the American pattern) work over the main north-south line. There are still some pockets of steam, one of which is at Temuco. This picture shows the modernized station, the yard shunter (a 2-6-0) and a typical diesel.

Right, bottom: A freight train crosses the Bio-Bio river to the freight yards at Concepcion, Chile.

CHILE

See map on pages 186-187.

CHILEAN STATE RAILWAYS
Ferrocarriles del Estado,
Casila 134-D,
Santiago.

The obstacle of the Andes running down the spine of South America has shaped Chile or, perhaps one should say, permitted it to exist. A country 2700 miles long but averaging only 110 miles wide would otherwise have serious problems when it came to defence against quarrelsome and aggressive neighbours. On the other hand it is a perfect shape for a railway system, the simplest possible one – a single route with some stub branches.

One of these stubs, leading to the port of Caldera was in fact the first railway in Chile, opened in 1852. The traditional first railway, connecting a country's capital with its port, linked Santiago with Valparaiso in 1863 and was the first state-owned line. Since then state and private ownership has gone hand in hand to build a very logical 5700-mile system but one which is currently only in moderate shape.

The longitudinal line, which puts off 35 branches in its 1700-mile length, divides into a broad-gauge (5ft 6in) section south of Valparaiso and a metre-gauge one north thereof. Only the broad-gauge section is shown as having a passenger service; and when one reaches its end at Puerto Montt there is still another 1000 miles of Chilean soil for one to traverse before one reaches Cape Horn. (A short line at a naval base at Cape Horn, now closed, was once the most southerly railway in the world – now the honours go to Argentina's RFIRT.)

Four lines run east into the high Andes. The lowest on the map, also the lowest in altitude, is the original Transandine line already mentioned. The line has been electrified on the Chilean side for many years and a two-mile tunnel at 10,400ft altitude takes the line 2000ft below the pass on which the great statue of Christ of the Andes marks the intention of two nations to live in peace with one another. One daily freight and the thrice-weekly passenger train do not occupy or keep the track busy – at other times it is used as a slightly dubious toll road for motor traffic. In its steam days the line introduced to Chile and indeed to the world, a type of double bogie articulated steam locomotive – in principle very similar to today's universal diesels and electrics – known as the Kitson-Meyer. Several Chilean lines used them, but they were never really used much anywhere else.

Travelling northwards (and upwards), that first line out of the port of Caldera was intended by its perpetrator, American William Wheelright, to cross the Andes by the 16,035ft San Francisco pass, which would have been the world's highest railroad had it ever been built. In fact it has remained a small, short branch. Of the Andes crossings which were constructed, the line eastwards out of Antofagasta to Salta in Argentina (with a 13,200ft summit in Chile) has been mentioned, but an interesting and independent line, the Ferrocarril Antofagasta (Chile) and Bolivia runs north-east. For many years the FCAB's Collahausi branch (maximum altitude 15,835ft), originally built to give access to the minerals in the mountains like most of Chile's expensive railways, gave Chile the world's height record, but the branch has now closed and a Peruvian line has taken the record. Even so, the FCAB main line reaches 12,800ft in Chile.

The FCAB (whose Bolivian section was nationalized in 1964) was begun in 1873 and laid as a 2ft 6in-gauge line, while the Bolivian section which followed was laid to metre gauge. In 1928 the whole 384 miles at the Chile end were converted to metre gauge during a closure period which lasted only six days. It is a pleasure to record that one can still travel by a dining- and sleeping-car express the 735 miles from Antofagasta to La Paz, the capital of Bolivia. Alas, the 37-hour timing of the diesel-hauled train cannot match the 31-hour schedule of steam days fifty years ago. One always assumes that it was this railway and its mining customers that figured in John Buchan's famous thriller *Courts of the Morning*.

So far distant from Cape Horn that it is in the tropics, this northern area of Chile is rich in nitrate deposits. Once upon a time (before Dr Haber discovered his process for fixing nitrogen from the air to make artificial fertilizers) these nitrate deposits brought the ships and sailors of the world to its strange-sounding but now half-deserted ports, Tocopilla, Iquique, and Pisagua. The reason for the deposits' existence

is that they have never been washed away by a drop of rain. However, this also means that nothing grows and no alternative traffic for the nitrate railways exists. Close to the Peruvian border runs the Arica-La Paz Railway, the shortest Bolivian outlet but, having rack-and-pinion working, the metre-gauge line is of limited capacity.

Since 1924 over 500 miles of main line between Valparasiso, Santiago and Concep-

cion, as well as the branch to Los Andes, have been electrified, at 3000v DC. On the state system, 160 electric, 300 diesel and 300 steam locomotives (the latter rather dilapidated and by no means all serviceable) haul 1000 passenger and 16,500 freight cars. Two million passengers and 1.1 million tons of freight (hauled an average distance of 84 miles) are carried annually at rates which mean that expenses are as much as 140 percent of the receipts.

COLOMBIA

See map on pages 186–187.

NATIONAL RAILWAYS OF COLOMBIA
Ferrocarriles Nacionales de Colombia,
Calle 13, No 18–24,
Bogota.

Like all South American countries with a Pacific Ocean coastline, Colombia's geography is dominated by the Andes. That these mountains have lost little of their fierceness, even at this the extreme northern end of the range, is shown by the fact that the highest point in the country, Mount Christopher Colombus (18,950ft) is close to the Caribbean coast. One benefit lies in the series of high plateaus between the mountains, cool and healthy in spite of the nearness of the equator, on which most of the population live.

All this added up to a difficult country in which to construct railways and the government was for many years in two minds whether to subsidize private investors or over-spend on its own account. In either case development was slow; the first railway in Colombia was opened in 1855 but it was not until 1961 that the traditional 'capital-to-port' line, normally the first to be built, was completed, linking Bogota to the Atlantic Ocean at Santa Marta. In 1962 the long drawn-out process, begun in 1901, of bringing all the railways into the National network was also completed. A few lines had to be converted from metre gauge to the Colombian standard of 3ft, so that all could be linked to make the current network of 2100 miles.

This new Atlantic Railway ran for much of its length along the valley of the Rio Magdalena, putting out of business many ex-Mississippi River steamboats. A direct link between Bogota and the Pacific was put in hand many years ago, but the project (and a good deal of finished grade in the mountains) was abandoned in 1913 and has not yet been revived although a very circuitous route is now available.

Steam (mostly of modern US origin, but including also Belgian) is almost gone with thirty engines still nominally on the books. The most recent record show 150 diesel units, 300 passenger and 8000 freight cars which handle 4.3 million passengers annually plus 2.7 million tons of freight, hauled an average distance of 270 miles.

Top centre: A Baldwin 2-8-2 crosses the Magdalena River at Girardot, Colombia.

Above: A well-maintained Baldwin 2-8-2 of the Colombian National Railways.

Top right: The Devil's Nose switchback at Sibambe, Ecuador.

Right: The inaugural train on the Atlantic railway. The line runs from Bogota to Santa Marta and the railcar is shown here crossing the new girder bridge over the Magdalena River at Puerto Berrio.

COSTA RICA

See map on pages 190–191.

NATIONAL ATLANTIC RAILROAD
San José.

PACIFIC ELECTRIC RAILROAD
San José.

Costa Rica has a rail link between the Pacific Ocean and the Caribbean. The network was originally built as two separate route systems, one serving each coast and its hinterland. The two lines meet at the capital, San José, and are now operated as a single system. The Pacific Line was electrified in 1934, is fully signalled, and provides a regular passenger service between the capital and Puntarenas. It also carries industrial traffic and a wide range of imported goods to the capital.

The so-called Atlantic line to Limon on the Caribbean coast is diesel-operated with no signalling apart from primitive semaphore arms at some of the principal stations and junctions. The principal traffic on this line and its three lengthy branches is bananas and spurs of considerable length extend through the banana plantations to each of the packing stations. There are no roads through much of the banana growing area and in only a few cases is it feasible to bring produce to the larger railheads by motorized road vehicle.

With this type of traffic the volume loaded at each station varies considerably from day to day, and the urgency of getting the bananas down the line to Limon and loaded into the ships in the shortest possible time to avoid deterioration of quality calls for a very flexible operating pattern with a different train schedule from day to day.

The daily passenger train from Limon to San José passes through spectacular scenery and despite its leisurely schedule is a remarkable experience for the tourist. Nevertheless it is a journey not without its risks for where else in the world would a passenger have his watch stolen from his wrist by an urchin running alongside the moving train.

CUBA

See map on pages 190-191.

CUBAN NATIONAL RAILWAYS
Ferrocarriles Nacionales de Cuba,
Havana.

Cuba is an island of substantial size, being almost 800 miles long. Railways came to it early; a line from Havana, the capital, to

Bejucal was opened on 19 November 1837. Development of the system was entirely in private hands. Havana and Santiago were joined in 1902 and twenty years later there were 3000 miles of public railway, divided mainly between two companies. There was the British-owned United Railways of Havana in the west (including that Bejucal line) and the US-owned Consolidated Railroads of Cuba in the east. The systems were nationalized in the 1950s and now operate under the title of National Railways of Cuba. The lines are and were almost entirely built to the standard gauge and North American style equipment was used, including – in the 1920s – cars supplied and operated by Pullman.

In addition, and highlighting one of the staple traffics of the system, there are 6200 miles of non-public railways, about half of which are narrow gauge, serving (mainly) the sugar industry.

Like all Communist countries, Cuba is shy on some railway statistics, although it is noted that eleven million tons of freight and eighteen million passengers are carried annually on the public system. Before the Castro regime took over there were 300 steam and 172 diesel locomotives, sixty railcars, 330 carriages and 8000 wagons; since then it is noted that forty Russian, twenty Canadian, thirty French and ten British diesels have arrived. Twenty electric locomotives were shown as operating on the ninety-mile erstwhile Hershey Cuban Railway, electrified at 1200v DC.

DOMINICAN REPUBLIC
See West Indies

DUTCH GUIANA
See Surinam

ECUADOR

See map on pages 186-187.

ECUADOR STATE RAILWAYS
Empresa de Nacional Ferrocarriles del Estado.
Carrera Bolivar No 443,
Quito.

Work began in 1871 on a 3ft 6in gauge line to link Quito, the capital of Ecuador (at 9375ft altitude) with the Pacific port of Guayaquil. It was to be 288 miles long, with a summit at 11,840ft. Various financial and engineering problems delayed construction and Quito was not finally reached until 1908.

Past a place called Devil's Nose there is a steep section 22 miles long, much of which is at the extremely severe gradient of one in eighteen, made worse by being combined with curvature down to 200ft radius. There are four zig-zags as well.

US and British staff were hired to work this problem road, but they must have enjoyed it, for the Guayaquil & Quito Railway was known in those days as the 'Good & Quick'.

When the railways were nationalized in 1960, the G&Q was the largest constituent of what is now a 700-mile system (it included an isolated 100-mile section of 2ft 5½in gauge), with 29 steam (nominally) and seventeen diesel locomotives on the books plus 35 carriages and 500 freight cars. A reported 1.7 million passengers and 600,000 tons of freight are carried annually.

EL SALVADOR
See Salvador

FALKLAND ISLANDS

See map on pages 186-187.

It is not known exactly when the Falkland Islands opened its 2ft gauge railroad which ran three miles from Port Stanley to the radio signal station. There was one small steam locomotive, which monopolized the provision of motive power in one direction. In the other, which coincided with the prevailing winds, an informal but more frequent service was provided by sail-driven rail cars. The railroad has since been abandoned.

GUATEMALA

See map on pages 190-191.

GUATEMALA RAILWAY – FEGUA
Ferrocarril de Guatemala,
Guatemala City.

Virtually all the railways in Guatemala originally belonged to a company called Interna-

Right: The crew of 4-6-0 No 57 gets a good view of Guatemala's 12,000ft volcano Agua in October 1961. Escuintla was the helper terminal for the loaded banana trains which have to work through a series of loops before reaching the high coastal plateau at Palin, near Guatemala City.

Extreme right, top: The 4-6-4T Sir Graeme *on Guyana's Georgetown-Rosignol train.*

Extreme right, below: Steam runs no more on Jamaica's standard-gauge railway system and Britain has stepped in with some modern Rolls-Royce engined railcars. This picture was taken at Spanish Town where the Port Antonio and Montego Bay lines divide.

Below right: Built in 1948, 2-8-2 No 199 is seen on the International Railways of Central America at Ipala Hill. The climb from here ascends the escarpment by means of six loops. This is the La Cuesta loop where, once the train emerges from the tunnel it immediately jumps across the steel trestle bridge on the upper left of the picture. There is a helper engine in the middle of the train.

tional Railways of Central America of Jersey City, USA (who, apparently, still dispute their ownership), which was incorporated in 1904. By 1970, when the state took them over, the IRCA had constructed over 500 miles of operational 3ft-gauge railroad plus other mileage in neighbouring Salvador. At that time there were ninety steam locomotives (many of modern construction) and seventeen diesels; 3.4 million passengers were carried each year using 150 carriages and 1.2 million tons of freight was hauled an average distance of 150 miles. It is understood that dieselization is now virtually complete although, in the disturbed state of the country, reliable information is not easy to come by. North American practice is followed.

GUIANA, BRITISH
See Guyana

GUIANA, DUTCH
See Surinam

GUYANA

See map on pages 186-187.

The first railroad to have been built in South America was constructed in what is now Guyana. On 3 November 1848, in the recent and tiny British colony of British Guiana, the Demerara Railway opened the first section of a 21-mile 4ft 8½in-gauge coastal line linking Georgetown with Mahiba. By 1900 the line had been extended to Rosignol (sixty miles), near the frontier with Dutch Guiana (now Surinam)

and there was also a short 3ft 6in-gauge coastal line west of the River Demerara. In 1922 the colonial government took over the working.

It is noted that the first locomotives to arrive were Sharp-Stewart 2-2-2Ts, named, significantly, *Mosquito*, *Sandfly* and *Scorpion*, and that the last (in 1946) were Hunslet 4-6-4Ts *Sir Gordon* and *Sir John*, a repeat order of two supplied in 1923. In 1972 six years after independence, the Guyana government closed both lines, which in 1962 had been carrying three million passengers a year, plus a small amount of freight.

A bauxite mining firm, the Demerara Bauxite Company operates a 3ft gauge fifty-mile line at Linden, which carries passengers as well as the firm's products.

HAITI
See West Indies

HONDURAS

See map on pages 190-191.

The railways of Honduras which began operation in 1869, are divided into three systems. First, there is a small system, the Ferrocarril Naçional, owned by the state; then there are two other railroads, the Vaccaro Railway and the Tela Railroad, owned by the Standard Fruit Company of San Francisco and the United Fruit Company of Boston respectively.

The scale of each's operation is indicated by the following:

Railways of Honduras	Nacional	Vaccaro	Tela
Length of route	128	270	210
Gauge	3ft 6in	3ft 0in	3ft 6in
Locomotives, steam	12	—	—
Locomotives, diesel	8	24	25
Passenger cars	150	25	90
Freight cars	600	700	1400
Passengers carried annually, millions	3.9	?	1.4
Freight carried annually, millions of tons	0.5	0.7	1.6

JAMAICA

See map on page 190.

JAMAICA RAILWAY CORPORATION
PO Box 489, 142 Barry Street,
Kingston.

The 205-mile Jamaica Railway is remarkable in two particular ways. First, it was the first railway in the British Colonial Empire when it opened on 21 November 1845 over the twelve miles between Kingston and Spanish Town. Second, that while nationalization is the common fate of railways the world over, one that has been nationalized twice is rare indeed. The government bought the 4ft 8½in gauge line in 1870 and did some extending; they found running a railway an expensive business (it was a time when tax-payers had a say in how their money was being spent) and sold out nineteen years later to American interests, by which time there were 108 miles of line.

Railroading on a small island did not suit the new owners either and the state had to take it over again in 1900.

Diesel railcars were introduced before World War II but current operations (one million passengers and four million tons of freight – mostly bauxite – annually) are handled by 25 diesel locomotives, 25 carriages and 380 wagons. After steam was phased out, one 4-8-0 was set aside for a tourist operation (Jamaica is a famous holiday isle) but boiler problems occurred and the scheme had to be abandoned.

MEXICO
See North America, Mexico

NICARAGUA

See map on pages 190–191.

PACIFIC RAILWAY OF NICARAGUA
Ferrocarril del Pacifico de Nicaragua,
Aparado Postal No 5,
Managua.

The 200-mile state-owned Pacific Railway was opened in 1886. It was intended to connect the capital, Managua, with the Pacific port of Corino. Until 1903 the journey down to the coast began with a long steamer trip on Lake Managua, but in that year the line was completed through to the capital. About 500,000 passengers ride annually in four diesel trains while nine steam and ten diesel locomotives look after the small amount of freight (60,000 tons) that is carried in the 100-strong wagon fleet.

PANAMA

See map on pages 190–191.

PANAMA RAILROAD
Box 5067,
Christobal, Canal Zone.

In spite of assertions to the contrary, the US does have a railroad that connects the Atlantic and the Pacific Oceans. Moreover, it is state-owned and it opened fourteen years before Union Pacific. The Panama Railroad is 5ft gauge, 47 miles long and was built, with heavy loss of life, between 1850 and 1855. The line provided, across the Isthmus of Panama, a land link in a route from the east to the west of the USA, which avoided the perils of the covered-wagon trail and the hazards of Cape Horn. The fare was $25.00 single, a month's pay in those days, perhaps.

It was used, re-aligned and finally doubled in connection with, first, de Lesseps and second, the US government's attempts to build the Panama Canal. Currently the now single-line road, which runs from Colon to Panama, has six diesel locomotives, 24 passenger and 274 freight cars, and handles one million passengers and 180,000 tons of freight annually.

The other railway in Panama, the 3ft-gauge 100-mile Chiriqui National Railroad, was intended to be part of a Pan-American railway link between North and South America. However, this was not to be and the line is now of local interest only; its operations are on a very small scale.

Right: A locomotive refuelling point at Asunción, Paraguay.

Extreme left, top: No 28, an Alco 2-8-0 of the FC del Pacífico de Nicaragua, heads a mixed train between Miraflores and Bella Vista. This mixed train ran between Corinto and Granada and was the only one to cover the 117-mile main line.

Left: In Paraguay today the ancient 2-6-0 wood-burning steam locomotives still creep (at an average speed of 14 mph) over the grass-grown tracks at the head of the 'International Train' consisting of stock built by the Birmingham Carriage & Wagon Company in 1910 plus a couple of more modern Argentine vehicles.

PARAGUAY

See map on pages 186-187.

PRESIDENT CARLOS ANTONIO LOPEZ RAILWAY
Ferrocarril Presidente Carlos Antonio Lopez, PO Box 453, Calle Mexico 145, Ascunión.

The first section of railway in Paraguay was put in hand as early as 1854 by Dictator Lopez; two British engineers were engaged for the purpose. The army provided labour and the first forty miles southwards from Asunción, the capital of Paraguay, was completed in 1861. War stopped further progress and in 1866 a British company, the Paraguay Central, took over. By 1911 the main objectives, the Parana River and the river port of Encarnación, were reached, 144 miles from Asunción, providing an outlet for Paraguay's farming products. After 1913 there was a connection by train ferry to Argentina's railways, here fortunately laid to the same standard gauge. Through sleeping cars were run to Buenos Aires until a few years ago, hauled over PC metals by handsome woodburning 2-6-0s of archetypical British appearance and design.

Equally archetypical political South American events then intervened and 65 years later the whole system is still there, almost as if it had been chemically preserved. It does demonstrate the extraordinary powers of survival of an old-fashioned steam railway. Since 1961, it has belonged to the state but funds for modernization have not been forthcoming. At the same time, the government is reluctant to close the line. It provides 500 jobs as well as a convenient way of regulating truckers and busmen on the parallel highway.

Meantime, Paraguay is the only all-steam country in the world; its 21 locomotives, thirteen carriages and 200 wagons handle 207,000 passengers and 144,000 tons of freight. Surprisingly, with expenses at only 84 percent of receipts, the financial results are in the top league among state-run railways.

PERU

See map on pages 186-187.

PERUVIAN NATIONAL RAILWAYS – ENAFER
Empresa Nacional de Ferrocarriles del Peru PO Box 1379, Ancash 207, Lima.

Railways came to Peru on 17 May 1851, when the nine-mile line from the Port of Callao to the capital city of Lima was opened. It was inspired by Richard Trevithick, the builder of the first steam locomotive, who had spent some time a few years earlier installing steam pumps to drain the silver mines in the high altitude area known as Cerro de Pasco in the Andes. The two factors which have dominated railway construction in Peru are the Andes mountains and their mineral deposits. No mountain range except the Himalayas matches them and the Himalayas have yet to be crossed by rail.

The second line essayed the foothills of the Andes, connecting 7500ft-high Arequipa, the second city of Peru, with the ocean at Mollendo. A man from San Francisco called Henry Meiggs (he had left there in a hurry fifteen years before) built the seventy-mile route, between 1868 and 1870. There was a £4000 per month bonus for completion in under three years, with a penalty of the same amount for time over, so he did reasonably well.

Already the Peruvian government had decided to carry the line on up into the mountains. Puno on Lake Titicaca (altitude: 12,500ft) was reached in 1874 and finally Cuzco in 1907. This line was later known as the Southern Railway. Via its steamers on Lake Titicaca, a connection into Bolivia was provided.

In the meantime Meiggs was occupied

further north on what was to be his greatest feat of railway construction. This was the Oroya Railroad, later the Central Line, which Brian Fawcett, its chronicler and one-time locomotive chief called 'the highest and hardest railway in the world'. The Southern rose to great altitudes, but approached the mountains gradually, while the Central went straight at them. All these railways were built to standard gauge.

Revolution, war, Meiggs death in 1877 and bad financial problems held up construction. In fact, the line was not completed through to Oroya until 1895. Peru had pledged its accumulation of bird droppings to get these railways built but there was a limit even to the guano. Now the country had to rely on direct foreign investment.

The concession to complete the Central fell to British investors, who also acquired the Southern; they took the name of the Peruvian Corporation. The mining concession for the Cerro de Pasco mines as well as a 75-mile railway feeder line to Oroya, remarkable in that its lowest point was above 12,000ft altitude, went to US interests.

By Andean standards, the grades on the first 25 miles from Lima to Chosica in the foothills are virtually flat, only 1 in 37: but over the next 75 miles the train has to climb 12,875ft to the summit in the three-quarter-mile Galera Tunnel at 15,693ft, just 155ft short of the world's highest. (This also is nearby, on a mine spur at La Cima.) On the climb there are eleven reversals at V-switches and a further two on the descent into Oroya. The ruling grade is a hideous and nearly continuous 1 in 22 and, combined with curvature as sharp as 330ft radius, it governs every move Andean railwaymen make; one careless moment and a runaway train is plunging to destruction down an unbelievable precipice. The wreckage of some of them can be seen today.

One must salute the bridges on the Central, not so much because of their span or length but because of the amazing locations in which they were erected. The Carrion Bridge over the

Above: An interior view of Uruguay's Montevideo Central Station.

Top extreme left: The summit station at Galera, Peru is 15,681ft above sea level.

Top centre: A Lima-bound train stops at Galera Station.

Centre, second from top: A switchback at Viso, Peru. The train will back up from the line in the foreground until it reaches the upper level from which it will proceed normally.

Centre, second from bottom: From the end of the 'most wonderful railway in the world' at Huancayo a 3ft 0in gauge line runs 92 miles to Huancavelica, dropping from 10,000ft to 8000ft and then climbing to 12,000ft. It was once intended to connect to Cuzco but this never materialized – the 150 miles, as the crow flies, which would link it with the terminus of the line out of Cuzco is too steep, hazardous and uneconomic. The line is worked by modern railcars together with steam locomotives.

Extreme left bottom: A daily train, forty miles out of Cuzco, awaits help.

Left: Uruguay's new Hungarian-built diesel train at Punta del Este station.

Verrugas Gorge, 572ft span and 252ft high, is named after Dr Daniel Carrion, who died after experimenting on himself in an attempt to find a cure for Verrugas fever which had carried away hundreds of workers. The great bridge called Chaupichaca (the name is onomatopoetic for steam locomotive) higher up, is notorious for having collapsed when, in 1909, a runaway hit a work train on the bridge.

Among operating features peculiar to these mountain lines should be mentioned the supplies of oxygen carried on the trains, to be administered to passengers suffering from mountain sickness. Another one, this time peculiar to the Central, which has a flow of copper downhill and a flow of oil uphill, is a combined gondola-tanker car. It can be loaded with copper or with oil, but not both without exceeding the permitted axle-load of 17.5 tons. Much empty-car movement is avoided by using this two-way system.

One objection to a zig-zag railway is that the length of the trains is governed by the length of the stalk of the reversing spur at each zig-zag and, by definition, there is almost always some major obstacle to extending them. If not, the extra distance available would already have been used in the first place to gain extra height. Hence, length of trains on the Central remained sensibly constant and, accordingly, the 2-8-0 served from first to last. The famous oil-fired 'Andes' 2-8-0, developed in 1935, was the result of forty years of traumatic operational experience. It combined the ruggedest North American design features with the best Beyer-Peacock English workmanship. BP went on getting repeat orders for 'Andes' locomotives from both the Central and Southern lines until the firm went out of the locomotive-building business. In fact, their very last steam locomotive order in 1957 was for a batch of 'Andes' engines for the Cerro de Pasco Railway.

The natural affinity of diesel locomotives to mountain railroading has been mentioned but, in contemplating dieselization, the Andean roads had a problem for some time. Like people, diesels cannot breathe properly at very great heights and the standard US products needed some refinements; on their home ground, they never got above 10,000ft. At the same time, the efficiency of steam locomotives gets better as they go higher. This has to do with the lower temperature at which water boils. These factors delayed dieselization until the mid-1960s. A loan from the World Bank was obtained for this and it proved the Peruvian Corporation's undoing. Under Andean conditions, the increase in productivity which is necessary to finance dieselization could not be obtained. For example, train lengths could not be increased. So, in the financial turmoil of 1973-74, a position was reached in which there was no money to pay the interest on the loans. The liability thus fell on the Peruvian government who, in return, confiscated the railways, adding them to a few short state lines that already existed.

There are now six separate and unconnected lines; of these, two include breaks of gauge. The last figures available show 1725 miles of route (1490 is standard, 210 is 3ft and 125 is 2ft) on which 29 steam and 146 diesel locomotives run, hauling 4050 freight and 200 passenger cars.

PUERTO RICO
See North America: United States of America: Ponce & Guyana Railway

SALVADOR

See map on pages 190-191.

NATIONAL RAILWAYS OF EL SALVADOR – FENADESAL
Ferrocarriles Nacional el Salvador,
Palacio Nacional,
San Salvador.

Two foreign-owned railway companies operated in El Salvador; the biggest was the 280-mile British Salvador Railway Company, dating from 1896. There was also 100 miles of the US-owned International Railways of Central America, whose main operations were centred in neighbouring Guatemala. The El Salvador Railway was taken over by the government in 1962, and the IRCA lines were taken over in 1973. In 1975 the present administration was formed, with 385 miles of route. The port of Cutuco is the southern end of continuous tracks which extend (with break of gauge at the Mexico-Guatemala frontier) to points in Northern Canada. Passenger trains are not, however, worked beyond the customs stations at any border except the US-Canada one, so a through-traveller faces three short taxi or bus rides, assuming his visas are in order.

FENADESAL has some twelve diesel and fifty steam locomotives, 85 passenger and 730 freight cars. Currently expenses are 120 percent of receipts; 400,000 tons of freight and 1.6 million passengers are moved annually.

SURINAM

See map on pages 186-187.

SURINAM GOVERNMENT RAILWAY
Oneverwacht, Paramaribo.

This small 83-mile metre-gauge railway operates out of Paramaribo, the capital of what was once called Dutch Guiana. There were eleven steam locomotives and a few diesel railcars, but the scale of its operations may be judged from the fact that fifteen passenger and fifty freight cars sufficed for the traffic. Recent information indicates that truncation to around fifty miles has taken place and it is not certain whether operation continues at all.

In compensation, some distance to the west at Apoera on the Guyana border, a 45-mile standard-gauge line is planned, in order to serve a bauxite mining area.

TRINIDAD
See West Indies

URUGUAY

See map on pages 186-187.

URUGUAYAN STATE RAILWAYS
Administracion de Ferrocarriles del Estado,
Calle La Paz 1095, Casilla de Correo 419,
Montevideo.

The Uruguayan State Railways was formed in 1952 from the British-owned 980-mile Central Uruguay and 505-mile, Midland Uruguay railways together with other previously state-owned lines; today's system is 1865 miles long, all on the 4ft 8½in gauge. The actual purchase was made by the government in 1948, using sterling funds earned by Uruguay during the war.

Work started on the Central in 1867; it was a line 127 miles long, running north from Montevideo, the capital and main port, to Durazno, in easy but pleasantly undulating country. Steady development over the next 45 years led to the present system of seven lines radiating out from Montevideo. Four go as far as the Brazilian frontier, to connect (with break-of-gauge) with the Brazilian Railways.

The frontier with Uruguay's other neighbour, Argentina, is the wide River Plate to the south and the Uruguay River to the west. The latter river is not at present bridged, although the Argentine railways on the other side have the same gauge.

Essentially, British 2-6-0s and 2-8-0s were the mainstay of the Uruguayan Railways for many years and even now provide a useful backup to diesel traction; in fact, they have out-

Left: Train ready to depart from Montevideo Station.

Below: View of buffer stops and circulating area at the main terminus at Montevideo.

Bottom: The Island of Haiti still collects its sugar together by rail though today little, if any, steam runs. Back in 1960 the Compagnie de la Plaine du Cul-de-Sac had a 2ft 6in gauge line which used some fascinating steam engines.

lasted not only postwar steam locomotives from other sources but many of the first batch of diesels acquired by Uruguay. It was in fact a sad example of how useless big new shiny diesels are on an old-fashioned railway, if no other steps are taken to provide for them, such as new workshops, permanent way and so on. When diesels first came, it was frequently the case that only one in five were serviceable. Currently there are twenty steam and (nominally) 110 diesel locomotives, 45 railcars (in fifteen modern three-car sets), ninety passenger coaches and 3000 wagons in service. Records show 6.4 million passengers and 1.6 million tons of freight are carried each year, the latter an average distance of 190 miles. British practices still prevail, other than in new motive power and rolling stock.

VENEZUELA

See map on pages 186-187.

VENEZUELA NATIONAL RAILWAYS
Ferrocarriles Naçionales de Venezuela, Estacion Camo Amarillo, Apartado 140, Caracas.

Venezuela, having divested itself of one railway system is presently going to market to buy another. During the last quarter of the nineteenth century fourteen narrow-gauge lines were opened, the longest – the 138-mile Ferrocarril Bolivar – had the narrowest gauge, of 2ft. However, 2ft 6in, 3ft, metre and 3ft 6in lines existed as well; two lines, the La Guira & Caracas and the Venezuela Central were partly electrified. The former had a rack section. The overall total length was 600 miles.

During the 1930s and 1940s many systems

closed; others survived to be nationalized in 1961 and then closed. The current mileage – in a country measuring 800 miles by 600 with twelve million inhabitants – is 170 miles of standard gauge plus a nine-mile 2ft gauge steam historical railway. This is the Empressa del Ferrocarril Historico del Encanto, Caracas.

Recently the Government asked for tenders for the first 700-mile stage in providing Venezuela with a 2100 mile national railway system; one strange omission – a line to Caracas, the capital, in which a thirty-mile rapid transit system is being built.

WEST INDIES

See map on pages 190-191.

Unless the rules are distorted by some random factors like state subsidies or a railway enthusiast in the royal house, the survival and, indeed, the original existence of a railway is

governed by its arithmetic. Railways are economic because many loads can be hauled by one locomotive; it is normally forgotten that it costs money to accumulate loads into trains. It follows that it is only worth forming up a train if it is to run a reasonable distance. By definition, on a small island this cannot be so and, hence, the small islands are the ones that lose their railways to the motorcar and lorry. Very small ones, of course, never got railways, even in horse transport days. Where the traffic can be accumulated into train loads at very small cost at, say, a coal mine, then short railways can survive.

All this is well illustrated by the railways of the West Indies; hence, the disappearance of railways from Antigua, Barbados, Haiti and Trinidad, as well as their degradation from a common-carrier role in Dominican Republic. Other and smaller islands, such as Grenada, Tobago and the Bahamas appear never to have had significant public railways; Cuba and Jamaica have systems of significance which merit their own entry.

The Cape to Cairo Railway

African Offshore Islands
Azores
Canaries
Madeira
Mauritius
Réunion

Algeria
Algerian Railways

Angola
Benguela Railway Company

Benin, People's Republic of
Benin Railways

Botswana

Cameroon
Cameroon National Railways Authority

Congo, People's Republic of the
Congo – Ocean Railway

Egypt
Egyptian Railways

Ethiopia
Northern Ethiopia Railways Share Company
Djibouti to Addis-Ababa Railway

Gabon
Gabon State Railway

Ghana
Ghana Railway and Ports

Kenya
Kenya Railways

Lesotho

Liberia
Bong Mining Company
Lamco J V Operating Company

Libya

Madagascar (Malagasy Republic)
Malagasy Railways

Malawi
Malawi Railways Limited

Mauritania, Islamic Republic of

Morocco
Moroccan Railways

Mozambique, People's Republic of
Mozambique State Railways

Namibia

Niger

Nigeria
Nigerian Railway Corporation

Rhodesia/Zimbabwe
Rhodesia Railways Board

Senegal, Mali, Guinea, Ivory Coast, Upper Volta
Senegal Railways
Mali Railway
Guinea Railways
Ivory Coast Railway (also serving Upper Volta)

Sierra Leone

South Africa
South African Railways

Sudan
Sudan Railways

Swaziland
Swaziland Railway

Tanzania
Tanzanian Railways Corporation
Tanzania Zambia Railway Authority – Tan-Zam Railway

Togo
Togo Railways

Tunisia
Tunisian National Railways

Zaïre
Zaïre National Railways

Zambia
Zambia Railways

THE CAPE TO CAIRO RAILWAY

There was a time when railways were regarded as a main influence in 'civilizing' and, it was implied, bringing 'peace and order' to 'savage' communities. Regarded years ago as the Dark Continent, Africa seemed to cry out for such a 'civilizing' railroad. A Cape to Cairo Railway was suggested by an English clergyman's son called Cecil Rhodes. He was born in 1853 and reached South Africa in 1870.

Rhodes, with the aid of a fortune acquired from diamond mining, got some way with his project. In fact, his railroad progressed as far as the Congo (Zaïre) town of Bukama, 2600 miles from Cape Town but still 3500 miles from his objective. He did it partly by financing the project himself and partly by bullying the government. When he died in 1902, much of the impetus was lost.

After World War I, when the whole distance was spanned by lands under British control and frontier problems were at a minimum, economic difficulties precluded construction. Since World War II, economic conditions have been better and new construction in Zambia, Tanzania and Uganda has filled in some of the missing sections. Alas, political problems have never been worse and border barriers have

Left: A typical South African steam-hauled train is headed by the customary 15E class 4-8-2. It is a fast train from Kroonstad to Harrismith and Durban.

Right: The Johannesburg main line out of Cape Town is now electrified. A coal train hauls its load through the Hex River Valley, Cape Province.

Below: Railway building in Uganda during quieter times (1964). The north-western extension reaches beyond Gulu towards the Nile not far from the Sudan border.

Below right: A diesel-hauled passenger train enters Ingumbi tunnel on the Tan-Zam Railway.

appeared at several points on the route.

Nowadays, a Cape to Cairo traveller who had sufficient political clout to break down these barriers, could travel by Rhodes' route from Cape Town via Kimberley and Mafeking as far as Bulawayo. Then across political barrier No 1, the Zambesi, at the Victoria Falls, the 'carriages washed by the spray' as Rhodes wished. One is diverted from Rhodes' originally proposed route at Kapiri Mposhi where one takes the new Chinese-built Tan-Zam line to Dar-es-Salaam. Every line so far has been laid to a uniform 3ft 6in gauge, but a change to metre gauge now ensues, although provision has been made for many years on East African railways for eventual conversion to 3ft 6in.

Kenya is entered close to Mount Kilimanjaro (or would be if Kenya and Tanzania were on speaking terms) whence the original Uganda Railway is taken via Nairobi and Tororo to East African Railways' furthest point north at Gulu, close to the Sudan border. The same line continues a little further west to Pakwach on the River Nile, but regular steamer services north from there no longer run.

A journey of a mere 100 miles by road brings one into the hands of the Sudan Railways at Juba. However, one must take one of its steamers not one of its trains, and after nine

days and 900 miles one would arrive at Kosti, 200 miles south of Khartoum. The SR is 3ft 6in gauge in anticipation of the first through express. Yet another Nile steamer is necessary before the last lap by Egyptian 4ft 8½in-gauge train to Cairo.

Other information on the Cape to Cairo route appears under South Africa, Botswana, Rhodesia, Zaïre, Zambia, Tanzania, Kenya, Uganda, Sudan and Egypt.

Apart from a rail link-up between Tunisia, Algeria and Morocco, the rest of Africa's nations are, with almost no exceptions, the possessors of isolated and fragmented systems. Most of them were constructed by their colonial owners to open up the hinterland and connect with the port and capital of the original European settlements. There are in fact 22 of these separate 'standard' colonial systems and one or two others which by-pass unnavigable reaches near the mouths of big rivers.

Page 210/211: The Casablanca to Marrakech express en route in typical country.

AFRICAN OFFSHORE ISLANDS

Some appear on map on pages 218-219.

AZORES, CANARIES, MADEIRA, MAURITIUS, REUNION

Of the smaller islands off the coasts of Africa, none currently offer public rail service, but in the past quite interesting systems existed. For example, the widest gauge used on any railway in the world was Isambard Brunel's 7ft 0¼in used by the Great Western Railway of England until 1892, after which it became extinct. Or so one thought, but it does appear that there is (or was until recently) a line of that gauge, complete with steam locomotive, used for repairing the harbour wall at Punta Delgada in the Azores, a group of islands in the Atlantic Ocean.

From 1890 to 1937, a 4.5-mile tramway of metre gauge ran between the port and the town of Las Palmas in the Canary Islands. It would not be mentioned but for the fact that when during the war, gasoline was in short supply, a steam locomotive was sent over from Spain to haul trains of dead electric tramcars over the line, the electric equipment having been dismantled on closure. Other tracks (but not of public railways, it is understood) have been observed at Santa Cruz on the island of Tenerife.

Funchal on the main island of Madeira had a steam rack railway known as the Monte Railway. It was built in 1892 (and extended in 1912) was 2.5 miles long, worked on the Riggenbach system and possessed five steam locomotives. It closed following an accident in 1939.

A 4ft 8½in gauge railway system, 111 miles in extent and based on Port Louis, existed on the island of Mauritius. In its heyday a fleet of 52 steam locomotives (including six Beyer-Garratts) nearly 200 carriages and 750 wagons handled the traffic. Passenger services ceased in 1956 and all traffic in 1967. British equipment and practice prevailed.

The island of Réunion of similar size to Mauritius, had a rail system of French origin smaller in gauge (one metre) and also proportionately smaller in extent and amount of equipment. This also has been closed recently.

ALGERIA

See map on pages 218-219.

ALGERIAN RAILWAYS – SNFT
Société Nationale des Transports Ferroviaires,
21 Boulevard Mohamed V,
Algiers.

The first railway in Algeria was a thirty-mile standard gauge line, running south-west from Algiers, which opened on 8 July 1862. Problems in working soon led to a take-over by the Paris-Lyons-Mediterranée Company; Algeria was then not just a colony but a department of France. The PLM completed the 260-mile route from Algiers to Oran in 1871. Another company, the Algerian Eastern, served the east, linking Algiers with Constantine by 1870. The eastern lines had to be taken over by the state in 1904.

Other lines, some 3ft 5½in gauge, led to the interior. By 1910 the town of Bechar, 500 miles from the sea and well out into the desert, had been reached. Leading south from this point, the proposed 1300-mile Trans-Saharan or, to give it its correct title, the Mediterranée-Niger Railway, almost put Tombouctou on the railway map. But tracklaying ceased in 1942 and has not been resumed.

In 1933 the railways in Algeria were unified

Extreme left, top: The famous steel-arched bridge at Victoria Falls on the Cape to Cairo Railway.

Extreme left, below: An 'open air' train on Monte Rack Railway at Funchal, Madeira.

Left: One of the powerful narrow-gauge Garratt locomotives in use on Algeria Railways during French rule. The locomotive is a 4-8-2 + 2-8-4 with a PLM number.

Below left: Benguela Railway woodburning Beyer Garratt 4-8-2 + 2-8-4 at Huambo (Nova Lisboa) in 1974.

Below: A diesel-hauled train on the Benguela Railway at Canocha in Angola.

and in 1939 their operation was finally nationalized. World War II and Independence in 1962 had only temporary effects on the rail network. Since then some narrow-gauge mileage has been converted to standard, but 750 miles still remain out of a total of 2400.

Locomotive Landmarks

The steam locomotive fleet was all based on and many were actual examples of current French designs, particularly the distinctive machinery of the PLM. A notable but somewhat brief episode was the introduction in 1934 of high-speed Garratts to work the Oran-Algiers-Constantine expresses. The Garratt type of articulated steam locomotive was generally built as a low-speed mountain climbing big puller, but its geometry, unlike that of other articulated types such as the Mallet, was eminently suited to high speed. The 29 4-6-2 + 2-6-4s could unassisted handle huge trains on the one-in-fifty grades as well as travel at up to 75mph on the level sections. Alas, the designers could not resist adding complications, such as an electrically worked reversing gear. This and a few other novel but unnecessary features proved to be the Achilles heel of these remarkable locomotives when, under wartime conditions, maintenance left a good deal to be desired.

Desert conditions in Algeria made the railways there a natural case for dieselization.

Before reliable French designs had been achieved, standard US diesels were imported. Steam was eliminated as early as 1955.

Electrification of iron-ore hauling lines in the east, based at the port of Annaba, began in 1932 and now extends 180 miles.

At the present time, on the standard gauge, forty electric and 137 diesel locomotives haul 400 passenger carriages and 10,000 wagons. The corresponding figures for the 3ft 5½in gauge are 0, 24, 33 and 1000 respectively. About 3.5 million passengers travel annually and 4.2 million tons of freight are hauled an average distance of 120 miles. Expenses are 99 percent of receipts.

ANGOLA

See map on pages 226–227.

Angola was a Portuguese colony dating from the sixteenth century, which achieved independence in 1976. Civil war broke out immediately afterwards and in 1977 the Communist side achieved control, although there is thought to be still some opposition outside main centres. There are three significant railway systems of which the principal was called the Benguela Railway.

BENGUELA RAILWAY COMPANY
*Cia do Caminho de Ferro de Benguela,
PO Box 32,
Lobito, Angola.*

The Benguela Railway was opened on 28 August 1928. Its principal *raison d'être* was to provide a direct outlet to the sea for copper, mined in what is now Zaïre and Zambia. For passengers from Europe to such places as Bulawayo or Salisbury, in Rhodesia/Zimbabwe, it saved three days in travel time compared to the route via Cape Town. Through trains were run – the gauge was the normal Southern African one of 3ft 6in. An Englishman called Robert Williams had obtained a 99-year concession from the Portuguese government in 1902 (a station on the railway is named after him) and accordingly the line was built with British capital. In theory at least, it still belongs to a British company.

Like most long-distance mineral hauling railways it has been financially successful – in some recent years expenses have been as low as 56 percent of receipts and the system has been maintained in top condition. This was, of course, before the recent war put it out of action.

The line runs inland due east from the port of Lobito, a distance of 840 miles to join the Zaïre railways at Dilolo. The principal operating problem was the climb from the coast to the 5000 + ft altitude of the inland plateau. The original alignment involved 1.5 miles of 1 in 16 grade and rack and pinion (Riggenbach) traction. A second, completed in 1948, involved a main climb at 1 in 33 and a much longer distance at 1 in 50. Yet a further one, completed in 1974, in spite of the uncertain future – kept the grade down to 1 in 80. The new line has 90 lb/yd rail but much 60 lb still exists elsewhere.

Like so many African Railways, especially those laid with lightish rails, the Benguela was faithful to the Beyer-Garratt articulated steam locomotives for hauling its principal traffic. Most of them in Angola are remarkable in one special way in that they use wood for fuel, the only case in the world in which a modern railway adopted *as deliberate policy* a primitive source of energy that in most other places did not out-last the first few puffs of steam.

The company planted eucalyptus forests at appropriate intervals along the line and they provide clean self-replacing and sweet-smelling fuel for its trains. The problem is that, while eucalyptus is little inferior to oil or coal in heat produced per *ton*, in terms of heat produced per *cubic yard* it is four or five times less effective. Although the locomotives carry huge cages in which the logs are stacked, not only are two firemen needed but wooding stops are required perhaps twice as often as coaling or oiling ones would be. Almost all the steam locomotives ever supplied to the railway – 107 in all – are still in service including some of the last ever to be built in England.

Near the coast where the heaviest grades are, eucalyptus does not grow and coal and oil burning power was used here even before the arrival of US standard diesels, 22 of which had been received by 1976.

In the early 1970s, problems between Zambia, Rhodesia and Mozambique had meant extra copper traffic on the Benguela, but since the Angolan troubles began, the railway has been closed to through traffic. At the same time the Tan Zam line provides another outlet for Zambian copper. A big question mark hangs over a line which four years ago was handling 2.5 million tons of traffic annually over its single line of metals.

Through passenger boat trains from Lobito to Elizabethville (now Lubumbashi) ceased several decades ago, but the daily passenger train which ran as far as the Congo border continued in service until 1975. There are 1830 freight cars, all equipped with the vacuum brake.

In Angola there are also three other separate smaller coast-to-inland systems, based on Luanda, Porto Amboin and Mossâmedes respectively. Prior to independence, these were separate entities, but it is likely that they are now administered as one. There are altogether 930 miles of 3ft 6in gauge and about 100 miles of 1ft 11½in with a fleet of 75 diesel and 35 steam locomotives (the latter mostly stored), sixty passenger cars and 2000 goods wagons.

AZORES
See African Offshore Islands

BASUTOLAND
See Lesotho

BECHUANALAND
See Botswana

BELGIAN CONGO
See Zaïre

BENIN

See map on pages 218-219.

BENIN RAILWAYS – OCBN
Organisation Commune Benin-Niger des Chemins de Fer et des Transports, PO Box 16, Cotonou.

The Benin Railways were begun in 1900 by a company which enjoyed a concession from the French government for a railway into the interior from the port of Cotonou. Its present terminus at Parakou, 275 miles from Cotonou, was achieved on 1 January 1935. There is talk of an extention to Gaya on the River Niger, which would double the length of the line. Currently eleven diesel locomotives and eight railcars haul 24 carriages and 350 wagons carrying 1.5 million passengers and 0.3 tons of freight. Receipts are 98 percent of expenses.

BOTSWANA

See map on pages 226-227.

A 400-mile stretch of the Cape to Cairo Railway has run through this sparsely populated country on its way from Mafeking to Bulawayo ever since 1897. Since independence in 1966 (Botswana was formerly the British Protectorate of Bechuanaland), Rhodesia Railways have operated the line. It is understood that the Botswana government has now taken over the line.

CAMEROON

See map on pages 226–227.

CAMEROON NATIONAL RAILWAYS AUTHORITY – REGIFERCAM
PO Box 304,
Douala.

In 1905, when Cameroon was a German colony, the Kamerun Eisenbahn Gesellschaft set out to build lines into the interior from Bonaberi and Douala, settlements on either side of the mouth of the River Wouri. The 100-mile western line was completed in 1911, but construction of the eastern one soldiered on into the days of the French mandate and then independence. The line was not opened to Ngaoundere, 585 miles from Douala, until 14 February 1974. There are presently 733 miles of metre-gauge route, 48 diesel locomotives, 94 carriages and 11,500 wagons in service. Expenses are 122 percent of receipts.

CANARIES
See African Offshore Islands

CONGO

See map on pages 226–227.

CONGO – OCEAN RAILWAY – CFCO
Chemin de Fer Congo – Ocean,
PO Box 651,
Pointe Noire.

This 3ft 6in gauge line, 320 miles long, was opened on 29 May 1934. It connected the port of Pointe Noire, on the Atlantic with Brazzaville on the Congo River, situated opposite Leopoldville (now Kinshasha, capital of Zaïre). The CFCO by-passed the barely navigable reaches of the river near its mouth. At one time the Wagons-Lits company provided sleeping and dining cars on the journey.

The CFCO provides common-carrier services on a 177-mile branch from Mont Belo to M'Bindo, built in 1962 by a mineral consortium known as COMILOG, who in turn operate their own ore trains through to Pointe Noire.

Statistics for the combined systems show 77 diesel locomotives with 58 passenger and 1540 freight cars, carrying 5.1 million tons of freight an average distance of 235 miles, in addition to 1.2 million passengers. The vacuum brake is used and the speed limit is 50 mph.

DAHOMEY
See Benin

Left, above: Mixed trains meet at Pobé, Benin.

Left: A Benguela Railway train on Angola's inland plateau. East of Huambo (Nova Lisboa) and Silva Porto most passenger trains were hauled by 4-6-0, 4-8-0 and 4-8-2 locomotives, the major hill-climbing having been accomplished.

Above: Multiple-unit railcars of French origin at Eséka, Cameroon.

Above centre, left: Construction work in the Congo.

Above centre, right: In days of steam, passengers await a steam train amid the banana plantations.

Top: A Rhodesian Railways 12th class 4-8-2 pulls a through Johannesburg–Bulawayo train.

Projection: Sanson Flamsteed's Sinusoidal

1:15 000 000

EGYPT

See map on pages 218–219.

EGYPTIAN RAILWAYS
Rameses Square,
Cairo.

The idea of a railway to connect the Mediterranean with the Red Sea was first mooted in 1834 but in fact it was not until 1858 that a standard-gauge railway was opened between Alexandria, Cairo (reached in 1856) and Suez. Before that time animal transport was relied on, the Peninsular Oriental Steam Navigation Company owning 3000 camels for this purpose. The railway, on the other hand, was state-owned.

Robert Stephenson, no less, was chief engineer and, when the first section out of Alexandria opened in 1854, railways had come not only to Egypt but also to Africa. After the Suez Canal was opened in 1869, the Cairo-Suez section across the desert was found to attract little traffic and accordingly closed. Extensions followed to cover all the fertile parts of the country (which is another way of saying that railway development was confined to the River Nile and its delta).

Asyût, 230 miles south of Cairo, was reached in 1874, Luxor (340 miles) in 1878. El Shellal, a point quite close to the present terminus at Sadd-el-Ali (561 miles from Cairo) was at that time accessible from Luxor on a 3ft 6in gauge military line; this was converted to standard gauge in 1926.

World Wars I and II, in both of which Egypt was a main base, brought temporary extensions into Palestine and Libya of what was effectively the Egyptian railway system.

Steam power was partly of British and partly of French design and construction for some reason, exceptionally handsome and well-proportioned. This applied particularly to the 4-4-2s and 4-6-0s, types very suitable for a flattish terrain. Little known were thirty noble high-stepping oil-fired 4-6-2s with 81in driving wheels, built in France during 1955; it is tragic to record that less than eight years later all these superb machines had gone to the torch in the face of diesel onslaught. By 1963 the system was entirely dieselized, except for a fifteen-mile suburban electrification in the Cairo area.

The Egyptians learned the art of comfort in rail travel from that master of the craft, the Compagnie Internationale des Wagons-Lits, who ran the sleepers, diners and Pullman saloons in the country for many years.

For both main-line and branch-line services, self-propelled diesel trains had been a feature for many years; currently these consist of 430 vehicles. There are 620 diesel locomotives, 1350 carriages and 17,500 wagons. Approximately 230 million passengers and 13.6 million tons of freight are transported annually. Expenses in the year 1978 are 103 percent of receipts.

There used to be a large system of 2ft 6in gauge light railways in the Nile Delta, developed by a British Company but state-owned after 1955. It extended at one time to 600 miles, but is now reported to be closing.

Right: One of the British LMS-designed 2-8-0s imported to Egypt by the War Department during World War II.

Centre right: An Egyptian electric train built by Siemens of Germany.

Bottom right: A scene at Djibouti in 1910.

Bottom: A British-built 2-6-0 at Geneifa in the Egyptian Canal Zone in 1950.

Below: With Cairo main station in the background, a British-built 4-4-0 heads a train of mixed six-wheeled and bogie coaches past the locomotive shed in 1946.

ETHIOPIA

See map on pages 218–219, 226–227, 250–251.

NORTHERN ETHIOPIA RAILWAYS SHARE COMPANY
PO Box 218,
Asmara.

DJIBOUTI TO ADDIS-ABABA RAILWAY
Compagnie du Chemin de Fer Franco-Ethiopien de Djibouti a Addis-Ababa,
PO Box 1051,
Addis Ababa.

The Ethiopians are a race whose military prowess has never led to easy colonial exploitation – the Italians paid dearly for their brief occupation from 1936 to 1941 – but both the railways that exist there are of the classic colonial port-to-interior pattern.

The oldest ran inland from the port of Mesewa, then in Eritrea, which was Italian territory at that time. It had not got far when the Italian defeat at Adowa held things up for twenty years. Work began again in 1907, Asmera was reached in 1911 and Agordat in 1922. At present, most of the railway is out of use due to terrorist activity, but there are nominally eighteen steam and three diesel locomotives, five railcars, nineteen passenger coaches and 600 wagons running on the 190-mile line.

The Eritrean Railway (later administered by the Northern Ethiopia Railways Share Company) was not absolutely the first line; in 1867 a British military railway was laid briefly in 1867 inland for eleven miles from Zula, a short distance south of Mesewa. Its purpose was to aid General Napier's expedition to rescue British prisoners held at Magdala and has gone down in history as an almost perfect example of how *not* to build a military railway. Although a tremendous effort had gone into the planning, much useless and incompatible equipment was supplied, with the result that four months work in easy territory produced only eleven miles of line.

The second permanent line in Ethiopia was a French enterprise, commenced in 1897, to connect the port of Djibouti in French territory (then called French Somaliland but recently independent Afars & Issas) with the Ethiopian capital. Bankruptcy intervened in 1902, when the line had reached Dire Dawa (296 miles). Work started again in 1909 and Addis Ababa (485 miles) was reached on 7 June 1917. The locomotive fleet came largely from Switzerland (a 2-8-0 is noted as being named *Tcher-Tcher* – presumably Abyssinian for puff-puff). Dieselization was complete by 1956; most unusually, some of the 26 diesel-electrics came from Switzerland. There are 42 passenger cars and 640 wagons; 600,000 passengers and 0.5 million tons of freight are handled in a typical year, although recently Somali insurgents have interrupted traffic.

FRENCH WEST AFRICA (SENEGAL, MALI, GUINEA, IVORY COAST AND UPPER VOLTA)
See Senegal *et al*

———GABON———

See map on pages 226-227.

GABON STATE RAILWAYS – OCTRA
Office du Chemin de Fer Transgabonais
BP 2198,
Libreville.

The August 1978 and 1979 issues of *Thomas Cook's International Timetable* offers, under the entry for Gabon, a blank table with the encouraging words 'Service to commence shortly'.

Output from manganese and uranium mines at Franceville in the southeast of the country had always been sent out by a 48-mile ropeway across the border to a railroad in the Congo Republic. The ropeway had limited capacity and was, of course, no use for the transport of anything other than minerals. The alternative of a 438 mile all-purpose railway to the Gabonese port of Libreville was naturally preferred by the government. Work began in March 1975.

Diesel power is supplied from the USA and France; many other countries have contributed materials. A very large loading gauge is provided; 20ft 4in high by 13ft wide – this eclipses the Soviet gauge, which had been the largest in the world. Fortunately the terrain is not exacting.

Top: A train from Pointe Noire arrives at Brazzaville in the Congo.

Above: A modern Ethiopian diesel-electric locomotive takes a freight towards the hills.

GERMAN EAST AFRICA
See Tanzania

GERMAN SOUTH WEST AFRICA
See Namibia

GHANA

See map on pages 218–219.

GHANA RAILWAY & PORTS – GRP
PO Box 251,
Takoradi.

Before independence in 1957, Ghana was known as the Gold Coast; it is thus not surprising that the first section of railway there was built to serve the gold mines at Tarkwa forty miles inland from what is now the port of Takoradi. Makeshift port facilities were provided at Sekondi nearby and work began in March 1898. The mines were reached in 1901.

It had been decided to continue the line a further 128 miles inland to the trading centre of Kumasi; and this was put in hand. The Gold Coast was the original 'White Man's Grave' and it is on record that ten chief railway engineers had been expended before Kumasi was reached on 1 October 1903.

A line connecting Kumasi with Accra, the capital, situated further along the coast, but then only a 'surf port', was begun in 1909, delayed by the war and completed in 1923. The great deep-water port at Takoradi was opened in 1928. Other connecting lines and branches followed, making up the 600-mile 3ft 6in gauge system of today.

A series of handsome 4-8-2s were the mainstay of the line in steam days. The GCR was not able to avoid Garratts entirely; some were supplied in World War II on a new branch financed by the British Ministry of Aircraft Production to serve bauxite mines. Sixty-four steam locomotives are still on the books.

Eighty-eight diesels haul the majority of the six million passengers and one million tons of freight (average length of haul – 180 miles) now carried. This traffic is, alas, insufficient for solvency, expenses being 180 percent of receipts. There are 230 coaches and 4000 freight cars.

Above: A steam locomotive in Ghana at the turn of the century.

Top: A US-built 2-8-2 sits on the turntable outside the shed at Kumasi, Ghana.

Above: A class 29 2-8-2 pulls a freight train bound for Nakuru, Kenya.

Right: Trainloads of hardwood from Ghana destined for Europe.

Centre top: A Kenyan 59 class 4-8-2 + 2-8-4 Garratt at Nairobi East signal gantry. Inherited from Britain is the practice of the signalman's waiting to take the electric token (for single line working) from the fireman.

Centre below: Henschel diesel-hydraulic 660 hp B-Bs stand in Nairobi station yard in their new blue livery, May 1978.

Extreme right, top: Masai warriors take a look at a North British Company 84 class diesel shunter.

Below: A 60 class 4-8-2 + 2-8-4 Garratt with roller bearings on all axles – a truly modern machine. These engines were in regular use until the late 1970s.

GOLD COAST
See Ghana

GUINEA
See Senegal *et al*

IVORY COAST
See Senegal *et al*

KENYA

See map on pages 226-227.

KENYA RAILWAYS
PO Box 30121,
Nairobi.

On 11 December 1895 George Whitehouse (later, Sir George Whitehouse, KCB) stepped ashore at Mombasa to commence construction of the British government's 580-mile Uganda Railway. It was a curiously reluctant piece of empire building, violently opposed at home, yet, in the end, one of the most successful. Against all reason the project soon became viable: the Arab slave-trade, the suppression of which was one of the objectives, came to an end; Nairobi, then just a survey peg in the scrub, became, seventy short years later, the capital of a great and respected independent nation.

The site of Nairobi was reached in 1899 and the objective, a landing place on Lake Victoria called Port Florence, later Kisumu, in 1901. Entebbe in Uganda was reached by a 150-mile steamer trip across one corner of the immense lake which is effectively a source of the River Nile. In 1931 the railway was extended across the Nile to Kampala, Kisumu then becoming the terminus of a 130-mile branch; it was finally extended to a point close to the Zaïre border and the Mountains of the Moon at Kasese (near Kilembe), 1080 miles from Mombasa, was reached in 1956. The 315-mile Tororo-Gulu-Pakwach branch reaches to within 100 miles of the Sudan border.

In 1926 the system became the Kenya-Uganda Railway and in 1948 the East African Railways & Harbours Administration, when the lines in what is now Tanzania became included. The system finally reached 3700 miles, the second largest in Africa, but in 1975 friction between what had in 1960 become three separate nations had reached a point where the administration of a single joint railway system became impossible. The railways in Tanzania had always been, in any case, a separate operating entity but, so far as Kenya and Uganda were concerned, any separation must be more *de jure* than *de facto* to start with.

Construction problems included marauding lions, hostile natives, disease and terrible supply difficulties. The now-regrettable decision to adopt a gauge other than the British Africa standard of 3ft 6in was taken at the last minute by the home government in order to permit the use of Indian equipment, conveniently to hand 'across the bay'; 32,000 Indians were brought over to do the construction work and 2500 died.

The traction problem in Kenya was a severe one. From sea level at Mombasa, the original railway climbed to over 6000ft. When the main line was extended into Uganda, more than 9000ft of altitude had to be surmounted. In fact Timboroa station, 9136ft, was the highest

railway location in the British Empire. Much easing of gradients was done – there are four spirals on the system – but the problems remained acute until the coming of the Beyer-Garratt locomotive, which in 1957 accounted for 129 out of a total stock of 450.

The first Garratts were supplied in 1926 and were basically two of the line's standard 4-8-0s joined together, inner pony trucks added, making them 4-8-2+2-8-4s. They shared the ten-ton axle-load of the 4-8-0s, enabling operation on 50 lb/yd rail. The Garratts marked the beginning of the end of eucalyptus wood-firing, although on some of the remoter lines it continued until after coal was superseded by oilburning at the end of World War II. The last Garratts supplied were the magnificent '59' class 4-8-2+2-8-4s of 1955, 104ft long, with 21-ton axle-load, now the most powerful steam locomotives running in the world and able to take full advantage of the heavier 95 lb/yd rail which by this time had been laid on the main line. They handle, in 1978, 1200-ton trains with ease between Mombasa and Nairobi. The overall cost of operation was then, less than would be involved in changing over to diesel traction. Their successors, were to have been the '61' class, the largest Garratts ever designed, 125ft long with 25-ton axle-load, but in the

end it was decided to dieselize instead. This process was to be completed by 1980 except for some minor operations.

An interesting feature of operation is the so-called 'caboose' system, whereby on long runs one train crew can rest while a second one takes over. In 1977 the East African administration was broken up and the three countries, Kenya, Uganda and Tanzania, resumed responsibility for their own systems. Kenya Railways Corporation began official operations on 20 January 1978. Kenya Railways operates a fleet of 103 steam and 130 diesel locomotives, 513 coaching stock vehicles and 6637 freight wagons. The last statistics available (1976) for the *whole* East African system show a fleet of 235 steam and 192 diesel locomotives, 16,000 freight and 530 passenger cars. The system carried six million tons of freight an average distance of 420 miles as well as 5.7 million passengers. Token working is used, with semaphore signalling. The air brake is used in Kenya and Uganda; both air and vacuum brakes are used in Tanzania.

225

SOUTHERN AFRICA

1:15 000 000

| 100 | 0 | 100 | 200 | 300 | 400 miles |

| 100 | 0 | 100 | 200 | 300 | 400 | 500 | 600 km |

MADAGASCAR
On same scale as General Map

INDIAN OCEAN

INDIAN OCEAN

ATLANTIC OCEAN

ANGOLA

ZAMBIA

MALAWI

MOZAMBIQUE

RHODESIA

BOTSWANA

NAMIBIA (SOUTH WEST AFRICA)

SOUTH AFRICA

CAPE PROVINCE

ORANGE FREE STATE

TRANSVAAL

NATAL

LESOTHO

SWAZILAND

TRANSKEI

Kalahari

Tropic of Capricorn

East from Greenwich

Projection : Sanson Flamsteed's Sinusoidal

LESOTHO

See map on pages 226–227.

One thing the Kingdom of Lesotho has in common with the Vatican City is an absurdly short railway (in this case 1.25 miles) belonging to a large and totally enclosing neighbour, in this case South Africa.

LIBERIA

See map on pages 218–219.

BONG MINING CO.
PO Box 538,
Monrovia.

LAMCO JV OPERATING CO.
PO Box 69,
Monrovia.

Not being anyone's colonial possession, the natural resources of Liberia were not exploited at all until shortly before World War II, when Firestone obtained concessions for rubber plantations on the coastal plain south of Monrovia. After that war other companies were allowed into the country and iron-ore deposits were discovered in the north and the south of the country. One railway was built from Monrovia to the Bong Mines in the north, and another from Buchanan to a mine in the Nimba range in the east of the country near the intersection of the Guinea, Ivory Coast and Liberia frontiers. The latter railway built in 1962 for Lamco was one of the first iron-ore railways to be deliberately designed for the operation of long trains and to be fully equipped with centrally controlled signalling and other modern aids to efficient operation.

The line is standard gauge with 130 lb/yd rail to American standards and the normal train size is ninety wagons each carrying about 94 tons of ore giving each a total gross load of 10,530 tons, hauled by three 2000hp locomotives. The 160-mile route is single track, and has eight intermediate stations with passing loops. The maximum tonnage of ore transported has been thirteen million tons/year. Since the total fleet is 510 ore cars and fourteen locomotives this calls for a very high standard of operations and maintenance.

Plans have been drawn up for increasing production at the mine to 16 million tons/year and for opening a new mine in Guinea with a production of 15.0 million tons/year. This will involve a 12-mile extension of the existing railway, lengthening of the train to 125 wagons, partial doubling of the main line and new terminal facilities at each end of the line.

LIBYA

See map on pages 218–219.

So far as railways are concerned, Libya has had a chequered history with independent ventures in various parts of the country. The earliest railway was constructed at 75cm (2ft $5\frac{1}{2}$in) gauge between 1911 and 1916 to serve Benghazi and the surrounding area. In 1918 it was converted to 95cm (3ft 1.4in) gauge and was gradually extended to a total of 69 miles reaching Barce in 1927; a separate 35-mile line was also built from Benghazi to Sulug.

In the west of the country a 95cm gauge line was built from Tripoli to Zuwarah between 1912 and 1915 with some branches inland and eastwards from Tripoli. Initially this group of lines was used for military purposes. Later it carried general freight and passenger traffic and in 1938 a diesel railcar service was introduced for the journey between Tripoli and Gharyan. During World War II these western lines were again taken over for military purposes and for a short period between 1943 and 1944 were converted to metre gauge to overcome a shortage of 95cm gauge stock. The lines out of Tripoli were closed in 1960 and much of the formation was used for the location of a new coastal highway. Several of the two-storey station buildings with their shady balconies and verandahs can still be seen beside the road.

The eastern lines radiating out of Benghazi were closed in 1965. The only other railway in Libya was a 60-mile standard-gauge wartime extension from Egypt to Tobruk. This line was cut short at Salûm in 1946 and the Libyan portion of the track was lifted.

More recently plans have been made for a standard-gauge line linking Tripoli with Sfax in southern Tunisia. This line will run slightly inland of the coastal highway and pass to the south of each of the principal towns; short branches to ports and other industrial developments are included in the proposals. The layout of the passenger and freight terminals in Tripoli will permit the line to be extended eastwards to Misratah at a later date. Preliminary designs have also been made for a 300 mile standard-gauge route from Misratah southwards to Brach to permit the exploitation of an iron-ore deposit there. The aspiration to create a continuous rail link along the Mediterranean coast from Morocco to Egypt is still a long way from being realized, but these new railways in Libya provide a vital link in the chain.

Extreme left: Mombasa mail train crosses the Nile Bridge at Jinja, Uganda hauled by a 60 class 4-8-2+2-8-4 Beyer-Garratt.

Left: A relic of Italian occupation, this metre-gauge 0-4-0+0-4-0 bears a British War Department number – 70640 – as it stands at Benghazi in 1950.

Bottom: North British Locomotive Company's No 49 – the last steam locomotive to run on Malawi Railways, 1973.

MADAGASCAR

(MALAGASY REPUBLIC)

See map on page 227.

MALAGASY RAILWAYS
PO Box 259,
Avenue de l'Independence,
Tananarive.

Madagascar is the only off-shore island around Africa to retain a public railway system, no doubt because of its great size.

A metre-gauge line runs from Tamatave, a port on the east coast of the island, to the capital Tananarive in the central highlands and then southwards along the mountain chain to Antsirabe. Since the line climbs to an altitude of 5500ft in the 100 miles from Brickaville on the coast to Tananarive it is not surprising that gradients as steep as 1 in 29 and curves as sharp as 164ft radius are involved, or that operating speeds are very low. However, the location of the capital city in the comparatively temperate climate of the mountain range in the centre of the island makes this inevitable. The main station in Tananarive has an ideal location across the end of the principal boulevard in the shopping district which indicates the greater importance the railway enjoyed in the days before domestic flights took over the bulk of inter-city passenger travel.

A separate railway on the island of Nossi Bé off the northwest coast of Madagascar provides a complete constrast to the national system. This serves a sugar estate and was constructed almost entirely of secondhand materials from other countries. Originally worked by steam locomotives designed to use bagasse, the waste-product from the sugar mills as fuel, the only recent acquisitions are two small diesel locomotives which now work the twelve-mile main line leaving the remaining octogenarian 0-6-0 tender engine to shunt to and from the cane yard and to make short trips to nearby stations. The cane wagons were adapted from ammunition carriers from the trenches of World War I and the rails generally date from the same period. The line includes a number of steep gradients where, despite the high axle-load of the locomotives, sanding is required to assist adhesion. The notorious unreliability of mechanical sanding devices is avoided by placing a sack of sand on the buffer beam and getting a member of the train crew to squat on the side-plates sprinkling handfuls of sand onto the rail whenever he hears the wheels begin to slip. This description may suggest a decrepit and run-down system unworthy of appearing in the same book as the sophisticated national networks, but the extreme enthusiasm of the train crews, the amazingly high utilization of its antiquated stock, and above all its picturesque setting make it a railway to remember.

MALAWI

See map on pages 226-227.

MALAWI RAILWAYS LTD.
PO Box 5144,
Limbe, Malawi.

The building of the railway in Nyasaland, as Malawi was then known, involved three stages. The Shire Highlands Railway, completed in 1908, ran up-country to Blantyre, the capital, from Nsanje on the Shire River, a tributary of the great Zambesi. A desire for more reliable movement when the river was low led to an extension, completed in 1914, and located partly in Portuguese territory, to Vila Fontes on the Zambesi. This section was known as the Central Africa Railway. A further desire to avoid transhipment from ocean-going ships into river barges led to a further project to extend the line across the Zambesi (hence the name Trans-Zambesi Railway) to the port of Beira. This was put in hand after World War I and completed in 1935, in which year the up-country line (by now called the Nyasaland Railways) was extended to Salima on Lake Nyasa. The Zambesi was crossed by the famous bridge at Sena, the longest in Africa, 12,064ft in length, with 33 spans. This structure is now in independent Mozambique but was effectively an integral part of the Nyasaland system.

The colonial settlers established their political and commercial centres on the southern highlands to avoid the risk of diseases then prevalent in the low-lying areas in the Shire River valley and around Lake Nyasa. As a result the railway had to climb very steeply to reach Blantyre and nearby Limbe, the headquarters. This section includes gradients of one in forty and curves as tight as $5\frac{1}{2}$ chains (363ft) radius, creating considerable operating and maintenance problems. The continuation of the line northwards from Blantyre to cross the Shire River near Matope and to approach the shore of Lake Nyasa involved similarly steep gradients and sharp curves which severely limit the operating capacity of the line. The new connection from Nkaya eastwards to cross the border into Mozambique at Nayuci has gentler gradients (one in 115 against exports) and has provided an opportunity for opening up the agricultural potential of the central part of the country. The system has recently been extended westwards to the new capital, Lilongwe, and a connection from there to Chipata in Zambia is planned.

In 1976 a Zambia Railways diesel locomotive and a number of Rhodesia Railway coaches were working in Malawi. Their return home was rendered virtually impossible by the political situation between neighbouring countries.

MALI
See Senegal *et al*

MAURITANIA

See map on pages 218-219.

MAURITANIA RAILWAY – SNIM-COMINOR
Chemin de Fer F'Derik a Nouadhibou,
PO Box 42,
Nouadhibou.

The Mauritania Railway is a newish iron-ore railway, 400 miles long, skirting the Western Sahara border. It was completed in 1963 and is owned by a mining organization, but passenger trains also operate. There are 37 diesel locomotives, fifteen passenger and over one thousand freight cars. Eighteen million tons, mostly minerals, are carried annually.

MAURITIUS
See African Offshore Islands

MOROCCO

See map on pages 218-219.

MOROCCAN RAILWAYS – ONCFM
Office National des Chemins de Fer du Maroc,
19 Avenue Allal ben Abdallah,
Rabat.

An extensive system of 1100 miles of 1ft $11\frac{1}{2}$in gauge military railways was built in Morocco during the period (1912 onwards) when it was being brought under the control of the French Army. In 1915 the principal links were opened for public service, including a 580-mile 'main line' on more or less the present route, from Oujda on the Algerian border via Fes, Rabat

and Casablanca to what is now the famous desert resort of Marrakech in the far southwest. A maximum speed of 15 mph made for rather tedious travel.

In 1914 an 85-year concession was given to a joint French and Spanish concern, for a standard-gauge railway joining Tangier to Fes. After delays due to World War I, this 200-mile line was completed in 1927. It still retains a nominal independence, although working is

Top left : New diesel-electric locomotives in Malawi in 1973.

Top centre : Diesel railcar No 198 UP rounds the bend to Chipoka station on its way to Salima from Blantyre. This trip of 160 miles was run twice weekly in 1962.

Left : A 1964-built diesel-electric set waits in the modern station at Casablanca with a train for Tangier in 1971.

Below centre : An electric train set nears Sule on the electrified route from Casablanca to Fez.

Below : The Fez-Rabat-Casablanca express. The route was electrified well before World War II.

in the hands of the Moroccan Railways. Further standard-gauge lines were by then also under construction, most superseding narrow-gauge ex-military ones and by 1934 there was a through route from Marrakech via Casablanca, Rabat and Fes to the Algerian border; it was part of a line running under French control all the way to Tunis, 1500 miles in all. A further line in the east running due south to Bouârfa, in an area where coal is mined, was constructed between 1927 and 1931 by a private company, the Morocco Eastern Railway. This was taken over by the state in 1963. The proposal to extend this line across the Sahara to Tombouctou was referred to in the Algerian section.

Electrification was envisaged from the start and the first contact wires were energized (at 3000v DC) as early as 1927 in the Casablanca area. At present all the main lines from Marrakech and Tangier to Fes are worked electrically, together with certain branches serving mining areas. Water power from the Atlas Mountains is used to generate current. About 440 miles (out of a total of 1090) of route are now electrified, with 61 locomotives; 81 diesels operate the remainder of the system and there are altogether 300 passenger and 8700 freight cars. Twenty-two million tons of freight and 4.3 million passengers are carried annually. Expenses are currently 104 percent of receipts.

MOZAMBIQUE

See map on pages 226-227.

MOZAMBIQUE STATE RAILWAYS
Caminhos de Ferro do Estado de Moçambique, Maputo.

A number of independent 3ft 6in gauge lines and one 2ft 5½in gauge line, were built at various times in the last eighty years to foster development of the country by providing connections to suitable port locations, at Maputo (formerly Lourenço Marques), Inhambane, Beira, Quelimane and Lumbo (near the town of Mozambique).

From Maputo there are connections to Swaziland (via Mlawula), the Republic of South Africa (via Komatipoort) and Rhodesia/Zimbabwe (via Malvernia). The latter line follows the river Limpopo. (Its construction crossed the routes taken by wild animals to their watering places. The animals were afraid to cross the new track formation and had to be herded across by game wardens to prevent them dying of thirst.) The line from Inhambane is narrow gauge and steam operated. Locomotives and rolling stock are shipped to Maputo for maintenance and the depot and workshops there incorporate mixed-gauge tracks for this purpose.

From Beira, there are connections to Rhodesia/Zimbabwe (via Umtali) – the sanction-breaking route closed by the Mozambique government early in 1976. At Dondo, some fifty miles from Beira is the junction with the Trans-Zambesi Railway which runs northwards to cross the River Zambesi between Sena and Dona Ana and continues northwards into Malawi. This was built and operated by a British Company but is now virtually nationalized. At Dona Ana, immediately north of the Zambesi bridge, is the junction with the Tete division of the Mozambique Railways which relies on the TZR for its connection with the rest of the system and which serves the coal mines at Moatize, Mozambique's only mineral resource to have been developed at the present time. Moatize is deep in the Zambesi valley near the regional capital of Tete whereas the main line is high on the north side of the valley on an alignment suitable for future extension into the northern plateau and across into Zambia. The gradients from Moatize to the highest point of the line at Caldas Xavier are very severe and present a considerable problem for expansion of production at the coal mine.

The railway bridge at Sena provides the only way of crossing the Zambesi for some considerable distance upstream and downstream. The TZR used to operate a form of motorail service across the bridge with end-loading docks in the stations at each end and a special flat wagon kept for the purpose. Cars could be carried on any train by application to the station-master at either end of the bridge but this was less convenient than it sounds because the flat-car had to be conveyed to a station some distance north of the bridge where it could be

shunted and brought back to be placed on the loading dock.

From Quelimane, there are no other connections and the line only serves agricultural areas in the coastal plain.

In the north a new port is being developed at Nacala and a branch line has been built from Rio Monapo to this port which has virtually replaced the service through Lumbo.

The working timetable for this branch includes a footnote that trains are not to cross at one particular station during the hours of darkness. The line is worked by telegraph and ticket with no signals and no staff at intermediate stations so that the guard has to change the switches for crossing movements. One night a guard getting down from the train to perform these duties was attacked and killed by a lion; this unfortunate event gives a macabre explanation for the timetable footnote.

The maintenance facilities for this route are located at Nampula, the regional capital; steam on this line is being superceded by diesel traction and a new servicing shed has recently been built. Major repairs would require locomotives to be shipped from Nacala or to be taken through Malawi and down the TZR to Beira and then via Rhodesia/Zimbabwe to Maputo, a total distance of over 2000 miles!

In its original form the northern line terminated at Nova Freixo some 300 miles from the coast and its purpose appears to have been to carry imported goods for the colonial settlers as much as exported products from the region since the track gradients are equally steep (1 in 52) against both imports and exports. Now that the line has been extended northwards to Vila Cabral and westwards via Entre Lagos into Malawi and is carrying copper from Zambia to replace the route through Rhodesia/Zimbabwe these severe gradients against exports are something of an embarrassment.

NAMIBIA

See map on pages 226-227.

As these words are written, Namibia (until recently Southwest Africa and before that German Southwest Africa) is undergoing a painful birth. Its railways are now a close-knit part of South African Railways but once upon a time they were remarkable enough to stand by themselves in any general book on railways. The reason is that most very narrow narrow gauge railways – in this case 1ft 11½in-gauge – are proportionately short; however, the Otavi Railway was 360 miles long. It was built in 1905-06 to serve a copper-mining area inland at Tsumeb; a sleeping car (thought to be the only one ever to operate on such a slim gauge as this) was provided to ease a two-day journey. Conversion to 3ft 6in took place in 1956, but locomotives and equipment from the Otavi can still be found running on the 2ft gauge lines in other parts of South Africa.

NIGER

See map on pages 218-219.

This land-locked state in the centre of the bulge of Africa has no railways as yet. However, its government has caught the railway disease sufficiently badly for study to be made of the feasibility of providing a railway system. It could connect with any or all of the systems of four neighbours: Benin, Ivory Coast (see Senegal), Togo or Nigeria.

Left, top: Mozambique has a fascinating 2ft 5½in gauge line powered by American Locomotive Company 2-6-0s and Baldwin 2-8-0s. The coastal terminus is at Joāo Bela (Xai-Xai), a small town near the north side of the mouth of the Limpopo.

NIGERIA

See map on pages 218-219.

NIGERIAN RAILWAY CORPORATION
Ebute Metta.

When the railway came to Nigeria, the country had been part of the British Empire for thirty years. In 1893 work began on the 3ft 6in gauge Lagos Railway, intended to run up-country for 700 miles to Kano. The first section to Ibadan (120 miles) was opened in 1901. This relatively slow progress did not satisfy the inlanders who stirred matters up by starting off on their own. Therefore work was also started from Baro on the north bank of the Niger River, which is navigable for shallow craft (as described in Edgar Wallace's famous *Sanders of the River* books) for hundreds of miles from its mouth. Kano was reached in 1911, but before this the southern section had reached the great river at Jebba. A new branch (shortly to become the main line) was built from a point opposite Jebba to Minna on the Baro-to-Kano line. A train ferry provided the connection.

In 1916 the Niger bridges were opened, crossing the two channels of the river with steel structures 66oft and 1525ft long respectively. This opened a through rail connection between Lagos and Kano via Kaduna. The Lagos Railway and the Baro-Kano railway were amalgamated to form the Nigerian Railway in 1912, becoming a typical colonial railway used for bringing raw materials from up-country down to the port of Lagos. Ground nuts and tin were two of the principal commodities.

In the meantime (1913) an eastern line was begun out of Port Harcourt, originally to serve coal fields 150 miles inland, but later it was extended. By 1934, when the 2625ft Benue River bridge was opened, there was through-communication between Port Harcourt and Kaduna. The present terminus, Nguru (850

miles from Lagos) was reached in 1930 and there have been other extensions since, one of which made redundant a 2ft 6in gauge line which, between 1914 and 1957, ran from Zaria to serve regional tin mines. Mileage presently stands at 2200.

In steam days 4-8-2s and 2-8-2s were the main types in use; the 'River' class 2-8-2s supplied from 1948 onwards was the standard in the latter days. Beyer-Garratts (also named and painted red) were supplied to haul on 45lb rails the same trains which had been brought up from the coast by 'straight' locomotives on 80 lb or 60 lb iron. Recently diesels have taken over more and more of the working; currently there are 180 such units on the books, against 133 steam. Since the main lines are shortly to be replaced by a 4ft 8½in gauge railway on new high-speed alignments, further diesel purchases will no doubt be for that system.

Currently around four million tons of freight and nine million passengers are carried at a cost which is two and a half times the receipts, but this position is expected to be transformed when the competitiveness and economy of the new standard-gauge railway comes into play.

NYASALAND
See Malawi

REUNION
See African Offshore Islands

Top centre: A new English-Electric diesel locomotive heading the Royal train prepares to depart from Lagos, Nigeria before independence.

Top right: A coal train arrives at Kaduna Junction in the heart of Nigeria behind the locomotive River Belwa *in May 1959.*

Left, centre: An ex-Rhodesian Railways 2-8-2 + 2-8-2 Beyer-Garratt – now a CFM locomotive – acts as station pilot at the frontier station with Rhodesia/Zimbabwe near Umtali.

RHODESIA/ ZIMBABWE

See map on pages 226–227.

RHODESIA RAILWAYS BOARD
PO Box 782,
Metcalfe Square,
Bulawayo.

At the time the city of Bulawayo was founded in 1893, it was a four month journey by ox-cart to travel there from the coast. When the dreaded rinderpest struck down the oxen even that was not possible. Accordingly the Cape to Cairo line, here known as the Bechuanaland Railway Company, was pressed forward over easy country to reach Bulawayo from the south on 19 October 1897.

Long before this line had reached the Rhodesian border, agreement had been reached with the Portuguese government for a line to the port of Beira in Mozambique. Construction began in 1892; a decisive reason for the slow progress was the heavy death rate, particularly among the white employees, imposed by indigenous fevers and disease. In both 1892 and 1893, over sixty percent of them died.

The 216-mile section in Portuguese territory was laid very lightly, using 2ft gauge and 20 lb/yd rail; that in Rhodesia was built to the normal African standard of 3ft 6in. Through communication from Beira – with break of gauge at Umtali – was possible from 22 May 1899; within the year, the Portuguese section was converted to 3ft 6in also, when operation (but not ownership) was taken over by the then Mashonaland Railway Company. Salisbury and Bulawayo were connected by rail in 1902, uniting the two lines in Rhodesia/Zimbabwe.

Towards the north, the railway reached the Victoria Falls in 1904 and then, by one of the world's most spectacular and spectacularly sited bridges, crossed into what is now Zambia. The Victoria Falls bridge built in a short eighteen months, is a steel arch of 500ft span, 400ft above the boiling waters of the Zambesi River at the foot of the great falls. It was opened on 12 September 1905.

The Bechuanaland (Bechuanaland is now Botswana) and Mashonaland Railways became in due time the privately owned 2436-mile Rhodesian Railways; the shares were bought by the government after World War II. Since then some contraction has taken place: Mozambique took over ownership and operation of the line to Beira in 1948; Zambia and the RR lines therein became independent in 1964. Additional connections with the outside world have been made, including the Rhodesian section of a route to the Mozambique port of Lourenço Marques (now Maputo) in 1951 and a line, independent of Botswana territory, completed in 1972 to connect with South African Railways at Beit Bridge in the extreme south. The current mileage is 2100.

As a country rich in coal but lacking oil, Rhodesia was naturally inclined to hold on to

Extreme left, top: A Beyer-Garratt locomotive takes on water at Victoria Falls, Rhodesia/Zimbabwe.

Left: A waiting room for third- and fourth-class passengers on the West Nicholson branch of Rhodesia Railways.

Below: A Rhodesian freight train double-headed with Beyer-Garratt locomotives.

steam. This tendency was increased by the United Nations' sanctions which have been applied to the country since its Unilateral Declaration of Independence (UDI) in 1965. The RR was also the extreme example of the use of Beyer-Garratt locomotives; these double-hinged monsters have formed three-quarters and more of the steam fleet in recent years. In Rhodesia/Zimbabwe, steam locomotives are Garratts unless described specifically as being 'straight'. The articulated fleet covered the whole spectrum of duties in a particularly well-arranged way. As a tribute to one of the most modern and logically designed collections of steam power, their significant dimensions are – quite exceptionally for this

book – given below.

In spite of sanctions the Rhodesia RR has succeeded in supplementing a few pre-UDI English Electric diesels with a substantial eighty-strong fleet which currently covers the operation of over one-half of the trains.

Unlike the situation in South Africa, there was no colour bar against coloured members of the population aspiring to responsible positions on Rhodesian Railways, such as locomotive drivers.

Rhodesian passenger trains are unusual in providing four classes of accommodation; again, there is no *apartheid* in respect of their use by various ethnically divided sections of the population. Approximately 500 brown-

and-cream cars cater for three million passengers each year, while 12,000 freight wagons are involved in carrying 12.8 million tons of freight an average distance of 300 miles; however, one should note that some of these figures are a little suspect because the division of rolling stock and other matters between Zambia and Rhodesia/Zimbabwe has yet to be agreed, even after fifteen years of separation.

Extreme left, bottom: This photograph, taken during the days of the Federation of Rhodesia and Nyasaland, shows a cross-border train on the then-new Bannockburn to Lourenço Marques (now Maputo) rail link.

Rhodesian Steam Power

Class	Type	Number Built	Cylinders (Bore × Stroke)	Coupled Wheel Diameter	Traction Effort lb	Grate Area sq ft	Maximum Axle-load in tons	Comments
14/14A	2-6-2 + 2-6-2	38	16in × 24in	48in	39,560	39	$13\frac{1}{2}$	Lightly built locomotives for lightly built branch lines
15/15A	4-6-4 + 4-6-4	74	$17\frac{1}{2}$in × 26in	57in	41,908	50	$15\frac{1}{4}$	Large-wheeled locomotives for passenger trains.
16/16A	2-8-2 + 2-8-2	50	$18\frac{1}{2}$in × 24in	48in	51,338	50	$14\frac{3}{4}$	General purpose
20/20A	4-8-2 + 2-8-4	61	20in × 26in	51in	61,176	63	$17\frac{1}{4}$	RR's heavy artillery

SENEGAL & NEIGHBOURS

See map on pages 218-219.

SENEGAL, MALI, GUINEA, IVORY COAST, UPPER VOLTA

SENEGAL RAILWAYS
BP 265, Dakar.

MALI RAILWAY
PO Box 260, Bamako.

GUINEA RAILWAYS
PO Box 581, Conakry.

IVORY COAST RAILWAY
PO Box 1394, Abidjan

UPPER VOLTA – served by the Ivory Coast Railway

Senegal, Mali, Guinea, Ivory Coast and Upper Volta are five adjoining countries that were formerly united and called French West Africa. Transport in the area is dominated by the River Niger, the source of which is not too far from the coast in the neighbourhood of Sierra Leone. The river then makes a vast loop into the interior of the bight of Africa before reaching the sea in distant Nigeria. For most of its length the river is navigable and runs through the vast area of what is now the Mali Republic.

One problem which faced the French was that the mouth of this river was in another power's hands, *viz* Britain. This occurred before the days of *entente cordiale*, so steps were taken in 1881 to connect the Senegal River with the Niger River by rail, thereby

providing – via another railway along the coast, which had been started the previous year – an all-steam route to the port of Dakar in what is now Senegal.

Navigation on the Senegal River was seasonal and in 1924 a direct connection to Dakar was completed, giving a 775-mile route from the coast to Bamako, now the capital of independent Mali.

During 1900 to 1913, another line was completed in what is now Guinea, connecting Conakry (the capital) with Kouroussa, (390 miles) the upper limit of navigation on the great river. Between 1903 and 1955, the third of these railways to be built runs inland 711 miles from Abidjan (the capital of what is now the Ivory Coast) eventually reaching not the River Niger but a place in the republic of Upper Volta called Ouagadougou. A connection is proposed between Bobo-Diouasso (the capital of Upper Volta) and Bamako in Mali, and another one as a link between Bamako and the Conakry line in Guinea.

At present there are three separate systems in four independent countries; statistically they stand up as follows:

All these lines are metre gauge. In Guinea some heavy-duty standard-gauge lines are being projected and built in order to exploit mineral resources, iron ore and bauxite. On these North American (Canadian) standards will prevail, replacing the French practices which have heretofore been the rule in all these countries.

Both the Senegal-Mali and Ivory Coast systems offer sleeping cars (first class only) and dining cars on their best train. In addition, the latter offers the very rare facility of a railcar train with sleeping accommodation; railcars in fact provide virtually all the ordinary train services on all three systems.

SIERRA LEONE

See map on pages 218-219.

Sierra Leone has the sad position of being the largest and most populous country in the world to have lost its railway system. Construction began out of Freetown in 1895. Kissy was

Statistics	Senegal	Mali	Guinea	Ivory Coast Upper Volta
Length of route, miles	642	400	540	730
Number of diesel locomotives	60	22	30	65
Railcars	10	3	16	20
Carriages	90	50	20	105
Wagons	930	330	500	1240
Annual Passenger traffic millions	3.6	0.6	*	2.8
Annual freight traffic, millions of tons	1.5	0.3	*	0.9
Length of haul	*	50	*	150
Expenses as % of receipts	*	115	*	*

* not available

Extreme left: A re-enaction of the first train at Dakar, Senegal.

Centre left: The Ocean-Niger Express from Dakar to Bamako in Mali – a long hot haul.

Left: Modern autorails in service on the main line out of Dakar show the French influence.

Bottom left: The 2ft 6in line out of Freetown in Sierra Leone was still pulled by steam in 1954. Here a train crosses the bridge at Hastings.

Bottom right: Cape Town's Table Mountain guards the city's modern station. Only clean electric trains frequent this station; steam does not begin until the shed at Parden Eiland.

reached the following year, Bo (135 miles) in 1903 and Pendembu, the terminus (226 miles), in 1905. Branches brought the system eventually up to 320 miles. There were no serious engineering problems.

As recently as 1955, new Beyer-Garratt 4-8-2 + 2-8-4 locomotives were supplied, providing 22,500 lb of tractive effort in spite of the five-ton axle-load limit imposed by 30lb/yd rails. Subsequently, a series of diesel hydraulic locomotives were provided.

After independence from Britain, the government lost enthusiasm and the railway closed in 1976. Since then a fifty-mile 3ft-6in-gauge private mineral-hauling line has all but closed; the Marampa Mineral Railway is still used occasionally to transport supplies to and from the port and the mine.

So, what school-children in the town of Kissy used to sing has finally come to pass . . .

> 'The train to Bo
> She no agree to go
> The engine she done tire
> For lack of plenty fire. . . .'

—SOUTH AFRICA—

See map on pages 226-227.

SOUTH AFRICAN RAILWAYS – SAS/SAR

Suid-Afrikaans Spoorweg,
Paul Kruger Building, Wolmanans Street,
12001, Johannesburg.

The South African railway system came into being on 26 June 1860, when a two-mile standard-gauge line from Durban to Point was opened. Another standard-gauge railway out of Cape Town to Wellington (45 miles) was the first line to be started (1859) but it was not to be completed until 1863. At this time what is now South Africa was divided into four political entities; British Cape Colony and Natal, as well as the Transvaal and the Orange Free State.

Diamonds were discovered at Kimberley in 1870 and this was an objective indeed. The

government produced the money and, from Wellington, after a slow start, Worcester was reached in 1876, Beaufort West (339 miles) in 1880 and De Aar in 1884, coinciding there with the completion of another line from Port Elizabeth, which had been started in 1874. Kimberley (653 miles) was reached in 1885. In the meantime, distant Westminster (London) felt that two colonies, so far away, did not quite rate standard gauge and suggested a slightly lesser one – not the indignity of two-foot-something narrow-gauge nor the foreign nonsense of metre gauge but 3ft 6in; a dimension which was to become standard in South Africa and many other countries. All these government railways were laid to the new gauge, a third rail being laid from Wellington into Cape Town, where 4ft 8½in held out until 1880.

The discovery of gold in the Johannesburg area led to a race between the various ports – Cape Town, Port Elizabeth and Durban – to be the first one connected. Furthermore, President Kruger of the Transvaal, wishing for an outlet independent of the British, promoted a line Lourenço Marques, now Maputo, in Portuguese territory. All these lines were completed by 1895. The mileage on the outbreak of the Boer War in 1899 was 7577 (Cape Province 3834; Natal 1043; Transvaal 1706; Orange Free State 994.)

All these railways were unified in 1910, when South African Railways were formed, then as now, the largest network in Africa. After 1918 the railways in German South West Africa (now Namibia) were included. They had been hurriedly joined to the SAR in connection with General Botha's campaign to occupy the territory. Completion of the Republic's network had led to the present day 14,600-mile system, all 3ft 6in gauge, except for 440 miles of feeder lines built to 2ft gauge.

South Africa joins India, China and Poland as the four nations who still operate steam locomotive fleets of 1000 plus. As if challenged by those distant politicians who specified a lesser gauge, straight steam locomotives are running in South Africa heavier, bigger and more powerful than ever ran on standard gauge in Britain. The '25' class 4-8-4 has tractive effort of 45,600 lb, a grate area of 70 sq ft and an overall weight of 208 tons. The condensing version of this locomotive, for use in bad water areas, is the world's only successful large-scale application of this advanced feature, producing puffers that do not puff.

In 1910 came the class 3A 4-8-2 'final form' steam locomotive, that is, with two piston-valve cylinders, outside Walschearts valve gear, wide firebox and superheater; successive versions, each more American looking than the

last, form the bulk of SAR steam power today.

Following trials in 1924 with Mallet and Garratt articulated locomotives, SAR went on to have both the largest number of Garratts as well as the largest Garratt design ever to see regular service. This was the GL class 4-8-2 + 2-8-4, tractive effort 89,140 lb, grate area 75 sq ft and weight 211 tons. On the 2ft gauge Natal lines, the sixteen NGG class 2-6-2 +

2-6-2s have a dainty six-ton axle-loading for 30 lb/yd rail, but can produce 17,000 lb tractive effort. A batch of these were the last steam locomotives supplied (1968). The total steam fleet currently numbers 1800 (including sixty 2ft gauge) and is maintained in first-rate order.

In a country which has cheap and ample coal, but is without indigenous oil, electrification is more attractive than dieselization. In operation, including twenty for the narrow gauge.

The original railways were built as single lines, largely following the contours of the land. More engineering work has been necessary to turn them into double-track arteries of commerce with reasonable curves and gradients than was necessary to build them in the first place. The five longest tunnels in the Republic of South Africa are all on these latter-day re-alignments. The actual longest is the 3.5-mile Cedara tunnel, completed in 1960. The longest bridge (3514ft) is at Upington, leading across the Orange River to Namibia. The highest is the Van Staaden's Gorge Bridge on the Avontuur 2ft-gauge line, 250ft high.

Apartheid, the segregation of the public according to skin colour, causes problems in station design. Small country stations need two foot-bridges, and the great stations of Cape Town, Durban and Johannesburg have to have duplicate concourses, with all that that entails. Trains are, of course, always marshalled so that the 'black' carriages (first, second and third class) are at the front and 'white' ones (first and second class) are at the rear.

The famous Blue Train, which runs twice a week on a 27-hour timing each way between Cape Town and Pretoria is, in sharp contrast with its namesake in Europe, one of the very few trains in the world that is *De Luxe* in the old-fashioned sense of the word. Comfort, food and service are impeccable and the train is fully booked ('whites' only, of course) weeks ahead.

Since the maximum permitted speed is 62.5 mph, passenger trains in South Africa are not fast; for example, the trip between Cape Town and Port Elizabeth, only 400 miles apart as the crow flies, means two nights in the train; not luxury, but wonderful scenery, clean accommodation and good food. SAR also provide worldwide and internal passenger air services – harbours and lighthouses too – so there is no incentive to run fast trains which interfere with freight-train operation.

South African Railways carry 140 million tons of freight an average distance of 325 miles as well as 635 million passengers annually, using a fleet of 10,300 passenger and 186,000 freight cars. Buck-eye type couplers are used and the vacuum brake; signalling is based on British practice, with much modernization. Expenses are eighty percent of receipts.

Extreme left, top: The 'Baby Garratt' in Natal.

Extreme left, below: South Africa's most powerful and perhaps most famous tender engines are the class 25 4-8-4s. Built for use in dry country, these huge water-saving machines are now almost all converted to non-condensing class 25NC.

Top left: A Beyer-Garratt with freight near Bethesdaweg on the Graaff-Reinet to Rosmead line.

Centre left: A South African Railways triple-headed electric freight train leaves Newcastle.

Left, bottom: An SAR 4-8-2 locomotive on the coaling stage at Burgersdorp in central Cape Province.

South Africa a beginning was made on the Natal main line in 1926, using the 3000v DC system. Since then steady progress has been made, including much suburban electrification in the Johannesburg and Cape Town areas. Since 1970, certain lines with lesser traffic have been electrified on the 25,000v fifty-cycle AC system. The electrified mileage now stands at 3440, on which 1691 electric locomotives run.

A start on dieselization was made with the lines in South West Africa (now Namibia), where traffic density was much too low for electrification and, moreover, absence of water plus remoteness from coal supplies made steam operation a problem. Accordingly 115 'World' diesel locomotives were ordered from General Electric (USA) in 1958, to be followed by many others. Currently 1200 diesel units are in

SOUTH WEST AFRICA
See Namibia

─── SUDAN ───

See map on pages 218–219.

SUDAN RAILWAYS
Atbara.

> So 'ere's to you, Fuzzy Wuzzy, at your
>   home in the Soudan;
> You're a poor benighted 'eathen but a
>   first class fighting man;
> An' 'ere's to you, Fuzzy Wuzzy, with
>   your 'ayrick head of hair;
> You big black boundin' beggar – for you
>   broke a British square!
>   Rudyard Kipling

The fighting qualities enshrined in Kipling's
famous words gave birth to the first section of
the Sudan Railways. Two short military lines
had in fact been constructed in connection with
the events described above, in 1881 and 1884,
but after the British withdrawal, the Mahdi
(the Dervish Leader) had the rails of the first
one flung into the River Nile, alongside which
it was built. The second, which ran inland
from Suakin on the Red Sea, was also destroyed.

The problem along this stretch of the river,
which connects Egypt with the Sudan, is that
the flow over the so-called cataracts is much too
fast for steamers to make headway against the
current. In 1895 General Kitchener was put in
charge of an expedition sent out to avenge the
death of General Gordon in Khartoum ten
years earlier. He had the utmost respect for his
adversaries' fighting ability and, accordingly,
determined that he would not offer battle until
an adequately equipped army could be put into
the field. The solution was a 3ft 6in gauge
railway, 385 miles long, starting at a place
called Wadi Halfa, just below the first cataract.
It ran for 200 miles across the desert, by-
passing a great loop of the river, then running
alongside a further bad stretch to reach a place

Extreme left, top: The line from Cape Town to Port Elizabeth has always been known as the Garden Route because of the magnificent scenery and the wonderful climb up over the Montague Pass. The station at George is the last stop before the climb really starts and the Beyer-Garratts took water here.

Extreme left, centre: The longest 2ft gauge line in South Africa takes a westerly line out of Port Elizabeth to the hills of Avontuur. New diesels now work the intensive service of stone trains to and from Loerie, but the NG15 class 2-8-2s take the through-train from Assegaabos to the upper terminal.

Left: A Sudanese Co Co diesel-electric locomotive leaves Atbara heading a Wadi Halfa to Khartoum express. Note the British style semaphore signals.

Below: An English Electric Co-Co locomotive of Sudan Railways.

Extreme left, bottom: Double-headed Beyer-Garratts pull a train on the southbound climb out of Rosmead on the Graaff-Reinet to Rosmead (via Middelburg) line in 1978. The mountains are crossed using the Lootsberg Pass.

Left: A Sudan Railways oilburning Pacific No 270 leaves Atbara with a train for Wadi Halfa.

called Atbara. The whole line was constructed in 1896–97 and is a classic of military engineering. It is interesting that some of the locomotives supplied for the run across the waterless Nubian Desert were equipped with condensing units to recover feed water from steam exhaust.

Well-equipped and fresh after a rail journey, the British defeated the Dervish army (a young soldier called Winston Churchill was there) at a place called Omdurman. The Sudan then became *de jure* an Anglo-Egyptian condominium, but *de facto* part of the British Empire, and so, of course, had to be provided with a well-run railway system.

Kitchener's railway – now extended to Khartoum – made a good starting point and, during the next sixty years, tentacles were sent out to such far corners of an enormous country as were fertile (by local standards) and inhabited. A new harbour – Port Sudan – on the Red Sea was set up and given rail access in 1906. The present system extends 2950 miles; Sudan Railway steamers on the Nile connect with the Egyptian Railways and – almost – with the Uganda Railways. The Sudan became peacefully independent in 1955, although malcontent groups caused trouble for a number of years after this, particularly in the west and south; the railways were not seriously affected. After independence in 1961, the network was extended into lion country to Wau in the far southwest, 873 miles from Khartoum and 1450 miles from Wadi Halfa.

In steam days, standard British colonial locomotives were supplied; now all that remain are some of the 42 oil-fired 4-8-2s supplied by North British Locomotive Works in 1956, that respected firm's last big steam order – also, of course, the last steam order placed by Sudan Railways. Water had always been a problem in the country, so it is not surprising that all principal trains are now in the charge of the 162-strong diesel fleet, the first of which was supplied in 1959.

Passenger traffic amounts to 2.6 million annually, freight to 2.5 million tons, hauled an average distance of 560 miles. There are 385 coaches, including excellent dining and first-class sleeping cars and 6600 freight wagons. Expenses are 108 percent of receipts.

South of Khartoum is the Gezira, an irrigated cotton-growing area whose crops are handled by a 1ft 11½in gauge railway system 500 miles in extent. There are seventy locomotives (all diesel) and trains of bagged cotton up to 400 tons are worked over the level terrain.

SWAZILAND

See map on pages 226–227.

SWAZILAND RAILWAY
PO Box 58, Mbabane.

A 3ft 6in gauge line was built in the early 1960s primarily to carry iron ore from Kadake in the northwest of the country through

Above: A Swaziland Railway double-headed iron-ore train near Mantenga Falls.

Right: Dar-es-Salaam on the Tan-Zam Railway.

Bottom extreme right: A Tunisian National Railway's diesel-hauled train at Bir Bou Regba.

Below: A class 30 2-8-4 of the then-East Africa Railways at Tabora, Tanzania.

Mlawula in the northeast to the port of Maputo (formerly Lourenço Marques) in Mozambique. The mountainous terrain in northern Swaziland necessitated a circuitous route passing well to the south of the two principal towns at Mbabane and Manzini. This means that there is no demand for passenger services, and none are provided. The western section of the line from Kadake to Sidvokodvo, the main depot and railway township, is steeply graded (1 in 50) and steam traction is used. At Sidvokodvo trains are re-marshalled and diesel traction is used over the gentler gradients to Maputo.

The iron ore at Kadake is virtually exhausted but new traffics have been established to ensure a future for the railway. These include wood pulp from the Usutu forests, said to be the largest manmade forests in the world, sugar products from Phuzumoya and Mlawula, and coal from Mpaka. Newly discovered coal deposits in the southeast of the country have prompted detailed investigation for a branch from Phuzumoya to the frontier at Gollel where it would join the South African Railway network and provide an alternative route in the event of political difficulties between Swaziland and Mozambique.

The line is controlled by a CTC system with coloured light signals but the tracks at intermediate passing stations are staggered so that trains always enter by the straight route and depart by the curved route through the switches. By spring-loading the switches in the straight position the need for point motors has been avoided, saving power generators.

TANGANYIKA
See Tanzania

TANZANIA

See map on pages 226–227.
**TANZANIAN RAILWAYS
CORPORATION**
Dar-es-Salaam.

**TANZANIA ZAMBIA RAILWAY
AUTHORITY – TAZARA – TAN-ZAM
RAILWAY**
Dar-es-Salaam.

In what was then called German East Africa, a company known as the Deutsch-Ostafrika Usambara-Eisenbahn began constructing a metre-gauge line out of the port of Tanga, 120 miles north of Dar-es-Salaam, in 1893. The objective was Lake Victoria, but the company went bankrupt in 1899, was taken over by the German government with a purely local objective. Moshi, 220 miles inland from Tanga, from where a connecting line now runs into Kenya, was reached in 1912.

In 1905 the present main line out of Dar-es-Salaam was begun. Lake Tanganyika was reached at Kigoma, 782 miles, in the fateful year of 1914. Surrounded by enemies, the meagre German forces did well to hold out until the Armistice, but the railway suffered.

After the war (1919), the country was granted a British League of Nations mandate and was called Tanganyika. In 1946 it became a United Nations territory under British administration. The railways were repaired and a new 245-mile line was laid, mostly on formation constructed by the Germans, north from Tabora to reach Lake Victoria at Mwanza.

Amalgamation with the Kenya-Uganda Railway took place in 1948 and the resulting East African Railways administration lasted until 1976. The ownership of the railways has now reverted to the individual governments. Tanzania's metre-gauge railroads are controlled by the Tanzanian Railways Corporation.

(In 1961 Tanganyika became self-governing and in 1964 became a people's republic and changed its name from the United Republic of Tanganyika and Zanzibar to the United Republic of Tanzania.)

Up until 1976 all railways had been built to the metre gauge. However in 1976 one of the most remarkable railway projects ever mounted in Africa was completed; this was the 3ft 6in gauge Tan-Zam Railway which connects Dar-es-Salaam with the main southern African rail systems. Primarily, of course, it is an alternative outlet for Zambian copper. The line was financed and constructed by China on the basis of an interest-free loan repayable over thirty years from 1983 onwards. Any doubts felt about the ability of the Chinese to build such a railway were unfounded; in fact, there are more engineers with large-scale railway-building experience in China than in any other country. Six hundred miles of the 1160-mile line are in Tanzania.

Motive power in Tanzania before 1914 was the typical German of the period; after 1919 it was British. Dieselization began under East African auspices in 1958, but one notes a surprising order to India for a batch of six standard steam YG 2-8-2s, rather secretively placed as late as 1974. The Tan-Zam line is reported to be worked by 102 Chinese diesel-hydraulic locomotives and to have 100 passenger and 2100 freight cars. Air brakes are used, but the freight stock also has vacuum brakes for working in Zambia and Zaïre. Apart from the locomotives, equipment is very simple; for example, most of the stations have oil-lit semaphore signals and working between stations is by train order. At Dar-es-Salaam a magnificent modern station is provided for but six passenger trains a week.

TOGO

See map on pages 218–219.

TOGO RAILWAYS – RCFT
*Régie des Chemins de Fer de Togo,
PO Box 340,
Lomé.*

Togoland – then a German Colony – entered the railway age early in the twentieth century when three typically colonial railways were constructed leading from the port of Lomé. The first one, running 28 miles eastward to Anécho, was opened on 18 July 1905, originally to 2ft 5½in gauge. Northward and northeastward lines (102 and 72 miles long respectively) followed quickly. The system was extended even further north to its present terminus at Blitta in 1934, during the period of the French mandate. Steam came to an end in 1960, coinciding with independence.

Current returns show twenty diesel locomotives, ten railcars, sixty passenger cars and 375 wagons. About 1.5 million passengers are carried annually and 112,000 tons of freight. Unusually passenger accommodation is designated first and third class.

TUNISIA

See map on pages 218–219.

**TUNISIAN NATIONAL RAILWAYS –
SNCFT**
*Société Nationale des Chemins de Fer Tunisiens,
67 Ave Farhat Hached,
Tunis.*

The earliest railways in Tunisia were built to serve the capital city and comprised a 2.5-mile line from Tunis to Bardo and a twelve-mile route from Tunis to La Marsa. These were built to standard gauge in 1874. The route to

La Marsa passed along the north side of Tunis Bay and a branch line served the industrial area at La Goulette. In 1905 a causeway was constructed across the bay and a new railway was laid along it to give direct access to La Goulette from a new terminus on the east side of the city. This route was electrified at about the same period, while the Bardo line was replaced by trams. The new line to La Goulette was later extended through Carthage and over the hill past Sidi Bou Said to provide an end-on connection with the earlier line at La Marsa. Subsequently the old route along the north side of the bay was abandoned, and the section through La Marsa itself was converted into a road by-passing the town centre. The electric trains working between Tunis and La Marsa have only recently been replaced by new stock and large portions of the track have been re-laid. A third-rail is used for current collection but in the depot area simple overhead catenary is provided. The old trains had a considerable variety of trolley booms, pantographs and bow collectors to enable them to move in and out of the depot.

Outside the capital and its immediate vicinity, standard gauge was adopted for the route westwards to Algeria, on which construction began in 1877, and for a local line to Hammam-Lif built in 1882. The latter was closed in 1897 and subsequently re-opened as a metre-gauge line. This was later doubled and now carries such a considerable volume of commuters, that there have been proposals for its electrification and extension of the commuter services to Bordj Cedria. A metre-gauge line was built southwards from Tunis to Sousse in 1896 and in 1912 this was extended to link up with other routes built slightly earlier to carry phosphate from deposits in the southwest of the country to the port at Sfax. The proposed standard-gauge line between Sfax and Tripoli in Libya will have an interchange station for passengers and freight at Sfax but provision is being made for the metre-gauge line to Tunis to become standard gauge at a later date.

The main terminus in Tunis, currently being replaced with a more extensive passenger concourse, already has two gauges with platforms for standard gauge on the west side of the station and platforms for metre gauge to the east. The routes diverge immediately south of the station but the maintenance depots and workshops southeast of the station cater for both gauges, and this necessitates some unusual 'diamond' crossings where the standard gauge crosses the metre-gauge track to gain access to the depot area. A similar series of hybrid gauge crossings is provided at Djebel Djelloud a few miles further south where the standard-gauge line crosses the metre-gauge main line again to enter a major freight depot and warehousing area.

UGANDA
See Kenya

UPPER VOLTA
See Senegal *et al*

ZAÏRE

See map on pages 226-227.

ZAÏRE NATIONAL RAILWAYS – SNCZ
Société Nationale des Chemins de Fer Zairois,
PO Box 297, Place de la Gare,
Lubumbashi.

The first railway in what is now Zaïre – but was then the Belgian Congo – was completed in 1892. It started at the port of Matadi, near (by African standards) the mouth of the great river after which the country was and is named, and ran inland 250 miles to the capital, then called Leopoldville, but now Kinshasa. The object was to avoid the rapids in the lower reaches. This role of a railway being handmaiden to noble woodburning stern-wheel steamers on one of the greatest rivers in the world was repeated twice (each time the gauge was different) over other un-navigable stretches, first past the Stanley Falls and then past the Hell's Gate Rapids. The limit of navigation is Bukama, 3050 steamer and 550 train miles from the river's mouth. From 1918 Bukama was connected by rail to the copper-belt area in the southeastern corner of the country (and also, of course, by Cecil Rhodes' route to Cape Town, as described earlier).

In the 1920s it was decided to build a line running diagonally across the country and connecting Bukama with the capital. It reached its present terminus at Ilebo (then called Port Francqui) in 1928; from here it was a mere week – instead of a month or so by the original route – by river steamer to Leopoldville (Kinshasa). Already in the 1930s the line from Port Francqui to Leopoldville (Kinshasa) was specified as 'surveyed and projected' a situation that appertains today.

In 1931 the Benguela Railway arrived at the Angola border at Dilolo and this, the shortest possible outlet to the Atlantic Ocean, was met by new construction in the then Belgian Congo.

A further international connection ran from the river at Kabalo to Albertville (now Kalemie) on Lake Tanganika; cross-lake steamers led to Kigoma and hence by rail to Dar-es-Salaam on the Indian Ocean. Since then isolated lines in the southwest have been connected to the main system, based at Bukama and Lubumbashi (previously Elisabethville), making it up to its present size of just over 2400 miles.

In this area in 1952 a very early example of what is now the world's standard system of electrification was inaugurated – high voltage AC at ordinary industrial frequency. The scheme covered the 64 miles between Jadotville (now Likasi) and Tenke; it has since been extended 400 miles into the copper-belt area. There are over seventy electric locomotives in use. Elsewhere in Zaïre a fleet of 250 diesels, supplemented by a small remnant of steam together with 260 carriages and 8400 wagons carry 3.2 million passengers and eleven million tons of freight annually.

Finally, in the remote northeast of Zaïre, appropriately situated right in the geographical centre of the 'Dark Continent', is an extraordinary mystery system comprising no less than 750 miles of 1ft 11½in gauge. This is the Vicicongo Railway or, in full, Chemin de Fer Vicinal de Zaïre (CVZ), whose nearest rail neighbour is in Uganda. It runs from Aketi and Bondo to Mungbere. Returns show it to have 29 steam and fifteen diesel locomotives, nineteen carriages and 350 wagons and to handle 300,000 tons of freight and 100,000 passengers each year; but otherwise, nothing seems to be known about it except that it not only appears on the map but also still functions.

ZAMBIA

See map on pages 226–227.

ZAMBIA RAILWAYS
PO Box RW65,
Ridgeway, Lusaka.

Until the breakdown of friendly relations with Rhodesia/Zimbabwe, the principal connection between Zambia and the outside world was the railway southwards through Rhodesia/Zimbabwe and South Africa. Now that the traffic working across the Victoria Bridge at Livingstone Falls is so restricted, the route southwards from Kabwe, the railway headquarters, through Lusaka is comparatively little used. Passenger traffic has also been lost with the creation of a good standard main road parallel to the railway providing a faster and more frequent express bus service.

The recently built Chinese-financed Tan-Zam railway, also known as the Tazara, from north of Kabwe, via Serenje, Mpika and Kasama to Dar-es-Salaam in Tanzania has provided a new outlet for Zambian copper and a route for essential imports of fuel and other commodities, but its capacity is limited and much traffic continues to be hauled by road throughout or to rail-heads in Malawi and Mozambique. The Chinese builders of the Tan-Zam did an extremely good job in constructing the railway quickly and cheaply, establishing their own townships and rice farms along the route to make themselves entirely self-supporting during the construction period. However, they took security of the operation extremely seriously even to the extent of refusing to allow the General Manager of Zambia Railways and other Board Members to inspect work at the junction with their railway at Kapiri Mposhi. Having been seen off at gun-point from the end of the new railway, the Zambia Railways' officials may be forgiven for any subsequent difficulty found in achieving satisfactory co-ordination of traffic movements between the two lines.

ZIMBABWE
See Rhodesia/Zimbabwe

Extreme left, top: Zaire in colonial days circa *1918. A locomotive of the Chemin de Fer du Katanga takes water near Bukama.*

Left, top: A train stands in Livingstone station, Zambia in the days of the federation with Rhodesia.

Left, centre and bottom: Two wayside stations, typical of the stops in Zambia on the Tan-Zam Railway.

The Baghdad Railway The Hedjaz Railway Overland to India **Iran** Iranian National Railways Company **Iraq** Iraqi Republic Railways **Israel** Israel Railways	**Jordan** Hedjaz-Jordan Railway **Lebanon** Lebanon State Railways **Saudi Arabia** Saudi Government Railroad Organization	**Syria** Syrian Railways Hedjaz-Syrian Railway **Turkey** Turkish State Railways **Yemen People's Democratic Republic**

The Baghdad Railway

More change has taken place in the political background to the railway situation in the Middle East than in any other part of the world. There is, in fact, considerable difficulty in describing its history within the framework of present-day boundaries. When a Baghdad railway was first mooted, as early as 1836, the whole route was under Turkish domination as part of the Ottoman Empire. The original motivation for the line was, however, British, with the objective of improving communications with India. Accordingly, the first concession to build a railway in Asia Minor went in 1856 to the British Ottoman Railway, for a line from Smyrna (now Izmir) to Aydin. But with the completion, acquisition and, later, the widening of the Suez Canal, the British dropped out.

France came to have considerable railway interests in the area, but mostly involving concerns of local interest. It was therefore left to the Germans to 'drive to the east' and promote the Baghdad Railway, intended to connect Haydarpasa, across the Golden Horn from Istanbul, with the Persian Gulf. Their Anatolian Railways (which seems to have been known officially under the fine old German name of *Société Ottomane des Chemins de Fer d'Anatolie*) was founded in 1889, completed to Ankara (305 miles) in 1892 and to Konya in 1895,

whence problems arose over choice of route. Kaiser Bill of Germany visited Constantinople (Istanbul) in 1899, causing a considerable flutter among the chancelleries of Europe; the outcome was the further extension, from Konya reaching Erigli in 1903, Aleppo (675 miles) in 1908. During the World War I, in which Turkey was an ally of Germany, construction was pressed forward through the Taurus mountains. Nusaybin (1230 miles) was reached in October 1918; simultaneously came the collapse of the Ottoman Empire. The existence of the railway did not prevent it, but it may have delayed it.

The easy section in what is now Iraq had almost been completed, but a gap between Tel Kotchek, north of Mosul, and Iraq's metre-gauge railhead at Kirkuk remained. In 1940 the standard-gauge line from Baghdad reached Tel Kotchek and so at last through running over the 1600 miles from Haydarpasa to Baghdad became possible, after just over a century of endeavour. At the time of writing, however, political problems have caused an interruption but it is expected that they will be resolved shortly.

Political problems have always precluded through running from Haydarpasa to Cairo, although 4ft 8½in metals have existed and a railway formation does exist, the whole length of the route. The bridge over the Suez Canal at

Kantara (El Qantara) was only allowed during the two World Wars, and other stretches such as Kantara-Gaza and Haifa-Beirut have only been laid down to be torn up again.

The Hedjaz Railway

Another international line, of considerable fame, derived entirely from the Islamic fanaticism of the Ottoman Empire. This was the pilgrim's Hedjaz Railway, whose 500-mile 3ft 5½in gauge line ran from Damascus, through what is now Jordan, down through Arabia to Medina. Medina is within reasonable walking distance of Mecca to which all good Mohammedans must make pilgrimage once in their lives. It is said that the whole cost was financed by contributions from the Faithful and, moreover, alone among the Turkish railway projects of the time, no bribes were either given or received in connection with the scheme. The railway was built between 1902 and 1906, possibly the only example of major railway construction to serve a religious rather than an economic, political or military objective.

The economic possibilities were virtually nil, while as a military line of communication the railway was a hindrance rather than an asset. The problem faced by the famous T E Lawrence ('Lawrence of Arabia'), who encouraged the nomadic Bedouin to throw off the Turkish yoke between 1915 and 1918, was not

Page 246/247: The inaugural train on the line connecting Iran with Turkey near the frontier.

to destroy the line, but to keep it open. His Arab friends just loved blowing up the trains, but he explains in *The Seven Pillars of Wisdom* that his strategy was to do just enough destruction to convince the Turks that they had a problem, but not enough to make them see that the game was not worth the candle. Lawrence was, of course, a very junior soldier when he achieved his amazing feats of arms – he had a profound contempt for all trappings of rank except the right to comfortable rail travel, for it is on record that he accepted promotion to the rank of colonel solely so he could travel back home (presumably from Taranto in Italy) in comfort by Wagons-Lit. Once abandoned by the Turks, the Hedjaz line has never re-opened south of the Jordan border. Although work was started on restoration in 1965, it was abandoned after the 1967 Middle-East war.

Overland to India

The only rail route across the region which is intact at time of writing is the one from Haydarpasa to Tehran, capital of Iran, completed in 1971 except for fifty miles by train ferry across Lake Van. Through sleeping cars run by this 1910-mile route, connection can be made with a train running 690 miles further west to Kerman, directly towards the Iranian town of Zahidan, 260 miles further on, which in turn is connected to Calcutta by 5ft 6in gauge metals.

ADEN
See Yemen

EGYPT
See Africa: Egypt

Extreme left: New in 1914 was this restaurant car of the Société Imperiale Ottomane du Chemin de Fer de Baghdad.

Left and below: Three views of the Hedjaz Railway during wartime: (top) a charge is detonated; (centre) a station, bombed in 1916; (below) repairs are made to under-line bridges.

─MIDDLE EAST─

Projection: Conical with two standard parallels

1:15 000 000

PALESTINE

- - - - Armistice boundaries between Arab States
and Israel, 1949-1967

1:1 500 000

East from Greenwich

COPYRIGHT. GEORGE PHILIP & SON. LTD.

IRAN

See map on pages 250-251.

IRANIAN NATIONAL RAILWAYS COMPANY
Sepahbod Zahedi Avenue,
Corner of Nasser Avenue,
Tehran.

Iran was late in entering the commercial railway age, as construction of the great Trans-Iranian Railway did not start until 1927. It was not the first actual railway in the country, as a short pilgrims' line had existed since 1887 to take devout Moslems to the mosque and shrine of Shah Abdul Azim on the outskirts of Tehran.

It was eleven years before the Trans-Iranian was completed and Tehran had rail connections with the Persian Gulf and the Caspian Sea – this was not because of any lack of forcefulness or commitment on the part of the now-deposed Shah's father (whose project it was) but because of the engineering problems presented by the mountain ranges over which the line had to pass.

In crossing the Elburz Mountains between Tehran and the Caspian on the northern side, a height of 7000ft had to be scaled, with the aid of many 'U' or spiral tunnels. There were forty miles of continuous 1 in 36 grade and a two mile tunnel near the summit. The southern ascent was nearly as exacting. In many places, the instability of the slopes on which the railway was built – and there were frequently three parallel sections of line on the same one – necessitated very heavy and lengthy retaining walls and stabilization works. Many of the viaducts are very beautiful, arched masonry structures. Nothing comparable was built elsewhere during those lean interwar years and very little either before or since. The opening day – 26 August 1938 – was a proud one indeed.

Since World War II, the system has expanded steadily from the 860 miles of the original trunk line to 2800 miles today, but the other three radial main lines have been a little less exacting than the original one from an engineering point of view. In addition to lines already mentioned extending to the Turkish and towards the Pakistan border, connection was made – with break of gauge from 4ft 8½in to 5ft – with the USSR's railway system in the far northwestern province. The ex-Soviet lines in this Iranian province of Azerbaijan were converted to standard gauge at the same time.

A programme of modernization and expansion has recently begun, on a scale unmatched in the world. It is a paradox that only a country with enormous oil wealth can afford to begin making its railways independent of oil, by electrifying (and at the same time doubling) many lines forming the system over a five year period. This is what Iran intended to do before the recent trouble, in addition to building hundreds of miles of new railway. New construction was to include connections with Pakistan and to Afganistan's projected railway

system. Journey times would become only one-half or even one-third of the present, while capacity would more than treble. These developments were regarded as an essential part of the process of changing a country of 33 million population from an agrarian to an industrial economy. Railroad policies in the new regime have not yet been made public.

A quaint little 0-6-0 from Turbize of Belgium worked on the Tehran pilgrim's line, but the fleet ordered for the opening of the first main line represented the best practice of the 1930s. Most notable were some 4-8-2+2-8-4 Beyer-Garratts from Manchester, built for the mountain section, certainly the largest and most powerful locomotive in the Middle East and (as regards locomotives in regular service) in Asia as a whole. Before 1941 traffic was very sparse, but in that year the Trans-Iranian became an artery of military supply to the armies of the USSR. The British military authorities flooded the line with London

Left: Iran-owned, American-built, diesel-electric locomotives double head a train at Tehran station, on the line leading to the USSR.

Below left: Before the direct connection was made, passenger stock for the Iranian Railways was transported on its own wheels over the standard gauge lines of Europe and, as seen here, loaded onto specially adapted metre-gauge flat cars in the marshalling yard at Baghdad for onward transportation to Basra and then to the Iranian port of Khorramshahr, 1958.

Below centre: The 'Taurus Express' at Baghdad in the 1950s. This steam-hauled train at the terminus comprises a Wagons Lits postal van and first and second class coaches from the Turkish State Railways.

Below: Niort station, Iraq State Railway, with a French built diesel-electric locomotive heading the train.

an average of 400 miles. The 1978 statistics allow 99 diesels, 350 diesel-electrics, 14,000 freight cars, 575 passenger cars and four turbotrains sets. This amounts to an increase of 65 percent in two years. At the time of writing the Ayatollah Homeine has just taken over the administration of Iran's government and his policies have not yet been made public.

IRAQ

See map on pages 250-251.

IRAQI REPUBLIC RAILWAYS
Baghdad Central Station Building, Baghdad.

Work on the Berlin-Baghdad railway began as early as 1902, but through running was not possible until 1940. In the interim, there was much metre-gauge construction by British forces. Like other Arab oil-producing countries, Iraq is embarking at present on a comprehensive programme of improving and extending its railway network. Unlike its immediate neighbours it has the problem of starting with two different gauges. The two most important 'links are from Baghdad to Mosul near the border with Turkey in the north, which is standard gauge and from Baghdad to Basra on the Persian Gulf in the

Midland & Scottish type 2-8-0s converted to oil firing which proved ineffective in Persian conditions. The Americans followed them with some early diesels, which produced better results but seemingly not sufficient reliability to induce the Iranian authorities to change over from steam to diesel at that time. Of course, oil was so plentiful and cheap in Iran that the savings emanating from such a change-over were small. Hence, orders continued for oil-fired steam in the years immediately following World War II.

Since 1958 the Iranians have dieselized with 375 standard General Motors units. Later models have pressurized engine rooms to keep the sand of a desert country out of sensitive machinery. Rapid expansion would make figures meaningless – it is expected that current traffic loads could treble over the next five years – but in 1975 (the Iranian year 1353) there were 4.8 million passenger journeys and the system carried eight million tons of freight south which used to be metre-gauge but which was converted to standard gauge a few years ago. The line to the north forms part of the land route from Europe and carries a considerable volume of freight in wagons from virtually every European country, while the line from the south links up with the shipping routes from the Far East and from the Mediterranean via Suez and the Red Sea.

Port congestion in the Gulf has been a considerable problem in recent years and new lines to alternative ports are required to relieve Basra. A branch has already been built to Umm Qasr near the border with Kuwait which may one day be extended southwards through Kuwait and Saudi Arabia. A new route from Baghdad to the Gulf to the east of the Tigris and Euphrates rivers is also planned.

The main passenger station in Baghdad still retains metre-gauge tracks as it is also the

terminus for the line to Kirkuk and Erbil in the northeast of the country. This line has a secondary terminus on the east side of Baghdad and a branch line to Khanaqin near the border with Iran. Plans have been drawn up for converting this remaining metre-gauge line to standard gauge and for extending it from Erbil to Mosul to provide an alternative route between Baghdad and the north. This would relieve pressure on the existing line which is virtually occupied to capacity.

Another proposed route is to be constructed westwards from Baghdad towards the border with Syria. Ultimately this may provide a direct link with Mediterranean ports and an alternative to the long sea passage through the Suez, but the railroad's more immediate purpose will be to permit development of mineral deposits in the western part of Iraq itself.

ISRAEL

See map on pages 250-251.

ISRAEL RAILWAYS
Central Station,
Haifa.

The first railway in the Holy Land went appropriately from Jaffa (the Joppa of the Bible) to Jerusalem and was the result of a concession obtained from the Turks in 1888 by a French company. This line, the *Chemin de Fer de Jaffa à Jerusalem et Prolongements*, 57 miles long and laid to the metre gauge, was opened in 1892.

The Hedjaz Railway from Damascus to Medina (described earlier) was the next and, although most of the route was outside what is now Israel, there was a branch to the port of Haifa, over which most of the material to build the main line was brought. The strange 3ft 5½in Hedjaz gauge (there is an apochryphal tale that it was due to the holes in the first consignment of steel sleepers being wrongly punched) was of course adopted. This line still exists but is no longer operated.

A long gruelling campaign was fought in Palestine during World War I and both sides were supported by a lot of railway construction.

A standard-gauge line of communication near the coast (to match the Egyptian railways) followed the British advance across Sinai and beyond, while the Turks built much military mileage to such familiar places as Beersheeba. They converted the Jerusalem branch from metre gauge to 3ft 5½in; British sappers then re-laid it to 2ft and finally, after the war, Palestine Railways altered it again to standard gauge. Four gauge conversions is possibly a world record.

So Israel's railways were born in conflict and in conflict they have been ever since. The connections with Egypt and Lebanon (built in World War II) have been abandoned, but since the formation of the state of Israel, 135 miles of other lines have been constructed, leading to today's 560-mile system, on which 55 diesel locomotives with 105 passenger and 2100 freight cars, handle 4.5 million passengers and three million tons of freight annually. Expenses are 140 percent of the receipts.

Above: An Israeli passenger train at Jerusalem.

Top left: A train on the Trans-Iranian Railway approaches Ahvaz.

Left: During World War II a number of British LMS railway designed Stanier-2-8-0s were specially built for service with the War Department. Many of the engines found their way to the Middle East and worked in Palestine, Egypt and Persia. Here is War Department No 70573 with a British freight train on the then-Palestine Railway at Jaffa.

JORDAN

See map on pages 250-251.

HEDJAZ – JORDAN RAILWAY
PO Box 1929,
Amman.

The railway system of Jordan is made up of the 230-mile section of the Damascus-Medina Hedjaz pilgrims' railway lying in that part of the Ottoman Empire which after 1918 became known as Trans-Jordan. The present King's grandfather, Abdullah, had been given the promise of a Kingdom by the British in the heat of the battles to drive out the Turks; one might imagine that after the war he would ride in out of the desert with his Bedouin robes flowing, to claim his throne. Not so, however; apparently he just bought a ticket (plus some for a few well-armed followers) and arrived unannounced at Ma'an on the Hedjaz train. All was well.

The railway in fact continued to be run by the British Palestine administration until 1948, when it became independent and known as the Jordan Royal Hashemite Railways. In due time help came for modernization in the form of a loan from the World Bank, but to their consternation the administration asked for new *steam* locomotives. This meant American dollars *not* going back to America, since locomotives of that sort were no longer built there. Some

excellent 4-6-2s (of that odd 3ft 5¼in gauge) from Mitsubishi of Japan were ordered and received, but since then diesels have in fact appeared. Currently the fleet consists of twelve steam and five diesel locomotives, with eight passenger and 370 freight cars; 7000 passengers and 56,000 tons of freight are carried each year.

In 1975 an extension was opened to the port of Aqaba on an arm of the Red Sea, giving Jordan long-dreamt-of access to the ocean and extending the rail system to 380 miles.

LEBANON

See map on pages 250-251.

LEBANON STATE RAILWAYS
Chemins de Fer de l'Etat Libanais,
PO Box 109,
Amar Beyhum Street,
Beirut.

The Lebanon as an independent state only came into existence in 1944 (before then it had been part of a French mandate which included Syria) but its railways were older. A 3ft 5¼in gauge line, 150 miles long and with rack-and-pinion sections, was built in 1895-97 to connect Beirut with Damascus. Locomotives were supplied from Switzerland and work on the Abt rack system.

Between the wars a standard-gauge line from

Aleppo to the port of Tripoli was opened and, during World War II, South African sappers built a standard-gauge railway northwards along the coast from Haifa to Beirut and Tripoli. At that time it formed a uniform gauge connection between Egypt, Israel, Syria and Turkey, but since then political disagreements have led to the dismantling of various sections.

The Lebanese government acquired the line from the British military authorities in 1947. Now the standard-gauge system consists of 210 miles of route with (nominally) thirteen steam and five diesel locomotives, although how many survive is problematical. On the narrow gauge there were fifteen rack-and-adhesion steam locomotives and four others. There were fifteen carriages and 900 wagons. Operations are currently either non-existent or limited. Even before the present civil war troubles it was an unusual taxi-driver who knew where the stations were in Beirut.

SAUDI ARABIA

See map on pages 250-251.

SAUDI GOVERNMENT RAILROAD ORGANIZATION
Dammam.

The late King Ibn Saud of Saudi Arabia, in his younger days, was one of those who had a good deal to do with the campaign to end the Turkish domination of Arabia which resulted in the destruction and hence closure of the Hedjaz Railway. He became a railway enthusiast in the process and much later became personally responsible for having a standard-gauge line built to connect his then-quite-small capital Riyadh with the port of Dammam, 370 miles away on the Persian Gulf. The oil company Aramco built it for him in 1951 because he asked them to, although it was at that time uneconomic in any commercial sense. Its soundness as a proposition lay wholly in the sense it made diplomatically.

There were no construction problems; troubles with blowing sand were overcome by spraying a wide swathe of the desert with a thick carpet of crude oil. Standard US equipment was acquired, including twenty cars from famous American trains. It is noted that at least one has been converted to a prayer car, for the Faithful to carry out their devotions en route.

Since the re-evaluation of oil, operations have expanded considerably – reflected in the fact that deep-water berths on the Port of Dammam have expanded from fifteen to over fifty – and there are now 26 locomotives and over a thousand freight wagons.

Below: Desert train: An early passenger suburban train enters Dhahran, Saudi Arabia behind an American-built diesel in 1951.

Bottom left: A Royal Hashemite Railway train, from Ma'an to Amman in Jordan, is headed by 2-8-2 No 258 in October 1955.

Below: In happier days a Swiss built 0-10-0 rack locomotive heads a Lebanese Government Railway mixed train out of Beirut.

SYRIA

See map on pages 250–251.

SYRIAN RAILWAYS
Chemins de Fer Syriens
BP 182,
Aleppo.

HEDJAZ-SYRIAN RAILWAY ADMINISTRATION
Chemin de Fer Hedjaz-Syrien
BP 134,
Damascus.

The first railway in what is now Syria was the 3ft-5½in-gauge rack-and-adhesion line to Damascus from Beirut (and now mainly in the Lebanon) completed in 1898. The next was the famous Hedjaz Railway (described earlier) leading south from Damascus, upon which construction began in 1901. Standard-gauge trackage had to wait until towards the end of World War I when Turkey, with German support, pressed on with the Baghdad Railway, the route of which passed through Aleppo, the present capital. The port of Tripoli was reached between the wars.

Since 1945, with Lebanon independent, extensions have taken place in other directions, notably along the bank of the Euphrates River towards the Iraq border, only 75 miles from Baghdad. Another line has also recently been reported as complete; this links Aleppo with the port of Latakia on the Mediterranean sea. A railway which will give an all-Syrian standard-gauge route to Damascus is currently under construction. A further 3500 miles is included in the current five-year plan.

Current Statistics

	Syrian Railways	Hedjaz-Syrian Railway
Gauge	4ft 8½in	3ft 5¼in
Route length, miles	560	125
Steam locomotives	36	45
Diesel locomotives	20	—
Railcars	10	5
Wagons	1200	450
Passengers carried	*	54,000
Freight carried, tons	*	175,000

* not disclosed.

TURKEY

See map on pages 250-251.

TURKISH STATE RAILWAYS – TCDD
Türkiye Cumhuriyeti Devlet Demiryollari Isletmesi,
Ankara.

The way in which Germany, before 1918, pushed forward railway projects in the then-primitive country of Turkey, in order to further the extension of German power eastwards, has been described. After 1918 the Turkish government had to return the British and French lines (mainly of local interest) to their former owners, but was able to retain the ex-German Anatolia and Baghdad railways. This 1200-mile route from Haydarpasa to the Iraq border became the core of the present Turkish State Railways

Left, top: A Syrian 2-8-2 locomotive leaves Damascus on a local working.

Left, bottom: A steam-hauled express leaves Izmir, Turkey.

Below: A Turkish State Railways train leaves Izmir for Afyonkarahisar.

Above: Hayderpasa station, Istanbul, with a diesel express bound for Ankara.

Top: The steam shed at Haydarpasa on the Asian shores of Istanbul with a green German 4-6-4 tank waiting for evening suburban duty, 1966.

Top centre: A diesel train passes through Florya on the electrified suburban line out of Sirkeci terminus en route for the Greek border at Edirne.

Top right: A German Kreigslok 2-10-0 takes water en route to Izmir with a train from Afyonkarahisar April 1977.

Right: A modern American diesel-electric locomotive stops briefly en route to Ankara in April 1977. The yard at this station was still being shunted by a British-built War Department Stanier 2-8-0.

(TCDD). However, modern Turkey under Kemal Attaturk, with Ankara as its capital, had first to be established and frontier disputes with Greece and Syria settled. The TCDD was not, in fact, formally established until 1927, the independent companies being absorbed over the next twenty years or so; the first railway in Turkey, the British Ottoman Railway, dating from 1860, was purchased in 1935. Since its formation, the TCDD has constructed over 2000 miles of new line to make up the present mileage of 6200, all (except for a short branch along the shore of the Black Sea) laid to standard gauge.

Turkish steam power favoured German practice, although locomotives from other sources have lingered on in service. Ten coupled motive power is particularly common, as befits a mountainous country. One fascinating oddity was a class of 2-6-0 by Hanomag which did not quite meet the axle-load limit and had to have a small pair of carrying wheels inserted between the second and third pair of drivers. Currently over 500 steam locomotives are reported as being in service although the main brunt of the work falls on 200 or so diesel locomotives. The Istanbul suburban services were electrified in 1955 and more recently a start has been made on the trunk line leading east from Haydarpasa towards Ankara.

There is much heavy construction in the mountainous regions which make up the greater part of the country, including the three-mile Amanus Tunnel southeast of Adana. Turkish railways presently carry some fourteen million tons of freight annually an average distance of 300 miles, using 19,000 freight cars. The annual passenger count is 128 million and there are 1100 carriages.

YEMEN

See map on pages 250-251.

In the days when Yemen was called Aden and ruled by the British, it had a 29-mile metre-gauge line running inland from the port. The line was built in 1916 for strategic reasons, since Arabia, as a rather loosely attached piece of the Turkish Empire, was then enemy territory. Indian equipment was used and an attempt to struggle on commercially after the war came to an end in 1929.

6——
ASIA

Afghanistan	**Kampuchea (Cambodia)** Kampuchea (Cambodia) Railways	**Philippines** Philippine National Railways
Bangladesh Bangladesh Railway	**Korea** Korean National Railroad (South Korea) Korean Railways (North Korea)	**Sri Lanka** Sri Lanka Government Railway
Burma Union of Burma Railways	**Malaysia** Malayan Railway Sabah State Railways	**Taiwan** Taiwan Railway Administration
China Railways of the People's Republic of China		**Thailand** State Railway of Thailand
Hong Kong Hong Kong Government Railways	**Nepal** Nepal Government Railway Janakpur Railway	**USSR** See Europe: USSR
India Indian Government Railways	**Pakistan** Pakistan Railways	**Vietnam** Vietnam Railways System
Japan Japan National Railways		

AFGHANISTAN

See map on pages 250–251 or 278–279.

AFGHANISTAN RAILWAYS
Kabul.

History is full of examples of railways being built to strengthen tenuous political links; occasionally the opposite, railways *NOT* being built in order to weaken them, also occurs. A prime example is Afghanistan, which has the distinction of being the most populous country in the world to be without railways. However, the government has recently approved plans for a network of 1100 miles of standard-gauge railway connecting the capital Kabul not with nearby Landi Kotal, terminus of the Khyber Pass Railway in Pakistan but with Chaman (giving, with a break of gauge, a direct route to the sea at Karachi) and two points on the frontier with Iran, whose railways are also standard gauge. There is no link proposed with the Soviet system (on yet another gauge) at Kushka in the north. Diesel-electric traction is intended; an initial fleet of fifty locomotives has been proposed.

BANGLADESH

See map on pages 278–279.

BANGLADESH RAILWAY
Chittagong.

As an indication of her status as a pathetic victim of power politics, Bangladesh has for a railway system a collection of disconnected left-over bits of line, most of which were part of the Bengal–Assam Railway. They are separated both by gauge and by the River Brahmaputra which remains unbridged in Bangladesh.

Nevertheless, there are some remarkable structures; the 1915 Hardinge Bridge over the

Ganges, on what was once the East Bengal Railway, the main line from Calcutta to Siligun (for Darjeeling), is 1.1 miles long and in the world class. There are fifteen spans and the pier foundations go down 160ft below low-water level.

Currently, on the metre gauge, 222 steam and 144 diesel-electric locomotives haul 926 passenger and 14,500 freight cars; on the broad gauge the figures are 115 steam locomotives, 34 diesel-electric, 276 passenger and 4300 freight cars. Seventy-two million passengers are carried; 2.7 million tons of freight are hauled an average distance of ninety miles. Expenses are 96 percent of receipts. In general Indian railway practice is followed.

BURMA

See map on pages 278–279.

UNION OF BURMA RAILWAYS
PO Box 118,
Rangoon.

Until 1937 Burma was part of India and the railways there had been constructed by the (British) Indian government, although initially leased for operation by a private company. The first line was opened in 1877, between Rangoon the capital and Prome on the Irrawaddy River. By 1934 it was possible to travel 723 miles up country from Rangoon to Myitkyina near the Chinese Border, crossing the Irrawaddy near Mandalay by the 3950ft-long Ava Bridge, of sixteen spans. It still remains the only bridge across this river. The 1900-mile system that then existed remains substantially the same today; there are several separate sections connected by river ferries. There has never (quite) been a connection with the railway system of any of Burma's neighbours.

There was heavy destruction of the Burmese Railways during World War II; the Ava Bridge was out of commission for over ten years, until 1954. Another great bridge, the Gokteik Viaduct up in the hills on the Lashio branch, was also out of use for nearly as long. The Gokteik Viaduct is a steel trestle structure 320ft high and 2250ft long, of ten spans. Equally remarkable is the alignment of this line, which includes four reversals and a spiral in its climb to 3800ft altitude.

The system is metre gauge and Indian practice generally prevails. Current returns show 280 steam and 75 diesel locomotives, 1160 passenger cars and 11,000 wagons. Garratt articulated locomotives were supplied for the heavily graded (1 in 25) hill sections, but standard Indian types handled traffic elsewhere in steam days.

A symptom of the generally discouraging attitude of the Burmese government towards visitors is the fact that notices and station names are written only in Burmese script.

CAMBODIA
See Kampuchea

CEYLON
See Sri Lanka

CHINA

See map on pages 266-267.

RAILWAYS OF THE PEOPLE'S REPUBLIC OF CHINA
Peking.

Chinese Railway history started when a British company sought and won a concession for a nine-mile line from Shanghai to Woosung. The nobility, like the Eton College authorities forty years before, felt – quite correctly, as it turned out – that such a devilish device would undermine their time-honoured top position in society, but were not able to prevent construc-

Bottom left: A Burma Railways 2-8-2 + 2-8-2 Beyer-Garratt hauls a mixed train out of Sedaw. Note the British type semaphore signals. The second reversing station of this ascent can just be seen through the locomotive's smoke.

Bottom right: Tangshan station, China, in July 1976, only two weeks prior to the disastrous earthquake. This row of SY class 2-8-2 locomotives had just been completed at the works there.

Below: Peking station, 1976, with a class RM 4-6-2, which has just come off a train from Tientsin.

Page 262/263: Two diesels await their turn at Peking central station.

Projection: Bonne

East from Greenwich

1:15 000 000

| 100 | 0 | 100 | 200 | 300 | 400 | miles |

| 100 | 0 | 100 | 200 | 300 | 400 | 500 | 600 | km |

C. Terpeniya

Blagoveshchensk
Khabarovsk
Sakhalin
Little Khingan Mts.
Yuzhno Sakhalinsk
Dolinsk
Kholmsk
Korsakov
Simushir
Urup
Kuril Is.
Tsitsihar
HEILUNGKIANG
Kiamusze
Hokang
Iturup
MANCHURIA
Kunashir
HARBIN (Pinkiang)
Hokkaido
2290
Mutankiang
Asahigawa
Changchun
Kirin
Sapporo
Otaru
Kushiro
Vladivostok
Nakhodka
Hakodate
C. Erimo
Muroran
PACIFIC
SHENYANG (Mukden)
NORTH
Tsuguru Str.
Aomori
Hachinohe
OCEAN
Antung
Sinuiju
KOREA
Akita
Miyako
Morioka
Pyongyang
Kamaishi
SEA OF
Sakata
Ishinomaki
Sado
Niigata
Sendai
JAPAN
Fukushima
SEOUL
SOUTH
Wajima
Toyama
Utsunomiya
Taegu
Kanazawa
Maebashi
Mito
Inchon
KOREA
Matsue
Tottori
KYOTO
NAGOYA
TOKYO
PUSAN
Okayama
KOBE
YOKOHAMA
YELLOW
Hiroshima
OSAKA
Shizuoka
Yokosuka
SEA
Shimonoseki
Kure
Taka-matsu
Sakai
Hamamatsu
Wakayama
Kitakyushu (Moji)
Shikoku
Tokushima
(Yawata)
Fukuoka
Kochi
Matsuyama
Sasebo
Kumamoto
Nagasaki
Omura
Kyushu
Miyazaki
JAPAN
Kagoshima
Tanega Shima
SHANGHAI
EAST CHINA
SEA
Amami O Shima
Hangchow
Ningpo
CHEKIANG
Ryukyu Islands
Okinawa
Naha
Taipei
Taichung
Hualien
Taiwan (Formosa)
Kaohsiung
Luzon

HONSHU, SHIKOKU AND KYUSHU

1:7 500 000

| 50 | 0 | 50 | 100 | 150 | miles |

| 50 | 0 | 50 | 100 | 150 | 200 | km |

REFERENCE TO PREFECTURES		
1 Aomori	16 Tokyo	32 Shimane
2 Akita	17 Saitama	33 Hiroshima
3 Iwate	18 Yamanashi	34 Yamaguchi
4 Yamagata	19 Shizuoka	35 Kagawa
5 Miyagi	20 Aichi	36 Tokushima
6 Fukushima	21 Gifu	37 Kochi
7 Niigata	22 Fukui	38 Ehime
8 Ishikawa	23 Shiga	39 Oita
9 Toyama	24 Mie	40 Fukuoka
10 Nagano	25 Nara	41 Saga
11 Gunma	26 Wakayama	42 Nagasaki
12 Tochigi	27 Osaka	43 Kumamoto
13 Ibaraki	28 Kyoto	44 Miyazaki
14 Chiba	29 Hyogo	45 Kagoshima
15 Kanagawa	30 Tottori	46 Hokkaido
	31 Okayama	

267

tion taking place. Accordingly, 2-4-os *Celestial Kingdom* and *Flowery Land* began operations on 30 June 1876. The Mandarins, however, still had cards to play; in this case it is said that they caused bound coolies to be thrown in front of the train, thereby bringing home to the common people in a very realistic way the dangers inherent in the adoption of mechanical transport. A public outcry led to an apparently munificent gesture on the part of the Mandarins, who bought out the owners and had the railway destroyed, after only fifteen months of operation.

The first lasting line in China was the first section of a line which was intended to carry coal from the mining areas of Tangshan, on the northeast coast, to Tientsin. It eventually became part of the main line from Peking to Manchuria.

Again there were problems with the authorities and originally permission was only given to use mule traction. However, the European manager managed to build a locomotive from surplus material on hand at the collieries – it is said that on one occasion it was buried in the ground to conceal it from visiting officials – and in this way the Railway Age came to China. The 'Foreign Devils' concerned were in this case again British, but later concessions for railway building were also obtained by American, Belgian, French, German and Japanese interests. In spite of this variety of ownership, all the lines of national importance were built to standard gauge, apart from a line leading into what was then French Indo-China (now Vietnam). In due course all the lines were absorbed into the Chinese National Railways. No new foreign concessions were granted after 1908, and the formation of the Republic in 1912 led the way to a gradual take-over of the foreign systems. By 1930 (the date of the notorious 'Manchuria Incident'), there were 7200 miles of railway, all forming part of the National system.

A long period of war and revolution then ensued, during which the Chinese Railways System functioned spasmodically, according to the ebb and flow of the fighting. By the time that the Communists took power in 1949, only an estimated 4000 miles of line were operable.

This was an absurdly small system for a nation with a population five times and a land area twice that of the US, which had thirty times the railway mileage. Tremendous efforts were made by the new regime to provide the new China with an adequate rail system. Its extension during the postwar years by nearly 20,000 miles has not been paralleled elsewhere. For example, the Yangtze River formed a gap in the Peking-Shanghai Railway until 1969, when the great bridge at Nanking (fourteen spans, totalling 1830ft) was opened. The river was not crossed by rail even up-stream until 1957, well into Communist times. Much new construction was carried out in appallingly difficult country, leading to feats of railway engineering which also have no counterpart elsewhere during the last thirty years. Not forgotten also must be the amount of upgrading and doubling of existing main lines. Railways now penetrate into the far corners of China; for example, there is a line to Urumchi in central Asia. Tibet, though, has still to be penetrated by rail. However, the Railway Technical Institute at Tientsin trains over 150 Railway Graduate Engineers each year and their work is gradually and literally leaving its mark in these tremendous but little known projects in the mountainous regions of western China. If present plans mature, there is little doubt that soon a 'Tibet Limited' will pull out of an enlarged Peking station on its journey to the still-forbidden city of Lhasa, crossing passes rivalling those of South America in the process.

In evaluating all this achievement, one must take account of the totalitarian nature of the regime, illustrated by the fact that Peking's magnificent central main station, completed twenty years ago, was planned, designed and built within twelve months. The democracies of the West could hardly do such a thing within twelve years! There are six platforms with twelve faces and, although it is a terminus, the main building is set at the side rather than the end, with the concourse at first floor level above the platform. Waiting rooms are provided for each main direction of travel, not only clean and comfortable, but almost luxurious. There are very fine dining rooms, nurseries and other amenities. The main signal box is just a room off one of the administrative corridors in the top floor of the block and above that there is a noble clock tower with a pagoda roof, which chimes 'The East is Red' at noon, three and six pm. There are 58 departures daily. Subtracting seven local ones, one finds that barely more than fifty main-line trains serve a capital city of some four million inhabitants, who have no private cars, no long-distance buses and only minimal air services.

Steam is very much in the fore in China, with around 5000 fiery dragons still in operation and 'March Forward' 2-10-2s still just (in 1978) rolling off the production lines at Tatung, northwest of Peking. It suits a country with much coal but little oil and a huge population to use this labour-intensive but simple machine for traction. 'People' 4-6-2s are used on passenger trains and a variety of 2-8-2s ('Liberation', 'Construction' and 'Aiming High') on shunting, trip and branch-line work. There are also some ex-Soviet 2-10-2s, secondhand after gauge conversion; their original name 'Friendship' is no longer appropriate. Most of the work is done with these very few types, the majority constructed since the rest of the world – except India – ceased to build steam.

During Mao Tse-Tung's 'Great Leap Forward' of 1958 to 1960, the Chinese Railways had some traumatic experience with do-it-yourself diesel locomotives and their premature large-scale production, so it is not surprising that they then set out to build the world's last steam locomotive factory as well as continuing steam production elsewhere. Although reliable diesel locomotives are now coming off Chinese production lines at the estimated rate of 200 per year, steam locomotives are also still being built on a reduced scale. It is thought that the diesel fleet is currently between 1000 and 2000, of which more than half are Chinese-built. Electrification is at present on a small scale, far away amidst the mountains of central China, between Paoki and Chengtu. Some French-built locomotives form the basis of this operation.

The passenger trains of the Chinese Railways have a good deal to commend them. The soft-class sleeping cars are similar to the European first-class couchette, but kept spotlessly clean. At the modest speeds run, the riding is excellent and the catering in the dining car very much in the Chinese tradition, simple, fresh and good. Air conditioning has only been noted on the prestige run from the Hong Kong frontier to Canton. Hard class cars, of which there are both the couchette and the open-sitting variety are plain but also clean. The only feature towards which the Westerner might display a little caution are hole-in-the-floor toilets.

Freight operations are very much in traditional US style with great long trains of buckeye coupled bogie cars, hauled at high speed by big black 2-10-2s. In statistical terms it is estimated that 900 million tons of freight are hauled an average distance of 220 miles in a fleet of 210,000 wagons, the majority eight-wheeled.

In contrast to the American style of the trains, left-hand running on double track and raised platforms take after Britain. More cosmopolitan is the signalling which on the main line is mostly conventional multi-aspect colour light. Semaphore areas do exist and here at first glance signals do appear to be of old-fashioned British lower quadrant pattern; a closer look shows the arms to be of the American type but, because of the left-hand running, seen as if in a looking glass. Still deeper examination gives the impression that, when several arms are mounted on the same post, the aspects displayed and their meanings owe something to German inspiration. To complete the international picture, it may be added that in the old days the whistle boards on the Peking-Hankow Railway bore the French legend '*Sifflez!*', the whole of this reflecting the piecemeal way the Chinese Railway system was developed before World War I by different foreign powers.

EAST PAKISTAN
See Bangladesh

FORMOSA
See Taiwan

HONG KONG ——INDIA——

See map on pages 266–267.

HONG KONG GOVERNMENT RAILWAY
Kowloon.

This 21.5-mile line is the stub end of the line from Kowloon – on the mainland just across from Victoria on Hong Kong island – to Canton in China. It was opened on 5 August 1911, was laid to standard gauge and was built with British capital. The new passenger station in Kowloon is very much after the style of and seemingly only a little smaller than Euston in London. One might expect something pretty grand in the way of trains to draw up at one of its six platforms. However, all there is is an hourly local train out to the frontier – as at Chicago, only pigs get a through ride. Passengers cross the border railway bridge on foot, noting (if they are so minded) the last Imperial four-bolt fishplate and the first Communist six-bolt one. A fleet of ten road-switcher diesels handles the traffic.

It should also be noted that Victoria is the last haunt of a once familiar rail-borne creature, the archetypical British double-decker street-car.

INDIAN GOVERNMENT RAILWAYS
Rail Bhawan,
Raisina Road,
New Delhi.

See map on pages 278–279.

When they evacuated their Empire, the Romans left behind them in Britain and elsewhere – a system of law and a system of roads; the British in their turn left behind in India a corresponding system of administration and a system of railways, which, improved and modernized since independence, still form a great united network, ranking second in the world in size.

It was in November 1852 that the first passenger train conveyed officials and their guests from Bombay 25 miles to Thana on the first section of the Great Indian Peninsula Railway, now known as the Central Railway. Like most subsequent construction in British India, the GIPR was built by a privately financed company under a concession and guarantee from the government of India. Under the terms, a five percent dividend on its capital was guaranteed; in return, government traffic was carried free or at reduced rates, a measure of state control was imposed and any further profit was divided between the government

Above: The late Prime Minister of India, Pandit Nehru, drives the first electric engine to be built at Chittaranjan in 1963.

Top: Modernization has brought the diesel locomotive to steamy India but the country scene changes little.

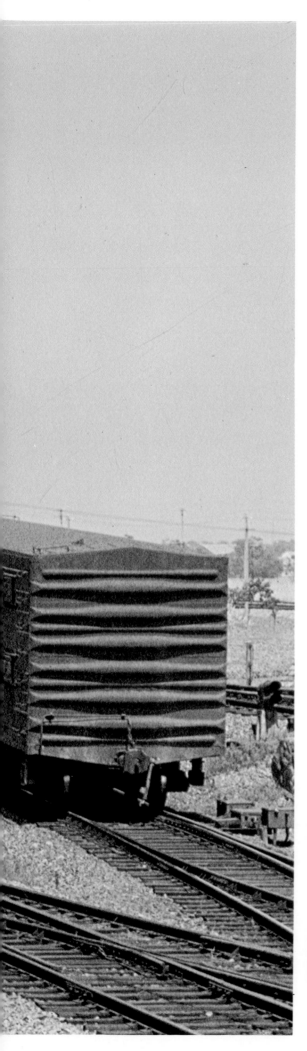

Left: Hump-shunting at a marshalling yard near Shanghai, China.

Below: A Darjeeling-Himalayan narrow-gauge train on the ascent. Note the sand-men on front.

and the shareholders. The government could exercise the right to take over the line after a certain passage of years.

Similar provisions applied to the East India Railway out of Calcutta, which opened its first section in 1854; the whole 1130 miles to Delhi began operating in 1864. A junction with the GIPR was formed at Allahabad in 1871, thereby opening rail communication right across the subcontinent. This was made easier by the foresight of the Governor-General, Lord Dalhousie (this was in the days before Viceroys), who imposed a uniform 5ft 6in gauge on the companies as a condition of granting the concessions.

The Indian Mutiny of 1857 came in the early stages of the period of railway construction. It has been argued that the coming of railways and the changes in the Indian way of life which their coming implied, was one major factor in sparking it off. Certainly one result of it was to ensure that the authorities did not drag their feet in providing India with a comprehensive railway system.

Alas, subsequent heads of government, Viceroys Lawrence and Mayo, did not maintain this insistence on a uniform gauge and introduced the metre-gauge for secondary lines. By the turn of the century there was even a through metre-gauge line between Delhi and Ahmadabad. Mayo is reputed to have said 'When we have an elephants load, we may use an elephant, but when we have only a donkey's load, we have to use a donkey', and the thinking behind this dubious analogy led not only to much metre-gauge construction but much narrow gauge as well, even in the plains where little advantage prevailed. In the mountains there were advantages; such lines as the Darjeeling-Himalayan with its 60ft radius curves would have been prohibitively costly as a broad- or even metre-gauge railway.

The military authorities stood no nonsense of this kind and strategic railways such as the Khyber Pass line (now in Pakistan) had to be broad-gauge to avoid the problems of transshipment from trains of one gauge to another.

The guarantee system (which later became considerably less advantageous to the investors) worked well and produced results; it by-passed government prevarication and took advantage of the Indian government's equally remarkable integrity and its ability to ensure that things were done properly. Even so, towards the end of the century there was some government-financed construction, particularly of so-called 'famine railways', which were built to bring in food quickly to areas where crops had failed. A few non-guarantee private companies also existed. In general there were few competitive or duplicated routes; one exception was be-

tween Bombay and Delhi, where both the GIPR and the Bombay, Baroda and Central India offered service.

In addition, the rulers of many of the larger princely states (that is one third of the total land area) constructed their own railway systems. On absorption in 1950 there were 7000 miles of such lines, of which the Nizam of Hyderabad's was the largest, extending 1375 miles.

From the 1920s onwards, the government exercised its option to take over the principal lines. First to go in 1925 were the GIPR and EIR companies. The Indianization of the lines was also begun. After 1925 the intake of young English engineers, for example, almost ceased. Subsequent recruitment was from India and, in fact, by 1947 there were a mere 200 British railway officers.

In 1947 came independence and partition, but, as stated earlier, well before this time the Indian government had acquired all the principal railways, although they still traded under the old names. Much mileage was lost to West Pakistan, East Pakistan (now Bangladesh) and Sri Lanka (Ceylon); in compensation, the lines in the princely states were acquired. The new boundaries were not convenient from a railway point of view and some otherwise pointless new construction was made necessary, particularly in order to maintain an all-Indian route to Assam. Alas, many refugees on trains crossing the new India–W Pakistan border were mas-

Extreme left, top: India's electrically hauled 'Sinhagad Express'. Note the bull-head track.

Extreme left, below: India's diesel-hauled 'Frontier Mail'.

Left: Chittaranjan (near Asansal, India) works in March 1965 where steam and electric locomotives are built side by side.

Below: A Western Railway of India train (shown here on the Northern Railway) from Delhi to Ahmadabad stops at Delhi Serai Rohilla station. The locomotive is YP class No 2750 – a 4-6-2 heading thirteen coaches.

sacred – as many as 3000 at a time – by opposing religious factions during this tragic period; rather strangely, British travellers were almost invariably spared.

Between 1950 and 1960 the old lines were reorganized into 'Railways' as generally shown below. Of course, the titles indicate administrative zones rather than separate systems:

Southern Railway[1]
Madras & Southern Mahratta, South Indian, Mysore*

South Central Railway
Indian peninsula, south-central area, south-west Maharashtra and Andhra Pradesh.

Central Railway[1]
Great Indian Peninsula, Nizam of Hyderabad's*, Scindia*, Dholpur*

Western Railway
Bombay, Baroda & Central India, Surashtra*, Jaipur*, Rajasthan*, Cutch*, Gaekwar of Baroda's*

Eastern Railway[2]
East India east of Moghal Sarai

South Eastern Railway[2]
Bengal–Nagpur

Northern Railway
Indian portion of the North Western Railway, Jodhpur*, Bikaner*

North East Frontier Railway[3]
Lines in Assam and approaches Darjeeling-Himalayan

Northern Eastern Railway[3]
Metre gauge lines north of the Ganges excluding lines in Assam and approaches.

Notes: * Princely State line.

1 In 1965 the South Central Railway was formed from parts of the Southern and Central Railways.
2 When originally formed the South Eastern Railway was included in the Eastern Railway.
3 In 1958 the Northern Frontier Railway was separated from the North Eastern Railway.

Aside from making good wartime neglect and going ahead with modernization, the greatest achievement since independence is self-sufficiency. In 1947 thirty percent of stores and equipment were obtained overseas; in 1977 the figure was five percent.

Civil Engineering

India is a country of great rivers and great rivers need great bridges. The story of the railway bridges of India is a book in itself. That strange story of Kipling's, *The Bridge Builders* ('The Day's Work') tells something of it. Among the problems are the unplumbed depths of alluvial soil, which means that foundations need to be sunk 150ft or more below water-level. The out-of-sight vertical height of a bridge's piers may total nearly a mile. Another difficulty is that rivers which are a trickle in the dry season and a mile or more wide in the wet, frequently decide to change their course.

Fortunately, from the earliest days, the Indians took effortlessly to the absorbing art of bridge building. One notes the retirement in 1945 of an Indian from the post of chief draughtsman in the Bridge Department of the North Western Railway and that he was the third generation of his family to be employed therein.

No problems are likely to arise which will overtax the skill and endurance of the bridge engineers and tradesmen. Indeed, the greatest river of Asia, the Brahmaputra, was not bridged at all until after Independence. The longest bridge in India – all but two miles in length – is over the little known Upper Sone River near Benares and dates from 1900. In all there are 111,000 bridges on Indian Railways, totalling over 680 miles in length.

Before independence, the principal seats of government moved into 'hill stations' during the hot summer. Most of these had railways, including Simla (the hot weather station for Delhi), Darjeeling (Calcutta), Ootacamund or 'Ooty' (Madras) and Matheran near Bombay. It is interesting to note the differing solutions adopted to solve the same problems on these world-famous lines.

Right: An Indian express train hauled by an Indian-built electric locomotive.

The Kalka-Simla line was a conventional, solidly built 2ft 6in gauge railway, sixty miles long. There are 103 tunnels including one three-quarters of a mile long. The ruling grade is one in 33 and the minimum curvature 120ft. Powerful 2-6-4 tank locomotives enabled train loads of the Viceroy's files and other traffic to be handled expeditiously. The line is now fully dieselized.

Between Siliguri and Darjeeling runs a line of similar length that conquers the mountains not by heavy engineering but by frequent spirals or Z-reverses and hideously sharp curvature, down in 60ft radius. The summit is at 8200ft altitude, the highest rails in India. The price paid is an average speed one-half of that of the Simla line.

The climb to 'Ooty' is achieved by the Abt rack and pinion arrangement. The gradient can be increased to one in ten; the forward speed is slow, but the speed with which height is gained is considerably higher. The original Swiss-built steam metre-gauge rack-and-adhesion 0-8-2 tank locomotives are still in service.

The 2ft-gauge Matheran line is remarkable in that problems on the mountain side are reduced to a minimum by using even sharper curves than on the Darjeeling line. Special locomotives were used, 0-6-Ts with a patent flexible wheel-base, and travellers are still startled to be met by notices saying (I quote) 'Oops, what a curve – 45ft radius!' Diesel traction is now used, with steam in reserve.

Indian railway stations both old and new are worthy of the great system they serve. Sonepur is noted for having the longest station platform in the world. The most magnificent is the Central Railway's terminus in Bombay. Incidentally, the actual Central Station, called Victoria Terminus, is a rather nondescript cinema-like 1930s structure, some distance from the centre of the city, serving another line.

Permanent way in early railways in India was of the British-chaired pattern with bullhead rails but soon the more usual spiked vignoles 'flat-bottom' became the norm. The signalling methods in use include the most modern colour light equipment, made in India under licence. The majority, however, is still mechanical and of great variety, but mostly British in origin. Staff, key and tablet working is usual on single lines and in addition, an Indian specialty – the use of ball-type tokens for this purpose.

Locomotive Landmarks

Indian Locomotive History can be divided into five overlapping periods; Primaeval (1852–1914); BESA (1903–1950); IRS (1926–1939); postwar steam (1947–1972); electric-diesel 1925 (to date).

Of the Primaeval period, *Fairy Queen*, an 1855 2-2-2 from the East India Railway is the most distinguished survivor, the grand old lady of the new railway museum at Delhi and still in working order. Otherwise 2-4-0s and 0-4-2s were the norm in the early days but outstanding was the 1880 'L' class 4-6-0 of the North Western and Bengal – Nagpur railways, built well before such behemoths were known in the home country. On the metre gauge, the 'F' type outside cylinder 0-6-0 was supplied to several systems. On the narrow gauge, one must salute the Darjeeling-Himalayan 0-4-0Ts of 1892 onwards, still in use on that most demanding line today.

The British Engineering Standards Association (BESA) designs were introduced in 1903, covering 4-6-0, 4-4-2 and 4-4-0 passenger designs and 2-8-0, 0-6-0 freight, etc. The 4-6-0s were still being built as late as 1950.

Corresponding 4-6-0s were constructed for the metre gauge. Many BESA locomotives – but not the 4-4-2s – are still to be found working, a tribute to their sound design.

Alas, the same comment cannot be applied to the IRS designs, mainly consisting of 4-6-2s of three different sizes (XA, XB, XC), and two 2-8-2s (XD, XE). The Pacifics had a reputation of being poor steamers, sluggish runners and – the XB particularly – bad riders to a point not only of discomfort but of danger. In the end, at Bihta, in 1937, one was derailed with the loss of 117 lives. An enquiry led to some modification, but the IRS broad-gauge designs never met the promises of their design committee, although some are still to be found in use. On the other hand the metre-gauge IRS YB 4-6-2 and YD 2-8-2 were satisfactory machines, while on the narrow gauge, generally the ZB 2-6-2 and ZE 2-8-2 remain the last word in steam power even today.

During World War II Lend-Lease brought quantities of American broad- and metre-gauge 2-8-2s to India. Their rugged characteristics showed up well in conditions there and led to an order being placed with Baldwins of the USA for the first batch of a new standard range of locomotives. So in 1946 there arrived in India the first WP 4-6-2. Later batches built in various countries brought the total to 755, to be eclipsed by the WG 2-8-2 which reached 2450. There was also a small WL 4-6-2 as well as three corresponding designs for the metre gauge, a YP 4-6-2, a YG 2-8-2 and a YL 2-6-2. A handful of ZP narrow-gauge 4-6-2s were also acquired, but insufficient for them to be regarded as a standard design. There are some 5000 of these excellent postwar locomotives in use, out of a total steam fleet of 8000. Many were built in India, in particular at the Chittaranjan Locomotive Works, set up in 1950

Extreme left: With an aluminium painted star on her smokebox, Western Railway 2ft 6in gauge No 574 crosses a river between Bilimora and Waghai south-east of Surat.

Left: Dharampuri station on the Kalka Simla Railway in steam days.

Below: A train on the Batasia Loop between Darjeeling and Ghum.

SOUTH ASIA

ft   m

18 000   6000

12 000   4000

9000   3000

6000   2000

4500   1500

3000   1000

1500   600

600   200

0   0

200   600

m   ft

Continuation Southwards
on same scale

Projection: Conical with two standard parallels

1:10 000 000

with British aid in order to give India self-sufficiency in locomotive construction. Locomotive building was no new thing for India; contrary to popular belief, even in the days of the *Raj* several of the old companies – the EIR and the BBCI particularly – built their own. The current steam fleet is by far the largest in the world.

Electrification in India began in 1925 with a 1500v DC installation on the GIPR out of Bombay, serving a suburban area, then up the *Ghat* (mountain) section towards Poona and Igatpuri. The original 'Crocodile' type C-C locomotives still survive in shunting and trip service. Since 1947 electrification (now standardized at 25,000v, fifty-cycle, AC) has gone on apace with the 3000 route miles now completed. Since 1962 Indian-built double-bogie locomotives of conventional type have been supplied. Electric locomotives now number 840.

Recent major off-shore oil finds in the Indian

Ocean may well speed dieselization, which so far has proceeded at a modest pace, although here again, India has shown remarkable enterprise and courage in constructing her own diesel-electric locomotives which – including some supplied from abroad – amount now to 1900.

Train Services

The most remarkable thing about Indian Railways' passenger traffic is its quantity – 3300 million passengers per year. The second most remarkable thing is its cheapness. A second-class ticket for a 400-mile journey costs a mere £1.20 ($2.50). (British Rail's corresponding fare is £18 or $36.) Indicative of social conditions in India is that the first-class fare is some five times the second and ten times the air-conditioned class (provided on only a few choice trains).

A fleet of 28,500 coaches, the majority built in India since the war, bears the burden of this

heavy usage. Means are provided to defend the occupants of each carriage against dust, the sun and the attentions of railway thieves who, alas, are a problem.

Regarding freight, 220 million tons are hauled each year an average of 400 miles, using a fleet of 406,000 freight cars, fitted with vacuum brakes; the majority are four-wheeled. Currently, expenses are 84 percent of receipts.

INDONESIA

See Australasia and Oceania: Indonesia

Above: Shin-Kansen – the high-speed New Tokaido Line bullet train passes Mount Fujiyama.

Top right: A double-headed electric train at Kumanodaira station, Japan.

Above right: A traditional Japanese express at speed.

Japan

See map on page 267.

JAPANESE NATIONAL RAILWAYS – JNR

1-6-5 Marunouchi,
Chiyoda-Ku,
Tokyo.

The first railway in Japan, very sensibly connected the capital with its port and the first train ran the eighteen miles between Tokyo and Yokohama on 14 October 1872. An English engineer was in charge and to him must go some of the credit of setting the Japanese off on a course which, a century later, was to lead to one of the world's finest railway systems. Apparently, this man insisted that his Japanese assistants learn everything about planning and building railways, in order to avoid future dependence on foreigners such as himself. No doubt he was influenced by a much loved Japanese wife but JNR officials to this day recount the tale to visiting railwaymen from Britain.

The first trunk railway in Japan was the original Tokaido line between Tokyo, Osaka and Kobe, completed in 1889, which established the 3ft 6in gauge as the Japanese standard. This marked the start of an intensive period of railway construction. In 1906 the trunk routes were nationalized by the purchase of 2800 miles belonging to seventeen companies and their consolidation with 1200 miles already owned by the state. Subsequent construction has taken the total to over 12,500, not counting the new Shin-Kansen high-speed passenger network. Almost 4000 miles of non-state railway also remain.

The Shin-Kansen ('new lines') railway is a remarkable concept. It consisted of overlapping an all-purpose utility railway with a completely separate system of different gauge dedicated to the long distance carriage of passengers in the daytime by high-speed self-propelled electric trains. The first line followed the route of the original trunk line between Tokyo and Osaka and it opened for business on 1 October 1964, offering its customers, for the first time in history, start-to-stop average speeds in excess of 100 mph. Railways will never be the same again.

In 1975 the Osaka line was extended not only to the western tip of Honshu, Japan's main island, but also under the sea by the 11.8 mile New Kanmon Tunnel to Fukuoka (735 miles from Tokyo) on the island of Kyushu. This is the longest undersea tunnel in the world.

The high average speeds owe less to anything special about the trains than to very heavy civil engineering; which keeps the curvature as flat as 2.5 miles radius. On the 1975 extension, 139 miles of the route are in tunnel and 73 miles on bridges and viaducts, leaving a mere 35 miles of ordinary railway. It is impossible to circumvent natural obstacles if you can only turn as slowly as that.

As remarkable as the high speed of Shin-Kansen trains is their frequency; every hour during the day a train (120mph average speed) leaves for Fukuoka on the hour; a 'stopper' (97mph average speed) at twelve minutes past. A local working to Osaka (346 miles) at sixteen minutes past the hour follows, then a fast to Hiroshima (560 miles) at 24 and a second local to Osaka at forty minutes past the hour completes the cycle of five hourly trains. All have buffet cars; those going beyond Osaka have dining cars also.

Extension of the network to other detached islands as well as other parts of the main

island is projected or proceeding. The Seikan tunnel, at present being bored beneath the sea in order to reach the northern island of Hokkaido, will be 31 miles long when it is complete in the early 1980s. It will also be the longest railway tunnel in the world of any kind – underwater, mountain or rapid-transit. Furthermore 3ft 6in gauge trains will be accommodated as well as the Shin-Kansen 4ft 8½in gauge ones. In the south, a pair of remarkable bridges, longer than any railway bridges so far built, are under consideration to connect the island of Shikoku with Honshu.

Even without the Shin-Kansen lines, the Japanese railways carry over twice as many passengers (7100 million) as any other railway system. Electrification began in 1925 using

American equipment and now extends to 4600 miles, carrying 75 percent of Japan's rail traffic. Older electrification is at 1500v DC, the newer at 25,000v AC.

In respect of steam, Japanese mechanical engineers soon found US designs more suitable than British for Japanese conditions. They also decided on standardization and placed an order in America around the turn of the century for a batch of locomotives of the then-new and interesting 2-8-2 type. Forty years later they found themselves with 1200 of them, 25 percent of the total JNR fleet. It is not surprising that the world calls a 2-8-2 a *Mikado* and since the type was invented, has built more of them than any other. The Japanese passion for steam is reflected in the fact that 128 Mikados were set aside – among 400 others – for preservation when steam finished in Japan on 14 December 1975. Eight thousand rail fans attended the last rites on Hokkaido Island.

Coal firing with oil supplement was the rule in Japan but in other ways the locomotives, were the simplest and easiest possible. Articulation, multiple cylinders, compounding and inaccessible mechanism were, it is a pleasure to relate, conspicuous by an almost complete absence. Indeed, the C62 4-6-4s the last word in JNR steam express power, were as uncomplicated as locomotives could be. Current traction needs are met by 2050 electric and 2134 diesel locomotives.

In addition to having the world's fastest commercial train service on the standard gauge,

the Japanese Railways have also the fastest narrow-gauge expresses in the world, with up to 75mph permitted on the 42in gauge rails. Most of them are of the self-propelled type and carry romantic sounding names. The carriage fleet on this gauge totals 29,000, including 12,000 power cars, electric and diesel.

A major commuter service is operated by JNR in various Japanese cities. In particular there is Tokyo, where electric suburban trains – brightly and contrastingly coloured to indicate the route – work the succession of rush hours that make up the Tokyo day. At a station called Shinjuku, the sight of white-gloved people-packers plying their trade during the morning peak, is one of the railway wonders of the world.

The compact geography of the overcrowded

Above: A Japanese 2-8-0 steam locomotive enters a station. Note high platforms and left-hand running.

Top: The fast Tokyo–Nikko electric train in the Tokyo suburbs.

Left: Repairs are made to the pantographs at Minakami Station, Gumma Prefecture, Japan.

Japanese islands, which does so much for JNR passenger traffic, is not so helpful when it comes to freight. Accordingly, traffic has fallen off in recent years, but still amounts to 158 million tons, carried an average distance of 200 miles in 125,000 freight cars. A notable event was the instantaneous conversion of the car fleet (then 55,000 strong) from manual to automatic coupling. This took place on 17 July 1925 and is a feat which has never been matched elsewhere.

Alas, all these wonders have not led to financial success; expenses currently run at 140 percent of receipts. This figure is both better and worse than it seems; in the first place the high-speed super railway covers its expenses comfortably. This in its turn means that the 3ft 6in gauge system is even worse off in respect of its losses.

Left: Japan's Tobu Railway sports both local electric and veteran steam.

Below: A French-built electric locomotive heads a passenger train in South Korea.

KAMPUCHEA

See map (Cambodia) on page 302.

KAMPUCHEA (CAMBODIA) RAILWAYS
Phnom Penh.

Railways did not come to what was then a province of French Indo-China until the early 1930s, when a railway from Phnom Penh, the capital, to the Siamese (Thai) border, was built. Its projected continuation towards Saigon was never begun. A second line, to connect Phnom Penh to the sea at Kompong Som was completed in 1969. Although the war in Southeast Asia has now been over for some time, much of the 400-mile system is believed still not to be in use. Its nominal returns show 24 steam and thirteen diesel locomotives, forty passenger and 680 freight cars.

Right: Workshops of the North Korean Railway at Tyongyang with 35 electric locomotives under construction in 1963.

Below: A North Korean survey team at work.

KOREA

See map on pages 266-267.
KOREAN NATIONAL RAILROAD – KNR
*168, 21a Bongrae-hong,
Jungku, Seoul,
South Korea.*

KOREAN RAILWAYS – KL
Pyongyang, North Korea.

The first railway in Korea, between Inchon and Seoul, was opened around the turn of the century. An American, James R Morse, was responsible. Subsequent development took place while the country was under Japanese rule, but was built to the European 4ft-8½in gauge instead of either the Soviet or Japanese standard. This was a little surprising because the main line from Manchuria to Pusan was to some extent operated as an extension of the Trans-Siberian Railway, which was to a different gauge anyway. The use of Pusan as an embarkation point involves a much shorter sea crossing to Japan than that from Vladivostok, and passengers were wooed to the Korean route by superb connecting trains of luxury cars built by Pullman.

When, in 1945, the Japanese were driven out, there were 4000 miles of railway in Korea, worked by over 1000 locomotives. Partition and destructive war followed and since that time little information has been available concerning the railways in the north. The fact that a through weekly train leaves Pyongyang twice weekly at 1205 for Peking is the only information available – except that on Saturdays the train carries a through-car for Moscow.

The South Korean railway system has developed in line with the rest of the fast-growing economy of the country. Eight dining car expresses now cover the 280 miles between Pusan and Seoul daily, 260 million passengers and 47 million tons of freight are now carried. This is expected to increase to over seventy million over the next five years. There is a fleet of 390 diesels, 66 electric and eighty steam locomotives plus 250 electric and diesel railcars, 1700 carriages and 16,000 wagons. Three hundred and twenty miles are electrified at 25,000v AC.

MALAYSIA

See map on page 302.

MALAYAN RAILWAY
Keretapi Tanah Melayu,
PO Box 1,
Kuala Lumpur.

In British colonial days before World War II, travellers from Europe might reasonably have expected to rough it a little when they travelled up country on what was then called the Federated Malay States Railway. In fact they were greatly surprised by a train whose facilities, comfort and smoothness rivalled anything 'back home'. Such a visible manifestation of efficiency also extended to the operations of the railway as a whole and was the tradition on which the present-day Keretapi Tanah Melayu has been built.

The full extent of the railway was reached in 1931 with the completion of the East Coast line from Gemas to Tumpat. Since then there have only been minor changes to the 1035 miles of route and 1339 miles of track that now comprise the system.

The first section of the present system, the seven miles of the Perak Government Railway from Keluang to Kuala Lumpur, was opened in 1886. Other states, such as Selangor and Malacca, had their own lines. In 1901, when some linking up had taken place, the FMSR was formed. Perai (for Pinang Island) was in rail communication with Johor Baharu, opposite Singapore island, by 1909. The Siam (Thailand) border was reached in 1918 and a three-quarter-mile causeway over the straits on to Singapore opened in 1923.

During the Japanese occupation, 157 miles of the 327 mile East Coast line together with certain short branches were removed to provide material for the infamous Burma–Siam 'death railway'. This East Coast line (which also links with Thailand) was re-opened in 1951. A short extension to a new station at Prai (Butterworth), completed in 1967, involved a swing bridge – the only one in Southeast Asia – and is, apart from two industrial branches, the only addition to the system in recent years.

A freight train in South Korea hauled by an electric Bo-Bo-Bo locomotive.

Independence from Britain, which came in 1957, hardly affected the railway; on the other hand, the secession of Singapore from the Federation in 1965 has meant customs and immigration formalities at the frontier point, Johor Baharu.

Civil Engineering

Malaysia is not a difficult country for railway building and the highest railway point is a mere 480ft above sea level and the longest tunnel – on the East Coast line – only 780yd long. Bridges are another matter and many rivers have had to be crossed. (In Malaya, a long narrow country, the rivers are mostly small but frequent). The longest bridge, over the Kelantan River in the northeast, has five 250ft and five 150ft spans.

On the main line 80 lb/yd flat-bottom rail is used and 60 lb on the East Coast line and branches, on hard-wood sleepers. Some continuously welded rail is in use. Speeds are limited by curvature to 45 mph, but the railcar sets can run up to 55 mph. Axle-loads are limited to 12.75 tons over the system generally, although for a period locomotives (the 'S' class) with sixteen tons axle-load were used, but confined to the main line.

Locomotive Landmarks

'A Railway of Pacifics' wrote the late Hugh le Fleming, once Assistant Chief Mechanical Engineer of the Malayan Railway. Indeed, during the fifty years preceding the onset of dieselization in 1957, 198 out of the 283 locomotives built for Malaysia were 4-6-2s: they, of course, handled all the principal trains.

A landmark was the first design of 4-6-2, the 'H' class, introduced in 1907 and of which sixty were built by Baldwins of US. Subsequent variations (the 'L's, 'K's and 'O's) came from Britain, mostly from North British Locomotive of Glasgow, within the same weight limitations. Before this, smaller 4-6-0s were the mainstay,

but the Pacifics preceded completion of the Pinang-Johor main line.

The first locomotive, which is preserved, is a little outside-cylinder 0-6-0T by Ransome & Rapier of England, one of the very few built by that firm. Exceptionally, a 'main-lines-only' class with heavier axle-load was tried in the late 1920s. These machines, eleven 'S' class of 1927–31, included five with three cylinders and poppet valves. This complex arrangement set the seal on the design of Malaysian steam locomotives to the end; but surprisingly and almost uniquely this cam-shaft driven valve gear multi-cylinder arrangement was a success and the 68 'O' (later '56') class of 1938–1946 remained the mainstay of steam in Malaysia until dieselization.

This was another indication of the quality of the Malayan Railway staff; many other, larger and better known administrations tried and failed to maintain multi-cylindered poppet-valve steam locomotives. The affection felt for the 4-6-2s is reflected in the presentation of two of them in working order, by a group of people connected with the railway. They are occasionally used on special trains, the regular use of steam having ended in 1975.

Names are a feature of all Malaysian road locomotives, steam and diesel; even the railcars carry them. A black livery with polished fittings and so on was standard before 1941; after the war, for a period, green lined in black and orange – with copper-capped chimney – was used. The steam fleet was converted from coal to oil during 1949–1953. Tests made in 1956 with a view to running faster trains showed that the '56' class Pacifics with 4ft 6in diameter wheels could run at speeds up to 70 mph; vindication of the three cylinder arrangement regarding balance, and of the poppet valves regarding freedom of steam and exhaust flow. At least it would have been had such speeds been needed in service.

Dieselization proceeded in a very orderly way. After experience with some diesel shunting locomotives which arrived in Malaysia as early as 1945, the first main-line diesels were the 26 1500 hp '20' class Co-Cos delivered from English Electric in 1957. In 1965 the Japanese manufacturer, Kisha Seizo Kaishu, sent fifteen 1000 hp '21' class Bo-Bos, followed by a further ten in 1968. Finally, English Electric in 1971 delivered a further forty Co-Cos (the '22' class), of 1700 hp. In addition to these 91 road diesel locomotives, there are 41 shunting locomotives and 22 railcars.

Passenger Trains and Statistics

Unusual nowadays among the world's railways are three classes of accommodation. It is true that the best night expresses 'Southern Cross' (Kuala Lumpur–Singapore) and 'North Star' (Kuala Lumpur–Butterworth) are only first and second class, while locals are second and third. Nevertheless the best day trains on the same routes ('Magic Arrow' and 'Golden Arrow' respectively) do cater for all three. An appropriately named 'Golden Blowpipe' serves the East Coast line. Through international trains run three times a week from Butterworth to Bangkok. Average speeds are in the 30–35 mph range, railcars being substantially quicker. Six million passengers are conveyed in a typical year using a fleet of 345 carriages. Brown and cream livery was the standard, but recently maroon with yellow lines has been used.

A recorded 8713 wagons (four-wheel and bogie) were used to convey 3.79 million tons of freight an average of seventy miles. Receipts are 97 percent of expenses.

The vacuum brake is used, together with chopper-type couplings. Wagons can be interchanged with the Thailand railways.

Above: One of the ubiquitous North British Locomotive Company Pacifics at work on the main west-coast line in days of steam.

Extreme left: A forest station on the metre-gauge Malayan Railway. Timber is a valuable export from the country.

The majesty of Kuala Lumpur Station, Malaysia.

Signalling and Operations

Present-day practice has evolved very much on British lines, with traditional semaphore signals and electric token working on most sections of the single line. Colour light installations also exist at Perai, Kuala Lumpur and Singapore.

Administration and Finance

The headquarters of the system are at Kuala Lumpur. It is administered as a public corporation under a general manager responsible to the Minister of Communications. Expenses in 1974 amounted to 87 percent of receipts. It is reported that studies are being made of the feasibility of constructing a transverse line running eastwards from Perai to the east coast.

SABAH STATE RAILWAYS

Kota Kinabalu,
Sabah.

The railway in Sabah, an outer province of Malaysia but then British North Borneo, was constructed between 1896 and 1905 and extends almost to 100 miles of metre-gauge line. It is situated on the west coast in the rice, rubber and timber producing areas. A quirk indicating its origin is that its trains provide first and third class accommodation only, as in pre-1950 Britain.

Five steam and fifteen diesel locomotives with ten railcar sets, 23 carriages and 150 wagons handle 175,000 passengers and 90,000 tons of freight annually. Expenses are 180 percent of receipts.

NEPAL

See map on pages 278-279.

NEPAL GOVERNMENT RAILWAY

Birganj,
Nepal.

JANAKPUR RAILWAY

Khajuri,
Nepal.

Nepal is a small mountainous kingdom on the northern frontier of India. Two short thirty-mile 2ft 6in gauge railways run from the border to rail-heads in the foothills. The older one, the 1927 Nepal Government Railway, which ran from Raxaul to Amlekhganj, is now reported chopped to a mere six miles. If true, even the naming of its seven steam locomotives (including two Garratts) after local gods has failed to avert this disaster. The other line, further to the west and known as the Janakpur Railway, appears still to be in operation from Jaynagar to Bizulpura.

Left: *Passengers arrive to travel on this North Borneo Railway (now Sabah, a province of Malaysia) railcar by boat.*

Bottom right: *Landi Kotal, the terminus of the Khyber Railway.*

PAKISTAN

See map on pages 278–279.

As a nation, Pakistan is barely thirty years old; the British Raj may have succeeded in giving the old India a reasonable railway system but failed to give her unity. Hence, two wars and for many years, good undisturbed grazing on part of the old Lahore–Delhi main line. It is pleasant to record the recent re-opening of this once busy artery of commerce to traffic.

Ignoring the lines in what is now Bangladesh, the railways which Pakistan inherited consisted of the lion's share of the old North Western Railway (in 1946 the longest in British India), plus the Western portion of the metre-gauge Jodhpur lines. All are now amalgamated into a single state system.

PAKISTAN RAILWAYS – PR
Lahore.

The first section of the Pakistan Railways was a line to by-pass the un-navigable reaches of the River Indus near its mouth. It went inland from the seaport of Karachi 108 miles to Kotri and was known as the Scinde Railway. The ceremonial first barrow-load of earth was moved on 29 April 1858 and the line was opened on 13 May 1861. It was part of a plan for a rail and river route from Karachi (and hence, London) 1250 miles to Delhi. At first almost half the distance was by paddle steamer on the River Indus. In winter there is barely enough water

Bottom, centre: *A 2ft 6in gauge passenger train on the Nepal Railway. The engine is typically British, an Avonside 0-6-2 tank, and the train a local from Raxaul to Amelkhganj (too small to appear on map).*

Below: *A modern Malaysian Railways diesel, the 8 a.m. 'Express Rakyat', leaves Singapore for Butterworth, 1978.*

An American Locomotive Company diesel at the head of the Bolan Mail at Mach station, Pakistan.

An American Locomotive Company diesel at the head of the Bolan Mail at Mach station, Pakistan.

295

to navigate; in summer the river can be up to fifteen miles wide without marked channels. Navigation was very much a hit and miss business and the consequence was that the Indus State Railway opened in 1878, giving a 2200-mile all-rail route – apart from the Indus ferry at Sukkur – from Karachi right across to Calcutta.

Because of the strategic importance of the legendary Northwest Frontier, then very much a live issue because of the aggressiveness of Imperial Russia (how history repeats itself), railways in this area were mainly financed and constructed by the government of India directly rather than by private enterprise.

The 1792-mile North Western Railway was formed in 1886 by the amalgamation of the state-owned lines and purchase of the private state-guaranteed ones. By 1947 it had grown to 6890 miles, including 53 miles across the Persian border. After partition, 1850 miles were lost to the new India, but 430 miles of metre gauge were to be added to make the new three-gauge Pakistan Western Railway. The old NWR had been solely broad and narrow (2ft 6in) gauge. In 1974, after East Pakistan had become the independent Bangladesh, the PWR became Pakistan Railways.

Large areas in the west of the country are devoid of railways (largely because they are virtually devoid of people also). One line which does thread this wilderness is the 455-mile Nushki Extension Railway out of Quetta, built for strategic reasons in World War I and (with the Germans approaching the Caucasus) re-

instated in World War II. Its terminus at Zahidan in Iran – the stretch across the border was recently handed over to the Iranians – may shortly be rail-connected, (except for three rail ferries) on standard gauge, to more familiar places such as Paris or London. The NER itself runs through country where stations are fifty miles apart and the whole annual rainfall of six to seven inches can fall in one day with dire results.

Civil Engineering

It is no accident that the civil engineering section dominates this account. Formidable and unpredictable adversaries which must be overcome are the River Indus and its tributaries, the Jhelum, the Ravi, the Sutlej and the Chenab. Furthermore, the unbending requirements of military strategy in demanding railways built to main-line standards in some of the most inhospitable country in the world, is another reason for civil engineers to come to the fore. The longest tunnel in British India, the 2.5-mile double-track broad-gauge Khojak tunnel, leads only to a dead end a few miles beyond the far portal, near the old fort of Chaman on the Afghan frontier.

Perhaps the very existence of this line, as well as that of its opposite number, the Khyber Pass Railway, meant that they never had to be used to transport troops in anger. On one occasion, the Amir of Afghanistan was invited to visit London and, in order to both honour and impress him, the great broad-gauge twelve-car Vice-regal special train was sent to Chaman

for his party to begin their journey. With four 2-8-0 engines, two at either end, the train set off up the 1 in 40 grade and entered the tunnel. Alas, in the smoke and darkness His Highness panicked and pulled the communication cord. It was some time before they got going again.

The Khyber Railway with its reversals, tunnels and spirals was an equally great achievement, partly because the engineering staff were, in a land where tribal custom rather than Imperial law prevailed, regarded by the tribesmen in the same light as a Victorian English gentleman might regard the pheasants and rabbits on his estate. In the end a 'close season' was negotiated for the daylight hours and the tribesmen made money as contractors for the building of the line.

It is possible that one or both of these strategic links (the former is the most likely) which now end at stop-blocks close to the frontier, might become commercial if Afghanistan goes ahead with her railway construction plan.

The overall length of the railway bridges on the PR exceeds 75 miles and their continued existence involves a constant battle against the forces of nature. Floods, earthquakes, winds, heat and cold are all on the grand scale. It should be noted that, at river crossings such as occur in Pakistan, not only has the bridge to be built but many miles of upstream containment works need to be constructed also. Even then a river may decide to seek new pastures, creating new gaps in the line, but leaving a great bridge high and dry.

The bridge with the greatest span is the

1962-built steel-arch Ayub Bridge across the Indus at Sukkur, replacing the Lansdowne Bridge, a cantilever structure, which when opened in 1889, held the record for the world's greatest span of 820ft. The longest bridge was the 1876-built Alexandra Bridge across the Chenab, on the line between Lahore and Rawalpindi, the length of which was originally 1.75 miles. There were 64 spans. As a result of river training works, the length was reduced by more than half in 1890, the girders being recovered and used elsewhere. The longest bridge then became the mile long Jhelum River bridge (on the same line) of fifty spans; it was completed in 1878.

Locomotive Landmarks

In common with the other railways in British India, the NWR took the standard BESA and IRS designs of steam locomotive. Some 600 (520 broad, forty metre and forty narrow gauge) are still in service, including the only BESA 4-4-0s that remain. Before 1947, the NWR was burning 3500 tons of coal daily, all of which had to be railed from faraway Bengal. So, after independence, the steam fleet was rapidly con-

verted to oilburning and plans laid to dieselize as quickly as possible. The current diesel fleet numbers 500, the majority being General Motors standard units and, of course imported. Two main-line diesels supplied by Armstrong-Whitworth with Sulzer engines in 1935 had teething troubles which were never overcome, but this early enthusiasm for diesel power was the result of having so much mileage in waterless country.

Pakistan has virtually unlimited and, of course, inexhaustible resources in the way of water power for generating electricity. The busiest lines, those centred on Lahore, have accordingly been electrified – the 100 miles to Khanewal in 1974 and the 150 miles to Rawalpindi currently in progress.

In the past passengers on what is now the Pakistan Railway have suffered death from heat-stroke in the Sind Desert and frost-bite in the Zhob Valley, the narrow-gauge line on which the 7212ft summit of the system lies. On the Nushki extension one could be days away from rescue if breakdown occurred and the victualling of the box-van 'buffet cars' took this into account.

The famous 'Frontier Mail', Bombay to Peshawar, no longer runs beyond Amritsar and the 'Quetta Mail' no longer needs four steam engines driven all out to climb the twelve miles at 1 in 25 leading to the Bolan Pass, but the PR's slightly more prosaic services are both cleaner and quicker, the best trains having air-conditioned as well as dining facilities and first- and second-class accommodation. Romance, however, 'still brings up the 9.15', as Kipling (who was born and worked in Lahore) put it – or rather the 0900 Fridays only, Khyber Pass train from Peshawar, still steams with 0-6-0s front and rear.

Currently the Pakistan Railway carries 28 million tons of freight an average of 190 miles each year. The annual passenger count is 318 million. Expenses are 76 percent of receipts.

Top left: A diesel-electric locomotive on the Karachi-Lahore express.

Top right: A British-built inside-cylinder 0-6-0 works hard at the head of the weekly mixed train from Peshawar to Landi Kotal, Pakistan.

A train leaves Columbo, Sri Lanka.

PHILIPPINES

See map on page 302.

PHILIPPINE NATIONAL RAILWAYS – PNR
943 Claro M. Recto Avenue, Manila.

The first railway in the Philippines was on the main island of Luzon. It was opened on 24 November 1892 and ran 123 miles northwards from the capital, Manila, to Dagupan. This was the 3ft 6in gauge Manila Railway Company, financed in Britain. Extensions followed, but bankruptcy and reorganization as the Manila Railroad took place in 1906. In 1917 the government was obliged to acquire the system. It was reorganized in 1967 under the present title.

Current returns show its extent as 'about 1052.679 km' (658 miles). Train services are unusual in that three classes of accommodation are provided plus first-class sleeping cars on overnight runs.

Seventy-six diesel locomotives, sixty diesel railcars, 140 carriages and 1700 freight cars handle 4.5 million passengers and 400,000 tons of freight, the latter hauled an average distance of 130 miles.

The small island of Panay has a seventy-mile public north-south line, dating from 1906; it was originally the Philippine Railway Company, but since 1975 it has been known as Phividec Incorporated; however, the scale of its operations may be judged from the fact that nine diesel locomotives do the work.

No public railways exist on the island of Negros, but there are numerous sugar plantation lines, believed still to exceed 1000 miles in total. Most are 3ft gauge, but the largest (the Victorias Milling Company at the northern tip of the island) was noted for having more than 200 miles of 2ft gauge line.

SRI LANKA

See map on page 278.

SRI LANKA GOVERNMENT RAILWAY
PO Box 355, Colombo.

Until independence in 1947, Ceylon (as Sri Lanka was then known to the world) was part of India. It is an extremely beautiful island 400 miles long by 200 miles wide, just off the southern tip of the sub-continent. Its railways were part of the Indian system, linked to the mainland by a rail ferry as well as by that strange tongue of land known as Adam's Bridge. Apart from one short line near Colombo – known as the Kelani Valley Railway and familiar from film scenes taken there in 'Bridge over the River Kwai' – the system is (rather surprisingly) of 5ft 6in gauge. One would have thought that metre gauge would have been more suitable in view of the mountainous nature of the country as well as its detachment.

The first railway ran 75 miles up into the hills between the capital Colombo and Kandy. It was opened in 1861; since then extensions under government auspices have increased it to almost 1000 miles.

Steam power followed Indian practice; dieselization in a coal-less land came early and currently 120 diesel locomotives cover the bulk of the work, the forty steam locomotives on the books seeing little use. There are 930 passenger and 3900 freight cars as well as 75 diesel railcars.

TAIWAN

See map on pages 266–267.

TAIWAN RAILWAY ADMINISTRATION
2 Yenping North Road, Taipei.

The beginning of railway construction in Taiwan (then known to the western world as Formosa) did in fact just precede its occupation by the Japanese in 1895; even so the main line from Taipei, the capital, down the west side of the island to Kaohsiung in the south was built entirely to Japanese standards, including its gauge of 3ft 6in, its rolling stock and the methods of operation.

A vast network of 2ft 6in gauge lines (with some 2ft) – estimated 1800 miles in extent – serves sugar plantations in the south-west, timber growing areas in the centre, coal mines

in the north and, until very recently anyway, offered public service along the east coast. The timber lines were (perhaps are still) one of the very last haunts 'in the wild' of the fascinating Shay-type geared steam logging locomotive.

The exploding economy of Taiwan is leading to extensive changes to the railways – electrification of the west-coast line, as well as gauge conversion and upgrading of the east coast line, together with its linking to the main system. Statistics are accordingly offered with more than the usual reserve, but current returns show 140 steam, 160 diesel and 74 electric locomotives, 1200 passenger and 7500 freight cars providing transport for 143 million passengers and seventeen million tons of freight (the latter hauled an average distance of 95 miles). Expenses are 84 percent of receipts.

Top: A three-cylinder Pacific heads the afternoon express for Manila out of Dau station on the old Manila Railway in the Philippines.

Bottom centre: A 4-4-2 Atlantic pulls a local train in the Philippines.

Below: A diesel-hauled local train in Taipei, Taiwan.

-SOUTHEAST ASIA-

1:15 000 000

THAILAND

See maps on pages 266–267 and 302.

STATE RAILWAYS OF THAILAND
Bangkok.

Thailand is an odd-shaped country, with a large head and a long tail. The northern part, roughly triangular with its southern and western sides each about 500 miles long, is generally hilly to mountainous, broken with some great rivers and large areas of plain in their valleys and deltas. The southern part, some 700 miles in length but often only twenty or thirty miles wide, occupies (or in the northern part shares with Burma) the isthmus joining Malaysia with the main continental landmass. Hills and tropical jungles compete with coastal plains for the territory of Thailand. Most of the land is fertile and rich, but not favoured with any significant mining or industrial development.

History

The Royal State Railways of Thailand have always been among the better-organized small systems of the world. Thailand maintained its independence through the colonial era, at the cost initially of remaining backward and undeveloped. One short isolated standard-gauge line was opened in 1893 but the main system, for which metre gauge was adopted, began in the late 1890s. The southern main line, to the Malaysian border at Padang Besar and so joining the Malaysian system was completed in 1918. The northern main line, from the capital Bangkok to Chiengmai (460 miles) was completed in 1926. Branch and secondary lines followed, and some construction is still continuing. The northern and southern lines, starting from terminals on opposite sites of the Chao Phraya River at Bangkok, remained unconnected until the great Rama VI Bridge some distance north of the city was built in the mid-1930s. Present route mileage is around 2500.

Locomotive Development

The Thais have not developed any particular style in locomotives. The majority in prewar days were of American build (although French, British and Swiss designs were also used in some number). After 1945 a large number of steam locomotives were obtained from Japan. None were very large; 2-8-2s and 4-6-2s predominated, designed for an axle-load of no more than 10.5 tons. However, they were remarkably well-maintained and until standards fell towards the end, Thailand must have had the most sparklingly clean and handsome fleet of steam locomotives anywhere in the world on a main-line system. Wood fuel was widely used, with oilburners latterly doing the hardest turns.

Thailand commenced dieselization very early, with a number of quite high-powered and successful diesel-electric main-line machines of Danish build as early as 1928. The changeover, however, was very deliberate, and not completed until a large order for French diesels was placed in the early 1970s.

Train Services and Rolling Stock

Passenger trains are relatively frequent, and the best of them quite fast (averaging around 35 mph overall) with a line speed limit of generally around 45 mph. There is sufficient modern rolling stock for most long-distance services, including air-conditioned sleeping cars for the minority of travellers wanting them. Branch lines and local workings around the capital city of Bangkok are often served with diesel railcars.

Operations and Signalling

The only double track occurs in the immediate neighbourhood of Bangkok, with automatic signalling. Principal lines are worked with the electric tablet system, together with the vacuum brake, one of the nearly universal British influences on Asian railway practice. Only the least important lines are worked by telegraph and train order.

Administration and Finance

One benefit of Thailand's continuing degree of partial economic insulation from the rest of the world is that inflation is not a very serious problem; a mattress would have done better filled with *baht* than most Western currencies in recent years. The railways were permitted in 1975 to raise their charges for the first time in twenty years, by less than five percent. As a result, the system which traditionally paid its way is now in deficit, to the tune of about ten percent of gross revenue. It is about twenty years since most Western railways did as well as this. Added to the impression of pleasantly unassuming all-round competence received by the traveller, the indication would seem to be that the Thais do not need lessons on how to run their railways.

USSR
See Europe: USSR

A Japanese-built 2-8-2 woodburner with polished brass and clean dark green livery approaches Bangkok with a mixed train. Steam has now been banished from virtually all trains in Thailand.

VIETNAM

See maps on pages 266–267 and 302.

VIETNAM RAILWAYS SYSTEM – RCFVN
Hanoi.

The first railway in what is now Vietnam – then a province of what was at that time French Indo-China – was the short tramway from Saigon to My Tho, constructed in 1885. Another small line near Hanoi appeared in 1890, but it was not until 1902 that a start was made on the 880-mile coastal line between the two main cities. Paul Doumer, who governed in Hanoi on behalf of France, had the vision of a national railway system which would connect

with one in Siam (Thailand) and hence with lines still to be built in Malaysia and Burma. This policy shows very clearly the unusually benign objectives of French colonial rule in this part of the world; instead of running inland from the principal ports to exploit the natural resources of the interior, the railway system was laid out for communications and trade internal to the country.

Alas, it did not do so for long; World War I and subsequent financial problems delayed completion of the line from Saigon to Hanoi until 1936. It functioned throughout only for a brief five years, when 37 years of bloodshed and destruction intervened to preclude through rail connections.

The line westwards to Phnom Penh in Cambodia was never built; on the other hand, lines running northwest and north from Hanoi into

China, completed in 1902 and 1903 respectively, have functioned fairly continuously ever since. The latter was converted to standard gauge to aid arms supplies during the recent North-South struggle and is the only part of the system laid to anything other than metre gauge.

Steam power was mostly supplied by French industry, although Germany sent locomotives between the wars as reparations and Switzerland obliged with cog-wheel power for the rack-and-pinion Dalat branch. The mainstays of the line were numerous 4-6-2s and 2-8-2s – scaled down and simplified but very neat versions of domestic French steam power, supplied during 1947-49. It had been reported that steam was now virtually finished in Vietnam, but it was at the centre of the stage on the occasion of that ceremonial first through

train from Ho Chi Minh City (Saigon), which
arrived at Hanoi, behind French built 2-8-2
No 141-121 on 1 January 1977. Twenty-three
US-built diesels were supplied in 1963, but
many would have been destroyed in the
fighting.

Having said earlier that the Himalayas are
the one mountain range to remain unconquered
by rail, one perhaps should have qualified this
by adding . . . 'except where they run down to
the sea in Vietnam'. Even so, the engineering
problems were formidable: ten tunnels including one 3600ft long and a river bridge
with 4100ft between abutments. This is why
this stretch south of Da-Nang was the last to
be completed and took so long.

Virtually none of the line was operational
when peace came in 1973. Very little destruction
was in fact due to enemy action – their 'own

troops' were much worse. Steel sleepers made
excellent bullet- and splinter-proof shelters
and strong points, and miles of track were
precipitately removed to facilitate the movement of tanks along the right-of-way. In 1964
a hurricane did terrible damage to the southern-
most section and the line was not sufficiently
valuable from a military point of view to be
worth the effort involved in restoration at the
time.

Since the through train service on the main
line comprises two trains a week, taking four
days for the 820-mile journey, the Vietnam
railways have a little way to go before they
reach the top league regarding service. But as
always, communications serve to integrate
dispersed communities and this no doubt
explains Hanoi's attitude that some sort of
train service is better than none.

*During the Vietnamese War a special passenger
train nears Thu Duc. The train has come from
Saigon (Ho Chi Minh City) and is en route to Bien
Hoa headed by a GE diesel electric pushing two flat
cars ahead of it as a protection from pressure mines
with armoured vehicles between the engine and
passenger coaches.*

AUSTRALIA

See map on pages 310-311.

General Introduction: History

Very roughly oval in shape, the Australian continent is something over 2000 miles from east to west and 1500 miles from north to south. Rainfall, and therefore the population, are both concentrated on the southeastern and eastern shores; the further north and west one goes, the drier the landscape, to such an extent that three-quarters of the area can be called desert. Recently important mineral workings in the northwest have begun to be developed on a very large scale; but even so, nearly thirteen million of the nation's 13.5 million inhabitants live in the eastern half of the country, and the majority of them in the great cities of Sydney, Melbourne, Adelaide and Brisbane. The landscape, though not without areas of hill, forest, mountain and scenic beauty, tends more often to be relatively featureless. The typical Australian railway scene is thus either a busy electrified urban commuter multiple-track, or a straggly single line running to the remote horizon and far beyond, though still hardly noticeable on the map – sometimes very busy but much more often carrying very little traffic indeed.

The picture is further complicated by the gauge problems. Australia has been a unified federation only since 1901, and the older states were not only responsible for the original development of the railway networks, but still retain much greater autonomy on railways and most other domestic policies than the otherwise comparable American states. At the beginning of construction in the 1850s, Irish engineers in Victoria and South Australia determined that the gauge in those states should be 5ft 3in. New South Wales refused to follow this lead, and insisted on 4ft 8½in instead. Coming along later, Queensland and Western Australia pleaded poverty and adopted the 3ft 6in gauge, and South Australia subsequently backslid and built over a third of its final mileage to that gauge too. Consequently state boundaries, with the one fortuitous exception between Melbourne and Adelaide, marked break-of-gauge.

Much has been said about the inconvenience of all this, and quite a lot done to mitigate it. A standard-gauge line reached Brisbane in the 1930s, on a new formation from the border

some seventy miles south; thirty years later standard-gauge track was laid beside the broad across Victoria from Albury to Melbourne, some 190 miles. The transcontinental link, completed in 1917, was always standard gauge between Port Augusta and Kalgoorlie, where it joined the Western Australian system; but at its eastern end it linked only with the South Australian narrow gauge. A junction with the 5ft 3in gauge at Port Pirie was not achieved until 1942, and the true transcontinental link did not really come into existence until 1969, with the completion of gauge conversions or construction of new routes between the NSW system at Broken Hill and Port Augusta, and Kalgoorlie and Perth. Adelaide still awaits the standard gauge.

The railway systems are, in general, still operated by the states. The Commonwealth government had the central desert sections of the east-west and still unfinished north-south transcontinental lines, but little else, until in 1973 an attempt was made to induce the states to transfer their railways to the newly formed Australian National Railways administration, which took over the Commonwealth lines. By 1978 only South Australia (for non-suburban lines) and Tasmania had done so, leaving the ANR with a scattered assortment of railways on all three gauges.

Further description will be more convenient state by state. However, two small general points remain to be noted. One is that, throughout, Australian railway practice is heavily influenced by British, although each state system has a very distinct style of its own. The other is that all the 3ft 6in gauge undertakings started from a position of inferiority, as poverty-stricken substitutes. In the steam age, Australia had no main lines of this gauge which would even stand comparison with those in New Zealand, and they were very poor relations when compared to those in Japan or South Africa. Modernization has not closed this gap by any means.

Top: In Australia's Northern Territory, the traditional steam train serves scattered communities.

Right: In Commonwealth Railway days, a diesel-hauled freight crosses the Nullarbor ('no trees') plain on the Trans-Australian Railway.

Page 306/307: A New Zealand freight hauled by a Japanese-built 'Dj' class Bo-Bo-Bo diesel-electric locomotive amidst the mountains of South Island.

AUSTRALIAN NATIONAL RAILWAYS
(Formerly Commonwealth Railways)
55 King William Road,
North Adelaide,
South Australia, 5006.

Before its recent reorganization and take-over of lines in South Australia and Tasmania, the old Commonwealth Railways system was in four sections. The most important was the Trans-Australian, completed in 1917: 1100 miles of 4ft 8½in track from Port Augusta to Kalgoorlie, serving no intermediate place of any importance whatever and including the famous 300-mile straight section on the Nullarbor Plains. It was crippled until 1969 by a break of gauge at each end and only since then has it achieved a useful flow of traffic; coastal shipping had most of the transcontinental business before, including passengers until the airlines took them. There is also the remarkable 'Indian Pacific' streamliner from Perth to Sydney, built in the image of the very best American long-distance passenger trains, years after most of them had disappeared, but booked solid months in advance (and still, be it added, losing money).

The second and third sections were the two parts of the never-completed 3ft 6in gauge north-south transcontinental; 770 miles from Port Augusta to Alice Springs, in the centre of the continent, and the now inoperative 300 miles from Darwin to a tin shed comprising what even a small map shows as the town of Birdum. The Alice Springs section is due to be replaced in 1981 by a new standard-gauge line on a different route; since the amount of traffic it carries does not in any way overload the weekly mixed, to relieve congestion with 500 brand-new miles of track built for no other purpose is incredible. The fourth section, four miles long, links Canberra with the New South Wales system.

PUBLIC TRANSPORT COMMISSION OF NEW SOUTH WALES
Transport House,
11 York Street,
Sydney.

This standard gauge system, with just over 6000 route-miles, is the most important in Australia. The principal main lines radiate from Sydney, northwards to Brisbane (600 miles) via the important coal-mining centre of Newcastle, westwards to Broken Hill (700 miles) and so beyond, and south-west to Albury (400 miles) connecting with the Victorian dual-separated gauge line to Melbourne, with a branch connecting to the Federal capital at Canberra, 200 miles from Sydney. The gaps between these main routes are well filled with secondary lines and branches so that except for the western third of the state, there is good geographical coverage. Very few branches have so far been closed; the total length of the network has declined by only forty miles in the last twenty years. But lately, since the railway management was assumed by the Public Transport Commission of New South Wales,

Australia

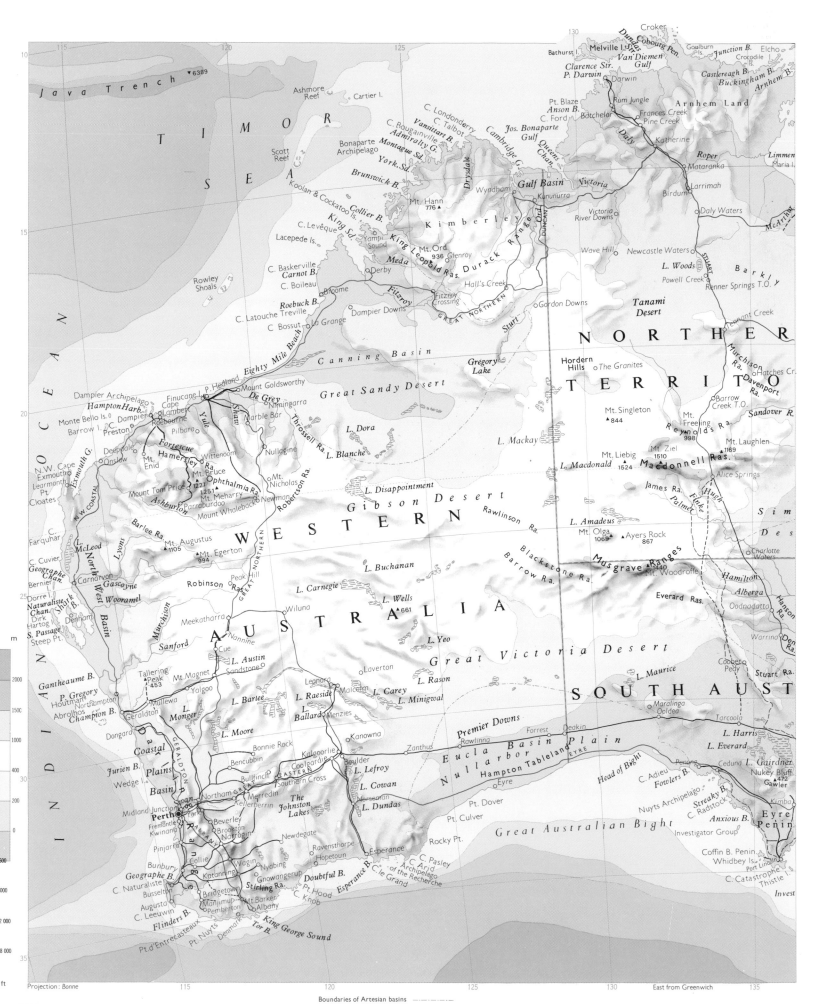

Projection: Bonne

Boundaries of Artesian basins

East from Greenwich

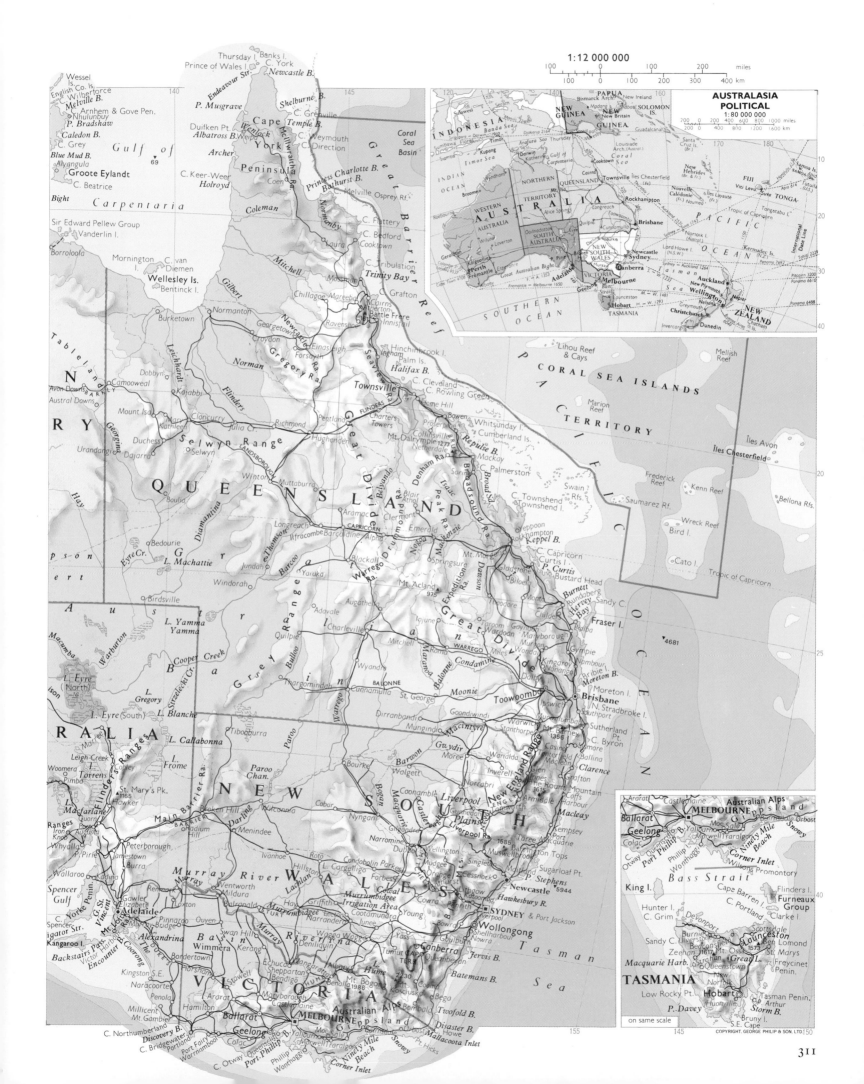

1:12 000 000

100   0   100   200 miles
100   0   100   200   300   400 km

AUSTRALASIA
POLITICAL
1:80 000 000

200   400   600   800   1000 miles
400   800   1200   1600 km

TASMANIA

on same scale

COPYRIGHT. GEORGE PHILIP & SON. LTD

many rural lines have had their passenger trains replaced by road services.

Of all Australian railways, the New South Wales system followed English precedents and practice most closely. Stations, signalling, and rolling stock could, until recent years, have almost passed for English. Until the 1920s the same was true of locomotives; Dugald Drummond spent some years in Sydney and left his mark on a fleet already much influenced by L&NWR practice. But with the larger, final, steam types, the resemblance was less marked, inevitably so perhaps when it came to heavy 4-8-2s and Garratts, although the rebuilt BR Bulleid Pacifics were strikingly like the final, unstreamlined, C38 class of 1943. Modern diesels are of American type, though built locally, and unremarkable. The Sydney suburban lines, including an underground section and of course two tracks across the famous Harbour Bridge, are electrified, with much use of double-deck multiple units, and some mainline electrification near Sydney includes the heavy and spectacular climb over the Blue Mountains.

Principal train services, though not particularly fast (not all main lines have speed limits as high as the maximum of 70 mph), are of a high standard with modern air-conditioned stock. Some less elegant main-line trains still survive, including some of the traditional all-stations overnight mails, and passengers on the rural branches which still cater for them may be carried in wooden-bodied railcars of what would be quite remarkable antiquity were it not that other states have equally venerable vehicles still in service.

As in most other states, New South Wales railways were built predominantly by the state for development purposes, originally very cheaply. In difficult areas main lines have been improved as money became available, often more than once, by deviations to ease gradients. Traditional policy has been to run the railways as a public service, holding down charges as much as possible; the trouble with this benevolence, as always, is that with the development of other modes of transport, the railways are left catering for the low-value end of the market without the capital to provide attractive competitive services. Particularly when politicians also lean on the level of charges in an endeavour to frighten away inflation, horrendous losses are the result, and New South Wales has not escaped or yet escaped from this predicament. Indeed, this paragraph can be applied without amendment to railways in all the other states.

Left: A new double-deck electric train for Sydney's suburban service.

Extreme left, centre: The Hawkesbury River Bridge situated 37 miles north of Sydney on the main northern line.

Extreme left, bottom: Sydney's famous Harbour Bridge, crossed by two lines of railway and six lanes of highway.

Below: This self-propelled diesel train is used between Sydney and Nowra on the south coast.

Above: A diesel locomotive (Australian-built but of American Locomotive Company design) waits at Sydney Central Station to take the 'Gold Coast Express'.

Top right: The 'Southern Aurora' Sydney to Melbourne express. Standard gauge was completed through to Melbourne in 1962.

Extreme right: An American 2-8-2 pulls a freight train near North Rockhampton, Queensland.

Right: A streamlined 4-6-2 locomotive pulls the 'South Coast Daylight Express'.

QUEENSLAND RAILWAYS
Railway Centre,
305 Edward Street,
Brisbane.

The present route mileage of the 3ft 6in gauge Queensland Railways system is just over 6000, which represents a decline of about five percent over the last twenty years. However, the culling of rural branch lines, though not too severe, has gone deeper than that; the figures mask a real growth in recent years with the construction of several hundred miles of new line in the Townsville, Mackay and Gladstone areas to serve new coal, phosphate and nickel mines. The effect of these flourishing new developments has meant that despite suffering the same difficulties as other states, the Queensland railways come within thirteen percent of meeting their expenditures with revenue.

The system is based on the long (1040-mile) main line along the coast from Brisbane to Cairns. Five lengthy branches run westwards and inland, up to 500 miles or so, and further branches give reasonably good geographical coverage of most of the state. Passenger services present a similar picture to other states, with a good modern train from Brisbane to Cairns and rather moderate ones still running elsewhere;

the Brisbane suburban lines are being electrified at present. A second generation of electric trains is being built to run on them; the first generation, built some thirty years ago, never had their motors fitted and were worn out being hauled round by 4-6-4Ts and later by diesel locomotives.

QR civil engineers were always extremely conservative in the matter of axle-loadings, and the system never had anything like a big steam locomotive, modern or otherwise, some unsuccessful latterday Garratts hardly excepted. Nowadays, and particularly on the heavily used mineral lines, the QR come nearer to making full use of the 3ft 6in gauge.

SOUTH AUSTRALIAN STATE TRANSPORT AUTHORITY – RAIL DIVISION
Railway Station,
North Terrace,
Adelaide.

The South Australian Railways system proper was mainly confined to the small area in the south-east corner of the state, less than a quarter of the whole, around the capital, Adelaide. The exception was the detached 3ft 6in gauge system based at Port Lincoln in the Eyre peninsula. The remainder of the state had only the two Commonwealth transcontinental routes.

The SAR was much the smallest mainland state system, with a peak length of only some 1600 route miles of 5ft 3in and under 1000 miles of 3ft 6in track so it made understandable sense for the undertaking to be transferred to the Australian National Railways (except for the unimportant Adelaide suburban lines) in 1978.

The SAR presented a more modern aspect earlier than most state systems; in part this was achieved during steam days with a fleet of big modern locomotives of marked and severe American appearance (although curiously enough most were built in Britain). These compared oddly with some brass-bound mid-nineteenth century relics which nevertheless survived into the diesel age. However, the short distances involved coupled with the policy of maintaining traditional services as far as possible meant that modernization did not avoid deficits proportionately heavier than any other state's, except Victoria, where revenue also currently covers only about 55 percent of expenses. Curiously enough, the narrower the gauge the lower the deficit, is the Australian rule at present.

Right: A C17 class locomotive pulls a freight train at Willowburn, South Australia.

Left: A Beyer-Garratt locomotive heads a ballast train en route to Yamba, New South Wales.

Below: The 5ft 3in gauge system in South Australia was one of the smallest on the continent, but had some of the most magnificent steam power, as exemplified by this streamlined 4-8-4.

Above: Australia's 'Overland Limited' hauled by trim English-Electric 1760 hp diesel locomotives.

Top: Crews change between Beyer-Garratt and diesel locomotives at Gladstone, South Australia.

Left: A South Australian streamlined steam locomotive.

TASMANIAN GOVERNMENT RAILWAYS

1 Collins Street,
Hobart 7000.

On a minute scale, the 520-mile 3ft 6in gauge system of the Tasmanian Government Railways (now a division of the Australian National Railways), exemplifies the Australian railway situation. Scenic, short-haul, not very busy, little abridged, and uneconomic, with its last quite good prestige passenger train recently axed, the system faces a rather questionable future, like a number of lines on the mainland.

Extreme left, top: Emu Bay Railway's 'The West Coaster' train at Rosebery station, Tasmania in steam days.

Left: The 'Tasman Limited' leaves the country station Ross in Tasmania.

Bottom left: The 'Tasman Limited' winds through typical Tasmanian countryside, 25 miles north of Hobart.

Below: The inaugural through-train from Sydney arrives at Dynon in the Melbourne suburbs on 3 January 1962.

VICTORIAN GOVERNMENT RAILWAYS – Vicrail
67 Spencer Street,
Melbourne 3000.

This is the smallest state, its greatest dimensions east to west some 500 miles and north to south some 250. Except for the mountainous region north-east of Melbourne, most of the area is well-served by the 4400-mile 5ft 3in-gauge network of the Victorian Railways; however many lines in the wheat-growing north-western plains carry little traffic and some limited cuts in mileage have taken place. Passenger services are still maintained over a high proportion of the network, although Vicrail's passenger rolling stock contains many elderly wooden-bodied vehicles, not all built since 1900. Even the suburban electric services in the Melbourne area, which are on a very large scale indeed, are still heavily dependent on coaches which before motorization fifty or so years ago had served many years behind steam power. There is some modern stock in suburban and inter-

city service, but not a great deal of it. Speeds are however somewhat higher than in other states, and the line maximum is 80 mph.

The steam locomotive fleet was a modern and up-to-date one, with handsome machines of individual character and unified style not much like those anywhere else in the world, although perhaps reminiscent of Indian practice. The broad gauge was, of course, one similarity. Dieselization, as always, has brought uniformity, although each state does possess a different colour scheme. Apart from the Melbourne area, where an underground line is now being built (Sydney's lead in this department having become intolerable), electrification is confined to one line running to the eastern coalfields area.

A brief account of this system's present situation would not differ *materially* from that of New South Wales (mentioned beforehand), although this compression misleads if it implies much uniformity in many other respects between very different operations. Revenue received is only 55 percent of expenses.

Top left: Victoria's only narrow-gauge Puffing Billy *passenger train has been restored to regular running from Belgrave to Menzies Creek in the Dandenong Ranges near Melbourne. It is the first time in the century-long history of the Victorian Railways that a narrow-gauge railway line has been re-opened. Restoration of the service was made possible by a volunteer organization – the Puffing Billy Preservation Society. This popular train runs to regular schedules at week-ends and public holidays, and is available also for special trips. It connects at Belgrave with electric trains. On the first trip into the hills, following restoration of the line on 28 July 1962,* Puffing Billy *is here seen, with steam and smoke belching from the funnel, crossing the Monbulk Creek trestle bridge in the Dandenong Ranges.*

Bottom left: A diesel-hauled train leaving Spencer Street Station, Melbourne, Australia.

Below: Melbourne's Jolimont passenger yard with the railway workshops to the right. Nearby is Flinders Street station which handles more traffic than any other Australian station.

WESTERN AUSTRALIAN GOVERNMENT RAILWAYS

Westrail Centre,
Box 5 1422, GPO,
Perth 6001.

This system, with a total of some 3800 route miles, eighty percent of which is 3ft 6in gauge and the rest 4ft 8½in (with about ninety miles of mixed gauge), is the exception to most Australian rules. Thirty years ago it was almost more typical than any other: then all-3ft 6in gauge, with a very large mileage of infinitesimally used branch lines, mostly loops circuitously joining points already connected, and a tiny centre of gravity around Perth. In 1957, at a stroke, over 800 miles were summarily closed, which had the effect of removing from the working timetable only those lines with less than one scheduled train *per week*. Then came the standard gauge, and conversion of the 400-mile Perth to Kalgoorlie section, including a brand-new

double-track mixed-gauge line up the mountain barrier outside Perth, followed by closure or conversion of other branches in the east of the state. Then came the mineral boom, and a great increase in business. And so, contrary to all reasonable expectation, the WAGR still earns its expenses.

As in Queensland, steam locomotives tended to be small, though not so excessively so; the V class heavy freight 2-8-2s of 1955, the last new steamers (ordered after sad experience with the first batch of diesels) would have passed muster on a minor branch line in South Africa. Modern power is adequate but unremarkable. Passenger services, surprisingly perhaps in view of the scanty population of the state, have always been a bit better. The old narrow-gauge transcontinental express on the Perth-Kalgoorlie leg offered its passengers hot showers in 1938; the same run now offers the fastest run in Australia (averaging just over 50 mph overall). Some very respectable trains

run on other routes (though understandably not very often).

Separate and distinct from the Western Australian Government Railways, and indeed a thousand miles distant in the northern part of the state, are four very new railways, all opened since the mid-1960s, and built to carry iron ore in large quantities from mines to ports, and nothing else. Extremely heavy trains, weighing up to 18,000 tons, on heavy track controlled by CTC (and busy enough in one case to need double line on heavy grades), all in desert or semi-desert with no town of any size within a thousand miles, clearly involve the managements of these concerns (for their railways operate only as a part of the mining undertaking) in a set of very different problems. One piquant illustration of this was the import of a 'Castle' class 4-6-0 from England to the Hamersley Iron Company's line in 1978, to work recreational trains and provide mechanically minded staff with harmless amusement.

Left : The 'Trans-Australian' express at Perth station soon after its arrival from Port Pirie.

Bottom left : The special ministerial train at the opening of the railway from Perth to Kalgoorlie on 1 January 1897.

Below : The combined 'Trans-Australian' and 'Indian-Pacific' trains en route to Perth. Note the 3ft 6in and 4ft 8½in gauge tracks alongside.

Above: Twin diesel units haul a 3800-ton train of grain hopper wagons somewhere in Western Australia.

Extreme left: One of Western Australia's northern and very modern iron-ore hauling railroads. Built to last using modern techniques, these tracks can carry 18,000 tons at a time.

Left: The giant Mt Tom Price iron-ore train is made up of either 175 ore cars with two locomotives hauling, or 200 cars with three locomotives hauling. In the latter form it is 1.25 miles long and transports 20,000 tons of ore. It reaches speeds of 80 mph. This Hamersley Iron Ore train runs between Mt Tom Price in the north of Western Australia and the port of Dampier. The locomotives were made in Canada and the 100-ton capacity ore cars were made in Japan.

Right: Iron ore in the West Australian outback on the Mount Newman Railroad.

Extreme right, top: A mixed train on the rack section between Solok and Bukittinggi on the island of Sumatra in Indonesia. The locomotive is a Japanese-built 0-10-0 of 1962.

Bottom: Villagers wait for the morning mixed train to Bukittinggi.

INDONESIA

See map on page 302.

INDONESIAN STATE RAILWAYS
Perusahaan Jawatan Kereta Api,
Jalan Gereja No 1,
Bandung, Java.

The Indonesian Republic includes a great many islands large and small, but most of them backward and undeveloped. Railways have always been confined to the three islands of Java, Sumatra and Madura. Java, some 750 miles long east and west and an average of 75 miles north and south, is a fertile, densely populated land with an ancient history of civilization; of volcanic origin, it is still studded with semi-active volcanoes and with many mountain ranges. There are some 3500 route-miles of railway in Java forming a single fairly dense system. Sumatra is much larger, but less fertile and less developed while every bit as mountainous; approximately 1000 route-miles of line survive in three widely separated systems. Madura, a small island off the Java coast, once had over 100 miles of railway but only one line now survives.

The first railway in Java was a standard-gauge line from Semarang to the central Java capital of Jogjakarta, and dates from 1864.

Development of the network in all islands was relatively unplanned, with most lines built by private capital to serve agricultural purposes; a state railway organization, however, came to control the main lines and some sixty percent of the mileage by 1939. The 3ft 6in gauge was soon chosen as standard, although the standard gauge survived at Jogjakarta until converted rather hurriedly during the Japanese occupation 1942–45; various relics of it remain.

By the 1930s the Javanese state railway system was extremely modern and well-equipped, with some electrification, automatic signalling, modern hump yards and well-maintained tracks on which ran absolutely the best and fastest 3ft 6in gauge express trains in the world. Twenty years later, after wars, revolutions, and a decade of highly quarrelsome and disorganized independence, not many of these high standards remained; in fact the system was by then perhaps the world's most ramshackle. Travellers' tales told of jungle creepers festooning catenary wires; photographs showed marshalling yards taken over as shanty towns, with families squatting in two-storied comfort in abandoned wagons (that is, inside the body and between the wheels); wheezing and antiquated woodburners dragged short trains of rotting coaches packed inside and outside with smiling customers. Since those years, a more stable administration has brought much recovery, and probably most of

the remaining dilapidations are due to competition from unrestricted road transport.

In Sumatra the course of events was much the same. However, although narrow-gauge lines in Java are strictly local affairs, the Atjeh Tramway of 2ft 5½in gauge, running some 300 miles in the northwest of Sumatra from north of Medan to Bandar Atjeh once had a much greater importance. This was closed in 1970 pending gauge conversion, and although some fifty miles have since reopened to 3ft 6in traffic it is uncertain what has become of the rest.

Locomotive Development
Early conditions favoured the use of small and lightweight, usually four-coupled, machines; an enormous variety once existed and many still survive and are occasionally active. Worth special note is a considerable number of van-bodied tram engines. Underlying this plethora, however, developed a fleet of powerful and advanced main-line steam locomotives, reaching a peak between about 1910 and 1930 with some compound Pacifics, some express passenger 4-6-4Ts, some impressive 2-12-2Ts for heavy freight haulage on mountain lines, and several varieties of Mallet culminating in some American 2-8-8-0s. After 1945 100 very workmanlike heavy 2-8-2s were acquired from Germany. The majority of locomotives, naturally, were Dutch, although there were also many British, German and Swiss products.

Many types were also to be found in Sumatra, though the Deli Railway at Medan had its own characteristic types and the system based at Padang, which had sections of rack line to reach coal mines, has some German-, Japanese- and Swiss-built ten-coupled rack-and-adhesion tanks, some built as late as the 1960s.

Political conditions ensured the survival, in a manner of speaking, of the steam fleet much longer than otherwise expected; even when cessation of 'confrontation' with the Western powers led to the commencement of loans and grants-in-aid from Western sources for the purchase of diesels, difficulties in keeping these more complex machines mobile has meant that steam has made some surprising comebacks. But very often the condition of the machines leads to deplorably bad performance and the results can give little pleasure. Diesels are in general European, and although a large number of diesel-hydraulics were acquired from Germany, more recent purchases have been diesel-electric. Much of the electrification in the Djakarta area was kept going rather in the manner of steam, but it is currently being refurbished although not extended.

Train Services and Rolling Stock
Main-line passenger services have never been quite as bad as they might have been, and some indication of pre-1939 standards survives. Sufficient new modern (though often spartan)

Above: Padang station is western Sumatra's port for the export of coal. A 2-6-2 tank shunts hopper wagons – note the poor condition of the passenger rolling stock on the left.

Top: Kisaran Junction, North Sumatra, in the midday sun. The locomotive is a woodburning 2-6-4T – the majority of locomotives on the northern railway system are woodburners.

Right: A steam idyll amidst lake and mountain in the heart of Indonesia.

steel coaches were acquired in the 1950s to relegate older stock to those minor and secondary services on which fares are so low that no real effort seems to be made to collect them. Speeds are not bad, in places up to the old 70 mph limit, although punctuality is not noticeable. However, main roads are usually good and buses considerably faster and more frequent; the train scores mainly in comfort, and the possibility to eat and sleep en route. Freight stock has seen much less change since the 1930s.

Operations and Signalling

Not all the advanced installations of prewar years are recommissioned; one can still see power signal-boxes inhabited by squatters, while trains run over unsignalled hand-worked points and the old cable conduits and point machines have left traces only. However, sufficient numbers survive for present purposes, and there is little point in reducing the number of employees.

Administration and Finance

Considerable funds are clearly being spent on improvements and rehabilitation, though a certain air of other-worldliness pervades the numerous published financial and other statistics. It is perhaps sufficient to remark that the Indonesians are a people of great charm and conscious of ancient tradition.

—NEW ZEALAND—

See map on page 335

NEW ZEALAND GOVERNMENT RAILWAYS
*Bunny Street,
Wellington.*

The two islands of New Zealand together make up a country whose land area is somewhat less than Britain's; from extreme north to extreme south is around 1500 miles, but for half that distance the land is less than 100 miles wide. The islands differ markedly; the North Island, much the more populous nowadays, is largely broken mountain country overshadowed by three central volcanic peaks, while the South Island's spine comprises the long granite chain of the Southern Alps as well as numerous lesser ranges. Flat country is not common in either island; much the largest level area, the Canterbury Plains around Christchurch, stretch for 200 miles north and south but are never more than thirty miles wide. The total population is some three million; the economy is mainly agricultural.

Geographical obstacles and the smallness of the population meant that railways in New Zealand were slow to get started and political fragmentation into five provinces before 1870 made matters worse. The first line to be opened, from Christchurch to Ferrymead in Canterbury in 1863, was built to 5ft 3in gauge, and during the next few years Southland

Extreme left: A smart C27 class 4-6-4 tank at the head of a freight train during Indonesia's Dutch colonial days. A few of these engines are still at work in Java.

Left: A New Zealand suburban electric train crosses the Paremata Harbour bridge near Wellington.

Below: An elderly 4-8-0 steam locomotive crosses a traditional timber trestle bridge.

opened Invercargill to Bluff on 4ft 8½in and Dunedin to Port Chalmers on 3ft 6in; meanwhile in the North Island the Wellington-Hutt Valley line used 3ft 6in and Auckland to Drury had been begun on 4ft 8½in. However, the Australian disaster was avoided by the central government in 1870 asserting its authority, imposing a standard 3ft 6in gauge and undertaking railway construction as a governmental responsibility, paid for by borrowing overseas.

Construction, in general, proceeded slowly. The 370 miles from Christchurch to Dunedin and Invercargill were completed in 1879; Wellington and Auckland were not linked until 1909, Christchurch and Greymouth until 1923, and Christchurch and Picton until 1946. Coastal shipping made a national rail network less essential, but encouraged the development of isolated sections serving different ports; as recently as 1930, there were still six detached lines. Branch line closures, particularly in the South Island, have reduced the route mileage by some fifteen percent from a peak of 3500 in the mid-1950s.

Civil Engineering

Among the major engineering works are three five-mile plus tunnels. The Otira tunnel between Christchurch and Greymouth is 5.3 miles long and dates from 1923. The new 5.5-mile Kaimai tunnel was opened in 1978 on the new line between Tauranga and Hamilton. The Rimutaka tunnel, also 5.5 miles in length, on the route from Wellington to Masterton, replaced (in 1955) a three-mile 1-in-15 gradient which had worked since 1878 on the Fell principle with a central rail gripped by horizontal driving wheels on the special steam locomotives. A normal length train needed four; this installation was the most significant long-lasting fully operational application of this unusual method of incline.

Steel trestle bridges are also a feature; the highest is the Mohaka viaduct between Napier and Gisborne (North Island) – 908ft long and 318ft high.

Locomotive Landmarks

For so small a system, New Zealand locomotive history presents great variety. In steam days practically every type or design was tried at least once, especially if the unconventional machines on industrial and logging lines are included. Almost the only absentee is a steam-turbine-electric. However, the Garratt was represented only by one unsuccessful class, and the Mallet only by a single example.

The earliest locomotives were small tanks built in England. During the period 1875 to 1900 larger machines, including 2-6-2s and 4-6-0s, of both English and American manufacture, ran side by side. By 1900 it was clear that the American product was better suited to New Zealand conditions, and from then until the last steamer was built in 1957 locomotive design was strongly based on American principles, though most of the actual construction was done in New Zealand. Design was generally advanced; the NZR was the first administration to standardize outside Walschaerts valve gear, and to place a batch of locomotives with the 4-6-2 wheel arrangement in service (1901); superheating was standardized early, and the 'Ab' class 4-6-2s introduced in 1915 then claimed at the time the highest ratio between horsepower developed and engine weight of any type in the world. The 'Abs', the 'K' and 'Ka' 4-8-4s (introduced 1931-39) and 'J' and 'Ja' 4-8-2s (1939-46) were all capable of speeds around 60 mph, inferior to no 3ft-6in-gauge machines anywhere.

Modern diesel locomotives are relatively conventional in comparison; British designs were tried first but superseded quickly by American and later by Japanese types, the latter in the South Island. Electrification (at

A New Zealand freight train hauled by a General Electric 'Dx' class, diesel-electric locomotive crosses the Hapawhenua viaduct on North Island.

NEW ZEALAND

NEW ZEALAND & DEPENDENCIES
1:60 000 000

New Zealand Territory
Self-governing Territory

SAMOA ISLANDS
1:12 000 000

FIJI AND TONGA ISLANDS
1:12 000 000

1:6 000 000

Projection: Conical with two standard parallels

COPYRIGHT. GEORGE PHILIP & SON, LTD.

1500v DC) has been on a small scale, although hydro-electric power could be made available; it is confined to working through the Otira tunnel and the Wellington suburban lines.

Train Services and Rolling Stock
The NZR has to a large extent got out of the passenger business. It has to run suburban trains in Wellington and Auckland; apart from these, it runs as few passenger trains as possible, but policy is that where they do run they must be good. The best is undoubtedly the 'Silver Star', an all-sleeping-car express between Auckland and Wellington, supported on the same route by a renovated mainly chair-car overnight train and a luxurious day railcar service. Locomotive-hauled trains, usually with dining car, also run from Wellington to Napier, and from Christchurch to Invercargill and to Picton. Apart from a few mainly railcar-worked services on secondary lines in the North Island and from Christchurch to Greymouth, that is all. Freight services are however still universal, and increasingly containerized, particularly for import or export traffic. Train ferries operate between Wellington and Picton linking the two island systems.

Operations and Signalling
Except for most of the 87-mile Auckland–Hamilton section and a few lengths near main cities, all railways are single track. Traditional British-style operation with electric tablet and semaphore signalling, once predominant, is now largely replaced by CTC or, in the case of secondary lines, a locally developed form of automatic signalling in which station staff are not required and crossings are handled, under colour-light signals, by train crews.

Administration and Finance
The New Zealand Railways have traditionally been run by a government department, presided over by the Minister of Railways. The disadvantage of this political dependence was not evident so long as the railways paid their way, but largely due to governmental pressure to keep down charges and so camouflage inflation, losses during the 1970s began to be significant. Passenger service cutbacks, due to inability to finance new rolling stock, were one result. The railways are protected from competition by prohibition of road haulage of freight (except livestock) parallel to any railway for more than 150 km (94 miles), a distance recently increased from 100 km (62.5 miles). Freight tonnage handled by rail has nevertheless increased markedly up to the mid-1970s.

Above: A diesel-hauled New Zealand freight ready to depart from Frankton.

Left: A New Zealand passenger train ascends the Rimutaka incline. A Fell locomotive heads the train, another trails the train and one is cut into the middle of the train.

New Zealand's 'Southerner' buffet-car express runs six days a week between Christchurch and Invercargill on South Island. Here it is hauled by a Japanese-built 'Dj' class Bo-Bo-Bo diesel-electric locomotive.

Above: A refurbished articulated two-car diesel train for the Hamilton–Auckland service.

Top left: The scene at the inauguration of the Greymouth–Hokitika line on New Zealand's South Island in 1893.

Bottom, extreme left: Oil-fired 4-8-4 and 4-6-4T locomotives pull a freight train which is ascending a 1 in 50 bank on New Zealand's Kinleith line, North Island.

Left: A local passenger train gets ready to leave Wellington, 1955.

A northbound container freight train, hauled by two General Motors 'Da' class AIA-AIA diesel-electric locomotives, leaves Wellington, New Zealand while a local electric passenger train, hauled by English-Electric 'EW' class Bo-Bo-Bo diesel passes below.

OCEANIA

See maps on pages 335 and 142.

The Pacific Ocean covers nearly a third of the earth's surface, but its thousands of scattered islands never mustered any very noticeable proportion of its railway mileage. The Hawaiian archipelago certainly had the best and biggest systems, with a very fine 3ft gauge network on Oahu and a shorter but spectacular standard-gauge line on Hawaii itself, both classic American operations. Each survived World War II, but neither for long. Apart therefore from a tourist reconstruction in Hawaii and mining lines on New Caledonia, Ocean Island and Nauru, the only surviving Pacific Island railway, is the two-foot gauge system in Fiji.

FIJI SUGAR CORPORATION RAILWAY
PO Box 283,
Suva.

Three sections of the Fiji system survive, with a total of some 500 miles of route. For many years the major part, centred on Lautoka in Viti Levu, was famous for having a free passenger train, which trundled along the 129 miles of main line behind a 4-4-0 to compensate the natives for the use of their land to build the line (whose main purpose was to carry sugar cane). Nationalization, of course, has ended this fine gesture of grateful capitalism, but less formal arrangements still subsist on the roadless area served by the lines in Vanua Levu. Australian diesels reign; some of the old British steamers have been taken to Disneyland.

Above: A train of the now-closed Kahalui Railroad on the island of Maui, Hawaii.

Left: One of the world's only free passenger trains (now nationalized and free no longer) climbs out of the Mba Valley on its way to Lautoka in Fiji.

INDEX

Figures in italics refer to tables in the text

PICTURE CREDITS

J H L Adams 37 (top 2)
Alaska Railroad 137, 138/139, 141 (bottom)
C J Allen Collection 12/13, 21, 92 (bottom), 109 (all 3), 110 (bottom and middle right), 113 (bottom), 149 (top), 154 (bottom 2), 156, 157 (top right and middle), 158 (bottom), 163 (bottom), 164, 165 (left), 167 (bottom) 170 (bottom), 177 (top 2), 181 (both), 317 (bottom), 319 (bottom), 320 (bottom), 321 (top)
G F Allen Collection/Association of American Railroads 151 (bottom), 203 (top)
P C Allen 108 (bottom left), 197 (top), 202 (both – Frank Barry), 204 (top – Frank Barry), 209 (bottom), 276, 332 (top)
AMTRAK 144 (both), 144/145, 146 (all 3)
Arabian American Oil Co/Courtesy K Westcott-Jones 257 (bottom)
ASEA 98
Marcel Aubert 45 (bottom), 48, 48/49
Bankverein 111
BART 148
P J Bawcutt 256
M Befeler 343 (top)
Benguela Railway Co (CFB) 216 (bottom)
E N Bewley 300/301 (both)
BMW 215 (bottom left)
K Bolton 166 (top)
Boston and Maine Railroad 149 (bottom), 150
Brazilian National Railways 182/183, 195 (top), 196, 196/197, 197 (bottom), 198 (top)
British Rail 70/71
Burlington Northern 151 (top 3), 152 (top 2), 153 (left)
B A Butt 105 (both)
Canadian National Railroad 124 (bottom)
Canadian Pacific 129 (bottom), 131, 132, 133 (top)
Central Office of Information Ghana 223 (top)
Central Office of Information London 292
Central Office of Information Sierra Leone 237 (bottom left)
Colourviews Picture Library 15 (bottom), 60 (top right), 67 (top), 68 (bottom 2), 73, 74 (bottom), 108 (bottom right), 110 (top left), 116, 116/117, 125 (middle left), 135, 234/235, 272 (both), 318/319, 320 (top), 328, 336/337, 340 (bottom), 343 (bottom)
Conrail 122/123, 159 (top), 160 (top)
Coras Iompair Eireann 88 (bottom 2)
Derek Cross 332/333
M S Cross 194
B F Cutler 165 (top right)
J M Davis 162 (top)
John C Dunn 315 (bottom), 316, 317 (top), 319 (top)
A E Durant 242 (top left)
East Africa Railways/Courtesy P B Whitehouse 224 (bottom), 225 (top left and right), 228, 242 (bottom)
English Electric Co. 233 (left)
ESR 30
N N Forbes 81 (top)
French National Railways (SNCF) 16/17, 43, 44 (top), 45 (top), 50
French National Railways (SNCF/CY Broncard) 44 (bottom)
Furka-Oberalp Railway 110 (top right)
German State Railways 57 (top)
S Gradidge 233 (right)
Greek Railways 81 (bottom)
E J Gulash 154 (top), 155 (top), 159 (bottom), 178/179 (top)
Ynguar Hansen 96 (both)
J D Harby 292/293
G F Heiron 72/73 (bottom), 74 (top), 113 (top right), 220 (bottom), 221 (top), 229 (top)

G G Hoare 96/97
C Hollingsworth 22
E Hollingsworth 271, 277 (bottom)
J B Hollingsworth 76 (top), 97, 107
Richard Hope 213 (bottom right), 242/243, 245 (bottom 2)
P J Howard 63, 71 (bottom), 90 (top), 129 (top), 130 (both), 134, 147 (top), 155, (bottom 2), 157 (bottom), 158 (top), 163 (top), 169 (middle), 170/171, 174 (both), 175 (top), 179 (bottom), 223 (bottom right), 225 (bottom left), 238 (top), 258 (top), 293 (top), 312 (bottom), 314 (top), 322 (bottom), 325 (top)
Illinois Central Gulf Railroad 169 (top)
'Illustrated London News' 171 (top)
Imperial War Museum 249 (all 3)
India Railways 277 (top)
Indian Railways/Courtesy K Westcott-Jones 272/273 (top)
Italian State Railways 90 (bottom), 91 (both)
J M Jarvis 156/157, 172 (top)
R G Jarvis 214 (bottom), 255 (bottom)
G J Jefferson 93 (bottom)
A A Jorgensen 212
Arthur E Loosley 75 (bottom)
Alfred Luft 35, 101, 121
Malayan Railways 290/291
Malayan Railways/P B Whitehouse Collection 288/289
Malawi Railway Ltd/P B Whitehouse Collection 229 (bottom), 230 (top left)
Mexican Railways 136 (top)
H Michimura 284 (top)
Ken Mills 184, 185 (all 4), 188, 189 (both), 192/193 (all 6), 199 (all 3), 200/201 (top 3), 203 (top), 206 (second from top), 208/209 (top 2)
Mitropa 57 (bottom left)
MoPAC 177 (bottom)
National Library, Dublin 88 (top)
H Nave 28 (bottom), 112/113, 257 (top)
A Nelthorpe 282/283
New South Wales Gort Railways 312 (top), 312/313
New Zealand Gort Railways 14, 306/307, 334, 338/339, 342
Norfolk and Western Railroad 171 (bottom), 172 (bottom), 172/173, 173 (both)
OBB 24, 25 (bottom), 28 (top)
Reinhold Palm 57 (bottom right)
The Post Office 79 (bottom)
Frank A Railton 252 (bottom)
J Ransom 77
Real Photographs Colourviews Collection 153 (right)
Rhodesian Railways 235 (bottom)
Trevor Rowe 33 (middle), 197 (middle), 206 (top 2)
E S Russell 93 (top)
Saburno Motojima 281 (bottom), 283 (bottom)
Santa Fe Railroad 145 (both), 147 (bottom)
H Säuberlich 56 (bottom)
Jim Shaughnessy 128, 136 (bottom), 162 (bottom)
Charles S Small 303
J B Snell 42 (top), 79 (top)
Shigeki Ohyama Jacket, 2/3
South African Railways 15 (top), 213 (top), 237 (bottom right), 238 (bottom)
Southern Pacific 175 (bottom), 176 (top)
Paul S Stephanus 272/273 (bottom), 304/305
D H Stuart 264
Swiss National Tourist Office 18/19
Swiss Foto 1
Eric Treacy 65
Union Pacific Railroad 124 (top), 180
Uruguayan State Railways 207 (both)
La Vie du Rail 9, 23, 36, 37 (bottom), 40 (both), 41 (top), 51, 55, 60 (top left), 82, 89 (bottom), 92 (top), 95 (bottom), 99 (bottom 2), 103 (bottom), 104 (both), 106/107, 108 (top), 114/115 (all 4), 117 (both), 125 (bottom), 141 (top), 152 (bottom), 157 (top left), 158 (middle), 160

(bottom 2), 161 (bottom left), 176 (bottom), 178/179 (bottom), 180/181, 195 (bottom), 210/211, 215 (top), 216 (top), 217 (bottom 3), 221 (bottom), 222 (both), 224 (top), 230/231, 231 (bottom), 236 (both), 237 (top), 240/241, 241 (both), 243, 244, 245 (top), 246/247, 248, 252/253, 253 (both), 254, 260, (bottom and top right), 274/275, 280/281, 281 (top), 283 (top), 284 (bottom), 285 (both), 286/287, 288, 293 (bottom), 294/295, 296, 297, 301, 309 (both), 314 (bottom), 321 (bottom), 322 (top), 327 (both), 333 (top), 337, 340 (top), 341 (both)
(ACEC Charlesroi) 31 (top)
(Association of American Railroads) 125 (middle right)
(Jean Bottin) 41 (middle)
(Y Broncard) 29, 56/57, 95 (top)
(F Fontaine) 31 (bottom)
(Illinois Central Railroad) 167, 168
(Guy Laforgerie) 60 (bottom)
(Noel Neumann) 59
(New York Times) 161 (top left and bottom right)
(A W Perry) 313 (top)
(Verkbild Siemens) 221 (middle)
Western Australian Government Railways 324, 325 (bottom)
Courtesy K Westcott-Jones 200 (bottom), 203 (bottom), 213 (left), 231 (top), 269 (bottom), 315 (top), 323 (bottom)
White Pass and Yukon 133 (bottom)
C M Whitehouse 32, 33 (bottom), 34, 42 (bottom), 66, 72, 75 (top), 83 (top), 89 (top), 100 (top), 103 (top), 105 (top), 169 (bottom), 198 (bottom), 206 (bottom), 215 (bottom right), 217 (top), 232 (both), 235 (top), 240 (all 3), 260/261, 261, 265 (top), 329 (both), 330 (bottom)
P B Whitehouse 11 (both), 25 (top), 33 (top), 41 (bottom), 49, 52, 53, 58, 59 (top), 62/63, 67 (bottom), 68 (top), 70 (bottom), 72/73 (top), 74/75, 76 (bottom), 78 (both), 80, 83 (bottom), 84 (both), 85, 99 (top), 100 (bottom), 161 (top right), 194/195, 204/205, 205, 206 (second from bottom), 214 (top), 220 (top), 223 (left), 230 (top right), 234 (bottom), 239 (all 3), 255 (top), 258 (bottom), 259, 260, 262/263, 265 (bottom), 269 (top), 270/271, 298/299, 330 (top) 330/331
Yugoslav Railways 120
Ron Ziel 165 (bottom right)